THE AMERICAN REVOLUTION:
A Compendium of Terms and Topics

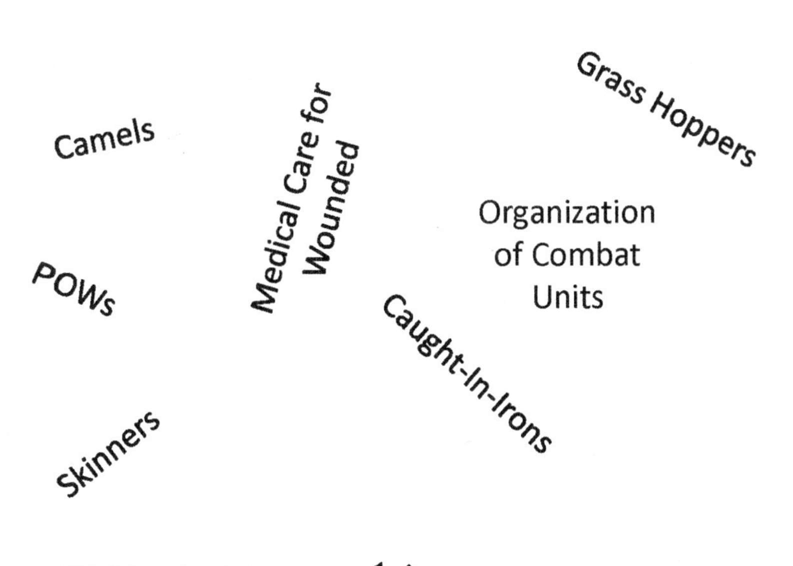

outskirts press

Author: Paul A. Chase

The American Revolution: A Compendium of Terms and Topics

v3.0

Outskirts Press, Inc.
http://www.outskirtspress.com

ISBN: 978-1-4787-9183-6

PRINTED IN THE UNITED STATES OF AMERICA

Compiled by Compatriot Paul A. Chase
Sons of the American Revolution (SAR)
Member (Primary): Colonel William Grayson SAR Chapter
Prince William Country Virginia
Member (Secondary): Colonel James Wood II SAR Chapter
Northwestern Virginia
Member Virginia Society SAR Color Guard
Lt. Col. USAF (Retired)
Vietnam Veteran 1971-1972
Former Director, DOD Agent Orange and PTSD Claims and Records
Research Group
Post Historian and Adjutant, Veterans of Foreign Wars
Post 7589 Manassas, VA

B.A. History and Political Science, Elizabethtown College 1964
Elizabethtown, PA
M.S. History and Secondary Education, Central Connecticut
State University 1974, New Britain, CT

TABLE OF CONTENTS

Purpose i
Organization iii
The Geology and Geography of the Colonies: 1
Pre-War Legislative Acts and Issues 4
  Bills of Credit 4
  Economic, Political and Social 4
  Enumeration 5
  Great Awakening (Religion) 6
  Mercantilism 6
  Proclamation of 1763 6
  Salutary Neglect (Taxes) 7
  Writs of Assistance 7
British Need for Revenue 9
  Sugar Act April 5, 1764 9
  Currency Act April 19, 1765 10
  Stamp Act March 22, 1765 10
  Quartering Act March 24, 1765 11
  Declaratory Act March 18, 1766 11
Townshend Acts 13
  Commissioner of Customs Act June 29, 1767 13
  Indemnity Act June 29, 1767 13
  New York Restraining Act June 15, 1767 14
  Revenue Act June 29, 1767 14
  Vice Admiralty Act June 29, 1767 14
Coercive & Intolerable Acts 16
  Boston Port Act March 30, 1774 16

Administration of Justice Act May 20, 1774 17
Massachusetts Governance Act May 20, 1774 17
Quebec Act October 7, 1774 17
Second Quartering Act June 2, 1774...................................... 17
American Prohibitory Act December 22, 1775 18
Incidents that Precipated the Revolution....................................... 19
Reinforcement of British Soldiers in Boston 1768.................... 19
Boston Massacre March 5, 1770... 19
HMS GASPEE Affair June 9, 1772 20
Boston Tea Party December 16, 1773 20
Lord Dumore's Wars #1 (1774) And # 2 (1775)............................ 21
Regional/Local Differences and Disputes in the Colonies 23
Economic 24
Religion.. 25
Revolutionary Fervor... 26
Slavery... 28
Subordination.. 30
Territorial/Border/Disputes 31
Conclusion.. 33
Collective Colonial Organizations 34
First Continental Congress - Sept 5 – Oct 22, 1774................ 34
Continental Association 1774.. 35
Second Continental Congress May 5, 1775............................ 36
Efforts to Negotiate an End to the Revolution 37
Galloway Plan 1774... 37
North Peace Plan February 20, 1775 37
Olive Branch Petition July 5, 1775.. 37
Staten Island Peace Conference Sept 11, 1776........................ 38
Carlisle Peace Commission June 13, 1778 38
Vergennes Peace Initiative Early 1779.................................... 39
Attempt to Make Quebec the Fourteenth Colony 40
American Army 43
American Navy 45
American Naval Privateers... 47

American Marines 49
African Americans 50
American Indians 52
American Militia 54
British Army 55
British Navy 56
British Royal Marines 58
French Army And Navy 59
German Army Mercenaries 61
Spanish Army And Navy 64
The Netherlands 66
Naval Influences and Terms of the Revolution 67
    Historical Analogies 67
    Naval Terminology 68
Notable Foreigners Who Fought for the American Cause 79
    Denmark 79
    France 80
    Germany 82
    Poland 83
Organization of American and British Armies 85
    Wings 85
    Divisions 85
    Brigades 86
    Regiments 86
    Battalions 86
    Companies 86
    Platoons 86
American and British Command Philosophy 88
    American Philosophy 88
    British Philosophy 89
American Infantry Tactics 90
    Continental Line 90
    Militia 91
British Infantry Tactics 92

Traditional "Line" Stand and Fight 92
Limited Loyalist Integration in British Army 93
American and British Infantry Weapons and Terms 94
American and British Cavalry Terms 102
American and British Cavalry During the Revolution 104
American Ranger and Legion/Cav Units 106
Light Horse Legion of Harry Lee 106
Pulaski's Continental Dragoons 106
British Ranger and Legion/Cav Units 108
Simcoe's Queen's Rangers 108
Banastre Tarleton's British Legion 108
Black Dragoons 109
American Recruiting and Enlistment 110
British Recruiting and Enlistment 113
American Stratgic Options At the Start of the Revolution 116
Draw Britain's Enemies into the Struggle 116
Wage Economic War with Naval Privateers 116
Fight a Delaying War/Avoid Major Battles 116
Organize American Army into Small Units 117
Fight a "War of Posts" 117
Offense-Defense 117
Perimeter Defense 117
Strategies Employed by Americans 118
Internationalize War with Britain's Enemies 1775- 1778 118
Wage a "War of Posts" 1778-1783 118
British Strategic Options at the Start of the Revolution 120
Divide and Conquer 120
Blockade Colonies 120
Use Terror and Destruction 120
Relentless Pursuit of Americans 120
Spreading Ink Stain 121
Have Loyalists assume Greater Fighting Role 121
Strategies Employed by the British 122
Divide and Conquer 1776-1777 122

Big Battle Strategy 1778-1780 ... 122
Southern Strategy 1780-1781 ... 123
American Logistics: Problems and Issues ... 124
No Large-Scale Logistics Experience ... 124
No Logistics Infrastructure ... 124
No Centralized Supply and Transportation System ... 125
British Logistics: Problems and Issues ... 126
British/German Food Stuffs Consumed from May 27, 1777 to November 11, 1781 ... 126
Annual Consumables ... 127
Faulty Assumptions And Issues ... 127
Assumed they could achieve a Quick Victory ... 127
Assumed they could use F&I War Logistics Model ... 127
Assumed Too Few Soldiers Were Needed to Win ... 127
Assumed Co-Operation between Army and Navy ... 128
Inexperienced Logistics Officials in Key Positions ... 128
Underestimated Problems of 3,000-mile Atlantic Supply... 128
Artillery Types ... 130
Cannons ... 131
Howitzers ... 132
Mortars ... 132
Artillery Terms ... 133
Pro-American Groups ... 138
Committees of Correspondence ... 138
Committees of Inspection and Compliance ... 138
Committees of Safety ... 138
Committees of Supply ... 139
First Rhode Island Infantry Regiment ... 139
Green Mountain Boys ... 139
League of Armed Neutrality ... 139
Liberty Boys ... 139
Monmouth Association for Retaliation ... 140
Over Mountain Men ... 140
Regulators ... 140

Scotch Irish ... 140
Skinners ... 141
Solemn League and Covenant ... 141
Sons of Liberty ... 141
Sons of Neptune ... 141
Sons of Violence ... 142
Whigs ... 142
Pro-British Groups ... 143
American Volunteers ... 143
Black Loyalists ... 143
Cowboys ... 143
Loyalists ... 144
New Jersey Board of Associated Loyalists ... 144
Provincials ... 144
Provincial American Loyalists ... 144
"River Gods" ... 144
Six Indian Nations Confederacy ... 145
Tories ... 145
Obedience of Orders, Rules and Regulations ... 146
General Information and Terms ... 149
Types of Soldiers and Units ... 195
Accoutrements of Non-Commissioned and Commissioned Officers ... 200
Siege Warfare ... 202
General Fortification Terms ... 204
Surrendering Terms ... 210
Prisoner of War (Pow) Issues, Terms and Statistics ... 215
Statistical Overview (Close Approximates) ... 215
Major Holding Facilities for American Pows ... 216
Major Holding Facilities for British and German Pows ... 218
American and British Pow Policies ... 219
British Pow Acts and Legislation: ... 220
Prisoner of War Terms: ... 221
Medical Care for American Rebels ... 225

Doctors and Hospitals 225
Scurvy 226
Smallpox 226
Treatment of Injuries 226
Venereal Disease 227
New Technologies During the Revolution 229
Breech Loading Rifle 229
Germ Warfare 229
Inoculation 229
Submarine 229
Torpedoes 230
Consumption of Alcohol 231
Jews During the Revolution 233
Women in the Revolution 235
Spying, Spies and Terms During the Revolution 237
Notable American and British Spies 237
Spy Terms 242
Miracle On The Hudson 245
The Joshua Huddy Affair 248
Succession of British Commanders-In-Chiefs (CINCs) During the Revolution 251
LTG Thomas Gage 1763-1775 251
LTG William Howe 1775-1778 251
LTG Henry Clinton 1778-1782 252
LTG Guy Carleton 1782-1783 252
Peace Negotiations 253
Post-Revolution War Debts 255
American National Debt 255
British National Debt 255
Dutch National Debt 255
French National Debt 256
German Princes' Debt 256
Spanish National Debt 256
Revolutionary War Pensions 257

Major Battles and Campaigns of the Revolution 260
Lexington/Concord 260
Bunker/Breeds Hill 262
Battle of Fort Moultrie 263
Battles for New York City 264
Battle of Valcour Island 266
Battle of Trenton New Jersey 268
Battles of Saratoga New York 270
Battle of Monmouth Courthouse 274
Siege of Savannah Georgia 275
Siege of Charles Town SC 276
Battle of Camden SC 278
Battle of King's Mountain 279
Battle of Cowpens 280
Race to The Dan River 282
Battle of Guilford Courthouse 283
Naval Battle of The Capes 284
Battle (Siege) of Yorktown 287
Bibliography 290
Index with "Quick Look Information" 381
Acknowledgements 442

PURPOSE

The purpose of this body of work is to amass for the record in a clear document the many relevant topics and terms that are important to know and learn about the American Revolution. Some of the issues resonate to these very times. The following are a few examples: The gap between the haves and have nots created social unrest then as it does now. Defense spending (especially naval construction) was driven by where jobs would be created just as it is now. Military service then was performed by the lower classes just as it is now. Massive war debts were accumulated then as they are now. Leaders were wildly over optimistic for military success then just as they have been in our recent conflicts, only to be shocked later when facing defeat.

Members of the SAR have an obligation to be informed about the Revolution and pass on to future generations how our independence was won and the incredible sacrifices it took by the men and women of America to achieve success. This document should help in this endeavor. The many unique terms explained in this document are the accumulation of reading tens of thousands of pages about the Revolution. Knowing the terms and having a way to learn their meaning in the context of the Revolution will make reading about the event more meaningful and enjoyable. For example: Where are you going to find the meanings of a "Liberty Jacket", "Hillsborough Treat" or "Adjutant's Daughter"? Not in Wikipedia and not in the dictionary. Liberty Jacket means tar and feathering, Hillsborough Treat means smearing excrement on the house of an official to send him a message and Adjutant's Daughter was the nickname given to the flogging post to which soldiers were tied when lashed. These and scores of other terms can be found in this document. There are no foot or end notes. However, the sources of the information for each section are noted in the Sources for the topic. The annotated Bibliography can serve as a resource for further reading. The "Summary" comments in the bibliography are solely mine.

ORGANIZATION

Common events are listed in chronological sequence. Terms are grouped by type and listed alphabetically. Military material as much as possible is grouped together. Bibliographical sources are listed in alphabetical order by the last name of the author(s). Where possible, references are made to indicate the source documents of the information and terms. This document can be used by teachers and students needing information about the Revolution. It is suggested that a CD of the document be provided to each new member of the SAR/CAR/DAR at the time of their induction. It is also a recommended source of information for individuals who desire to make presentations about the Revolution. The Index is formatted to provide "Quick Look" information about the line item and page numbers where there is more information. The authors and their books that are mentioned in the Index can all be found in the annotated Bibliography.

THE GEOLOGY AND GEOGRAPHY OF THE COLONIES:

The geology of the Colonies/States worked to the benefit of the British during the Revolution. The geography of the Colonies/States worked to the benefit of the American Rebels during the Revolution.

Geology of the Colonies/States: The geology of the Colonies/States is hardly mentioned in the histories of the Revolution. The rock formations of the mountains from Maine (then a territory of Massachusetts) south to Florida (then a possession of the British after the French and Indian War) were severely deficient in the kind of ores that could produce native American specie (gold and silver). Today there are many small Revolutionary Era mines throughout New England especially, where people of the time tried unsuccessfully to obtain silver and gold. The result is that the Colonies/States had to rely on imported foreign and British specie. The absence of native produced specie was used by the British to their huge economic advantage during the Revolution. If the Colonies/States had the geology of Mexico for example, where gold and silver deposits were plentiful, the Americans could not have been held hostage to the British mercantile system. In addition to the shortage of gold and silver there was a significant shortage of American mined lead. There was also a near complete lack of sulphur which was critical to the manufacture of black powder. The French and Spanish loaned or donated millions of Livres and Reales to American Rebels throughout the War but most of that money went to pay the European suppliers of war materials. The Americans saw precious little of the actual specie. The British formalized their economic dominance over the Americans starting even before the French and Indian War with the passage of the first Currency Act of 1751 which regulated the American production of paper money most commonly known as Bills of Credit which were easily counterfeited and produced in huge volumes and thus quickly devalued. The British further formalized their policies requiring the States/Colonies to pay for British goods with specie or material goods such as tobacco, rum or wood products with subsequent Currency Acts of 1764 and 1773. The fact that British bled the Americans of specie and forced Americans to rely on paper money caused hyper-inflation and created the situation where American soldiers could not be paid, uniformed and the inability to procure food and supplies because they had mostly worthless money. This economic warfare by the British waged against the Americans almost caused the Revolution to fail.

Geography of the Colonies/States: The geography of the Colonies/States has been noted occasionally by historians as a factor in favor of the American Rebels during the Revolution. The reality is that it was a significant plus for the Americans. America's 3,000-mile-long Atlantic Coastline stretched British Naval forces when they were already under stress worldwide. This great area made it difficult to concentrate their forces at critical times. The thousands of American Rivers mostly flowing to the Atlantic Coastline provided opportunities for privateers to hide and launch attacks. These same rivers made it difficult for the British to move through inland areas as demonstrated by the Race to the Dan when British General Cornwallis was attempting to capture American General Greene after the Battle of Cowpens. The heavily forested and mountainous areas, such as were found in the Battles of Saratoga NY, were foreign to the British military to their detriment. The alluring geographical fault but deadly "Great Warpath" down Lake Champlain twice resulted in British defeats. The American coastal cities of Boston, New York, Philadelphia, Charles Town, and Savannah all posed tempting targets that were ultimately occupied at times by the British, but sucked up their forces without causing the Americans to surrender. Too many Americans lived in inland areas to surrender by the loss of the coastal cities. Ironically, it was the British Army being trapped in the coastal enclave of Yorktown which caused their ultimate defeat. The Appalachian Mountains were too porous to provide a barrier to the westward expansion of American settlers which was a geopolitical objective of the British as evidenced by the 1763 Proclamation Act. The dramatic climate changes to the southern tip of the Atlantic coastline subjected British soldiers to debilitating diseases and adverse health.

Sources:

Aaron, Larry: *Race to the Dan*

Butler, Judge Edward: *Spain – Our Forgotten Ally In The American Revolutionary War: A Concise Summary of Spain's Assistance.*

Ferreiro, Larrie D. *Bothers At Arms. American Independence and the Men of France and. Spain Who Saved It.*

PRE-WAR LEGISLATIVE ACTS AND ISSUES

Other than taxes, there were issues that festered and contributed to the discontent of the British control over the American Colonies. These issues are shown below:_

Bills of Credit: To the extent possible the British paid for the goods and services from Americans with "Bills of Credit" rather than specie. For example: the British might contract with an American merchant for 1,000 cords of firewood and pay for it with a Bill of Credit which was in effect paper money. The Bills of Credit quickly became devalued. They were traded between merchants. Americans who owed the British for goods or services were forced to the extent possible to pay with specie or valuable commodities. This created a financial hardship on Americans which soured relations between Britain and the Colonies.

Economic, Political, Religious, Governance and Social Conditions in America: Europeans fled to America to achieve economic opportunity, escape poverty, depravity, militarism and immorality they experienced in Europe. They wanted religious freedom, release from heavy handed government control and to live in a social structure without domination by the upper class. Increasingly, Americans in the 13 Colonies began to experience the things that made them flee

Europe. Their daily activities were controlled more and more by officialdom from across the seas. The poor were getting poorer and the wealthy rich. Since the beginning of 1700 the wealthiest Americans increased their taxable income from 30% to 49%. At the same time wealth owned by the poorest half decreased from 9% to 5%. There we more and more crowds of homeless and jobless wandering the landscape who were being victimized by the upper classes. The government from afar not only failed to protect the common folk it inflicted more pain and suffering on them. Landed proprietors victimized their workers and kept them in a state of perpetual poverty. Corrupt judges used small debts to justify foreclosures and dishonest officials were protected from accountability. Tens of thousands of indentured servants worked in abusive conditions that were barely tolerable. Hard work alone could not allow these individuals to rise above their miserable conditions. The common folk gained confidence in their growing numbers and became bolder. The conditions in America were ripe for change and Britain was seen as the roadblock to make the changes that were so badly needed.

Enumeration: Enumerations were the "lists" of American commodities subject to British control mentioned in multiple acts. An example of an "Enumeration" would be a British order saying: "The following "enumerated" items are prohibited for export by the Colonies except to Britain: tobacco, indigo, iron, copper etc."; or an order "enumerating" the non-importation of gun powder, flints, muskets, tents etc. from any country except Britain. The Continental Congress issued its own "enumeration" lists banning the consumption and or purchase of British goods such as glass, silk, ceramics etc. The enumerations by the British were far more common than those of the colonies. Enumerations by the British were used for economic leverage and punishment with at best moderate success and were a source of great hate and discontent by Americans towards the British. In accordance with the Staple Act of 1763 American goods could not be exported directly to Europe without first being transshipped through

Great Britain. Goods from Europe destined for America also had to be transshipped through Great Britain. Maryland and Virginia lost over 250,000 pounds sterling each year from the added costs of transshipping tobacco through Britain to Europe.

Great Awakening: This was a religious movement that began in mid-18th Century in New England where established authority began to be questioned. According to the "New Lights" the authority of the Crown and the Anglican Church were no longer to be slavishly obeyed. This set up a contest between the "New Lights" and "Old Lights" of the movement. The New Lights were at the forefront of this new way of thinking and the Old Lights supported the Crown. Religion was a white-hot issue among the New England Colonists of the time which is where the Revolution actually started. New Light thinking had a significant impact on justifying the Revolution.

Mercantilism: This was the economic policy of the European Colonial powers which postulated that these powers could accumulate wealth by administratively and militarily ruling their colonies through restrictive and favorable trade policies. These policies most frequently worked to the economic disadvantage of the colonies and advantage of the colonial power which created hate and discontent, that in the case of the Thirteen American Colonies, helped give birth to the American Revolution.

Proclamation Act of October 7, 1763: This Act created the western boundaries of the colonies along the Appalachian Mountains at the end of the French and Indian War. Land west of the boundary was reserved for the British to administer for regulation of trade, control of Native Americans and profitable sale. The Act outlawed the purchase of Native American lands by Americans and called for some of the land to be given to **British** veterans of the French and Indian War. Some of the land west of the boundary had already been settled by American Colonists and some of the land had been promised to

Americans who had fought with the British during the war. Those whites who already occupied the territory were told to leave. The boundary was never thought to be permanent but the Act put the vast area under control of the British Crown. The Americans considered the Act a huge violation of American territorial rights and turned many of the colonies and their people against the British.

Salutary Neglect: During the period 1720 – 1756 British administration of the colonies was done with a "light hand" (salutary neglect) and so customs duties, taxes, administrative requirements, judicial and legal proceedings etc., were frequently ignored without accountability or punishment; therefore, many Americans did not feel burdened or bothered by them. During and after the French and Indian War, primarily to raise revenue, the British began to enforce these restrictions that had been on the books for many years. This suddenly and greatly angered the colonists. Classic examples of this situation were the sudden enforcement of old tax and regulatory acts such as: The 1733 Sugar Act, 1732, Hat Act, 1750 Iron Act, Woolens Act of 1699, King Tree Acts of 1711/1722 and many more. Where previously there was ambivalence there now was increasing friction between the Colonies and Britain.

Writs of Assistance: Writs of Assistance were search and seizure actions that allowed British sheriffs and customs officials to conduct these activities in the homes and businesses of Americans without an approved specific court ordered search warrant. This led to abuse of the system by the British. If they wanted to harass a suspected American Rebel, they would trash his home on the pretext he was breaking the law. This was especially troublesome in the Massachusetts Colony which led the forefront of opposition to the British in the pre-Revolutionary years. The opposition to search and seizure actions without specific court approved warrants ultimately led to the Fourth Amendment of the U.S. Constitution which made such actions illegal.

Sources:

Alden, John R. *A History of the American Revolution.*

Archer, Richard. *As If an Enemy's Country.*

Breen, T. H. *American Insurgents, American Patriots.*_

Ferling, John. *Almost a Miracle.*

Ferling, John. *INDEPENDENCE: The Struggle to Set America Free.*

McCullough, David. *1776.*

Middlekauff, Robert. *The Glorious Cause. The American Revolution.*

Miller, John C. *Origins of the American Revolution.*

Phillips, Kevin. 1775, *A Good Year for Revolution.*

Rae, Noel. *The People's War, Original Voices of the American Revolution.*

Raphael, Ray. *A People's History of the American Revolution, How Common People Shaped the Fight for Independence.*

BRITISH NEED FOR REVENUE

The Seven Years War which is commonly known in America as The French and Indian War left Britain 130,000,000 pounds sterling in debt. Although victorious, Britain needed to maintain a standing army in America to enforce the peace and maintain British rule. The occupation was costing Britain more money than it was gaining through trade with the American Colonies. The British people were far and away more burdened by taxes than Americans. For example: The British "Land Tax" was at an annual rate of 20% of the value of the land; so, a British land owner whose land was worth $10,000 was paying $2,000 in annual land taxes. The average Britisher paid 200 shillings taxes a year and an American one shilling. In view of the above it was felt by British authorities that Americans should shoulder more of the financial burden needed to repay its debts and for maintaining its forces in America. Parliament undertook to remedy this funding gap by passing the following acts shown in chronological sequence:

Sugar Act April 5, 1764: This Act was also known as the **American Duties Act or American Revenue Act**. Rum was one of the most favored alcoholic drinks in America. Its production required great amounts of sugar from molasses, primarily produced from sugar cane grown in the British West Indies of the Caribbean. The original Sugar

Act of 1733 levied a tax of six pence per gallon of molasses. The Act of 1733 was never enforced. The Sugar Act of 1764 halved the tax on molasses but greatly increased the enforcement against the smuggling of it which was widely done and was very profitable for the colonies. The enforcement against the smuggling of molasses angered the colonists. The Act also prohibited the sale of American products, such as lumber to countries other than Britain and put into the hands of British appointed judges' trials for violations of the Act. These judges were obviously biased which further angered Americans.

Currency Act April 19, 1765: The purposes of this Act (actually there were several acts) were to reduce smuggling, get control over Colonial trade and reduce British debt from the French and Indian War. It restricted the use of Colonial paper money which was commonly substituted with **bills of credit** which the British used to pay debts to American merchants. The Colonists felt this was another intrusion in their affairs and a back-door example of "taxation without representation".

Stamp Act March 22, 1765: Life during the 18th Century revolved around paper transactions, such as court documents, licenses, business agreements, certificates and endless other matters. In order to raise revenue, the Act required that these documents have "stamps" most often in the form of ink stamped certifications that taxes had been paid for the transaction. In other instances, the paperwork had to be done on British produced "stamped" paper much like watermark paper. This process greatly annoyed the colonists, slowed business processes, depressed trade and resulted in a financial burden. A firestorm of protest erupted over the Act which led to its repeal on March 18, 1766. The Act also raised the issue of taxation without representation which the British hoped to settle in their favor with the **Declaratory Act of 1766**.

Quartering Act March 24, 1765: This Act required that the Colonies provide "quarters" (lodging) and provisions for British soldiers stationed in America. The lodging was to be done in vacant buildings, taverns and barns, not in the private homes of Americans as is commonly said. Free provisions to be provided by the colonists included beer, cider, vinegar, firewood, food and fodder for animals. This decreased the cost of the British for maintaining their forces in America and shifted the cost burden to the Americans who considered this a wrongful practice. The Act was mostly ignored by the Colonies, except for New York, which outright refused to comply. The Act expired on March 24, 1767. It was replaced in 1774 by a new Quartering Act which was part of the 1774 "Townshend Acts".

Declaratory Act March 18, 1766: This Act is less well known as the **American Colonies Act**. This Act followed the repeal of the Stamp Act and declared that Britain could in effect rule over the colonies as it sought fit, especially as it pertained to taxes. The Stamp Act would not have been repealed by Parliament without the Declaratory Act. In Britain, they were called the "Twin Brothers". The Stamp Act was repealed on March 18, 1766 and the Declaratory Act enacted on the **same day.** In the minds of the British Government this seemed to settle the issue of taxation without representation. In the minds of the Colonists it was felt that Britain could tax the colonies at will which created much discontent among Americans. The Act declared that Britain had the same right to rule over the colonies as it did to its homeland citizens, but the Americans keenly knew they had no representation in Parliament.

Sources:

Alden, John R. *A History of the American Revolution.*

Ellis, Joseph J. *American Creation, Triumphs and Tragedies at the Founding of the Republic.*

Middlekauff, Robert. *The Glorious Cause. The American Revolution.*

O'Shaughnessy, Andrew Jackson. *The Men Who Lost America, British Leadership, the American Revolution and the Fate of the Empire.*

Phillips, Kevin. *1775. A Good Year for Revolution.*

Rae, Noel. *The People's War, Original Voices of the American Revolution.*

TOWNSHEND ACTS

By 1767 it was clear additional revenue was needed from the colonies. Lord Charles Townshend was appointed on August 4, 1766 as Chancellor of the Exchequer (Britain's Finance Minister) with the mission to solve the debts from the French and Indian War and eliminate the deficits from the stationing of British forces in America which were nearly 400,000 pounds per year. From his leadership five new revenue acts were passed by Parliament which were commonly referred to as the "Townshend Acts":

Commissioner of Customs Act June 29, 1767: This Act created the American Customs Board whose membership was appointed exclusively by the British. This powerful board could rule on trade cases from individuals and Colonies and since the board members were appointed by the Crown, its bias was always apparent. There was a similar board in Britain which was notoriously corrupt. The decisions of the board could not be appealed and were done without juries. The members of the board got a percentage of the merchant goods they seized.

Indemnity Act June 29, 1767: This Act raised the price of tea in America through support of the British East India Tea Company. Americans were "hooked" on tea which meant that every day use of this product was unnecessarily more expensive by means of the

British East India Company which was given exclusive rights to import its tea to the Colonies.

New York Restraining Act June 15, 1767: This Act restricted the powers of the New York Colonial Assembly until it complied with the 1765 Quartering Act. The colony of New York openly opposed the Quartering Act and ultimately relented and provided some assistance to British soldiers and therefore avoided the penalties of the act.

Revenue Act June 29, 1767: This Act levied taxes on the importation of goods from Britain. Many industrial goods used in the colonies could only be legally imported from Britain, such as: metals, glass, exotic fabrics and so on. The taxes on these goods were an immediate burden on every day Americans. The Act also expanded the search and seizure capabilities of British officials to seek out violators such as smugglers and those who brought these goods into the colonies without paying the required taxes.

Vice Admiralty Act June 29, 1767: This Act created courts throughout the Colonies whose members were appointed by the Crown to prosecute accused smugglers and avoiders of the revenue acts. Decisions of the courts were done without the benefit of juries and could not be appealed. Americans who were brought to the court were presumed guilty until they could prove themselves innocent. Worse yet the salaries of the judges were paid by the taxes levied on the Americans.

Lord Townshend never saw the full reaction of the Colonies to these acts. He died unexpectedly at the age of 42 on September 4, 1767. He was replaced by Frederick Lord North who held the titles of Prime Minister and Chancellor of the Exchequer until his resignation in 1782 after the American victory at the Battle of Yorktown in October 1781. The irony is the fact that the Townshend Acts were only projected to result in 40,000 pounds additional annual revenue for the Crown. This was at the same time, when due to tax riots in Britain, there was an annual reduction in British Land Tax revenue of 400,000 pounds, which put further pressure on Parliament to raise revenue from the American Colonies.

Sources:

Alden, John R. *A History of the American Revolution.*

Archer. Richard. *As If an Enemy's Country. The British Occupation of Boston and the Origins of the American Revolution.*

Bobrick, Benson. *Angel in the Whirlwind.*

Middlekauff, Robert. *The Glorious Cause. The American Revolution.*

Miller, John C. *Origins of the American Revolution*

O'Shaughnessy, Patrick. *The Men Who Lost America. British Leadership, the American Revolution and the Fate of the Empire.*

COERCIVE &
INTOLERABLE ACTS

The opposition by the colonies to the Townshend Acts led to the passage by the British Parliament in March 1774 of what they called the **"Coercive Acts"** which were meant to coerce the colonies into compliance. In America, they became known as the **"Intolerable Acts"** which were as follows:

Boston Port Act March 30, 1774: Of all the Coercive Acts the Boston Port Act was the most damaging and inflammatory. It required almost all Boston Port traffic to be routed through Salem, Massachusetts, which added enormous expenses to the people of the colony. The Act was to remain in force until repayment was made for the December 16, 1773 Boston Tea Party. The additional expenses of routing trade out of Boston were especially hard on the middle and working-class families which constituted many Americans. This galvanized people of all the colonies to support opposition to Britain. A massive effort was made by communities of all the Colonies to provide money and charity to the people of Massachusetts who were hurt by the Act. The immediate response to the Port Act by the radical leadership of Boston was to propose a Solemn League and Covenant whereby all the Colonies would promise: (1) Non-importation of British goods (2) Non-consumption of British made goods and (3) Non-exportation of goods to Britain. Such actions would have a very uneven and in some cases detrimental effect on the individual Colonies. Because the Solemn League and Covenant was too confrontational for the likes of many leaders, especially those from Philadelphia, and too damaging to American commercial interests, a compromise proposal was created by a group called the Committee of 51. Their proposal was to create a Continental Congress which initially had a more moderate response. Thus, the Boston Port Act was the spring-board for the First Continental Congress which was the first unified body of Colonies in opposition to Britain.

Administration of Justice Act of May 20, 1774: This Act allowed the British appointed Colonial Governors to move the trials of individuals to other colonies and even to Britain, which rightfully gave the appearance of the violation of local justice.

Massachusetts Government Act May 20, 1774: This Act mandated that all the Colony's government positions be appointed by the Crown and limited the activities of their "Town Meetings" which were a uniquely American democratic institution that were widely popular. Massachusetts was a hotbed of resistance to British rule so it was the focus of their punishing acts.

Quebec Act of October 7, 1774: This Act expanded the province of Quebec (ruled by Britain) into parts of what are today Wisconsin, Ohio, Illinois and Michigan. This Act ceded to Quebec lands that were being claimed and settled by the American Colonists. It was easier for Britain to administer this area as part of Quebec than it was to deal with the claims to the area, which was already occupied in many cases by Americans. The Colonists also felt that this Act would result in the expansion of Catholic influence in America which was opposed by most non-Catholic colonists.

Second Quartering Act June 2, 1774: This Act specifically targeted the New York Colony, which openly opposed the original 1765

Quartering Act. This new Act required the quartering of the previous Act, but lifted the requirement to provide provisions for the British soldiers.

American Prohibitory Act December 22, 1775: This act passed by Parliament created a world-wide blockade of all American commerce. Under international law a blockade is an "act of war". This was the final step in Britain's attempt to quell the American Revolution short of military force.

Sources:

Alden, John R. *A History of the American Revolution.*

Archer, Richard. *As If an Enemy's Country. The British Occupation of Boston and the Origins of the American Revolution.*

Bobrick, Benson. *Angel in the Whirlwind.*

Middlekauff, Robert. *The Glorious Cause. The American Revolution.*

Miller, John C. *Origins of the American Revolution.*

O'Shaughnessy, Andrew Jackson. *The Men Who Lost America, British Leadership, the American Revolution and the Fate of the Empire.*

Phillips, Kevin. 1775, *A Good Year for Revolution.*

INCIDENTS THAT PRECIPATED THE REVOLUTION

Reinforcement of British Soldiers in Boston: In 1768 the British sent 4,000 British soldiers to Boston, MA. This was far and away more than the number need for basic security and control of the Americans there. There were not enough billets to house the soldiers, a shortage of appropriate logistics, and the soldiers and local population were constantly in conflict with each other over petty incidents that enraged both groups. The non-stop "friction" between the Americans and British soldiers who were everywhere all the time made it impossible to prevent conflict between them.

Boston Massacre: This was known by the British and Loyalists as The Incident on King Street. On March 5, 1770, a squad of British soldiers on King Street in Boston was being harassed, abused, threatened and hit with thrown objects. Either by accident or purposely they fired on the crowd of Americans killing five and wounding several others. It is not exactly clear whether the shooting started unintentionally, but to the Americans, throughout the Colonies, it was an intentional massacre. The word of it spread like wildfire and incited Americans to further permanent hostility against the British. John Adams, much to his credit, defended the soldiers and got the charges against six acquitted and found two only guilty of manslaughter with reduced sentences. Americans were highly literate throughout the Colonies so newspapers and flyers were used to inflame public opinion about this British atrocity.

HMS *GASPEE* Affair: The HMS *Gaspee* was a British schooner that was attempting to enforce British customs and was chasing an American ship which it suspected of violating regulations against smuggling. The British ship ran aground in Warwick, Rhode Island on June 9, 1772. It was boarded by angry Americans many of whom made their livings by avoiding British anti-smuggling regulations. These Americans shot the captain, looted the cargo and burned the ship to the waterline. The perpetrators were charged with treason but found not guilty for lack of evidence. The incident showed the increasing boldness by Americans and the inability of the British to control events.

Boston Tea Party: On December 16, 1773 members of the Sons of Liberty, poorly disguised as American Indians, boarded three British ships (*Dartmouth*, *Eleanor* and *Beaver*) and dumped their hundreds of cases of British East India tea into Boston Harbor. As part of the punishment the British Parliament passed the Intolerable Acts described above. The British actions ratcheted up the ante and further widened the divide between Loyalists and Whigs in America and abroad.

Sources:

Alden, John R. *A History of the American Revolution.*
Archer, Richard. *As If an Enemy's Country. The British Occupation of Boston and the Origins of the American Revolution, 1763-1789.*
Middlekauff, Robert. *The Glorious Cause. The American Revolution.*

LORD DUMORE'S WARS #1 (1774) AND # 2 (1775)

The significance of Lord Dunmore's Wars, especially Number Two merits detailed explanation. John Murray was the Fourth Earl of Dunmore and was thus one of the very few titled royal governors of the American Colonies. He was first named Royal Governor of New York where he earned a reputation for unbridled greed, an uncontrolled ego and incompetence. He was deeply involved in the illegal selling of New Hampshire Grants to settlers of the land between New York and New Hampshire. In 1771, he was named by the Crown as Royal Governor of Virginia. In 1774, he organized militia to fight Indians who were opposing the westward expansion of Virginians. In a clash on October 10, 1774 called the Battle of Point Pleasant the Indians were defeated. Many historians consider this as the first battle of the American Revolution. This is commonly called "Lord Dunmore's First War". Lord Dunmore's Second War is less well known but was far and away more significant for the American Cause than his first war. Seemingly nervous about the security of munitions in the capitol of Virginia (then Williamsburg) and knowing that the Lexington and Concord battles two months prior were about munitions, Dunmore had the munitions secretly evacuated to British ships off shore. This put him in conflict with many local Virginians. Dunmore also made incautious remarks about possible slave revolts and escapes of indentured servants. All this made Virginia's slave owners and indentured servant holders leery of his policies. In late November 1775 Dunmore declared martial law and announced freedom for slaves and indentured servants who would join the British cause. Thinking freedom was at hand they flocked to him. On December 9, 1775, British Redcoats from the 14th Regiment along with 300-400 ex-slaves from Dunmore's Ethiopian Regiment and 300 or so Loyalists clashed with Colonel William Woolford's 2nd Virginia Regiment at Great Bridge 30 miles south of Norfolk. The British lost 102 killed and wounded with the Americans one wounded. The British fled north to Norfolk on board ships in the harbor. The Americans then occupied the Port of Norfolk which had great strategic value and immense logistics infrastructure to support major naval operations. The British began a bombardment of Norfolk, but seemingly not with the intent of destroying the city. Despite its great potential for the American Cause the Americans burned the city, blaming it on the British.

This event had profound positive implications for the American Rebels as is shown in the following: (1) Fearing possible slave revolts instigated by the British, southern landowners almost universally sided with the Americans. (2) The Port of Norfolk became ruined and abandoned by the British. Had they continued to occupy Norfolk they might have not needed to move to Yorktown which led to the disaster there. (3) The more than two-year hiatus of the British from southern Virginia gave the rebels of Virginia time to support their compatriots both north and south without major opposition.

Sources:

Alden, John R. *A History of the American Revolution.*

David, James Corbett. *Dunmore's New World. The Extraordinary Life of a Royal Governor in Revolutionary America.*

Hoock, Holger, *SCARS of INDEPENDENCE. America's Violent Birth.*

Middlekauff, Robert. *The Glorious Cause. The American Revolution.*

Winkler, John F. *Point Pleasant 1774. Prelude to the American Revolution.*

REGIONAL/LOCAL DIFFERENCES AND DISPUTES IN THE COLONIES

Up, into and beyond the Revolutionary War, there were significant territorial conflicts and differences between the individual colonies/states. There were three large blocks of colonies/states where the differences were most pronounced: The Northern Colonies of Massachusetts, New Hampshire, Connecticut, Rhode Island and New York; The Middle Colonies of Maryland, Delaware, Pennsylvania and New Jersey and The Southern Colonies of Virginia, North Carolina, South Carolina and Georgia. While there was some blurring, the differences can be delineated into the following categories: subordination, religion, territorial, economic, cultural, revolutionary fervor and slavery.

The regional and individual differences were well known by the British and gave them the belief that the colonies could never coalesce into powerful military and political entities. This gave them confidence the American Rebels could be defeated with relative ease. For example: Benjamin Franklin saw the need for the colonies to bond together and in 1754 proposed The Albany Plan of Union. It called for the union of 11 colonies with a president appointed by the Crown. The recommendations were submitted by their delegates but seven of the colonial legislators rejected them because it would have taken away some of their powers. To the British this was emblematic of the non-cooperation between the colonies that would make them easy prey.

The following are discussions of each of the major issues and differences between the colonies which could have spelled disaster for the Revolution:

ECONOMIC

Northern Colonies: While land was plentiful and relatively inexpensive in the Northern Colonies it was not suitable for large scale enterprise farming and was mostly forested mountains with rocky and fairly poor soil. The hard and cold northern climate made for relatively short growing seasons. Most farms there were local subsistence enterprises. However, because these colonies had a long coastline with many excellent harbors and inland rivers ship building and repair was a major business there. The British policy of reserving without compensation the highly prized 27-inch diameter trees for use as masts for their navy was a significant irritant to these colonies (See King Tree Acts). Smuggling was also a major profit generator in the Northern Colonies. British attempts to control smuggling turned many in these colonies into hard core revolutionaries. Fishing in the outer banks of the Atlantic was also a large-scale business. Trade was a major factor in the Northern Colonies which made Britain's boycotts, embargoes, and enumerations especially hurtful to these colonies. Because of Britain's Navigation Acts which restricted trade, its mercantilist policies, anti-smuggling efforts, taxation policies, and thoughtless actions the Northern Colonies became a hot-bed of revolutionary fervor.

Middle Colonies: Despite the more moderate climate and less mountainous rugged terrain of the Middle Colonies large scale plantation farming in these Colonies not at all like the Southern Colonies. Wheat was a significant agricultural product along with growing tobacco in some parts of Maryland, but large-scale plantation farming was not prevalent in the area. Like the Northern Colonies import/export trade was a major economic element in these colonies. Therefore, Britain's policies regarding trade and taxation were major factors in these colonies joining the American Cause.

Southern Colonies: The piedmont areas of these colonies were perfectly suited for large scale profit plantation farming of labor intensive crops such as rice, tobacco and indigo. The great need for low cost labor for these farming operations made the slave trade a significant economic element for these colonies. Although British trade policies were irksome to these colonies, Britain was a major importer of the agricultural products of the area. The result was that the Southern Colonies except for Virginia, up to the start of the Revolution, were not as rabid in their desire to break with Britain as were the Middle and Northern Colonies. This all was significantly and irrevocably changed at the outset of the war when the British proposed freedom for slaves who fought against the Rebel Americans which turned Southern Colonial white landowners against the British.

RELIGION

Northern Colonies: These colonies absorbed the bulk of immigrants fleeing the hostile Anglican Church in Britain which was effectively an arm of the Crown. From these immigrants spawned the Puritan and Congregationalist movements unique to this area. These strict groups were intolerant of the rule by the Anglicans which among other things preached predestination. Anglicanism preached that specific groups were "predestined" for heavenly bliss while others were to live lives of misery, poverty and hardship. The Puritan and Congregationalist ethic espoused Deism which said man was the master of his own destiny and that salvation, hard work and good acts could result in improving one's lot. This created the "leveling" as it was frequently called and lack of social stratification, equality and democratic culture typical of the region that pervades to this very day.

Middle Colonies: Theses colonies had three distinct religious groups: German Lutherans in Pennsylvania, Quakers in Pennsylvania and New Jersey and Catholics in Maryland. The Quakers were prominent in their anti-war philosophy which put them in the no-win position of supporting neither the British nor American Rebels. The Lutheran Dutch and Germans had no particular ax to grind but in general they supported the American cause because they too had fled their home countries to escape the oppression they had experienced there. Because the Catholics in Maryland were persecuted in Britain they supported the American cause.

Southern Colonies: In this group of colonies Presbyterianism was dominant which preached tolerance and anti-Anglican thought. These individuals were mostly Scotch/Irish who had fled the oppression of the British in Scotland and Ireland. Their brand of religion was mostly centered on the western areas of the Carolinas and Georgia.

REVOLUTIONARY FERVOR

Northern Colonies: The American Revolution was sparked in the Northern Colonies for multiple reasons. They were the first highly populated colonies and the people mostly came from Britain. The inhabitants left Britain because of the highly-stratified class structure there where there was little opportunity for economic mobility. They were highly educated and knew the rights of Englishmen under the English constitution which were being abridged in America. They opposed taxation without representation. They knew their rights of local justice and illegal search and seizure. They left Britain where corruption was rampant, immorality prevalent and was now being tolerated by the British officials in America. The Anglican Church acted as an arm of the crown rather than as a place for comfort, salvation and healing. The British stationed far and away too many of its soldiers than were needed in the Northern Colonies. This was unique to these colonies. These British soldiers were a burden and constant serious irritant to those of the Northern Colonies. The British Navigation Acts were particularly burdensome on these colonies where trade was critical to their economic well-being. British trade and anti-smuggling policies were particularly hurtful to the Northern Colonies. The result of these long-term issues was that the Northern Colonies took the early lead in the break with Britain even if by military means.

Middle Colonies: These colonies were more of a mix of immigrants from other European counties than the Northern Colonies. Therefore, there was less inherent hostility to Britain than from the Northern Colonies. There was more religious diversity in these colonies with Lutheranism from German and Dutch immigrants, Quakers in Pennsylvania and Catholics in Maryland. Trade was highly important to these colonies which meant British mercantilist and preferential trade policies drove these colonies to the American Cause.

Southern Colonies: Boston was the center for Revolutionary fervor in the Northern Colonies and Williamsburg Virginia was so for the Southern Colonies. The capitol of Virginia was moved from Williamsburg to Richmond at the request of Thomas Jefferson in 1780. The hostility and Revolutionary fervor of Boston was more due to direct action by the British such as quartering of their troops there, anti-smuggling, King Tree Acts and enumeration of products. In Virginia, it was more a matter of principles such as taxation without representation, and interference by the Crown in local affairs. Patrick Henry raised the issue to Colonial-wide notice with his famous speech on May 29, 1765 comparing George III to Brutus and saying: "If this be treason, make the most of it". What immediately followed was the Virginia Resolves which focused their opposition to taxation without representation. Thereafter, there were a series of escalating actions in the Southern Colonies such as the formation of a Committee of Correspondence in 1773 to coordinate actions in support of Massachusetts Port Act and election of delegates to the First Continental Congress, the President of which was Virginia's Payton Randolph.

SLAVERY

Northern Colonies: By the time of the Revolution there were individual instances of slavery in all these colonies, but on a whole, the practice was disparaged and thought badly of. The slave trade was made illegal in Connecticut and Rhode Island in 1774. The Puritan and Congregational Churches of these colonies preached against the practice of slavery. Slavery was contrary to the classlessness of these colonies and emphasis on equality and humanity. The early immigrants of these colonies in a large part came to America to better themselves and rise above their miserable existence in Britain which was inconsistent with slavery. The anti-slavery culture of the Northern Colonies had been entrenched by the time slaves began arriving in America in significant numbers. The absence of large landholders in the area and harsh winter climate made slavery impractical on a large-scale basis in the Northern Colonies. There was also the lack of large scale labor intensive agricultural enterprises (rice, tobacco and indigo cultivation) that could have made slavery profitable in the Northern Colonies. The anti-slavery sentiment was so pronounced by the soldiers from these colonies that they opposed campaigning in the Southern Colonies because they felt they would be supporting slavery.

Middle Colonies: Except for some parts of eastern Maryland where plantations existed to cultivate tobacco, slavery and wheat, slavery in these colonies was not practiced on a significant basis. Pennsylvania became the first colony to prohibit the slave trade in 1773. The Quakers, Lutherans, and Catholics of these colonies all opposed slavery on religious and moral grounds.

Southern Colonies: The first shipload of Blacks to America arrived in Virginia aboard a Dutch ship which had captured them from a Spanish ship destined for the West Indies. Slavery in the Southern Colonies actually started with large numbers of white indentured servants from Europe that were treated no better than slaves. However, these individuals served only for specified periods (usually no more than seven years) which made their use in a plantation environment difficult. Slavery was permanent and self-sustaining which made it ideal for plantation agriculture where there was an insatiable need for labor to work the fields of tobacco, rice and indigo. In 1770 slaves constituted 40% of the population in Virginia and 30% in Maryland. By the start of the Revolution, South Carolina had 100,000 slaves and 70,000 whites. The economies of the Southern Colonies were highly dependent on slave labor. Although British trade policies were irritants to the Southern Colonies the trade with Britain in agricultural products from slave labor made the southern plantation owners extremely wealthy. Lord Dunmore Royal Governor of Virginia in November 1775 then made the catastrophic strategic mistake of announcing freedom for slaves who would fight against American Rebels. The prospect of their slaves fleeing their plantations and possibly rising against them terrified Southern colonial landholders and drove them permanently into the American Rebel camp. The mistake was compounded by General Clinton on June 30, 1779 with his Philipsburg Proclamation which promised freedom and amnesty for slaves who left their masters and joined against the American Rebels. The adverse consequences for the British were huge. The tens of thousands of slaves who tried to flee their masters could not be supported by the British and died by the score of disease and starvation. The American Revolution was in fact won in the Southern Colonies as shown by the Battles of Kings Mountain, Cowpens, Guilford Courthouse, Race for the Dan River and Yorktown.

SUBORDINATION

Subordination refers to the social stratification of the peoples of three colonial groups.

Northern Colonies: The colonists of these colonies left Britain in a significant way to escape the brutal class structure that existed there. The result was that in the northern colonies there evolved a culture where there was a significant absence of class structure. Puritan and Congregationalist teachings stressed fairness and equality. This classlessness was a serious drawback for the creation of military units from this area. Officers were elected by the men (soldiers – enlisted men) from their units who were often their best friends. Officers did not know how to issue orders and soldiers had little inclination to follow those they did not like. Officers who were barbers before the Revolution would cut the hair of their men. The result was chaos and a near complete breakdown of discipline which is the backbone of all effective military units. General Washington and his generals were appalled at the lack of subordination demonstrated by soldiers of New England. One of the fundamental elements in the creation of military units is "Basic Military Training" where soldiers learn without hesitation to obey the orders of their "superiors". There was no such basic military training for the soldiers of New England which seriously degraded their performance. This helps explain the very important contribution of MG Baron von Steuben who with the blessing of Washington upon his arrival in America on December 1, 1777 effectively created a basic military training program for American soldiers. The results of this training were dramatic and very positive.

Middle Colonies: The settlers of the Middle Colonies were mostly from Germany and the Netherlands where subordination was more part of their cultural make-up and background. There was not the "culture shock" of becoming disciplined soldiers in the Middle Colonies soldiers like there was in Northern Colonies.

Southern Colonies: Social stratification was part of the culture of the Southern Colonies. This came in part from the many Scotch Irish who came to the area and the plantation culture where land owners were the law of the land there. Slavery also had an impact on social stratification. Southern soldiers adapted to military structured life far better than the men of the North. This was so pronounced that southern soldiers openly disparaged the soldiers of the north as "Damn Yankees".

TERRITORIAL/BORDER/DISPUTES

New York/New Hampshire: The most notable and potentially explosive border dispute during the Revolution was between the colonies of New York and New Hampshire. New York claimed the land east of Lake Champlain to the Connecticut River which was the western border of New Hampshire; the land that is now the state of Vermont. New Hampshire claimed the same land west to the border of Lake Champlain. At the time, the land was called the "New Hampshire Grants". Technically, by Royal decree the land did belong to New York, but the Royal Governor of New Hampshire (Benning Wentworth) sold plots (grants) of land in the disputed territory to settlers mostly from Connecticut and Massachusetts. The Royal Governor of New York (William Tryon) tried to sell grants for the same property which meant these settlers would have had to pay twice for the same land. Ethan Allen made it his mission to resolve the situation in favor of the individuals who had bought land from New Hampshire. Threats of open warfare between New York and New Hampshire simmered throughout the Revolution to the great consternation of

Gen Washington. Allen actually made serious threats to invite British troops from Canada to the contested land. Vermont declared itself an independent republic in January 1777. After protracted debate in the U.S. Congress Vermont was declared a state of the U.S. in 1791.

Connecticut/Pennsylvania: Connecticut claimed territory in the Susquehanna Valley of Pennsylvania (then frequently called the Wyoming Territory). Connecticut and Pennsylvania both started selling tracks to the same land. This actually led to armed conflict called the Pennamite War which was not settled in favor of Pennsylvania until 1788.

Connecticut/Massachusetts: These two states were in conflict over the northern border of Connecticut which was not settled until 1804.

Maryland/Virginia: The borders of these two states were in dispute until 1877.

Maryland/Pennsylvania: It was not unit 1763 that Maryland and Pennsylvania agreed to accept the border survey lines of Charles Dixon and Jeremiah Mason which had been hired by Britain to resolve their territorial disputes.

Delaware/Maryland/Pennsylvania: Delaware was originally settled by the Dutch but they were expelled by the British in 1674 which created the colony of Delaware over the protests of Maryland which wanted that land.

New Jersey/Pennsylvania/New York: The western borders of New Jersey and New York were contested throughout the Revolution. It was not until 1833 that New York and New Jersey came to agreement on their eastern border along the Hudson River.

New Hampshire/Massachusetts Territory of Maine: The New Hampshire border with the Massachusetts Territory of Maine was not settled until the Treaty of Paris in 1783.

Georgia/North Carolina: In 1732 King George II granted the colonial charter for Georgia. Both Georgia and North Carolina claimed the same land on their northern borders which led to periodic bloodshed until 1803.

North Carolina/South Carolina: Due to errors in the original surveys of the Royal Charters for these colonies their borders needed to be significantly redrawn which led to long standing disputes.

CONCLUSION

It is frequently said that it was a miracle the Thirteen Colonies could bind together to pass the Declaration of Independence and defeat the largest and most professional Army and Navy in the world and then agree on the U.S. Constitution that has passed the test of time. It is even more amazing that they could cooperate and get this done in the face of all the above obstacles to cooperation, coordinated effort and joint sacrifice.

Sources:

Miller, John C. *Origins of the American Revolution.*
Randall, William. *Ethan Allen, His Life and Times.*
Smith, Page. *A New Age Begins, Vols I & II.*
Stein, Mark. *How the States got their Shapes.*

COLLECTIVE COLONIAL ORGANIZATIONS

First Continental Congress: This group met at Carpenter's Hall in Philadelphia from September 5 – October 22, 1774. All thirteen colonies had a minimum of two and a maximum of seven representatives each, except Georgia which did not send representatives because it sought British forces to control American Indian attacks there. No representative could serve more than three years out of a period of six years. Each colony no matter how large or small had only one vote. There were no "branches" of government in the Congress. The votes of nine representatives were required for important votes and seven votes for more minor matters. Congress had the exclusive right to make treaties and declare war and or peace. The States/Colonies appointed all regimental officers from colonel on down. All members were elected by their colonies. Virginia representative Peyton Randolph was president of the First Continental Congress. One of its goals was to agree on issues to present to the Crown to prevent a break with Britain. Pennsylvania's Representative Joseph Galloway proposed a plan (sometimes referred to the Galloway Plan) to create a governing body that was to be called the **Grand Council**. It would have a body similar to Parliament elected by the Colonies and a President General appointed by the Crown. There was considerable support for the plan in Philadelphia but not in Boston which suffered the worst of Britain's restrictions. Sensing that the Galloway

Plan might be adopted Dr. Joseph Warren a Boston firebrand wrote a document called the **Suffolk County (Boston) Resolves** and had Paul Revere make a last-minute ride from Boston to Philadelphia to present it to the Congress which proposed:

1. A boycott of British goods, curtailment of exports to Britain and limits of the use of British goods by Americans. This would create economic hardship on merchants in Britain.
2. Non-compliance with the Boston Port Act.
3. Demands for the resignation of British appointed Massachusetts officials.
4. Refusal to pay taxes until the Massachusetts Government Act was repealed
5. Creation of a Massachusetts Colonial Government until the Intolerable Acts were repealed.
6. The Colonies raise militia to protect their rights.

The Suffolk Resolves stiffened the spine of the delegates which defeated the Grand Council plan by a narrow vote. The members agreed to meet again next year but by then the Revolution was in full swing. The Congress also voted to boycott British goods in response to the Coercive/Intolerable Acts.

Continental Association: To oppose the heavy-handed policies of the British the First Continental Congress created the Continental Association which coordinated the actions, information sharing, reactions and policies of the thirteen colonies. Enforcement of the Resolves was left to local "Committees" of Safety, Correspondence, Communications, Enforcement and Inspection". The committees used various methods such as intimidation, destruction of property, threats and sometimes violence (tar and feathering and riding the rail) and other extra-legal activities to ensure compliance. Boycotts of British goods by Americans caused economic hardship in Britain and political opposition in Parliament to oppression of the colonies. It also greatly widened the divide in America between "Loyalists" (supporters of the Crown), and "Whigs" (those who supported independence for the Colonies). This hardened divide helped make possible the armed resistance and rebellion by the American Colonists.

Second Continental Congress: War with Britain had already broken out by the time this group met in Philadelphia on May 5, 1775. All thirteen colonies were represented including Georgia with a total of 56 delegates. It was from this Congress that the Declaration of Independence was created and signed. The Congress managed the war effort through the Board of War to which General Washington reported. It administered other colonial activities through boards and committees. During the War, the Congress moved from Philadelphia to Baltimore to Lancaster to York and back to Philadelphia to avoid capture by the British. On November 17, 1777, the Congress passed the Articles of Confederation which were ultimately adopted on March 1, 1781. This created the Congress of the Confederation (sometimes called the Continental Congress or Congress of the U.S.) which took over the responsibilities of governing the country until March 4, 1789.

Sources:

Alden, John R. *A History of the American Revolution.*

Ferling, John. *Almost a Miracle. The American Victory in the War for Independence.*_

Middlekauff, Robert. *The Glorious Cause. The American Revolution.*

Mitchell, Broadus. *The Price of Independence. A Realistic View of the American Revolution.*

EFFORTS TO NEGOTIATE AN END TO THE REVOLUTION

Galloway Plan: See First Continental Congress above.

North Peace Plan: Sometimes known as the **Conciliatory Proposal** it was a last-ditch effort by Prime Minister Lord Frederick North to avoid war with the American Colonies. He made the proposal on February 20, 1775 to Parliament without approval of King George III. It called for the colonies to pay proportional taxes levied as they sought fit from an overall amount determined by the Crown which would spend the money as it saw fit. The Crown would not apply additional taxes on the colonies if they approved the plan. The plan was to be presented separately to each of the colonies possibly to sow dissention among them. War broke out on April 19, 1775 at Concord/Lexington and the proposal was sent by the colonies to the Continental Congress where it was dead on arrival.

Olive Branch Petition: This was a last-ditch effort of the Colonists by a petition to King George III on July 5, 1775 to prevent outright war with Britain. The British were confident that they would win any war with the Americans. In the petition the Americans stated their continued loyalty to the Crown, but George III refused to even read the it and on August 23, 1775 issued the **Proclamation of Rebellion,** otherwise known as the: "Proclamation for Suppressing Rebellion and Sedition" which rejected peace with the colonies and was in effect a declaration of war.

Staten Island Peace Conference: This was a peace conference instigated by British Commander-In-Chief General William Howe and his brother Admiral Richard Howe Commander of British Naval forces in America after their arrival in New York. Both brothers had insisted they be given diplomatic powers to end the Revolution before they would serve in America. George III and Lord George Germain Minister of Colonies only gave them powers to grant pardons and amnesty. American Major General John Sullivan who had been captured at the Battle of Long Island on August 27, 1776 was paroled to facilitate the meeting. The meeting was held on September 11, 1776 in a home on Staten Island. Benjamin Franklin, John Adams and John Rutledge from the Second Continental Congress attended representing the Colonies. Franklin and Adams both insisted on British recognition of American independence which the Howe brothers had no authority to grant; therefore, the conference ended in failure. General Sullivan was later exchanged just before the Battle of Trenton for British Brigadier General Richard Prescott who had been captured at the Battle of Montreal on November 17, 1775.

Carlisle Peace Commission: The Carlisle Commission was a group of British negotiators headed by the Earl of Carlisle that were sent aboard the *HMS ANDROMEDA* arriving in New York on April 14, 1778. The treaty of alliance with France which was delivered aboard the *USS SENSIBLE* by Simeon Deane, the son of Silas Deane, arrived Casco Bay Maine on April 13, 1778. The British Commission which was presented on June 13, 1778, proposed to end the war and offered self-rule for America. The Americans insisted on independence and withdrawal of all British troops in America, especially in light of the French alliance. The American terms were unacceptable to the British so the effort failed.

French Foreign Minister Vergennes Peace Initiative: At the urging of French Foreign Minister Charles compte de Vergennes in early 1779 the Continental Congress began discussing terms of a possible peace initiative. France which had been bankrolling the American Revolution for three years saw no end to the conflict. Russia and Austria indicated they would act as mediators. Britain indicated it was possibly receptive to peace if it could retain the territory currently under their control which was New York City and much of the coastal cities of the Southern States which understandably balked at the idea they might be sold out to the British. Congress ultimately sent a clear message to Vergennes that America would never surrender any of its territory for a peace agreement which was the death knell of the initiative.

Sources:

Alden, John R. *A History of the American Revolution.*
Daughan, George C. *REVOLUTION on the HUDSON. New York City and the Hudson River Valley in the American War of Independence.*
Ellis, Joseph J. *Revolutionary Summer. The Birth of American Independence.*
Ferling, John. *Almost a Miracle. The American Victory in the War for Independence.*
Ferreiro, Larrie D. *Brothers At Arms. American Independence and the Men of France and Spain Who Saved It.*
Hooch, Holger. *SCARS of INDEPENDENCE. America's Violent Birth.*
Isaacson, Walter. *Benjamin Franklin. An American Life.*
Mackesy, Piers. *The War for America 1775-1783.*
McCullough, David. *1776.*
Middlekauff, Robert. *The Glorious Cause. The American Revolution.*
O'Shaughnessy, Andrew Jackson. *The Men Who Lost America. British Leadership, the American Revolution and the Fate of the Empire.*
Rappleye, Charles. *Robert Morris.*

ATTEMPT TO MAKE QUEBEC THE FOURTEENTH COLONY

Overcome with a false sense of confidence from the early military victories over the British at Lexington/Concord (April 19, 1775), Fort Ticonderoga (May 10, 1775) and Bunker Hill (June 17, 1775) the Americans set their eyes on conquering the British Province of Quebec which had been created by the Proclamation Act of 1763. Quebec had many divisions among its people just as existed in the Thirteen Colonies. The "Old Subjects" were the British that lived in Quebec after the French and Indian War. They naturally preferred rule by the British Crown. The "New Subjects" were the French that remained after the War and preferred the former forms of French government. Quebec was primarily agrarian with the peasants known as "Habitants" tilling the land as tenant farmers for major wealthy land owners known as "Seigneurs". The Habitants and Seigneurs were primarily Roman Catholics. Parish Priests were known as "Cures" and had great influence over the people of the province.

With the establishment of the Continental Army on June 16, 1775 a "Northern Department" was created under the command of Maj Gen Philip Schuyler to lead military operations in the north. On

June 27, 1775, he was given orders to take possession of Montreal, St. John's and surrounding area. The campaign north to Quebec via St. John's and Montreal began in late August. The Americans tried to enlist the Habitants in their campaign. The British tried to enlist the Old Subjects to repel the Americans. Due to illness and other commitments, command of the attack was given to American BG Richard Montgomery. Due to bad weather, difficult terrain and expiration of enlistments the campaign went very slowly. Colonel Ethan Allen was captured on September 25, 1775 outside of Montreal attempting to attack the city against his orders. St. John's finally fell to the Americans on November 3, 1775 followed by Montreal on November 13, 1775.

Benedict Arnold, who had participated in the capture of Fort Ticonderoga, left for Boston after the Northern Department was given to Gen Schuyler. He proposed to Gen Washington an attack on Quebec via the Kennebec River through the territory of Maine. The attack was approved with 1,000+ men starting on September 25, 1775. In an epic journey through unmapped land and horrific weather Arnold's group lost 200 men to disease, desertion, starvation and accidents. He finally arrived south of Quebec on November 11, 1775. Bad weather, lack of food and supplies hindered the joint attack on Quebec by Arnold and Montgomery which finally occurred during a blizzard on December 31, 1775. Despite near success the Americans were defeated with Montgomery being killed in the battle and Arnold seriously wounded. Many of Arnold's men were taken prisoner and incarcerated for six months before their release. This ended the major attempt to make Quebec America's fourteenth colony.

Sources:

Anderson, Mark R. *The Battle for the Fourteenth Colony. America's War of Liberation in Canada 1774-1776.*

Leake, Isaac Q. *Memoir of the Life and Times of General John Lamb. An Officer of the American Revolution.*
Lefkowitz, Arnold S. *Benedict Arnold in the Company of Heroes.*
Shelton, Hal T. *General Richard Montgomery and the American Revolution from Redcoat to Rebel.*

AMERICAN ARMY

Because there was no "unity" between the 13 Colonies before the Revolution there was no American National Army. However, there were two parts which would eventually work with the National Army: (1) Local Militia and (2) State Militia. (See Chapter on American Militia for further details). The American Army was called the Continental Line and was created by the Second Continental Congress on June 16, 1775. It was the equivalent of today's Regular Army. It initially consisted of four departments (Corps): (1) Adjutant General (2) Engineer (3) Finance and (4) Quartermaster. Very soon thereafter Cavalry and Field Artillery corps were added. General George Washington became the first Commander of the Continental Army. The Continental Line was organized into six combat brigades totaling 27,000 soldiers. The ranks were filled by volunteers or "draftees" that came from "levies" placed on the Colonies by the Continental Congress. Because there was no universal tax system among the colonies, the pay for these soldiers was supposed to come from levies imposed on the colonies, which frequently failed to meet their obligations to pay their soldiers. The detailed history of the Continental Army is currently maintained at the U.S. Army Infantry Center, Fort Benning, Georgia. According to these records the Continental Army lost 4,044 killed in action and 6,004 wounded during the Revolution. At its height in 1776 the Continental Army consisted of 46,891 soldiers. At the end of the Revolution the Army was mostly disbanded due to extreme funding shortages, but soon resurrected as the United States Army when it was realized a standing army was needed to enforce borders and protect against American Indian raids.

Sources:

Ferling, John. *Almost A Miracle. The American Victory in the War of Independence.*

Ketchum, Richard M. *The Winter Soldiers. The Battles of Trenton and Princeton.*

Martin, James K. & Mark E. Lender. *A Respectable Army. The Military Origins of the Republic 1763-1789.*

Savas, Theodore P. & J. David Dameron. *A Guide to the Battles of the American Revolution.*

Smith, Page. *A New Age Now Begins.* (Volumes 1 & 2)

AMERICAN NAVY

Because there was also no "unity" between the 13 Colonies before the Revolution America did not have a National Navy. Therefore, it had to start from scratch to build one under combat conditions, which was a daunting task. However, eleven of the 13 colonies had their own militia navies. Their mission was to control piracy, lawlessness and maintain order on their coasts. The Continental Navy was established by the Second Continental Congress on October 13, 1775. On December 13, 1775, the Congress authorized 13 frigates for the Navy: five with 32 guns, five with 28 guns and three with 24 guns. The estimated cost for these ships was $866,666. By 1780 the cost had spiraled to $13 million. America did not lack ship building expertise or capacity. It lacked military ship building ability. The American Revolution was a naval war. The thirteen colonies had a 3,000-mile Atlantic coastline. The Colonies had their own Privateer fleets, so in reality America eventually had three parts to its navy: Continental Navy, State Naval Militia and State Sponsored Privateers. The Mississippi River was increasingly becoming a critical water way for international commerce. American products: indigo, tobacco, iron and rum and more were increasingly in demand on international markets which required global water transport. The mission was to build a navy with the capability to fight the British head to head on the high seas and protect America's merchant fleets. By 1780 only five of the initial warships were left floating: The *Alliance, Confederacy, Deane, Trumbull* and *Saratoga*. They were eventually all lost or de-commissioned. America relied on the Spanish and French Navies to do head to head combat with the British Navy so the American Navy mostly relied on privateers to inflict pain and damage to the British. The first significant success of the Continental Navy was at the Battle of Valcour Island on Lake Champlain in October 1776. At the battle, General Benedict Arnold with his little fleet of boats and vessels delayed the movement of the British Army of the North from advancing from Canada towards Albany, NY until it was too late in October for the British to proceed further. This caused a critical one year delay for a second attempt to capture Lake Champlain and drive down the Hudson River to Albany. After peace was signed in 1783 the American Navy was disbanded in 1785 due to lack of funds and fear of a standing military force. It was reconstituted as the United States Navy in 1789.

Sources:

Bratten, John R. *The Gondola PHILADELPHIA & Battle of Lake Champlain.*

Ferling, John. *Almost a Miracle. The American Victory in the War of Independence.*

Fowler, William M. *The American Navy during the Revolution.*

McGrath, Tim. *Give Me a Fast Ship. America's Continental Navy and America's Revolution at Sea.*

Nelson, James L. *Benedict Arnold's Navy. The Ragtag Fleet that Lost the Battle of Lake Champlain but Won the Revolution.*

Nelson, James L. *George Washington's Great Gamble and the Sea Battle that Won the American Revolution.*

Patton, Robert H. *Patriot Pirates. The Privateer War for Freedom and Fortune in the American Revolution.*

Savas, Theodore P. & J. David Dameron. *A Guide to the Battles of the American Revolution.*

Shomette, Donald Grady. *PRIVATEERS of the REVOLUTION. War on the New Jersey Coast 1775-1783.*

Smith, Page. *A New Age Now Begins.* (Volumes 1 & 2)

AMERICAN NAVAL PRIVATEERS

Privateering was a practice whereby privately owned and operated ships with official State provided authorization papers called "Letters of Marque" could attack and seize enemy cargo and warships called "Prizes". The crews, owners and investors who provided the money to "fit and crew" the ships would share in the profits from the sale of the prizes and their cargoes. It is estimated that American Privateers captured 3,000+ prizes during the Revolution for a cost to Britain of up to $60 million. Because of privateering British merchant marine insurance increased 20% due to the estimated 10% ship losses they experienced. The arms captured by privateers provided a lifeline to America's armed forces. For example: the British cargo ship *NANCY* captured on November 27, 1775 by a privateer off Massachusetts contained 2,000 muskets, 31 tons of musket shot, 100,000 musket flints, 30,000 cannon shot and more. Privateering had its down side though because it made crewing American Naval ships extremely difficult resulting from the competition for crewmembers. Privateers who were captured by the British faced prison for life without the possibility of exchange according to the Pirate Act of March 1777. In the final analysis privateering was more costly and damaging to Britain than the American Navy and played an important role in the success of the Revolution.

Another good example of the success of American privateers is the September convoy of Hessian soldiers out of NYC in 1779. Nearly 1,000 Hessians were loaded onto six British troop transports: *TRITON, ADAMANT, BADGER, POLLY,* and two un-named ships for a secret destination, most probably Canada. These Hessians had mostly been captured at the Battle of Trenton on December 27th, 1776. They had subsequently been exchanged. The whole convoy ran into a hurricane four days out of NYC. All the ships were severely damaged. Two, one of which was the *ADAMANT* and an un-named ship were lost with all hands in the storm. The *TRITON* nearly sank and was captured by a privateer with 214 Hessians aboard. Despite the efforts of the British Navy to recapture the ship, it was towed successfully back to American waters where the Hessians became POWs again. The *POLLY* shared the same fate with the passengers becoming POWs again. The *BADGER* was captured by privateers and recaptured by a British war ship and towed back to British control in NYC. One of the un-named ships with 150 Hessians aboard was captured by an American privateer and the passengers made POWs again. Only one of the six ships in the convoy made it safely back to NYC without being captured. The ships with their Hessian passengers and British crews lost at sea and made POWs again by the Americans represented the equivalent of a significant battlefield loss by the enemy.

Sources:

Martin, James K. & Mark E. Lender. *A Respectable Army. The Military Origins of the Republic, 1763-1789.*

McGrath, Tim. *Give Me a Fast Ship. America's Continental Navy and America's Revolution at Sea.*

Patton, Robert H. *Patriot Pirates. The Privateer War for Freedom and Fortune in the American Revolution.*

Shomette, Donald Grady. *PRIVATEERS of the REVOLUTION. War on the New Jersey Coast 1775-1783.*

Smith, Page. *A New Age Now Begins.* (Volumes 1 & 2).

AMERICAN MARINES

American Marines were founded on November 10, 1775 as Naval Infantry. Their initial mission was ship security and for boarding enemy ships and repelling enemy boarders. On March 3, 1776, the Marines had their first significant action during the Revolution with their capture of the British Forts Montague and Nassau in the Bahamas. The largest and most extensive land combat action by the Marines during the Revolution was at the Battle of Penobscot Bay in the Massachusetts territory of Maine in August 1779. The Marines distinguished themselves but the expedition ended in failure due to poor leadership by the expedition commander, Commodore Dudley Saltonstall. Like the Navy, the Marines were disbanded after the Revolution due to funding shortages and then resurrected.

Sources:

Buker, George E. *The Penobscot Expedition.*

Savas, Theodore P. & J. David Dameron. *A Guide to the Battles of the American Revolution.*

AFRICAN AMERICANS

Britain outlawed slave trade in 1772. The Royal Governor of Virginia, Lord Dunmore, in the fall of 1775 organized 300 African Americans into what became as known as Dunmore's "Ethiopian Regiment" for duty against American rebels. The Ethiopian Regiment and their Loyalist comrades and British officers were demolished at the Battle of Great Bridge on December 6, 1775 south of Norfolk, VA. In 1776 British General Sir William Howe ordered all African Americans discharged from the British Army. Due to shortages of manpower they were later encouraged to rejoin the British Army by Gen Howe with his Philipsburg Proclamation of June 30, 1779. This proclamation promised security for Negroes who fled their masters and prohibited their sale. It also indicated that Negroes who were captured supporting the rebel Americans would be sold. Ultimately blacks served with distinction on both sides of the conflict. The largest and most distinguished African American combat unit that fought for the American Cause was the First Rhode Island Infantry Regiment. Because of the promises made by the British thousands of Negroes did in fact flee for British protection which never materialized when the British were defeated. The fear of recapture and return to slavery in a large part explains why so many thousands of Negroes fled America at the end of the War. Most African Americans who joined the British were used in support roles such as digging trenches, building fortifications and hauling supplies rather than direct combat.

General Washington in early 1776 initially prohibited the enlistment of Blacks into the American forces. Later that same year, seriously short of soldiers, he permitted the enlistment of Black freemen (not escaped slaves). A former slave of General Washington by the name of Harry Washington escaped from General Washington in 1771 and in 1776 joined the British forces in 1776 and served mostly in Charles Town SC. When the British evacuated Charles Town in 1782 Harry Washington fled to the British enclave in NYC. The 1783 Treaty of Paris prohibited the British from evacuating Blacks from NYC with their soldiers from the city. Washington strongly argued to have the Blacks prohibited from evacuation. LTG Guy Carleton in command of the British evacuation forcefully argued that it was impossible to prohibit the evacuation of Blacks with British troops which was fully underway. The result was that thousands of Blacks departed America with the British in 1783. Harry Washington along with thousands of British soldiers and Loyalists successfully evacuated NYC to Nova Scotia.

Sources:

Aron, Paul. *FOUNDING FEUDS. The Rivalries, Clashes, and Conflicts That Forged a Nation.*

Ferling, John. *Almost A Miracle. The American Victory in the War of Independence.*

Hooch, Holger. *SCARS of INDEPENDENCE. America's Violent Past.*

Jasanoff, Maya. *Liberty's Exiles. American Loyalists in the Revolutionary World.*

Raphael, Ray. *A People's History of the American Revolution, How Common People Shaped the Fight for Independence.*

Savas, Theodore P. & J. David Dameron. *A Guide to Battles of the American Revolution.*

Smith, Page. *A New Age Now Begins.* (Volumes 1 & 2)

AMERICAN INDIANS

At the end of the French and Indian War in accordance with King George's Proclamation of 1763 all lands west of the Allegheny Mountains were declared off limits for American settlers and reserved for the British to administer in part for American Indians. However, there was an inevitable push westward by American settlers which created constant conflict with the Indians. The American Colonists, not the British, were settling western lands so the logical thing for most of the Indian tribes to do was to tilt to side with the British. Up to 1772 there was a loose Indian organization known as the Iroquois Confederacy which with the addition of the Tuscarora became the Six Nations Confederacy. The Indians of the West and North slaughtered American Colonists to such a degree that in 1779 Gen Washington sent MG John Sullivan with 4,000 soldiers to devastate the American Indian settlements in Pennsylvania and upper New York. He did this job with ruthlessness in order to effectively end the predatory acts of the American Indians in the region. The British used American Indians for scouting, reconnaissance, ambush and direct combat, much to their detriment. The Indians were guilty of incredible atrocities against militia, American Rebels, prisoners and non-combatant civilians. These actions worked against the British by playing into the Whig factions in Britain who were appalled that the British Army in America would countenance these acts. Some individual Indian tribes attached themselves to various sides of the conflict. In fact, the Tuscarora and Oneida tilted to the Americans. The chief of the

Oneida, Han Yerry, and members of his tribe brought 600 bushels of white corn through British and Loyalist controlled lines to help feed the starving Americans at Valley Forge in 1777. From the start to the end of the Revolution and beyond, the Indians, North, West and South, fought the expansion of the American Colonists and paid a significant price for the ultimate victory of the Americans over the British.

Sources:

Blackmon, Richard D. *Dark and Bloody Ground.*

Ferling, John. *Almost A. Miracle. The American Victory in the War of Independence.*

Hooch, Holger. *SCARS of INDEPENDENCE. America's Violent Past.*

Martin, James K. & Mark E. Lender. *A Respectable Army. The Military Origins of the Republic, 1763-1789.*

Raphael, Ray. *A People's History of the American Revolution, How Common People Shaped the Fight for Independence.*

AMERICAN MILITIA

There were two kinds of American Militia: local and state. Local Militia were soldiers that signed up for very brief periods, up to 60 days and were paid from very local sources. They responded to local situations where their help was needed to fight loyalists, Indians or the British. State militia were raised and paid for by the state and commanded by state officers. Their enlistments were usually longer, up to one year. They could operate independently or in conjunction with the Continental Army. The intent was for them to operate within the borders of their state, but that was frequently not the case. General Washington did not respect militia because they did not possess the discipline and steadiness that existed in the Continental Army. Too often they would flee from the enemy before fighting hard.

Sources:

Breen, T. H. *American Insurgents, American Patriots. The Revolution of the People.*

Brown, Wallace. *The Good Americans. The Loyalists in the Revolution.*

Cox, Caroline. *A Proper Sense of Honor. Service in General Washington's Army.*

Gross, Robert A. *Minutemen and their World.*

Middlekauff, Robert A. *The Glorious Cause. The American Revolution 1763-1789.*

BRITISH ARMY

At the height of the American Revolution the British Army had 84 infantry regiments in America. Each regiment was composed of 811 officers and men under command of a colonel. Within the regiment there were 40 officers, 72, non-commissioned officers, 24 drummers, two fifers and 672 privates. The British Army enlistment criterion at the start of the Revolution had a minimum age of 17 and maximum of 30 and minimum height of 5′ 6″. Later, the manpower demands of the war were such that the height restriction was dropped and the minimum age lowered to 16 and maximum age increased to 50 years.

Sources:

Hagist, Don N. *British Soldiers, American War.*

O'Shaughnessy, Andrew Jackson. *The Men Who Lost America. British Leadership, the American Revolution and the Fate of the Empire.*

Stephenson, Michael. *Patriot Battles. How the War of Independence Was Fought.*

Urban, Mark. *Fusiliers. The Saga of a British Redcoat Regiment in the American* Revolution.

BRITISH NAVY

At the beginning of the Revolution Britain had a total of 270 warships of which 131 were "Ships of the Line" – those with two or more gun decks and 60 or more guns. By the end of the war she had 468 warships of which 164 were ships of the line. However, under the corrupt administration of the Minister of the Navy Earl Sandwich, the British Navy was in deep trouble. During the war 76 naval ships were lost to grounding, capsizing or wrecked, of which 14 had 64 or more guns. Of the 175,990 sailors recruited and impressed during the war 42,000 deserted, 18,541 died of disease and only 1,243 were killed in action.

British rules of Naval combat were outdated and inflexible. Admirals were afraid to innovate or deviate from the rules of engagement. This was in stark contrast with the French Navy where new formations were tried and practiced. This lack of flexibility would come back to haunt the British at the Battle of the Capes.

The British Navy was still without question the strongest in the world, but it was expensive and had global commitments which strained its ability to provide the critical naval power needed to defeat the Americans. It not only had to provide convoys for ships travelling back and forth across the Atlantic it also had to protect the home islands which were threatened by French and Spanish fleets and even

American warships as was demonstrated by Captain John Paul Jones in his attacks on the British coastline.

Sources:

Ferreiro, Larrie D. *Bothers At Arms. American Independence and the Men of France and Spain Who Saved It.*

Nelson, James L. *George Washington's Great Gamble and the Sea Battle that Won the American Revolution.*

O'Shaughnessy, Andrew Jackson. *The Men Who Lost America. British Leadership, the American Revolution and the Fate of the Empire.*

Patton, Robert H. *Patriot Pirates. The Privateer War for Freedom and Fortune in the American Revolution.*

Savas, Theodore P. & J. David Dameron. *A Guide to the Battles of the American Revolution.*

Smith, Page. *A New Age Now Begins.* (Volumes 1 & 2)

BRITISH ROYAL MARINES

British Royal Marines originally had the mission of Naval Infantry and thus served mostly in American coastal battles. The first detachment of 460 Royal Marines came to America in 1774 at Boston. An additional 700 came to America in 1775 at New York City. They fought in separate battalions with light infantry and grenadiers. They fought at Lexington, Concord and Bunker Hill where they endured heavy casualties. Their commanding officer, Major John Pitcairn was killed at Bunker Hill. The only serious battle where American and British Marines fought head to head was at the Battle of Penobscot Bay in 1779 where the Americans were routed. Throughout the Revolution the Royal Marines distinguished themselves along the American coastal cities and ports. A detachment of Royal Marines was captured with LTG Cornwallis at the Siege of Yorktown in October 1781.

Sources:

Buker, George E. *The Penobscot Expedition, Commodore Saltonstall and the Massachusetts Conspiracy of 1779.*

FRENCH ARMY AND NAVY

French Army: In June of 1776 France began to provide covert financial and logistical (weapons, clothing, tents, equipment etc.) assistance to the Colonies. France signed a formal alliance with the Colonies on February 6, 1778 and formally recognized American independence on May 4, 1778. The first contingent of 4,000 French Army forces arrived in America in September 1779 under and command of Admiral d'Estaing and the second contingent of 6,000 soldiers arrived in July 1780 under the command of Comte de Rochambeau and finally an additional 3,500 troops in August 1781 under the command of Major General Comte de Saint-Simon. These forces in addition to the French Navy were critical to the ultimate success of the American Revolution. French Army forces were subordinated to American Army forces during the Revolution.

French Navy: The French Navy was the wild card in the poker game of the American Revolution. Since her defeat by the Britain in the Seven Years War in 1763 France had modernized her navy but not to the extent or size of Britain. At the height of the American Revolution, Britain had 311 warships, supply vessels and transports. France had 211. Spain which worked in cooperation with France had a total of 144 so there was relative parity in total naval strength between the ships of Britain and the combined total of Spain and France. Britain had more global naval commitments than France so it was more stretched than France. Britain also had to protect its supply ships from

French warships and American Privateers which further weakened its ability to support its army in America. The British home islands were also under threat of invasion from the French Navy which was a high concern of the Crown. French Naval leaders were also willing to take more aggressive and bold action than the British. The French Naval and Army leaders worked together better than the British who barely talked to each other. A key element in the success of the French Navy in the Battle of the Capes in September 1781 was the willingness of Spanish Naval Admiral Don Jose Solano to protect France's interests in the Caribbean while French Admiral Francois-Joseph de Grasse moved his Navy north to the Chesapeake to do battle with British Admiral Sir Thomas Graves. Because the British had divided their fleet at the Battle of the Capes, the British had 19 ships of the line with 1,800 guns vs France's 24 ships and 2,000 guns. French Admiral Jacques-Melchior de Barras also in a bold move sailed with the French siege cannon and supplies from Newport Rhode Island to Yorktown without being detected by the British.

Sources:

Bonnel, Ulane. *The French Navy and the American War of Independence.*

Ferreiro, Larrie D. *Brothers At Arms. American Independence and the Men of France and Spain Who Saved It.*

Nelson, James L. *George Washington's Greatest Gamble and the Sea Battle that Won the American Revolution.*

O'Shaughnessy, Andrew Jackson. *The Men Who Lost America. British Leadership, the American Revolution and the Fate of the Empire.*

Savas, Theodore P. & J. David Dameron. *A Guide to the American Revolution.*

Tuchman, Barbara W. *The First Salute. A View of the American Revolution.*

GERMAN ARMY MERCENARIES

Due to manpower shortages and opposition to forced service in the Army and Navy among British civilians, George III tried to hire Hessians for service in America even before the start of the Revolution. The costs stated by the German states were too high so an agreement could not initially be reached. Next, the British approached Catherine the Great of Russia for soldiers for service in America and she wisely declined, as did the Netherlands and even the Moors of Morocco. With the outbreak of fighting in America the British again turned to the German states for soldiers to serve in America. Agreements were made throughout the War for the following German states to ultimately provide soldiers for duty in America as indicated below:

Anhalt-Zerbst	1,160
Anspach-Bayreuth	2,353
Brunswick	5,723
Hesse-Hanau	2,422
Hesse-Cassel	16,992
Waldeck	1,225
TOTAL	**29,875**

The costs to the British for German mercenaries were astronomical considering the already burdensome expenses of funding the costs of their own soldiers in America. The money paid to the German Princes was called "Levy Money". For each German soldier the British paid over four Shillings. Each German soldier killed cost Britain over seven pounds sterling. For every three wounded German soldiers, it cost the price of one killed. Annual subsidies of approximately 16,000 pounds were paid to the German princes for the services of their soldiers in America. It was estimated that the German mercenaries cost Britain 4.5 million pounds sterling. One third of the annual payment was due at signing of the agreement, with the other two thirds due within 60 days. The agreements required the British had to pay their annual payments for two years after the Germans returned from America. There was no compensation paid by anyone to the families of Germans who were killed or remained in America after the war.

Because Hesse-Cassel and Hessel-Hanau provided two thirds of all the Germans who served in America all the German mercenaries were called "Hessians". German officers and professional soldiers gladly signed-up for service in America; however, there was considerable opposition among low ranking soldiers, a great many of whom had to be drafted, impressed and forced against their will into American service. Mutinies, revolts, desertions and some suicides were recorded from German units as they assembled for transport to America. German officers were paid handsomely and even privates were paid a pound sterling a month which was an unheard of large sum at those times. Training for German soldiers was harsh but professional. However, due in part to their lack of cultural connection with Americans they had a reputation for brutality, plunder and rapine treatment of civilians which had a detrimental effect on British efforts to win over those Americans who might otherwise have supported the Crown. German soldiers who consumed British rations had the cost of the rations deducted from their pay. If they consumed their food from plunder they did not have such deductions. This created a unique incentive for the Germans to plunder Americans.

German Prisoners Of War were less problematic than British. The German POWs frequently hired themselves out as farm laborers which ultimately helped their assimilation into America. This in part explains why so many declined to return to Germany where life was infinitely harder and prospects for betterment were very slim. The following reflects the statistical summary of the German experience in America during the Revolution:

Killed and died of wounds	1,200
Died of illness and accidents	6,354
Deserted	5,000
TOTAL	**12,554**

Thus, 40% of all who came to America in the service of Britain failed to return to Germany which represents a huge loss for the German Princes and a huge gain for America. To gain a perspective of the significant losses the German mercenaries suffered at the hands of American privateers see the discussion contained in this document in the chapter: AMERICAN NAVAL PRIVATEERS.

Sources:

Hooch, Holger. SCARS of INDEPENCE. America's Violent Birth.

Ketchum, Richard M. *The Winter Soldiers. The Battles for Trenton and Princeton.*

Lowell, Edward J. *The Hessians and the other German Auxiliaries of Great Britain in the Revolutionary War.*

Rae, Noel. *The People's War, Original Voices of the American Revolution.*

Savas, Theodore P. & J. David Dameron. *A Guide to the Battles of the American Revolution.*

Shomette, David Grady. *PRIVATEERS of the REVOLUTION. War on the New Jersey Coast 1775-1783.*

SPANISH ARMY AND NAVY

At the start of the Revolution Spain was still at war with Britain. Like the French, the Spanish began providing covert material and financial support to the Colonies in 1776. The provisions of weapons and gunpowder were especially important. Through the Treaty of Aranjuez on June 21, 1779 Spain formally declared war against Britain and allied itself with France. Spain did not enter into a formal alliance with America during the Revolution. The areas of Louisiana, Florida and Mississippi River were the main battlegrounds for the Spanish Army in America. Spain had infantry regiments in Louisiana and Florida which attacked the British in West Florida and provided assistance in attacking British forces up the Mississippi River. The Spanish Army ultimately captured 2,000 British soldiers in and around St Augustine Florida. The Spanish Navy although in need of modernization was a potent force in the West Indies which caused the British to deploy scarce naval forces to the region. Spanish King Carlos III sent his fleet of 40 ships and thousands of soldiers to attack the British in Florida and Louisiana. In addition to Army and Naval forces King Carlos provided considerable and critical financial support for the Revolution. Critical logistical support consisting of weapons and gunpowder were provided up the Mississippi River by Spain which helped defeat the British forts in the Mississippi River Valley. The material was also funneled east over the mountains to George Washington's forces fighting the British on Atlantic Coast. Probably the most important contribution of the Spanish Navy was to "backstop" French Admiral de Grasse's decision to move his ships north from the West Indies where he could meet and attack the British with all his fleet at the crucial at the Battle of the Capes which sealed the fate of Cornwallis at Yorktown. In the final analysis, Spain's financial, material and military assistance to the American Cause rivals that of France's without which the Revolution would not have succeeded.

Sources:

Butler, Judge Ed. *Galvez. Spain – Our Forgotten Ally in the American Revolutionary War: A Concise Summary of Spain's Assistance.*

Ferling, John. *Almost A Miracle. The American Victory in the War of Independence.*

Ferreiro, Larrie D. *Bothers At Arms. American Independence and the Men of France and Spain Who Saved It.*

Nelson, James L. *George Washington's Great Gamble and the Sea Battle that Won the American Revolution.*

O'Shaughnessy, Andrew Jackson. *The Men Who Lost America. British Leadership, the American Revolution and the Fate of the Empire.*

Savas, Theodore P. & J. David Dameron. *A Guide to the Battles of the American Revolution.*

Tuchman, Barbara W. *The First Salute; A View of the American Revolution.*

THE NETHERLANDS

The Netherlands like the French was a long-term enemy of the British. They saw the American Revolution as an opportunity to fight the British and make a lot of money from supporting America through trade. Throughout the Revolution the Dutch were a major weapons supplier of the American cause especially through the port of St. Eustatius in the West Indies. Gunpowder was the most important supply element which was in chronic short supply by the American rebels and was brought through the Port of St. Eustatius in massive quantities. Ultimately, the British declared war on the Netherlands in 1780 after intercepting secret communications being transported from the Netherlands by Henry Laurens who became a POW and was then held in the Tower of London. The declaration of war by the British on the Dutch further increased their burden during the Revolution.

Sources:

Tuchman, Barbara W. *The First Salute. A View of the American Revolution.*

NAVAL INFLUENCES AND TERMS OF THE REVOLUTION

HISTORICAL ANALOGIES

It can be said the American Revolution was fought in reverse of World Wars One and Two. In the Revolution, the land fighting was done on the American Continent with the British and German Mercenaries coming across the Atlantic to do the fighting. In World Wars One and Two it was the Americans coming across the Atlantic to fight in Europe with Britain against the Germans. The common element in these two scenarios was control of the Atlantic between Europe and America. The Americans and her naval allies fought for control the Atlantic during the Revolution just as the British tried to do. In the Revolution America's fledging navy and naval Privateers (see chapter on Privateers) disrupted British forces and logistics coming across the Atlantic to America. In the World Wars, it was German submarines which disrupted and almost choked American supplies going to Britain. The British in the Revolution learned an expensive lesson in that their ships going to America needed to be "convoyed" with armed naval ships. In World Wars I & II the Americans had to learn the same lesson. The British had no naval allies in Europe during the Revolution. The Germans had no naval Atlantic allies during the World Wars. America had powerful Atlantic naval allies such as France and Spain and to a lesser extent the Dutch during the Revolution. The British during the Revolution not only had to protect its forces transiting the Atlantic it had legitimate concerns about the security of its home islands. The manpower strains of maintaining the British Navy were such that it resorted to impressment. The prohibitive cost of maintaining a huge navy with such extensive commitments contributed to the anti-war effort in Britain. The common factor in all of this was the decisive influence of Naval Power and the Atlantic. This was ultimately shown in the entrapment of General Cornwallis at Yorktown which effectively ended the War in favor of the Americans. Therefore, knowing about the Revolution requires a deep read of Naval Power and understanding of its terms during this epic event.

NAVAL TERMINOLOGY

Bateaux: Bateaux (sometimes spelled batteaux) were flat bottomed, flat sided, double square bowed American boats used to transport commercial goods on inland waterways and lakes. They could be as long as 60 feet. They figured prominently in the battles of Lake Champlain where they transported soldiers and cannon. Occasionally they were armed with cannon and had a single sail. They could be on loaded and off loaded from the bow or stern.

Bomb Ketch: A bomb ketch was a two masted sturdily built vessel with cannons and mortars for armament. They were used in fighting by the Americans and British on Lake Champlain.

Breaming: This was the process of cleaning the vegetation and marine growth from the wooden hulls of ships that severely hampered their sailing performance. The breaming process involved laying the ship on its side (careening), exposing the hull to burn and scrape the growth and making repairs as necessary.

Brigantines: Brigantines were two masted vessels with square sails. They were smaller than sloops or cutters. They were armed with swivel cannons and infantrymen with guns.

"Camels": Camels were large watertight casks which were lashed to the hulls and sides of ships to lift ships off sand bars and those which needed to be lightened to cross shallow waters.

Careening: Careening was the process of laying a ship over on its side so the hull could be cleaned (breamed) of vegetation and marine growth. The rigging had to be removed along with the cannons. This was a time consuming and expensive process. It had to be done periodically, especially if the ship operated in warm ocean waters.

"Caught-in-Irons": This was the situation where a ship was caught with its bow into the wind without momentum to turn. This made the ship vulnerable in battle and risked the ship being de-masted by the force of the wind blowing head on.

Chevaux-de-Frise: These were underwater obstructions made of logs with sharp iron spikes usually placed in rivers to pierce the hulls of British ships trying to move along the waterways. They were used prominently in the Hudson and Delaware Rivers by the Americans with varying degrees of success.

Clippers: These were fast multiple masted vessels used for reconnaissance, sending communications and quick response action. Sometimes they were lightly armed.

Close Hauling: This was a ship that was sailing between 75 to 85 degrees into the wind, which was the maximum before head on which could become very destructive to rigging and masts.

Coppering: Eighteenth century ships suffered from the growth of vegetation and barnacles on their wooden hulls which greatly impeded their maneuverability and speed and led to the fast deterioration of their hulls. The British learned that by copper plating the hulls of their ships this would greatly reduce the barnacles and growth of vegetation on their hulls. This expensive process was employed by the British and less so by the French which gave the British a significant wartime naval advantage. An example of the advantage of "coppering" came in March 1781 when the French warship *EVEILLE'* which was coppered overtook and captured the un-coppered British warship *ROMULUS* off the American coast. The much heavier *EVEILLE'* with 50 guns should have been much slower than the lighter *ROMULUS* with only 40 guns. Coppering made the difference, which resulted in the *EVEILLE'* capturing the *ROMULUS* that carried the bonanza of the payroll for the British Army in Southern Virginia.

Cutter: Cutters were the smallest of commissioned vessels just below sloops. They had single masts with a long bowsprit with large aft sail and multiple foresails. They were fast and could be armed with small swivel cannons or gun boats.

Doctrine of "Free Ships, Free Goods": Under this doctrine a neutral country could, without interference, trade in non-warlike goods with belligerents. Conversely belligerent countries could prevent by armed measures the trade by neutral countries of war-materials with adversaries. This led to great confusion especially with the Netherlands which was officially neutral for most of the American Revolution but was a world-wide trading power, especially in weapons and gun powder with America.

Durham Boats: These were commercial flat-bottomed boats with flat bows and sterns primarily used on the Delaware River to transport coal, iron and lumber. They were made famous in their use by General Washington to transport his army across the Delaware River to attack Trenton on December 26, 1776. They were very much like bateaux.

Fathom; A fathom was a measure of distance equal to six feet. The term was pretty much exclusively used by the Navy.

Fire Ships: These were rafts filled with hay, tar, wood and pitch and would be then floated by Americans in the dark of night against moored British ships. They would be attached to the British ships by grappling hooks and set afire. The six or eight American oarsmen aboard the fire ships would then swim ashore and hopefully the British ship would burn. These were used with varying degrees of success on the Hudson River, James River, Lake Champlain and at Yorktown.

Frigate: A frigate was a three masted warship with a single gun deck with no more than 24 guns. The frigate was the largest warship built during the Revolution by the Americans.

Gondolas: Gondolas were quickly and inexpensively built vessels with flat sides and bottoms with double ends which allowed them to be off and on loaded from the stern or bow. They sometimes had sails and were from 40 to 60 feet in length. In combat on Lake Champlain they frequently had a large cannon on the bow and smaller cannons on the starboard and port sides. They were sometimes called GUNDALOES or GUNLOES.

Great Masts: These were the 27+ inch diameter pine and hemlock masts used for ships of the line which were in high demand by all the major naval powers of Europe. The usual supply from the Baltic States was becoming scarce so the British turned to the superb trees of New Hampshire and the Massachusetts District of Maine. The British reserved these trees for their own use and cut them down without compensation which greatly angered New Englanders.

Halyard: A Halyard was a line (rope) used to lower or raise sails.

Heaving Down: This was the process of rolling a ship on its side so the growth of vegetation and barnacles could be "Breamed" off.

Heeling: A ship would heel (lean) when wind would catch its sails. When a war ship would "heel" hard it would be very difficult to fire its cannons because they could not fire direct (line of sight) at the enemy. The cannons on the windward side of the ship would shoot high and the cannons on the leeward side of the ship would shoot into the water.

Iron-Sick: Wooden ships became Iron Sick when the iron bolts and nails which held the hull and structure of the ship together became loose after the iron rusted and corroded. Iron Sickness caused ships to become un-seaworthy after a long time.

Keel Haul: This was a punishment for sailors consisting of dragging the individual under the hull of a ship from one side to another. This punishment was sometimes fatal.

Ketch: A Ketch was a two masted vessel with the mizzenmast (much shorter mast) in the rear. They were used by the British and Americans on Lake Champlain.

Lanteen Sail: This was a single triangle shaped sail mounted on a single mast of a small boat. They were used mostly in combat on Lake Champlain.

Lee Gauge: This is the opposite of Weather Gauge which is the Windward (upwind) position in battle. The Lee Gauge is the Leeward (downwind) position in battle. In combat, there are generally more advantages to obtaining the Weather Gauge. The Lee Gauge allowed a ship to more easily flee the enemy through quick maneuvers.

Leeward: This is an important nautical term which means the direction the wind is blowing **TO;** such as the shore or a fleet or line of ships.

Light-Ball: A Light-Ball was a shot of combustible material fired by a mortar to light up the area for night fighting by ships.

"Made Masts": The demand for masts for ships of the line was so intense that "made masts" were constructed of slabs of wood which were bound together with glue and cables.

Man of War: Technically a Man of War was any ship with at least 20 guns.

Naval Fighting Tactics: Generally the British fired their ship's cannons at the hulls of adversaries. This would possibly sink the ship or set it on fire. The French generally fired their cannons at the sails and rigging of their adversaries which would disable the ship and possibly set it up for boarding and capture. Most 18th Century naval battles were fought at close range (less than 1,000 yards). At 500 yards, the ship's cannons were set for "Double Shot Range", 300 yards range was called "Musket Range" and 50 yards range was called "Pistol Range".

Oakum: Oakum was a combination of tar and hemp used to "chink" (seal) the planks of ships under construction.

Packet Ships: Packet ships were used to carry mail and messages mostly across the Atlantic. They usually were cutters because of their speed. On land, a "packet rider" was a horse mounted mail or message carrier. They were also sometimes called "express riders".

PHILADELPHIA: The *PHILADELPHIA* was one of the first gondolas built for the Northern American Navy during the earliest days of the Revolution. It was built on the orders of the Second Continental Congress and launched at the southern terminus of Lake Champlain on July 30, 1776. The ship was built in 45 days with a length of 54 feet. It weighed 54 tons, and had 24-pound cannon on the bow and two 6 pound cannons on the sides. General Benedict Arnold who had significant experience as a blue water navy captain was named as commander of the American Lake Champlain Navy. At the critical battle of Valcour Island on October 13-14, 1776 General Arnold and his small fleet of boats, gondolas and galleys were defeated. However, the significant time it took the British to build their Lake Champlain Fleet to fight Arnold's fleet caused them to withdraw back to Canada due to the onset of winter weather. This allowed the Americans a full year to recover and prepare for Britain's second assault from Lake Champlain towards Albany, NY, which ultimately led to the catastrophic defeat of LTG Burgoyne in October 1777. The *PHILADELPHIA* was sunk at the Battle of Valcour Island and was raised intact from the bottom of Lake Champlain in 1935. In 1961 the ship was acquired by the Smithsonian Museum where it remains today as one of the largest relics of the Revolutionary War.

Poop-Deck: The Poop-Deck was a short deck on the very aft of the ship.

Port Side: The port side of a ship is the left side of the vessel when facing the bow from the stern.

Powder Monkeys: Power monkeys were young boy sailors who worked in the powder magazines of British warships who handled the large leather-bound sacks of black powder for the guns.

Press Gangs: These were British Naval officers and sailors who would grab men to involuntarily serve on British ships. This showed how desperate the British Navy was for manpower during the American Revolution. It was actually done on a smaller extent by the Americans.

Some American naval POWs were "pressed" into British naval service in lieu of serving as POWs of the British. The offer was made to many such POWs but only a few accepted.

Prize Money: Prize money was the money that was accrued from the sale of ships and their cargos captured by privateers. Frequently the distribution of the money was subject to approval by Prize Courts. Usually the prize money was split up into 1/8th parts between the captain, senior officers, junior officers and crew and the investor who put up the money to equip the privateer ship. The money paid to crewmen was frequently far above what U.S. Navy sailors were paid which made recruiting for the Navy very difficult.

Prize Ship: A Prize was an enemy ship that was captured by the Americans privateers, usually with the intent of selling it and its cargo.

Quarter-Bills: Quarter-bills were lists of officers and crewmen on a ship much like muster rolls for the Army.

Ratlines: Ratlines were horizontal lines woven together in a vertical step-like fashion for sailors to climb a ship's rigging.

Schooners: Schooners were sailing vessels with at least two masts with the lower sails rigged fore and aft.

Ships of the Line: Ships of the Line were large fighting ships that were sometimes called "Rated" ships. They were rated as follows:

1st Rate: 100 or more guns with three or more gun decks.
2nd Rate: 90-98 guns with three decks.
3rd Rate: 64-80 guns on two decks.
4th Rate: 50-60 guns on two decks.
5th Rate: 32-48 guns on a single deck.
6th Rate: 20 guns on a single deck.

Shipwrights: Shipwrights were ship carpenters and craftsmen who were skilled in the building of ships. They were paid bounties and were in high demand. Benedict Arnold went to great length to obtain shipwrights to build his fleet on Lake Champlain in the summer of 1776.

Shrouds: Shrouds were a set of lines (ropes) forming part of the rigging of a sailing vessel.

Sloops: Sloops were vessels bigger in size and with greater capability than Cutters. They had one mast and two large fore and aft sails. They were armed with small cannon and gun boats and were used mostly for inland river and waterway missions. The most famous sloop of the Revolution was the HMS *VULTURE* which operated on the Hudson River and figured prominently in the Andre'/Arnold affair.

Spider Catchers: This was the name given to American privateers who operated from whale boats close in shore to the coast of New Jersey. They attacked British supply ships outside the harbors or when they were unloading off shore. Their primary armament was muskets and sometimes small cannon. Sometimes they attacked in groups._

Starboard Side: The starboard side of a ship is the right side of the vessel when facing the bow from the stern.

Sweeps: Sweeps were oars which were used to row small craft that did not have sails. "Sweep Locks" were oar locks. "Long Sweeps" were very long oars used to row very large craft such as bateaux, gondolas and occasionally sloops when they were stuck without wind. The sweeps were generally made of ash trees which were plentiful in America.

Turtle: The *TURTLE* was America's first "submarine" the invention of David Bushnell of Connecticut. It was given its first and only operational combat mission against British General Howe's flagship HMS *EAGLE* on September 6, 1776 in New York Harbor. Due to bad luck, the operator failed to attach the bomb (torpedo) to the hull of the British ship. After the attempt, the *TURTLE* was swept away by the current of the river from the British fleet and never used again.

Weather Gauge: This is the nautical term for the upward wind position in naval combat. The ship that held the weather gauge could adversely affect the wind for enemy ships down-wind usually by "stealing" the wind of opponents. Jockeying for the weather gauge figured prominently in the famous British/French naval battles of the Capes in early September 1781 which sealed the fate of Cornwallis at Yorktown.

White Ash Sail: A ship said to be under "White Ash Sail" was being rowed by oars which were almost exclusively made of white ash.

Windward: This is an important nautical term indicating the direction the wind is blowing **FROM**, such as a fleet or line of ships or body of land.

Xebecs: Xebecs were armored two masted sail boats with overhanging bows and sterns. They were used in the Lake Champlain campaigns.

Sources:

Bratten, John R. *The Gondola PHILADELPHIA & Battle of Lake Champlain.*

Ferreiro, Larrie D. *Brothers At Arms. American Independence and the Men of France and Spain Who Saved It.*

Fowler, William M. Jr. *The American Navy during the Revolution.*

Nelson, James L. *Benedict Arnold's Navy. The Ragtag Fleet that Lost the Battle of Lake Champlain but Won the Revolution.*

Nelson, James L. *George Washington's Great Gamble and the Sea Battle that Won the American Revolution.*

Patton, Robert H. *Patriot Pirates. The Privateer War for Freedom and Fortune in the American Revolution.*
Savas, Theodore P. & J. David Dameron. *A Guide to the Battles of the American Revolution.*

NOTABLE FOREIGNERS WHO FOUGHT FOR THE AMERICAN CAUSE

America was blessed by the services of foreigners from Europe most of whom made significant contributions to the success of the Revolution. The majority of these individuals came from France totaling as many as 85. The major conduit of these individuals was through Silas Deane, America's agent in Paris. The motivations for most of these individuals were to further the cause of liberty, freedom and democracy. For a small portion, it was adventure and a minority self-promotion. The following are brief sketches of these individuals listed alphabetically by country.

DENMARK

Fibiger, Hans Christian: Fibiger came to America from Denmark in 1772 as a businessman and became a Massachusetts Militiaman at the outbreak of the Revolution. He fought with distinction at the Battle of Bunker Hill. He then joined Benedict Arnold's expedition through the territory of Maine to attack Quebec. At that battle he was captured and held prisoner for six months. After his exchange Fibiger he was promoted to Lt Colonel of the 11th Virginia Regiment under Colonel Daniel Morgan. He further distinguished himself at the

Battles of Germantown, Monmouth Courthouse and particularly at Stony Point where he personally captured the British commander of the fort. He later went on to serve at the Battle of Yorktown. Following the war he settled in Philadelphia and held important civilian positions and died there in 1796.

FRANCE

Conway, Joseph: General Conway was born in Ireland and at age 8 moved to France where he went to school and served twenty years in the French Army. He came to America in 1777 via the Silas Deane connection. He was appointed a Brigadier General and distinguished himself at the Battle of Germantown. He desired a promotion to Major General which was opposed by General Washington. He was not popular among the military and civilian leaders of America, primarily because of his arrogant personality. He was critical of Washington's generalship and favored General Horatio Gates as commander of the American Army. He was very critical of Washington in what was supposed to be a private letter which when disclosed caused him to be discredited. It is thought he was trying to engineer a "cabal" to have Washington ousted. His reported effort to oust Washington in cahoots with Brigadier General Wilkinson is commonly known as the "Conway Cabal". After his criticism of Washington was disclosed he apologized and resigned his commission and returned to France for further service in the French Army.

Fleury, de Francois: De Fleury was another Frenchman who volunteered to join the Continental Army in 1777 through the famed Silas Deane connection in Paris. By profession he was an engineer, a skill severely lacking in the American military. He was appointed an officer of engineers by Washington. He was wounded at the Battles of Germantown and Fort Mifflin and served as an assistant to von Steuben and fought at the Battle of Monmouth Courthouse. At the Battle of

Stoney Point in 1779 he led the charge through the British defenses with General "Mad" Anthony Wayne and was again recognized for his bravery. He finally fought at the Battle of Yorktown. Because of his serious wounds he returned to France and was pensioned in 1796. The de Fleury Medal is named for him and is awarded each year by the U.S. Army to its most outstanding engineering officer.

Kalb, de Johan: Born in poverty in Bavaria on June 29, 1721 he had a strong desire to become a career soldier. After many years of distinguished service in German units he eventually joined the French Army. He came to America in June 1777 via the famed Silas Deane connection. When France entered the war against Britain de Kalb reverted from "observer" status to service as a French General in America. He moved to the southern theatre of operations under the command of Horatio Gates who disregarded de Kalb's strong advice to proceed with caution in approaching a battle with British General Cornwallis. Gates badly formed his soldiers and was soon severely defeated at the Battle of Camden on August 16, 1780. During the battle, de Kalb distinguished himself with great valor but was fatally wounded.

Lafayette, Marquis: Lafayette was born in a wealthy French family on September 6, 1757. He came to America motivated by genuine concerns to be part of overturning the corrupt and debased monarchical systems that pervaded Europe. He was drawn to service in the army and was named a captain of French Dragoons. He saw the war in America as the method to achieve that vision. At age 20 and newly married he came to America against the wishes of his family. He paid for his own travel and the travel of those who came with him. He arrived in America in June 1777. Washington was quickly smitten by him and confirmed him a major general. He helped save Washington from defeat at the Battle of Brandywine where he was wounded. He then participated with distinction in the Battle of Monmouth Courthouse in 1778. In 1779, he returned to France to recruit new talented Frenchmen to come and serve in America and came back in 1780. He played a crucial part in the Battle of Yorktown by standing firm in the face of Cornwallis' over whelming numbers causing Cornwallis to think he could not break out of the trap he had created for himself. At the Battle of Yorktown, he and Alexander Hamilton led the capture of British Redoubt #10 which helped win the battle. After the Revolution, he fell on hard times for his support of republican values, barely escaped execution, spent five years in prison in Belgium and Prussia and was finally allowed to return to France.

Ponceau, Peter Stephen: Du Ponceau came to America also via the Silas Deane connection in 1777 with Baron von Steuben. Du Ponceau was multi lingual and served as von Steuben's interpreter who only spoke German and French. Throughout the war du Ponceau served with von Steuben. Although he was a not a combat officer, he suffered the same privations as other Americas at Valley Forge and on campaigns. After the Revolution du Ponceau stayed in America and died in Philadelphia in 1827.

GERMANY

Steuben, Freidrich William: Steuben had a military background in Germany that was largely inflated and even non-existent. He actually had a tenuous claim to royalty hence the "von" in his name. He was dismissed from several military positions in Germany. If nothing else, he was very good at self-promotion and soon convinced Silas Deane of his ability to make a significant contribution to the American Cause. He said he would serve only for his expenses in America. He arrived in New Hampshire on December 1, 1777 and went to the Continental Congress in Philadelphia and met Gen Washington. It was agreed he would be paid at the end of the war according to the contributions he made to the effort. Because the Americans lacked a position for him Washington came up with the ingenious solution by making him the "Inspector of the Army" which was perfect for him because it gave him a position to identify weaknesses in the Continental Army and implement solutions which he did with alacrity. He implemented battlefield training routines which greatly improved the combat effectiveness of American soldiers. In addition, he implemented camp routines which improved sanitation and healthfulness of soldiers. His development of travelling teams of trainers to units exists to this very day. By the spring of 1778 the American Continental Army had been transformed into a disciplined fighting machine capable of head to head combat with the British Army.

POLAND

Kosciuszko, Tadeusz: Kosciuszko came to America in 1776 through France and the services of Silas Deane. He was an accomplished engineer which were in short supply in America and was quickly appointed Colonel of Engineers. He was put to work supervising the construction of defensive positions, especially in the northern sector of America. As British General Burgoyne approached Fort Ticonderoga he advised American General Arthur St. Clair to fortify the commanding mountain of Sugar Loaf, advice which was ignored. The result is that the British quickly took command of the mountain which resulted in the capitulation of the fort in a matter of just a few days. Kosciuszko then performed crucial services in managing the construction of defensive structures and impediments to Burgoyne's move south from Fort Ticonderoga, which ultimately were keys to the surrender of the British Army at the Battle of Saratoga. He supervised construction of some of the walls at West Point which can still be seen there. He then went on to distinguished service with General Greene in the southern theatre of operations. He eventually commanded an infantry unit and two cavalry troops at the end of the war. In July 1784, he returned to Poland for a life of service in the Polish Army.

Pulaski, Casimir: Pulaski was born 1745 into an aristocratic family in Poland. With a strong desire to reform he came to America in July 1777 via the Silas Deane and Benjamin Franklin connection in Paris. After an initial delay, he was named the First Commander of the Cavalry in the American Army. At the Battle of Brandywine he distinguished himself by his bravery and expert battlefield management of his troopers. He wintered with the American Army at Valley Forge but resigned his commission for lack of receiving a command. He then formed his own unit called Pulaski's Legion in March 1778. On October 9, 1779 with French Admiral D'Estaing and 4,000 French soldiers he attacked British held Savannah Georgia. After D'Estaing was seriously wounded Pulaski attempted to rally the Americans and French only to be seriously wounded himself and die six days later.

Sources:

Ferreiro, Larrie D. *Brothers At Arms. American Independence and the Men of France and Spain Who Saved It.*

Leepson, Marc. *Lafayette, Lessons in Leadership from the Idealist General.*

Lockhart, Paul. *The Drillmaster of Valley Forge. The Baron de Steuben and the Making of an American Army.*

Nash, Gary B. & Graham R. Gao. *Friends of Liberty.*

Sirey, Steven E. *Liberty's Fallen Generals. Leadership and Sacrifice in the American War of Independence.*

ORGANIZATION OF AMERICAN AND BRITISH ARMIES

Over a period of several hundreds of years the European military powers developed a highly efficient hierarchical organizational structure for their armies. Because most senior American military leaders fought for Britain during the French and Indian War the American Revolutionary Army was structured basically the on the British model. With some modifications, the same structure currently exists in America's Army. The following shows the British and American Army structure during the Revolution.

WINGS

(COMMANDED BY MAJ GENs)

Composed by two or more Divisions

DIVISIONS

(COMMANDED BY MAJ GENs)

Composed of two or more Brigades

(Approximately 3,240 soldiers)

BRIGADES

(COMMANDED BY BRIG GENs)

Composed of two Regiments

(Approximately 1,620 soldiers)

REGIMENTS

(COMMANDED BY COLONELS)

Composed of 10 Companies.

(Approximately 810 soldiers)

During the war with America the British regiments maintained two units called "Additional Companies" for recruiting duty and basic training in Britain

BATTALIONS

(COMMANDED BY MAJORS)

Composed of 4 Companies

(Approximately 260 soldiers)

COMPANIES

(COMMANDED BY CAPTAINS)

Composed of approximately 65 soldiers

G F F F F F F F LF

Grenadier (G) and Light Foot (LF) companies were stationed at the flanks of regimental formations and were thus commonly called "flanking companies". In between them were common Foot (F) companies.

PLATOONS

(COMMANDED BY LIEUTENANTS, ENSIGNS OR SERGEANTS)

Composed of 10 to fifteen soldiers

British and American Armies and units commonly operated at far less than their authorized "Strength" levels due to illness, desertion, casualties and expiration of enlistments.

Sources:

Locus, Michael. *With Musket and Tomahawk. The Saratoga Campaign and the Wilderness War.*

Savas, Theodore P. & J. David Dameron. *A Guide to the Battles of the American Revolution.*

AMERICAN AND BRITISH COMMAND PHILOSOPHY

The American military commanders under Washington's example had a diametrically different approach to decision making which is shown in the following:

American Command Philosophy: The command philosophy fostered under George Washington was to frequently call councils of war in times of important decisions to conduct a "collaborative decision making" process. He would frame a problem and ask for input without first revealing his preference. Sometimes junior officers and soldiers would be present. There was true "give and take" in these sessions. An excellent example of the successful application of Washington's collaborative approach came after the Second Battle of Trenton, sometimes called the Battle of Assunpink on January 2, 1777. The American Army was exhausted after a week of hard marching and combat. The British and Germans were thirsting for revenge after their disaster at Trenton and assembled their large forces for a crushing blow against Washington. Washington called a council of war. Some of the generals were for further headlong attacks against the stunned enemy. Other generals were for withdrawing and avoiding further combat to retreat and rest. General Washington seemed to prefer rest and retreat, being concerned that a failed general engagement would result in the total destruction of the American Army.

General Arthur St. Clair suggested a forward flanking maneuver to catch the British by surprise. It had manageable risk with the possibility of significant reward. Washington chose St. Clair's proposal. The result was the Battle of Princeton which was another American victory. Having suffered two defeats in quick succession caused the British to be forever more cautious to their detriment. The two successive American victories caught the attention of foreign governments, spurred recruitment and raised American morale.

British Command Philosophy: The British senior commanders, both Army and Navy, believed in a "top down" approach to command. British generals would frequently call councils of war with their senior leaders at times of critical decisions, but the decisions were commonly dictated by the senior officer present. Dissent was not favored or encouraged. This could lead to disastrous consequences such as the time where British Commander in Chief William Howe decided against further offensive operations in the winter of 1776 when his subordinate generals favored a final campaign against the Americans in the dead of winter. This in hind sight would probably have resulted in crushing the American Rebellion.

Sources:

Fischer, David Hackett. *Washington's Crossings.*

O'Shaughnessy, Andrew Jackson. *The Men Who Lost America. British Leadership, the American Revolution and the Fate of the Empire.*

AMERICAN INFANTRY TACTICS

Continental Line Infantry Tactics: The Continental Line was organized in the same manner as the British Army; therefore, it frequently adopted the same stand and fight tactics as the British with some modifications. American Continental Line tactics were more fluid and used concealment and terrain more than the British. Because the British frequently had more soldiers in battles they could hold their ground more than Americans. American Militia units were fairly frequently integrated into the Continental Line. Loyalists were rarely integrated in the British Army. Continental Army tactics were less rigid than British rules of engagement and were more non-traditional, innovative and spontaneous then the rigid European systems. Quick attacks, faints, maneuvers, and disengagements were common in the Continental Army. Line tactics were used with modifications that prevented the slaughter that came from "stand and fight" tactics of the British. A good example of the difference between American and British infantry fighting was British "Line Firing" vs American "Platoon Firing". In British Line Firing a whole "Line" would fire on command in the direction of the enemy which would create a lull until the line reloaded. In American "Platoon Firing" separate platoons would fire at specific targets which would not create lulls that would present opportunities for bayonet charges by the British.

American Militia: Most American militia units were subordinated to the commanders of the Continental Army and fought directly with the Continentals which enhanced their effectiveness. A good example of how American Militia were successfully integrated into the Continental Army battle plans was the Battles of Saratoga and Cowpens. Their skills were frequently different but worked to their advantage. Militia were more often frontiersmen who were expert marksmen and skilled in rough country fighting. They were familiar with "Indian Style" fighting which emphasized, aimed fire, especially at enemy officers, concealment, ambushes, sniping and close quarters fighting with knives and especially hatchets. Militia units usually fought in local area campaigns and battles and were active in the ugly "Civil War" within the American Revolution.

Sources:

Ferling, John. *Almost A Miracle. The American Victory in the War of Independence.*

Martin, James K. & Mark E. Lender. *A Respectable Army. The Military Origins of the Republic 1763-1789.*

Savas, Theodore P. & J. David Dameron. *A Guide to the Battles of the American Revolution*

BRITISH INFANTRY TACTICS

Traditional Line Stand and Fight: The British used "Line Tactics" where the soldiers would stand in lines and shoot at their adversaries. This was a relatively new tactic vs the earlier "Block Fighting" used in Europe where the soldiers would form in squares, not unlike Roman soldiers. Block fighting limited flanking maneuvers by the enemy but it made the soldiers vulnerable to accurate musket, rifle and artillery fire. Line tactics enabled the British to bring more soldiers into the fight and to maneuver for advantage. The downside of Line Fighting was that it required more training. Columns formed into "files" (lines) two deep (sometimes three) facing the enemy about 18" between the shoulders of each shoulder. The first line would fire and then kneel and start reloading while the second line fired with the goal of firing 7 rounds a minute. The emphasis was "volume" fire (maximum firepower in a given space and time). Americans preferred fire by "Company" and was known as the "Loose File and American Scramble" formation. By the end of the eight years of the American Revolution the British Army had significantly adopted American tactics of fighting from concealment, small unit maneuver, camouflage and with non-descript uniforms and fighting "light" – fighting with minimal equipment.

Limited Loyalist Integration into British Army: Loyalists were not well integrated into British army units which limited their contributions that was, in hindsight a mistake. Regular British Army leaders disparaged the fighting qualities of American Loyalists. Unlike Loyalist militia which did not fight alongside British infantry, American militia forces commonly fought side by side with regular American Continental soldiers which increased their effectiveness. Loyalists and American militia were frequently involved in local actions and were also deeply involved in the ugly "Civil War" within the American Revolution.

Sources:

Ferling, John. *Almost A Miracle. The American Victory in the War of Independence.*

Martin, James K. & Mark E. Lender. *A Respectable Army. The Military Origins of the Republic 1763-1789.*

Savas, Theodore P. & J. David Dameron. *A Guide to the Battles of the American Revolution.*

AMERICAN AND BRITISH INFANTRY WEAPONS AND TERMS

Bayonets: The bayonet was the terror weapon of the British Army. Frequently the British would fire a volley and then charge the Americans with bayonets which usually caused the Americans to flee the battlefield. In the Seventeenth Century, British muskets could not be fitted with bayonets because the bayonet was inserted in the barrel of the gun by means of a "plug". This was later solved with the creation of "sockets" to hold the bayonet which allowed the musket to fire a bullet along with holding a bayonet. Some bayonet blades were triangular shaped which were good for slashing and stabbing. Most were 14 to 16 inches long. Others were round with a sharp point. These were not good for slashing but the puncture wounds they could inflict were nearly impossible to resolve by surgery and caused frequent fatal internal bleeding. There is little evidence of bayonet to bayonet combat. The major value of the bayonet on the battlefield was to make the enemy flee.

Bill Hook: This was a weapon used to clear abatis (sharp tree branches tangled in front of fortified positions). The bill hooks had a sturdy short curved blade with a hook at the end to enable infantrymen (frequently Forlorn Hopes) to chop and hook the abatis away so the infantrymen could charge through the breech in the enemy line.

Bore: The bore was the diameter of the hole in the barrel of a rifle or musket. The bore had to be slightly larger than the caliber (diameter) of the bullet.

Breech Loading: A breech loading rifle was one that was loaded from the back (breech) of the barrel. Muskets were loaded from the front of the barrel. There were only a few breech loading rifles used by the British during the Revolution. The first operational breech loading rifle was invented by British Major Patrick Ferguson. After demonstration tests in Britain 100 soldiers were trained to use the weapon and sent to America under Major Ferguson. Breech loading weapons were being developed as early as 1700 but most performed unsatisfactorily until the Ferguson version was developed. The new gun had significant manufacturing problems which limited its adoption. Few saw actual combat during the Revolution.

Buck and Ball: Buck and ball consisted of a musket load of several (up to 10) small shots (bucks) and a main ball bullet. These multiple projectiles from a single shot created a higher opportunity to hit an enemy soldier, especially in close quarters shooting.

Caliber: The caliber was the diameter of the bullet fired by a musket or rifle. Most muskets and rifles during the Revolution shot .69 to .73-inch caliber bullets.

Carbines: Carbines were muskets with short barrels that were commonly used by cavalry and dragoons. Their shorter length made it easier to fight in wooded areas and from horseback where long barrel guns were cumbersome and difficult to load quickly. The cavalry and dragoons mostly fought "dismounted" with these weapons.

Cartouche Box: Cartouche boxes were box like containers worn on the belts of soldiers containing the pre-made bullets for their guns. They could contain up to 30 pre-made bullets in slots drilled in the box. British infantry soldiers frequently had two ammo boxes, the first called a "Belly Box" with 7-18 bullets fastened by a waist belt. The second box was called the "Battalion Box" containing as many as 36 bullets fastened by means of a shoulder strap.

Charleville: The Charleville musket was the most common French made musket imported for American soldiers. It was frequently copied by American gunsmiths. It fired a .69 caliber bullet. It has been estimated that France imported over 100,000 of these rifles for use by American rebels during the Revolution.

Cutlass: A cutlass was a sword used mostly by mounted cavalry and dragoons. The cutlass was a shorter version of the common sword used in infantry combat. The longer infantry sword was too cumbersome to use on horseback.

Ferguson Rifle: The Ferguson Rifle was invented by Major (later Lt Col Patrick Ferguson) of the British Army. It was of revolutionary design in that it loaded the bullets from the "breech" end of the barrel (the end next to the stock). Earlier attempts at by others to invent breech loading rifles resulted in too many problems for their rifles to be adopted. Ferguson's rifle for example did not need a ramrod which eliminated that time-consuming step in the loading process. Because it was loaded from the breech it was not necessary to load the weapon from a standing position. This allowed it to be loaded and fired from the "prone" (laying down position) which had huge advantages. In the hands of a trained infantryman it could be loaded and fired seven times a minute, far greater than the rate of three shots a minute from a musket. Its drawbacks were that it was more expensive to produce, had a fragile stock, required new training and was 'NEW". Then as now, anything "new" in the infantry world is met with opposition.

After impressing George III in Britain at a firing exposition in 1777 Ferguson was sent to America with 100 trained riflemen. At the Battle of Brandywine on September 11, 1777 the Ferguson Rifle had its first battle test. It is not exactly known what happened to the 100 Ferguson Riflemen who were sent to America, but Patrick Ferguson suffered a disabling wound to his elbow at the Battle of Brandywine which thereafter caused him to use the weapon (albeit successfully) with only one arm. Ferguson was killed at the Battle of King's Mountain on October 7, 1780 while leading a Loyalist group of more than 1,000 soldiers in the British Southern campaign.

Flint: The flint was commonly called the "pebble" by soldiers. When the hammer which held the flint struck the steel frizzen it would create sparks to ignite the gun powder in the "pan" of the gun. American flint was mostly inferior to British and French flint so it was commonly imported from Europe to America during the war. An excellent British "black" flint could last as long as 35 shots. Most flints lasted for much fewer shots.

Flintlock Muskets: Flintlock Muskets were the common infantry gun used by almost all soldiers of European nations during the Revolution. They were muzzle loaded smooth bore guns which were fired by the hammer that held the flint which would strike the frizzen. This would cause sparks that would ignite the powder in the "pan" to fire the bullet. A common flintlock musket would weigh about 11 pounds and fire a .75 to .69 caliber round. The first of these weapons were introduced into the British Army in 1722 and were called the Long "Land Pattern" muskets, which were 69 inches long. Short "Land Pattern" muskets began to be introduced into the British Army in 1768 and had a length of 42 inches. The Continental Army used some of these weapons left over from the French and Indian War and locally manufactured variants. The Continental Army also used French muskets donated to the Colonies. The common British infantry weapon during the American Revolution was known as the "Brown Bess". A highly trained and proficient British infantryman could load and shoot 3 shots a minute with a Brown Bess. The maximum effective range of most muskets was 100 yards. The loading sequence for muskets was very structured and consisted of the following steps:

1. Raise the gun vertically until the hammer was about shoulder level and pulled back.
2. Pull back the hammer to the half cock position which opened the pan by activating a spring that lifted the frizzen.
3. Lower the gun until the butt was grounded somewhat behind the shooter steading the gun away from him.
4. Obtain a cartridge from his bullet box or cartridge pouch.
5. Bite off the soft end of the pre-made cartridge.
6. Pour a little of the powder into the pan.
7. Pour the rest of the powder down the barrel.
8. Insert the ball down the barrel.
9. Shove the remaining paper with powder down the barrel.
10. Ram the bullet and wadding with the metal rammer.
11. Remove the rammer and slide it into the housing of the gun.
12. Raise the gun to the shoulder.
13. Close the pan.
14. Close the frizzen.
15. Pull the hammer back to full-cock position.

Fowling Pieces: Early in the Revolution Continental soldiers and especially militia brought their own guns to the War. Sometimes the only weapons they could bring were "Fowling" pieces, which were in effect "shot guns" used for bird hunting that were mostly useless on the battle fields of the Revolution. Usually these weapons were discarded for muskets provided to soldiers by their units upon their arrival.

Frizzen: The frizzen of a musket or rifle was the piece of steel which would be struck by the flint held by the hammer to create the sparks to ignite the gun powder in the "pan" to fire the weapon.

Gun Powder: Gun powder was a mixture of salt peter (potassium nitrate), sulfur and charcoal. Due to the shortage of potassium nitrate in America 2/3 of all gun powder used by Americans had to be imported from France and other countries. The shortage of good gun powder was a chronic problem for Americans during the War.

Hammer: The "hammer" of a gun was the hammer shaped part of the firing mechanism which held the flint which when triggered would strike the frizzen.

Hanger: A hanger was a sword almost identical to a cutlass. It was short, easily handled and good for close quarters combat.

Matchlock Muskets: A matchlock musket was a muzzle loaded smooth bore gun that was fired by means of a slow burning potassium nitrate cord (a wick) which when triggered would cause the slow burning cord to touch the gunpowder in the flash-pan of the musket to ignite the gun powder to fire the bullet. The matchlock system was slowly outmoded and replaced by flintlock muskets after 1742.

Muskets: See Flintlock Muskets above. American soldiers used a variety of domestically manufactured muskets and captured British guns. Their main source of foreign muskets was from France, primarily the French Charleville musket which was cheap to produce. It is reported that the French sent 100,000 Charleville muskets to America before the end of the War.

Pistols: Pistols were usually the personal weapon of officers. Some were dual barreled. They were also used by cavalry officers.

Powder Horns: Much of the ammunition used for muskets by the British consisted of pre-made bullets. As the war went on this was also true for the Americans. Powder horns were not needed for muskets because the powder was contained in the pre-made bullets. However, powder horns were needed for rifles because they did not use pre-made bullets.

Rifles: Revolutionary War era rifles were muzzle loaded guns that had spiral grooves cut inside the barrel. The grooves would cause the bullet to spin from the barrel which gave the gun greater accuracy and range. There were downsides to rifles. They were far more expensive and time consuming to make and far slower to load. They were excellent for sniping at long range, but not good for massive line infantry combat. They and their shooters were not at all favored by Washington and his generals because they were so slow to load and had limited use except to snipe and pick off officers in uncommon circumstances. Their shooters were primarily back country woodsmen who did not comply with the strict discipline and standards required by senior officers. The best rifles made in America were from the Pennsylvania gunsmiths. Soldiers who sought to join rifle units had to compete in shooting contests to prove their shooting skills.

"Sleeping in/on Arms": When on high alert for quick combat soldiers would literally sleep on their arms to be ready for instant action. This was called "Sleeping in/on Arms" and could not be done for extended time because of the inability of soldiers to get adequate rest.

Spontoon: A spontoon was a spear like weapon on a long pole commonly used by Ensigns during the Revolution for close quarters combat. It could stop soldiers charging with bayonets.

Stacking Arms: Stacking arms was a method of keeping guns ready for use by placing the stocks on the ground and interlocking the bayonets teepee like.

Swords: Swords were used by officers and Non-Commissioned Officers (NCOs) in infantry combat as well as cavalry combat. Officer swords were curved and had gilded hand cages. NCO swords were straight bladed and had bar hand cages. Many American swords were made from worn out logging saw blades.

Tomahawk: This was a much-feared weapon of American Indians adopted by many American and British soldiers for close quarters fighting. It was carried by a waist band holder belt loop called a "frog". It could be thrown or hand held.

Tow: A "tow" was coarse fiber used to clean the barrels of guns and for wadding in ammunition.

Trench Pikes: Trench pikes were spears with a double edge iron knife like top. They were used in trench warfare and in defending against bayonet attacks.

Windage: Windage was the difference in the diameter of the bullet and diameter of the bore of the gun. The greater the windage, the greater amount of gas that would escape from the barrel, which would cause the bullet to have lower velocity and less range.

Sources:

Lenk, Torsten. *The Flintlock. Its Origin, Development and Use.*

McGuire, Thomas J. *Battle of Paoli. The Revolutionary War "Massacre" Near Philadelphia, September 1777.*

Savas, Theodore P. & J. David Dameron. *A Guide to the Battles of the American Revolution.*

Ward, Christopher. *War of the Revolution.*

Wilbur, Keith C. *The Revolutionary Soldier.*

AMERICAN AND BRITISH CAVALRY TERMS

Carbine: A carbine is a smaller and lighter version of an infantryman's musket that could be used by cavalry on horseback.

Dragoons: These were the horse mounted American, British, French, German and Spanish soldiers who served in the Revolution. Due to the chronic shortage of horses it was common for dragoons to serve in a dismounted mode. The shortage of horses and equipage and fodder requirements resulted in limited cavalry capability by American and British forces during the Revolution.

Heavy Cavalry: Heavy cavalry was primarily used in conjunction with massed infantry and artillery. It was mostly used by the British. It was used for shock effect by headlong charges into the enemy to punch holes in their lines to allow infantry to follow through.

Legions: Cavalry units regardless of nationality were frequently identified as "Legions" such as Light Horse Harry Lee's American Legion. Legions were mostly composed of militia and loyalist soldiers who were led by Regular Army officers such as Tarleton and Lee. The most famous British Legion during the Revolution was Banastre Tarleton's British Legion.

Light Cavalry: Light cavalry was mostly used for quick strike, recon, and flanking maneuvers on the battlefield. It was almost exclusively used by the Americans.

Rangers: British cavalry units were commonly known as "Rangers" such as Simcoe's Queen's Rangers which were a combination of British and Loyalist soldiers. Ranger units were traditionally smaller than Legions and consisted of a combination of infantry and mounted soldiers.

Reconnaissance: The role of cavalry quickly evolved to a reconnaissance role for much of the Revolution. While cavalry could and did perform a "quick strike" capability it was mostly useful in determining the movement and disposition of enemy forces in preparation for battles. Cavalry on the battlefield was also used to attack the rear and flanks of enemy lines.

Sabre: A sabre is the equivalent of an infantrymen's sword, except that a sabre is shorter and lighter so it can be used easily by troopers on horseback.

Troop: The word "troop" is the cavalry equivalent to a "company" of infantry. The "troop" was the basic fighting unit in cavalry operations. Troops typically consisted of 68 troopers including officers, farriers and support personnel.

Troopers: Cavalrymen were called "Troopers" not soldiers.

Sources:

Cecere. Michael. *Wedded to My Sword. The Revolutionary War Service of Light Horse Harry Lee.*

Piecuch, Jim (Editor). *Cavalry of the American Revolution.*

AMERICAN AND BRITISH CAVALRY DURING THE REVOLUTION

Cavalry during the American Revolution referred to horse mounted soldiers commonly called Dragoons. The British, German, French, Spanish, American Militia and American Continental forces all had cavalry units. However, there was a chronic shortage of horses for everyone in America which meant that most cavalry forces were a combination of mounted and dismounted soldiers. The basic cavalry fighting unit was called a "Troop". This was the equivalent a "Company" the basic infantry fighting unit, and "Battery" the basic fighting unit of the artillery. The tactics of using cavalry were evolving as the war was fought. There was "Heavy Cavalry" defined below which was used for "shock effect" by charging headlong into the enemy. There was "Light Cavalry" defined below which was used for rapid flanking, scouting and reconnaissance. How they were used was determined by available resources, the decisions of the battlefield commanders and the situation.

There were two major cavalry fighting units in the Revolution: "Rangers" and "Legions". They consisted mostly of Loyalists combined with British regulars or American Militia combined with Continental soldiers. Ranger and Legion units consisted of cavalrymen who were mounted and dismounted soldiers. A Ranger was unit was composed similarly to a Legion unit but much smaller, far less than 1,000 men. A Legion was also composed of dismounted infantry and mounted solders but composed of up to 1,000 men so it could operate more independently from the main army. Because of the shortage of resources American Ranger and Legion units were smaller than similar British units.

AMERICAN RANGER AND LEGION/CAV UNITS

Light Horse Legion of Harry Lee: From the start of the Revolution this celebrated unit consisted primarily of Virginia horsemen commanded by Major Light Horse Harry Lee the father of Robert Lee of Civil War fame. Because it was created early in the War Lee's Legion participated in most of the battles of the "Middle Colonies" of New Jersey, and Pennsylvania and later in Virginia and the southern colonies. Harry Lee's Legion provided critical support to defeat the British "Southern Campaign" from 1780-1783.

Pulaski's Continental Light Dragoons: This unit was commanded by the volunteer Polish officer Count Casimir Pulaski who came to America on July 23, 1777 without pay from Europe. His unit distinguished itself in the battles of Brandywine and others. He soon became a favorite of Gen Washington who admired his discipline and daring exploits. During the southern campaign, he was a key player in the American/French assault on the city of Savannah, Georgia in October 1779. His unit was notable in the action there. While covering the withdrawal of the American and French forces at Savannah he was killed in October 1777.

Sources:

Cecere, Michael. *Wedded To My Sword. The Revolutionary War Service of Light Horse Harry Lee.*

Piecuch, Jim (Editor). *Cavalry of the American Revolution.*

Savas, Theodore P. & J. David Dameron. *A Guide to the Battles of the American Revolution.*

Ward, Christopher. *War of the Revolution.*

BRITISH RANGER AND LEGION/CAV UNITS

Simcoe's Queen's Rangers: Lt Col John Simcoe fought in the French and American War. After the Battle of Brandywine in 1777 where his unit suffered heavy casualties he was named commander of a unit called Simcoe's Rangers. He was captured in October 1779 and exchanged in December where he again assumed command of his unit. He successfully fought with British Brigadier General Benedict Arnold in southern Virginia in the spring of 1781. He was captured with Cornwallis on October 17, 1781 after the Battle of Yorktown. He eventually became commander of British forces in Canada after the war.

Banastre Tarleton's British Legion: This unit was formed by British General Clinton in 1778 and was mostly composed of American Loyalist infantry and cavalry lead by British officers. It was larger than Simcoe's Rangers and more heavily equipped with light artillery (3 pound grasshoppers). It was more capable of head to head combat with American units than Ranger units. Under the command of Lt Col Banastre Tarleton it had a reputation of cruelty and slaughter of soldiers who were surrendering on the battlefield. It mostly operated in the British southern campaign. Under the command of Colonel Daniel Morgan, the Americans severely mauled Tarleton's Legion at the Battle of Cowpens on January 17, 1781. As part of General

Cornwallis' army the British Legion and Tarleton were captured at the Battle of Yorktown in October 1781. After the War, he served in Parliament and became a full British General in India.

"Black Dragoons": The Black Dragoons were a horse mounted group of slaves who were given their freedom in November 1781 to fight for the British and Loyalists around Charles Town, SC. This reflects the desperation of the Loyalists after the disastrous battle of Yorktown in October 1781. The Black Dragoons were known for their ruthlessness. They continued to fight with the British until November 1782.

Sources:

Cecere, Michael. *Wedded To My Sword. The Revolutionary War Service of Light Horse Harry Lee.*
Piecuch, Jim (Editor). *Cavalry of the American Revolution.*
Savas, Theodore P. & J. David Dameron. *A Guide to the Battles of the American Revolution.*
Ward, Christopher. *War of the Revolution.*

AMERICAN RECRUITING AND ENLISTMENT

Enlistment in America's armed forces was far more complicated than in Britain because there were Local militia, State troops and Continental Army soldiers. American recruits were paid "Bounties" (bonuses) just like British recruits. The hyper-inflation caused by the uncontrolled printing of American currency greatly depressed the value of the bounties. In part to counteract this problem recruits were promised 100 acres of land along with a bounty if they enlisted for the duration of the War. Enlistments for as short as 60 days or less were common for the Militia. Enlistments in the Continental Army were usually for a minimum of one year, or three years or the duration of the War. Some recruits would enlist, collect their bounty, then desert and enlist in another unit. This "Bounty Jumping" as it was called was so damaging that Washington ordered the immediate execution of individuals guilty of this practice. Different States had different bounties for enlisting which set up in effect "bidding wars" for recruits. Recruiters were usually from the area where they did their recruiting which helped their credibility among local folk. Recruiting in the New England States was easier than in the Southern States. In New England, there was a strong family and local loyalty to those who enlisted. Brothers, sons, father and uncles were motivated to enlist out of a sense of family service to the new nation. Local towns were in competition to see which could enlist the most recruits. Recruiting in the southern States was far more difficult. Southern land holders felt no obligation to serve in the Army. They felt it was the duty of the landless, poor and destitute to serve. The draft was instituted by the Continental Congress at the urging of Washington very early in the Revolution. Each State was levied to produce draftees in proportion to the number of their militia. The States were told to pay for the costs of those who were drafted from their State, which they rarely did. This in a large part explains why so many American soldiers went unpaid. Because of the requirement to fill the draft quotas, southern landholders paid increasingly higher "Bounties" for recruits. For both the Northern and Southern States as the War wore on enlistees came increasingly from the lowest classes which resulted in training, performance and conduct problems. Individuals who received a draft notice could also pay someone to be a "Substitute" for their draft. Initially blacks were not permitted as "Substitutes" for the draft but by 1777 the manpower shortages of the American Army were so severe that black substitutes were permitted. Indentured servants who were drafted into the American Army were called "Redemptioners". Their service in the American Army relieved them from their indenture. The period of service for a draftee was usually one year. After the War was over some of the most generous promises made to those who served were not honored which created tension between those who served and those who did not.

Sources:

Broadus, Mitchell. *The Price of Independence. A Realistic View of the American Revolution*

Cox, Caroline. *A Proper Sense of Honor. Service and Sacrifice in George Washington's Army.*

Ferling, Don N. *Almost A Miracle. The American Victory in the War of Independence.*

Kranish, Michael. *Flight From Monticello. Jefferson at War.*

Mayers, Robert A. *The War Man. The True Story of a Citizen-Soldier Who Fought from Quebec to Yorktown.*

Raphael, Ray. *A People's History of the American Revolution – How Common Peoples Shaped the Fight for Independence.*

Royster, Charles. *A Revolutionary People at War. The Continental Army & American Character, 1775-1783.*

Stephenson, Michael. *Patriot Battles. How the War of Independence Was Fought.*

BRITISH RECRUITING AND ENLISTMENT

The British Army was an "All Volunteer" force. During periods of deployment from the home islands British regiments left behind two recruiting companies called "Additional Companies" primarily to recruit and conduct basic training for new soldiers. That basic training could last over a year. Like recruiting offices to this current day "quotas" were applied so there was pressure to meet the numbers. The recruiters were not limited to geographical areas. They concentrated their efforts in bars, saloons, markets and country fairs where potential recruits would congregate. Up until 1775 Roman Catholics were barred from serving. Recruits had to meet age and height minimums initially set at 5′6″ height and 17 years of age. As manpower requirements became more severe these criteria were relaxed. Bounties (bonuses) were paid to new recruits. Recruiters were paid bonuses for each successful recruit they enlisted. Newly signed recruits had to appear before a magistrate no sooner than one day and no later than four days after signing up to confirm they voluntarily enlisted and "Attest" they had not been tricked into signing and had been read the Articles of War, which among other things specified the punishments for violations of military regulations, especially desertion. It was also the magistrate's job to ensure the enlistee was qualified for military duty. If the recruit changed his mind about enlisting during the four-day period, he had to pay back the bounty he had been paid at the time of enlistment: usually a shilling. He also had to pay the cost of his recruitment plus what was called "Smart Money" of 24 shillings for the trouble the Army had gone to recruit him. If it was found that a recruit had been fraudulently enlisted by a recruiter the recruiter was required to pay for all the expenses invested in the recruit. When and if a soldier was Court Martialed for desertion, which was fairly common, proof that he "Attested" to having been read the Articles of War was crucial to his conviction or innocence. It is true that some criminals were given the opportunity to enlist in lieu of jail time, but that was quite rare. Manpower requirements were so severe that "Press Acts" of May 28, 1778 and February 9, 1779 were passed by Parliament to get new recruits. Voters, those who owned property, were excluded from impressment. It is estimated that no more than 2,000 recruits were "pressed" into service. The Acts were overturned in 1780. The Acts scarfed up mostly poorly qualified individuals who ultimately were usually discipline problems and just plain bad soldiers. The Acts were very unpopular within the officer corps and British population. There were some instances of self-mutilation to avoid the draft. All voters (land holders) were exempt from impressment. The Acts did motivate a fair number of individuals to voluntarily enlist so they could collect their bounty. Recruits who voluntarily enlisted were also given their choice of regiment most of which had celebrated and valorous traditions. This was a big motivator and also included the place where the regiment was located. The minimum period of enlistment was three years. Most recruits were motivated to enlist with the prospect of improving their economic plight. British soldiers were paid 8 pence per day, (12 pence equaled one shilling). Much the same in the American Army, most of the pay for the British soldiers went for their food, uniforms, repair of weapons, medical care and overhead which meant the soldier had little to spend for himself or send home to his family. The prospects of steady employment, regular pay, a pension (five pence a day after twenty years or service or disability) and most importantly adventure were the biggest reasons for enlistment by the British.

Sources:

Hagist, Don N. *British Soldiers, American War.*
Urban, Mark. *Fusiliers, The Saga of a British Redcoat Regiment in the American Revolution.*

AMERICAN STRATGIC OPTIONS AT THE START OF THE REVOLUTION

Draw Britain's Enemies to Fight with America: The object of this effort was to internationalize the war which would require Britain to fight a global war. This strategy was ultimately successful after the American triumphs at the battles of Trenton, Princeton and Saratoga which gave France the confidence to formally join the American battle against the British.

Wage Economic War on Britain through Naval Privateers: This tactic would severely disrupt British trade which was critical for its economic survival. While this was attempted with some success. However, the bite cut both ways and in the end privateering did not have enough impact to sway the Crown's decision makers to abandon the effort to subdue America.

Fight a Delaying War and avoid any Major Battles: The plan here was to maneuver and avoid entrapment in a major battle that might result in the destruction of the American army. This strategy was designed to wear down the British with a "Fabian Defense", militarily and politically.

Organize the American Army into Small Mobile Units: The thought here was to make it impossible for the British to consolidate their forces to catch and defeat in a single battle the whole American Army.

Fight a "War of Posts": This is what General Washington called his strategy. This was a defensive approach where very much like the Fabian strategy. It would make the British waste their time and resources in futile efforts to attack the American strong points (posts).

"Offensive-Defensive" Strategy: With this approach the Americans would attack when they had superior forces and then go on the defense in the face of superior enemy forces.

Perimeter Defense: The thought here was for all towns and cities to be protected from the British. This was never seriously considered because it required too many American soldiers.

STRATEGIES EMPLOYED BY AMERICANS

Colonial Strategy of 1775-1777: The plan during this period was to internationalize the Revolutionary War through strategic alliances. This military strategy was also as old as warfare and consisted of bringing enemies of your enemy to support you in your cause. The Greeks used this strategy in Grecian City State wars. The implementation plan for this strategy was to send high level emissaries from the Continental Congress to France, Spain and the Netherlands to encourage these long-term enemies of Britain to support the Colonial cause or declare war on the British. Silas Deane and Benjamin Franklin were sent to France, John Adams to the Netherlands and John Jay to Spain for long term assignments and were ultimately successful to the great detriment of the British war effort against the Colonies. It took the American battlefield successes of Trenton, Princeton and Saratoga to convince the Europeans that the Americans with their help could defeat the British. Ultimately the strategy worked because France signed an alliance with the Americans in 1778, the Spanish declared war on Britain in 1779 and the British declared war on the Netherlands in 1780.

Colonial Strategy of 1778-1781: The American strategy during this period was to avoid major battles of potential catastrophic consequence and wear down the British Army through constant maneuver and use the French Navy to deny the British Army the ability to be supported from coastal ports. The French Navy ultimately proved decisive by bottling up the British Army of Lord Cornwallis at Yorktown, Virginia in the early fall of 1781.

Sources:

Ferreiro, Larrie D. *Brothers At Arms. American Independence and the Men of France and Spain Who Saved It.*

Hackett, David Fischer. *Washington's Crossing.*

Martin, James K. & Mark E. Lender. *A Respectable Army. The Military Origins of the Republic, 1763-1789.*

BRITISH STRATEGIC OPTIONS AT THE START OF THE REVOLUTION

Divide and Conquer: A good look at the map of North America showed what was known for centuries. Lake Champlain was called for a very long time "The Great Warpath" and presented what seemed as a logical way to accomplish the classic Divide and Conquer strategy of separating the northern colonies from those down south.

Blockade: The American colonies were coastal entities and depended on trade for their survival so a blockade was considered but rejected because it would be ruinous to British industry and unenforceable because of the length of the American coastline. In addition, the British Navy had too many other world-wide naval commitments to fulfill.

Deliberate use of Terror and Destruction: The Germans called this strategy *shrecklichkeit* or total war. Although there were some adherents to this approach the British Commanders in Chief considered this immoral and inhumane and prohibited it.

Relentless Pursuit of the American Rebels: This was rejected as too dangerous after the British experience of Bunker Hill. American

Rebels could disappear into the civilian population and then assemble to fight again with ease, which made this approach unworkable.

Spreading Ink Stain Strategy: This plan called for the British to occupy the major cities in America and from there to spread their control to ever greater areas. This approach would take too much time and too many soldiers to be viable.

Have Loyalists do the Fighting: Here the thought was to let the Loyalists take the burden of defeating the American Rebels. Loyalists who fought for the British never had a major impact on the course of the Revolution. They were poorly organized and not integrated into the British Army. The fact that the British wrongly assumed that huge numbers of Loyalists would flock to support the Crown is credited as a **major** cause of their failure to defeat the Americans.

STRATEGIES EMPLOYED BY THE BRITISH

Divide and Conquer 1776-1777: The object here was to divide the northern American States from the others by driving a wedge between them through campaigns south from Canada through Lake Champlain to the Hudson River then Albany, NY eventually to NYC. This was first tried by MG Sir Guy Carleton Commander of the British Army in Canada in 1776, which failed because winter was about to set in by the time they arrived at the southern end of Lake Champlain. Under the command of British LTG General John Burgoyne the strategy was again attempted in 1777. Here the plan was to have him link up with General William Howe who would move up the Hudson River from New York City. This second attempt failed in October 1777 when Burgoyne's force became bogged down in the forests around Saratoga, NY and was defeated by overwhelming American forces.

Big Battle Strategy of 1778-1780: With the defeat of Burgoyne the Revolution became an international war with the entry of France in 1778 and later Spain in 1779 and the Netherlands in 1780. This caused the British to reduce their forces in America and withdraw from Philadelphia. Occasionally called the **Big Battle** or *coup de main* strategy, the plan during this period was to trap the Americans in a take-all battle that would crush the rebellion. Due to the superb generalship of Washington and his subordinate commanders the Americans were able to avoid such a catastrophic battle.

Southern Strategy 1780-1781: With their failure to win over the Americans in the north and inability to bring the war to a successful conclusion with a major battle over Washington's, Army, the British sought victory with a new approach called the **Southern Strategy** which brought the war to the Southern Colonies. The British had the false hope that multitudes of Loyalists would join them in the south. They initially met with success with the capture of Charles Town, SC on May 12, 1780 which resulted in the surrender of the largest number of American soldiers during the War. This victory for the British was followed by the catastrophic defeat of the Americans at the Battle of Camden, SC on August 16, 1780. However, the expected and critically needed Loyalist support never really materialized in the south. The British then began suffering a series of devastating defeats: King's Mountain (October 1780), Blackstock's Plantation (November 1780), Cowpens (January 1781), the ruin of Cornwallis' army in its unsuccessful pursuit of General Greene to the Dan River (February 1781) and Guilford Courthouse (March 1781) all of which caused the British to suffer irreplaceable losses. Finally, there came the entrapment and surrender of Cornwallis at Yorktown, VA (October 17, 1781) which effectively ended any further chances of the British defeating the American Revolution.

Sources:

Ferling, John. *Almost A. Miracle. The American Victory in the War of Independence.*

Ferreiro, Larrie D. *Brothers At Arms. American Independence and the Men of France and Spain Who Saved It.*

Hackett, David Fischer. *Washington's Crossing.*

Martin, James K. & Mark E. Lender. *A Respectable Army. The Military Origins of the Republic.*

AMERICAN LOGISTICS: PROBLEMS AND ISSUES

There was no "unity" between the colonies before the Revolution which is reflected in the severe logistics problems the Americans had during the conflict which are shown in the following:

No Large-Scale Logistics Experience: Both the Americans and British faced daunting but very different problems in supplying and feeding their armies. Flawed as it was, the British at least had a logistics framework to start with. The Americans had nothing to start with and thirteen separate colonies with very individual agendas and priorities. The critical problem for the Americans was the fact that they had no central power to raise taxes to pay for supplies and food stuffs and no power to force the colonies to pony up needed provisions. Because America never had an army of its own it had no experience in feeding and provisioning tens of thousands of soldiers encamped in a single area. Washington estimated it would take 100,000 barrels of flour and 20,000 pounds of meat to feed the 15,000 Americans surrounding the British at Boston in 1775. These were staggering amounts during these times.

No Logistics Infrastructure or Organization: Upon the establishment of the American Army in July 1775 the Second Continental Congress created the Board of War to direct the management of American forces. The Board was a collection of committees with various assignments.

A "Commissary General" was created to coordinate and manage the procurement of food stuffs for the Army. A "Quartermaster General" was created to coordinate and manage the overall procurement of supplies. The British had similar officials. During the War the Americans had four Quartermaster Generals and four Commissary Generals. These were impossible jobs that no one wanted or could do. To begin with Americans got their food stuffs and provisions from merchants who charged fees up to 7.5% for their services. It was a system that made fraud and corruption all too easy. Later in the war the system was changed to provisioning by "contracts" which helped some.

No Centralized Supply Transportation System: The problems of transporting supplies and provisions were vexing for both the Americans and British. Wagons sent from Britain were not suited for rough American roads. The British had civilian wagon masters under contract who were unpredictable during combat. A substantial number of American wagon masters were soldiers which helped some, but recruiting wagon masters for the Army was a problem because as civilians got paid twice as much as soldiers. The Americans in an effort to solve the problem on May 14, 1778 separated the responsibilities for wagons from the Quartermaster General and created a "Wagon Department" which sounded good on paper but did not have a measurable positive impact. Bread was the mainstay of the diets of the American and British soldiers. All too often the flour was adulterated with chalk or dirt or some other foreign substances. In 1777 Congress appointed a Superintendent of Bakers for the Continental Army. He developed portable ovens to bake bread for soldiers in the field. Salt was prized for bread and preservation of meat which explains the battles over the salt mines in the hills of North Carolina and evaporation ponds on the New Jersey coastline.

Sources:

Stephenson, Michael. *Patriot Battles. How the War for Independence was Fought.*

BRITISH LOGISTICS: PROBLEMS AND ISSUES

One of the primary reasons for the failure of the British to crush the American Revolution was the challenge they faced with logistics and their failure to adequately address them. The logistics requirements for the British Army (including their German mercenaries) in America were unprecedented for that period and are still impressive as shown by the following metrics:

BRITISH/GERMAN FOOD STUFFS CONSUMED FROM MAY 27, 1777 TO NOVEMBER 11, 1781

79,465,184 pounds of bread, flour and rice
10,711,820 pounds of salt beef
38,202,081 pounds of salt pork
3,093,952 pounds of fresh meat
3,997,043 pounds of butter
7,282,071 pounds of oatmeal
2,865,782 gallons of rum
176,672 gallons of molasses
134,378 gallons of vinegar
427,452 bushels of peas
63 tons of candles

ANNUAL CONSUMABLES

70,000 cords of wood
14,000 tons of hay (4,500 tons in NYC alone)
6,000 tons of oats

FAULTY ASSUMPTIONS AND ISSUES

Assumed a Quick Victory: The British assumed that they would achieve a quick victory over the Americans who were not unified and had no army or navy and would be facing the world's most professional British forces. The colonies united quicker than the British anticipated with the Declaration of Independence and immediately formed a continental army and navy supplemented by privateers.

Assumed French and Indian War Logistics Model Would Work: They believed the logistics model used in the French and Indian War (F&I) would suffice for the Revolution. The logistics requirements and situation for the F&I War were dramatically different for the Revolution. During the F&I War the local Americans were mostly supportive of the British which meant they could obtain local supplies from Americans which was not the case during the Revolution. As a result, most of the supplies needed by the British had to be transported across the Atlantic.

Assumed Too Few Soldiers Would be Needed: Early on the British did not anticipate the number of soldiers that would be required to tame the Revolution. As 1776 drew to a close, more and more troop requests were submitted by the British which strained the logistics system from the start. They assumed they would get high levels of support from Loyalists which never materialized. As the British plundered and confiscated local supplies to unburden their own logistics system, more and more Loyalists turned to the side of the American Rebels. German mercenaries were known to be especially predatory which aggravated the situation.

Assumed Army and Navy Would Co-Operate: The British logistics model was badly flawed. The British Treasury department was responsible for Army logistics and the Navy had responsibility for it is own logistics. The British Army and Navy competed for the same limited resources. There were no clear top to bottom lines of responsibility and authority. The Treasury hired victual ships which were unarmed from the start which made them fairly easy game for American Naval ships and privateers. Later when they were armed they then came to be in competition for experienced crewmen by the navy. Losses continued so arrangements were made for the navy to protect the victual ships with armed convoys. This complicated logistics arrangements because armed convoys could not be frequently synchronized with the sailing of victual ships.

Lacked Key Military Logistics Experience: Key logistics officials were appointed based on their connections rather than any relevant experience. Until 1779 the British had faulty "Strength Accounting" from the "Returns – Muster Rolls" to determine the volume of food stuffs and supplies needed for planning purposes. They did not know how many Loyalists should be counted in their logistics planning. Corruption among British logistics officials was well known. Corrupt suppliers provided goods that were found to be spoiled when inspected upon arrival in America. There was a shortage of warehouses so victual ships which were in short supply were used to store goods for long periods of time increasing the chances of spoilage. There was a perpetual shortage of wagons which were critical for campaigns. The wagons shipped from Britain were too big and unwieldy for practical use in America. Wagon teamsters were hired civilians who fled at critical times in combat. Most American wagon teamsters were soldiers and subject to military order and training. Shipping horses by sea from Britain turned into a disaster. Of the 845 horses shipped from Britain to America in 1776, 532 died en-route or on their arrival. A similar mortality rate was experienced among the hundreds of horses shipped by sea from New York City to Head of Elk Maryland when the British moved to capture Philadelphia in 1777. Throughout the war the British were critically short of horses.

Underestimated Thousand Mile Ocean Transport Difficulties: The three-thousand-mile ocean distance between America and Britain made effective communications a nightmare. Ships sailing from Britain to America "up-hill" as it was called could take 60 or even 90 days. Ships sailing from America to Britain "down-hill" as it was called would take a minimum of three weeks. Bad weather could delay the departure of convoys for weeks and weeks completely upsetting logistics schedules. British CINCs Howe and Clinton who were naturally inclined to be cautious, became ever more so with the unpredictable arrival of supplies. They felt they needed a minimum of six months reserve of supplies to undertake major campaigns. Rarely did they ever have one third of that and at one point in 1778 were down to just a few days of food rations. German soldiers were particularly prone to deserting when they were "short rationed". As a result, both Howe and Clinton missed great opportunities to strike forth against the Americans for lack of confidence in their supply situation. For the most part, the British did not suffer from shortages of arms except for muskets. They had enough muskets to supply their own forces but frequently lacked enough to arm Loyalists which limited their ability to fight the American rebels.

Sources:

Bowler, R. Arthur. *Logistics and the Failure of the British Army in America.*

Braisted, Todd W. *Grand Forage 1778, The Battleground Around New York City.*

Ferling, John. *Almost A Miracle. The American Victory in the War of Independence.*

Ketchum, Richard M. *The Winter Soldiers. The Battles of Trenton and Princeton.*

ARTILLERY TYPES

Worldwide there were three types of artillery described below. Cannons were not generally accurate, although individual gun crews prided themselves on their ability to hit targets at long range. A six-pound cannon firing at a company of infantry (six feet tall by 30 feet wide) would score nearly 100% hits at 520 yards, which was reduced to 31% at 950 yards and 17 % at 1,200 yards. A good gun crew firing six pound balls could get off two or three rounds a minute. A six-pound gun crew usually consisted of nine to twelve soldiers. One soldier would stand to the right of the gun with a sponger/rammer device. Another stood to the left and was responsible for loading the gun. To the left and right at the back of the gun was the igniter-man holding the linstock and the vents man. The gun crew chief stood at the back of the gun. The first action to fire the gun was to aim it which was done by moving it around with crowbar like spikes and then properly elevating the muzzle. The ammo for six pounders usually consisted of the ball and sack of powder tied together in a charge which would be placed in the barrel with the powder at the back. The rammer would ram the charge fully down the barrel. The vents man would then puncture the powder sack inside the barrel by shoving a sharp device down the vent hole called a "pricker". He then inserted a tube of powder into the vent hole. The firer on command to fire would pass the lighted linstock at the vent hole to ignite the charge. For the next shot the cannon had to be re-aimed, and the rammer would shove a water soaked sheep skin down the barrel to clean and extinguish any sparks that were left. The next charge would be rammed down the barrel. Care always had to be taken to ensure no sparks or flames prematurely ignited ammunition.

Cannons: Cannons were smooth bore muzzle loaded artillery weapons that fired non-explosive rounds, such as solid shot, canister and grape shot. They were identified by the weight of the solid shot they fired; i.e., 2 pounders, 4 pounders, 12 pounders etc. Four and six pounder cannons were the most popular cannons used by the Americans during ordinary campaign operations. Canister shot were iron balls loaded in a can which when fired spread a broad path of destruction into enemy infantry. Grape shot was a canvas bag of iron bullets which when fired also spread a broad path of destruction into enemy infantry. Cannon can be readily identified by their long barrels with "bulbous" ends. Because of their long barrels, they could only be with fired with a small elevation of the barrel. They were mostly made of iron but the most durable, expensive and highly prized ones were made of brass. Three pound cannons were commonly known as GRASSHOPPERS because, unlike most other cannons, they were fired from a tripod which made them look like a GRASSHOPPER and would "jump" like a grasshopper when fired. Because they had no wheels they were moved around by horseback. Cannons most commonly fired "line of sight", meaning they fired in a straight line to their target. Another cannon 2 to 3-pound cannon was called the SWIVEL and was mounted and fired from a post which allowed it to be fired from a point and aimed around the battlefield. Swivel cannons were commonly used aboard ships. They were of lower caliber than PIVOT guns which fired from a moveable frame.

Howitzers: Howitzers were a smooth bore muzzle loaded artillery weapons that fired explosive shells that either detonated when they hit their target or burst in the air via a fuse over the heads of troops. They were identified by the size of the diameter of the hole (bore) of the barrel i.e., 2 inch, 4 inch etc. They can be readily identified by their shorter barrel and lack of the "Bulbous" rear end. Howitzers could fire rounds over fortifications and hills. On average, they weighed considerably less than cannons. Howitzers were not commonly used aboard ships.

Mortars: Mortars were stubby heavy muzzle loaded artillery weapons that would "lob" shells, shot and grenades high in the air to fall into the forts and redoubts of the enemy, mostly in siege situations. They were also identified by the size of the hole of their barrel, i.e. 2 inch 4 inch etc. and had a fixed elevation of 45 degrees. The American Revolution was primarily a war of maneuver rather than siege battles where mortars could destroy fortifications, so their use was fairly infrequent. Small mortars which threw grenades (explosive shells) were known as COHORNS. Large mortars were also known as ROYALS. Some boats were heavily constructed to fire mortars.

Sources:

Greene, Jerome A. *The Guns of Independence, The Siege of Yorktown.*
Puls, Mark. *Henry Knox. Visionary General of the American Revolution.*
Ward, Christopher. *War of the Revolution.*

ARTILLERY TERMS

Artillery Carcase: The carcase was an incendiary shot intended to set the targets on fire. The shots would be hollowed out and filled with flammable material which would spread fire on impact. The hollowed-out shell looked like a carcase hence its nickname.

Artillery Parks: Artillery "Parks" were the places where the British and or Americans and French would consolidate their artillery before a siege or major attack. At the "Parks" the artillery would be repaired as necessary and supplies consolidated for the forthcoming battle. The most famous "Artillery Parks" for the Americans and French during the Revolution were at the siege of Yorktown.

Bar Shot: Bar shot consisted of two balls of iron attached together by a bar which when fired would swing through the air ripping sails and rigging of ships. They were mostly used in naval fighting.

Batteries: These were groups of artillery guns which operated usually in groups of three. They were the basic artillery fighting unit similar to a "company" in infantry. They were manned by crews of nine to twelve specially trained men. Early in the war they operated independently but later were integrated into infantry units to increase their effectiveness.

Cannon Fever: This was a derisive term for cowardice on the battlefield related to the fear of artillery.

Cannons: Cannons were large guns which would shoot non-explosive "shots". On average, they were heavier than howitzers. They were named for the caliber (weight of their shots) – three pounds, 4 pounds, 8 pounds etc. Their tubes were longer and had a distinctive "bulbous" end (breech).

Carriage: The carriage was the wheeled gun assembly on which the cannon or howitzer **trunnion** (frame) was mounted.

Case Shot: Case shot were balls of iron enclosed in a "case" which would burst from the case when fired to wound and kill opposing infantry. It was very similar to grape or canister shot.

Caisson: Caissons were two wheel carts towed behind the limbers of cannons and howitzers. They carried the ammunition and equipment needed to fire and service the guns. During combat the limbers and caissons of these guns would be detached from the guns.

Chain Shot: Chain shots were two iron shots linked by chain and shot from cannons primarily to rip and tear sails and rigging of enemy ships.

Cohorn: Cohorns were small 4 ½ inch mortars. Due to their relatively light weight they could be easily transported by two men which made them popular.

Field Artillery: Field artillery was smaller and lighter artillery which could be towed on two wheeled carriages with two horses. They were mobile on a battle field. Heavy artillery were larger guns which usually required four or more horses and were carried on four wheel carriages and were not commonly used in fluid battlefield conditions.

Grape Shot: Grape shot was similar to Case Shot and Canister Shot except that the iron balls would be wrapped in canvas which would burst to spread death and destruction to enemy infantry.

Grasshoppers: These were two and three-pound artillery pieces which could be moved without the need for wheeled apparatus. They could be transported between supports of horses which greatly improved their mobility. They got their name from the fact that they looked like a "grasshopper" when ready to fire and when fired would "jump" like a grasshopper.

Handspikes: Handspikes were large wooden crowbars shielded in iron to lift the breech of cannons to help insertion of "Quoins" which were screw like devices to lower or elevate cannons as necessary for proper aiming.

Heurtoirs: Heurtoirs were the wood platforms where artillery was placed in the embrasures of parapets.

Howitzers: Howitzers were artillery guns which would shoot "Shells" (explosive) munitions. They had shorter barrels than cannon and could shoot their shells in arcs vs cannons which mostly could shoot "line of sight". They were named for their caliber (4 inch, 6 inch, 8 inch etc.) which referred to the diameter of the hole (bore) in the muzzle of the barrel.

Langrage: Sometimes when lead balls for grape and canister shot were not available fragments of metal, rock and debris was fired from cannons. This material was called langrage.

Limber: The Limber was the two-wheeled carriage attached to the tongue of a cannon or howitzer which allowed the gun to be pulled by horses or oxen.

"Long Arm" of the Army: Artillery during the Revolution and to this current day is known as the Long Army of the Army due to its ability to bring fire to the enemy at very long distances.

Merlons: Merlons were the part of the parapet between embrasures (openings in the parapet) where cannon or howitzers were placed.

Pivot Guns: These were guns mounted on a pivot so they could be fired in an arc rather than a 360-degree swivel cannon. They were commonly used on ships and were of far greater caliber than swivel guns.

Quaker Guns: These were logs painted black and mounted to look like cannon. They were made to fool an enemy into thinking they were facing artillery.

Quoins: Quoins were screw like devices which were placed below the breeches of cannons which when turned would elevate or lower the cannon to assure proper aiming.

Ricochet Firing: Ricochet firing was one of the most deadly and destructive methods of shooting cannons (not howitzers). The shots from cannons would be deliberately aimed so as to "ricochet" off walls, buildings, trenches and the ground which would create great destruction from a single shot.

"Royal": A Royal was a 5 ½ inch mortar.

Sabots: Sabots were wooden disks slightly hollowed in the center and placed in the barrels of cannons to accommodate "shots – rounds" when they were loaded in cannons.

Siege Artillery: Siege artillery were heavy gage cannons (24 + pound) which were not mobile and could be transported best on heavy wagons and then assembled for action. In many cases, they were placed in fixed positions on fortifications. In cases where they were moved it was to conduct a "siege" of a fortification.

Spider Shot: Spider shot was Chain Shot with multiple chains and balls. This was used mostly in ship to ship fighting. It would rip rigging, sails and lines.

Spiking Guns: When in the heat of battle and the enemy captured the cannons and howitzers of opponents, they would frequently attempt to make the guns useless by driving their bayonets down the "Vent Holes" of the guns which would prevent them from being fired. This was called "Spiking". Bayonets were not suited for this purpose because the broken tips of the bayonets could be pried out fairly easily which would make the guns serviceable again. A more permanent method of Spiking consisted of driving a special soft iron rod down the Vent Holes. This soft iron would be very difficult to remove.

Swivel Guns: These were small caliber cannons (three pounds or less) mounted on a vertical device whereby the gun could be swung around the vertical post and fired at any point in a 360-degree circle.

Trunnion: The trunnion was the frame of a gun carriage.

Vent Holes: The Vent Holes of cannon and howitzers were the holes through which the powder would ignite the charge of the weapon.

Sources:

Greene, Jerome A. *The Guns of Independence. The Siege of Yorktown.*
Puls, Mark. *Henry Knox. Visionary General of the American Revolution.*
Ward, Christopher. *War of the Revolution.*

PRO-AMERICAN GROUPS

The Revolution seriously fractured the Colonies and States into antagonistic groups which led to the ugly "civil war" that was a serious component of the Revolution. Many of the hard feelings between these groups continued long after the war. The following are the American groups which were so prominent during the Revolution.

Association for Retribution: This was the New Jersey group of American Rebels who fought against the Association Loyalists in New Jersey's civil war during the Revolution.

Committees of Correspondence: These were groups within each colony to coordinate their actions and share information. They became very powerful and influential.

Committees of Inspection and Compliance: These were groups within the colonies and states to ensure enforcement of anti-British colonial agreements such as boycotts.

Committees of Safety: These were groups within each colony to manage the resistance or military action against British rule. These committees frequently used strong-arm tactics against British officials.

Committees of Supply: These were the committees that had the special responsibility for procuring food, supplies, and armaments for the Americans, especially gunpowder.

First Rhode Island Infantry Regiment: This pro-rebel unit was organized in late 1776 and early 1777 and was the first all-Black military unit in America. It was commanded by white officers and distinguished itself in the Battle of Newport, RI on August 29, 1778 and participated in the famous assault on Redoubt 10 at Yorktown in October 1781. Its veterans never received pensions for their service but their distinguished combat record helped dispel the notion that Blacks were incapable of military discipline or valor in combat.

Green Mountain Boys: These were New England militia from Connecticut, Massachusetts, and New Hampshire initially led by Colonel Ethan Allen. They were prominent in the capture of Fort Ticonderoga on May 10, 1775 and later participated in the Battles of Hubbarton, and Bennington in Vermont and Saratoga, NY. They later became known as The Green Mountain Rangers under the command of Colonel Seth Warner after Ethan Allen had been captured and made a long-term POW of the British.

League of Armed Neutrality: The question of neutrality of trading ships became more important as the Revolution dragged on and involved more of the European powers. The League was proposed by Catherine II of Russia and eventually was accepted by most of the neutral countries of Europe. While it did not have military enforcement powers, it did work to the advantage of the Americans. Its purpose was to protect the shipping of neutrals from search and seizure by the British navy.

Liberty Boys: The Liberty Boys were close cousins to the Sons of Liberty except that Liberty Boys were mostly located in NYC and were more prone to rough tactics such as death threats, intimidation and beatings. The Liberty Boys were for the most part led by John Lamb who later became a celebrated combat artillery commander (Colonel) during the Revolution.

Monmouth Association for Retaliation: New Jersey was one of the most fractured States in America. The Monmouth Association for Retaliation was formed to retaliate against the New Jersey Board of Associated of Loyalists which conducted raids on American rebels, held executions and helped fill the British POW hell holes of NYC.

Over Mountain Men: These were rugged Colonial Militia from the western Appalachian and Smokey Mountains who were expert marksmen. They were driven to the American cause because of Britain's pro-Indian land policies which restricted west-ward expansion. They were the majority of the American soldiers who fought against the Loyalists at the critical and successful Battle of King's Mountain on October 7, 1780.

"Regulators": Regulators were a large group of highly dissatisfied citizens of western South and North Carolina who were being victimized by the Crown's appointed colonial leaders. The British appointed colonial courts failed to enforce regulations to protect local citizens from criminal behavior and subjected them to unfair taxes. The Regulators protested their systematic victimization and started to resort to violence. The revolt of the Regulators against the British appointed Colonial Governments of North and South Carolina caused these governments to raise volunteer Loyalist militia which crushed the Regulator army with heavy casualties at the Battle of Alamance on May 16, 1771. This was an early indicator of the growing high level of anti-Crown sentiments which ultimately led to the American Revolution.

Scotch Irish: Other than the original settlers of America from Europe and slaves from Africa the next largest group of immigrants to

America was the "Scots Irish". These were the descendants of Scots and English Presbyterians who moved to Ireland who drove Irish Catholics from their land. They were then subjected to harsh British control. Unwilling to accept taxes to be paid to the Anglican Church, and bars of Presbyterians from holding judicial positions and trading discrimination, the Scots Irish immigrated in mass to America. They connected well with the conservative Congregationalist settlers of New England. They had a fearsome warrior reputation. They became a backbone of the Americans fighters during the War.

Skinners: These were American Militia operating north of New York City. They were part renegade but fought for the American cause. They got their name "Skinners" from their habit of burning the skin of Loyalists they captured. It was a band of three Skinners who caught Major John Andre' on September 23, 1780 as he tried to enter British territory above New York. Their Loyalist opposite counterparts were called the "Cowboys".

Solemn League and Covenant: See Boston Port Act.

Sons of Liberty: These were early vocal supporters of the American cause, primarily in Boston. They staged rallies, demonstrations and public events to promote the defiance of Americans against British aggression. The foremost American Revolutionary leaders were members of the group. They rallied around the "Liberty Tree" and kept the British on the defensive. They were tamer than their similarly named "Liberty Boys" in New York City.

Sons of Neptune: These were the seamen equivalents of Sons of Liberty and Liberty Boys. They were made up of sailors and seamen who almost to a man opposed the British and fought with the American rebels because of British "Impressment" of American sailors and British trade policies which frequently put them out of work.

They were known for their brutal treatment of Loyalists and British customs officials.

Sons of Violence: British customs officials, tax collectors, judges and administrators were frequently subject to threats, beatings, tar and feathering, property destruction and harassment by American Rebels. The Loyalists and British referred to the Sons of Liberty, Sons of Neptune and Liberty Boys as "Sons of Violence

Whigs: This is the term frequently given to those who politically opposed Britain's rule over the Colonies. It was used both in Britain and America. It was identified with democratic ideals, lower sociographic groups and anti-Crown policies.

Sources:

Ferling, John. *Almost a Miracle. The American Victory in the War for Independence*

Hoock, Holgarth. *SCARS of INDEPENDENCE. America's Violent Birth.*

Langguth, A. J. *Patriots. The Men Who Started the American Revolution.*

Middlekauff, Robert. *The Glorious Cause. The American Revolution 1763-1789.*

Mitchell, Broadus. *The Price of Independence. A Realistic View of the American Revolution.*

PRO-BRITISH GROUPS

American Volunteers: American Volunteers were formal groups of Loyalists who fought on the side of the British. They were mostly found in the southern states of Georgia, South Carolina and North Carolina.

Black Loyalists: On November 7, 1775 Lord John M. Dunmore, Governor of Virginia issued a proclamation declaring freedom for slaves who joined the British to fight American rebels. Ultimately, 300 former slaves joined the "Ethiopian Regiment" to fight for the British. Slave land holders in Virginia were very opposed to the prospect of freeing slaves to the point that Dunmore was forced to flee to a British ship off shore for fear of retribution by the slave owners. In 1776 General Henry Clinton formed a unit of runaway slaves known as the "Black Pioneers" to help the fight against American rebels. Eventually approximately 20,000 black slaves joined the British but they never had a significant impact on Britain's combat capability in America.

Cowboys: This was the name given to local Loyalist outlaws who operated in contested territory north of New York City. They got their name from their practice of rustling the cattle and sheep of local patriots and driving the herds for sale to the British in New York City. Their local American Militia counterparts were called the "Skinners".

Loyalists: This was the term used by the British in America for those who opposed the Revolution and wanted to remain "Loyal" to the Crown.

New Jersey Board of Associated Loyalists: This was a group of rabid Loyalists in New Jersey created by Benjamin Franklin's son (William) who was the British appointed Governor General of New Jersey. This group was also known as the **Refugee Club** and consisted of armed Loyalists whose aim was to destroy Colonial farms and towns. The estrangement of Benjamin Franklin and his son William was permanent and was particularly hurtful to Benjamin. They never reconciled even after the revolution.

Provincials: This was a common name by the British for supporters of the Crown in the Colonies. Provincial military units fought for the British against the Americans.

Provisional American Loyalists: At least 25,000 American men fought for the British as Loyalists (Tories). In general, they were known as Provisional American Loyalists. They were mostly located in the southern colonies. They frequently served as partisans fighting against American rebels. They contributed to the "Civil War" that was fought within the American Revolution. A prime example of this civil war was the Battle of King's Mountain, South Carolina which was fought exclusively by American Militia against Loyalists. The Loyalist force which was commanded by the famous British officer Major Patrick Ferguson was destroyed at the October 7, 1780 battle of King's Mountain.

"River Gods": This was the name given to the wealthy large land owners in Connecticut River Valley of western Massachusetts and those of the Hudson River Valley. They saw advantages in remaining with the Crown and thus opposed the Revolution. They made their fortunes by trade on the major rivers in the area. They opposed the American boycotts of trade with Britain.

Six Indian Nations Confederacy: The Native American tribes (Nations) for centuries were at war with each other before the arrival of European settlers. Facing inexorable pressure from colonists who were moving westward they saw the need to band together to protect their interests. Initially they were known as the Iroquois Confederacy and became the Six Nations in 1772 with the addition of the Iroquois. They then consisted of the: Onondaga, Seneca, Mohawk, Cayuga, Tuscarora and Oneida tribes. Their leader during the early Revolutionary times was Joseph Brant an English educated Indian. The tribes were promised land and protection if they supported the British during the Revolution. Because their land was being taken from them by Colonists they assaulted American settlers which benefited the British. This caused General Washington to organize a retaliatory expedition in the summer of 1779 led by General John Sullivan into Northern New York and Pennsylvania. This campaign intentionally devastated Indian settlements there and effectively ended organized Indian resistance against Americans in the Northern States during the Revolution.

Tories: This was the name frequently used by Colonials to designate supporters of the Crown and opponents of American Revolution. The term "Loyalist" was synonymous with privilege, wealth, conservativism, superior class and inherited social status.

Sources:

Ferling, John. *Almost a Miracle. The American Victory in the War for Independence.*

Hoock, Holger. SCARS of INDEPENDENCE. America's Violent Birth.

Langguth, A. J. *Patriots. The Men Who Started the American Revolution.*

Middlekauff, Robert. *The Glorious Cause. The American Revolution 1763-1789.*

Mitchell, Broadus. *The Price of Independence. A Realistic View of the American Revolution.*

OBEDIENCE OF ORDERS, RULES AND REGULATIONS

At the time of the Revolution and to this current day, military personnel sign a contract (enlistment) where for faithful and honorable service they are to be: paid, trained, fed, equipped, uniformed, competently led and treated in accordance with the Articles of War. Because the British and their German comrades were better resourced than American soldiers they were better fed, paid, uniformed and professionally led than American soldiers. On the negative side, the British served in a far-away country where many of the local inhabitants were hostile and in a war that seemed without end. American rebel soldiers lacked uniforms, regular pay, had poor food and inadequate equipment. The problems experienced by the British, Germans and American soldiers led to discipline, desertion, morale and conduct problems. Various forms of discipline were imposed to correct non-compliance with orders and regulations. American officers who failed to demonstrate valor on the battlefield or were guilty of fraternization or did not demonstrate appropriate "officer-ship" were "drummed" out of the service in a humiliating ceremony. British and Germans soldiers were subjected to the lash of up to 1,000 strokes which could be fatal. There was also the "gauntlet" where the offender would run repeatedly through lines of his fellow soldiers and be beaten with fist and clubs. A drummer would precede the victim between the lines and officers would ensure the victim did not go too fast through the gauntlet and other officers would ensure the beaters would inflict punishment as hard as possible. Congress restricted to 100 the number of strokes that could be inflicted on an American soldier. Washington was a stern disciplinarian and requested permission to increase the number to 500 which was denied. Most lashing of Americans was limited to 39. Deuteronomy 25.3 laid out maximum strokes at 40 so it was most common to inflict one short of the maximum indicated in the Bible. Offending American soldiers were subjected to humiliation by tying them naked to trees and having them wear their clothing inside out. A punishment called the "Picquet", involved hanging the victim by one hand over his head with nothing to stand on but a sharp stick. Some men were required to wear women's clothing and be chained to a log which they had to drag around or wear a sign advertising their guilt. Others had their enlistments extended or were fined. In some instances, the names of those who were guilty of offences or desertion were published in hometown newspapers to humiliate them. There were mock executions where an individual would be led to the gallows or execution pit only to be pardoned at the last moment. Punishments for blacks exceeded those of whites. Major Harry Lee asked permission to behead serious offenders which was denied by Washington. Executions were not common except in cases of mutiny which were fairly rare. The most prominent and horrific executions of American soldiers occurred on May 25, 1781 when six soldiers of the Pennsylvania Line were executed by firing squad in front of their fellow comrades for mutiny by order of their commanding officer MG Madd Anthony Wayne.

Sources:

Cox, Caroline. *A Proper Sense of Honor. Service and Sacrifice in George Washington's Army.*

Ferling, John. *Almost A Miracle. The American Victory in the War of Independence.*

Hagist, Don N. *British Soldiers, American War.*
Hoock, Holger. *SCARS of INDEPENDENCE. America's Violent Birth.*
Royster, Charles. *A Revolutionary People at War. The Continental Army & American Character, 1775-1783.*
Urban, Mark. *Fusiliers, The Saga of a British Redcoat Regiment in the American Revolution.*
Van Doren, Carl. *Mutiny In January.*

GENERAL INFORMATION AND TERMS

The following reflects the common and not so common terms shown in the literature of the Revolution:

"Additional Companies": British regiments typically consisted of 10 companies. When on deployment overseas the regiments had two more companies on the home front called "Additional Companies". The roles of the additional companies were to recruit new soldiers and conduct their initial training which could last up to a year or more before the recruits were sent to the deployed regiment.

"Adjutant's Daughter": This was the American nickname for the flogging post used to tie members for the "lash". It got its name from the fact that the unit Adjutant recorded the proceedings and number of lashes inflicted.

Ague: The ague was a high fever with debilitating chills sometimes associated with malaria or what is commonly now known as the "flu" which was frequently deadly.

Albion: This is one of the oldest terms referring to the Island of Great Britain. Occasionally, it will be mentioned in the literature of the British archives relating to the Revolution.

Allowances: The portions of an American soldier's/sailor's pay that were deducted for food, uniforms and medical care etc. were called "Allowances".

Ambuscade: This was the word that was used for **ambush** during the time of the Revolution.

"Amuse the Enemy": This was a military term used at the time of the American Revolution which meant to deceive or confuse or occupy the attention of the enemy.

Articles of Agreement: These were so called "contracts" with privateer captains as to the methods of discipline, the crewmember's duties, work station and the split of the proceeds of any "prizes" the ship captured.

Articles of War: These were the military disciplinary codes which described the punishments for violations of military rules and regulations by soldiers. The modern equivalent of them is the current Uniform Code of Military Justice. The Articles also established codes of conduct for the treatment of civilians in war and codified the rights of solders to protest their mistreatment by superiors.

Artificers: These were the skilled craftsmen primarily in weapons repair, munitions and medical instruments. They did not play an active combat role and were usually assigned to the depots and magazines.

"Attesting": Attesting was the process of a new British recruit appearing before a judge or magistrate to affirm that he was read his rights to decline his enlistment and was enlisting voluntarily. Some soldiers when undergoing court-martials would claim fraudulent enlistment (involuntary enlistment). This was counteracted by the attestment of a fellow soldier or officer who would swear the soldier voluntarily enlisted and had been read his rights and Articles of War.

Attrition From Atlantic Crossings: During the war eleven percent of soldiers shipped to the colonies from England did not survive the journey, which could take as long as 90 days. Occasionally whole ships were lost at sea during the crossings. Some soldiers committed suicide by jumping overboard. Many others perished from diseases during transit. The attrition of horses sent to America was particularly gruesome as indicated by the fact that of the 845 horses sent to American from Britain in 1776, 532 died enroute or on their arrival.

Barge: A barge was a Flag Officer's (General/Admiral) personal boat usually with 10 oarsmen.

Barrel Fever: Barrel Fever was the debilitating effects of alcoholism which frequently made, British, German and American soldiers unfit for duty.

Batman: This was an attendant who assisted a senior officer with his horse and riding equipment. They were exclusively employed in the British Army during the Revolution. Servant Soldiers would assist the senior officers with their uniforms, meals, personal supplies etc. See "Soldier Servants" for further details.

Bills of Credit/Exchange: The use of gold and silver coins (specie) for currency was fairly rare during the Revolution. The British used "Bills of Credit" also sometimes called Bills of Exchange, which were the equivalent of paper money. For example: to pay an American merchant for tents the British would pay for them with a Bill of Credit/ Exchange. In theory, the Bills of Exchange could be traded and used like paper money. The trouble was that the Bills of Credit were not backed by the banks which should have guaranteed their value. The result was that they badly depreciated in value which made it difficult for the Americans to receive fair value for their goods and services provided to the British. This increased opposition to the British on the home front. The Americans were not much better and issued

"Continental Dollars" which eventually became worthless. To accept British "Bills of Credit" or "Continental Dollars" as payment for services or goods was foolhardy in the extreme.

Black Powder: Black powder used during the Revolution consisted of saltpeter (potassium nitrate), charcoal and sulphur at a 75/15/10 ratio. Most the black powder used by the Americans was imported from Europe. At the siege of Yorktown, the Americans and French used approximately 300,000 pounds of black powder shooting 15,437 rounds/shells at the British during the siege that lasted three weeks.

Blockade: A blockade was to reduce a fort, port or country by denying it sustenance or supplies to force it to surrender. The blockade of a port was an act of war under international law.

Bloody Flux: Bloody flux was bloody dysentery which could result in fatal consequences for a soldier or sailor who was weak from poor diet and excessive exposure to the elements.

"Blue Book": Baron von Steuben's training manual for American soldiers was called the Blue Book. It contained just about everything soldiers needed to know about marching, weapons care, encampments etc. It remained the US Army's standard training manual well into the 19th Century.

"Bounty Jumping": This was the practice of recruits signing up for service in the American Army and collecting their enlistment bounty (bonus). They would then desert, sign up for another unit and collect another bounty and do this several times over. This was damaging to morale and financially destructive. General Washington demanded the immediate execution of individuals found guilty of this practice. Both British and American recruits were guilty of this practice.

Branding: Branding an offender's thumb or foot was done to show that an individual had been punished for an offense or a crime.

Brevet: A brevet was a temporary rank promotion for a specific particular campaign. Major General Burgoyne after his successful capture of Fort Ticonderoga was given a brevet promotion to Lieutenant General.

British Currency: At the time of the American Revolution British currency was valued as follows:

Two farthings equaled one halfpenny
Four farthings equaled one penny
Twelve pennies equaled one shilling
Five shillings equaled one crown
Four crowns equaled one pound
Twenty shillings equaled one pound
Twenty-one shillings equaled 1 guinea

The British also used Portuguese coins called Half-Johannes sometimes called "Half-Joes" which were silver coins that were worth one pound sterling, 16 shillings.

British Moral Depravity: There was serious moral depravity among the leading members of British society and government during and before the Revolution. Pedophilia, sex slaves, prostitution and flaunted paramours were common. That sort of behavior was brought to American by leading British generals such as Henry Clinton and John Burgoyne which disgusted Americans.

British Sergeant's System: This was the British method where by Sergeants taught soldiers the art of being a soldier. This was vastly different from the American system where Officers taught soldiers the art of being soldiers. The American system was criticized because it created too much "familiarity" between Officers and soldiers.

Broadsheets: These were "broadsides" printed on both sides of the paper.

Broadsides: These were single page news releases or documents printed on large paper that were commonly nailed to walls for the public to read. Sometimes they were used to display muster rolls of soldiers or accounts of battles.

"Bumper": A Bumper was a glass or mug filled with spirits for making a toast.

"Camp Difficulty": This was the American term for severe diarrhea experienced by many American soldiers.

"Canadiens": This was the general term used to identify French descendants living in Quebec.

Cantonment: A cantonment was a winter quarters "stand down" for an army where training and preparation for fair weather military action was undertaken. Valley Forge is an example of a winter cantonment and so was the British occupation of Philadelphia during the winter of 1777.

"Carolina Gamecock": This was the nickname given by the British to American South Carolina militia leader Brigadier General Thomas Sumter who was known for his fierce fighting style. Because he fought with such determination and zeal he was feared by Loyalists and British alike.

Castrametation: This was the process for setting up a military encampment. Under this process a military encampment would be structured so that soldier tents would be erected at the front of the encampment followed next by junior officer tents and then senior officer tents. In the far back would be the tents for supply, equipment, medical munitions personnel and camp followers.

Charles Town SC. During and before the Revolution the proper name for the city was Charles Town, not Charleston. The name was changed to Charleston in 1783 after the Revolution.

Chemade: This was a drum beat indicating the desire to have a parley for surrender negotiations.

Club: The club was a male soldier's hair style with the long hair bundled in a bun at the back of the neck. The bun was frequently powdered.

Colors of British and German Uniforms: British and German units wore distinctively colored uniforms to identify their units and military functions. German uniforms were forest green. British infantry wore red coats. British artillerists wore dark blue coats and British cavalry wore green coats. Cavalry sometimes wore white with blue uniforms.

Committees of Safety and Correspondence: Committees of Safety and Correspondence were local town assemblies where anti-British activities were organized, coordinated and enforced. They served as extra-legal bodies that intimidated and often punished loyalists. These committees also served as a local "Draft Board". A quote from the Keene New Hampshire Committee of Safety for my Revolutionary War ancestor says in part: "In order to carry the underwritten Resolve of the Honorable Continental Congress into execution, you are requested to desire all males above twenty-one years of age (lunatics, idiots and Negroes excepted) to sign to the declaration on the paper..."

"Common Sense" and "The Crisis": "Common Sense" was written in very late 1775 by Thomas Paine and first anonymously published in January 1776. By March 1776 over 300,000 copies had been printed and Paine was identified as the author who contributed all the profits to the Revolution. The book provided rationale for a complete split with Britain. It was a fifty-page pamphlet written in the style of common Americans which greatly helped persuade tens of thousands that the break with Britain was not only inevitable but necessary. Paine joined the American Army in late 1776 and wrote the "American Crisis" more commonly known as "The Crisis". Its publication came just at the time when it appeared the Revolution was imploding and stirred the 13 States into new support for the Revolution. George Washington required that all his commanders read The Crisis to all their American soldiers. It became the most widely read pamphlet of the American Revolution with an estimated 500,000 copies printed and circulated. It begins with the following stirring words:

"These are the times that try men's souls. The summer soldier and sunshine patriot, in this crisis, may shrink from the service of their country; but he that stands it now, deserves the love and thanks of man and woman. Tyranny, like Hell, is not easily conquered; yet the harder the conflict, the more glorious the triumph. What we obtain too cheap, we esteem too lightly: it is dearness only that gives everything its value."

Paine returned to Britain in 1787 and continued his pamphleteering and in January 1791 wrote the "Rights of Man" which was as sensational in Britain as Common Sense was in America. It espoused representative government, social reform and progressive taxes to resolve grinding poverty. These things made him the enemy of the powerful, rich, and influential royalists who had him indicted for treason which caused him to flee to France where he was arrested and imprisoned and ultimately released in 1794, barely escaping the wrath of the French Revolution.

Commutation: This was the one-time payment for services rendered to soldiers, particularly officers, during the War in lieu of pensions. This was not favored by most officers because the payments were usually in the form of mostly worthless paper money.

Continental Army Signing Bonus Commonly Known as "Rifle Dress": This was the uniform allowance "supposedly" given to new American enlistees which consisted of the following:

Two linen hunting shirts.
Two pair of stockings.
Two pair of shoes.
Two pair of overalls.
A leather or woolen jacket.
A leather or woolen cap.

Continental Army Enlistment Bonus: This was the bonus promised to soldiers for enlisting in the Continental Army which consisted of:

Forty dollars (twenty of which was withheld for the Rifle Dress).
One hundred acres of land at the end of the war.

The depreciated state of the Continental Dollar made the signing bonus nearly worthless. Additionally, the State Militia signing bonus sometimes exceeded the Continental Army signing bonus. All this made Continental Army recruiting extremely difficult.

Continental Dollars: Each of the colonies/states issued their own Continental Dollars for a total of $209,524,766. The Continental Congress issued $241,550,780. None of this money was secured (backed) by the states or a national bank. Further aggravating this situation was the counterfeiting of Continentals by the British and Loyalists. At War's end, the Continental Dollar was basically worthless from which sprang the saying: "Not Worth a Continental". The depreciation of the Continental Dollar was particularly damaging to Rebel American soldiers.

Conway Cabal: This was an under-cover attempt by Brigadier General Thomas Conway in late 1777 to solicit support from members of the Continental Congress and other influential patriots to have General George Washington relieved as Commander in Chief of the Continental Army due to the series of defeats the Army suffered at the hands of the British early in the War. The plan was to have Major General Horatio Gates the so called "Hero of Saratoga" whose forces had recently defeated Burgoyne to replace Washington. The plot was exposed and Conway discredited. He moved to France where he died in 1800. General Gates was ultimately disgraced by his incompetence and cowardice at the Battle of Camden in 1780.

Counterfeiting: During the Revolutionary War the British undertook a deliberate campaign to debase the American "Continental Dollar" by printing it in huge quantities to the point where it became almost completely worthless. Whereby local American citizens had to revert to bartering their services to survive, this was not possible for soldiers, which made their pay worthless. British counterfeiting was a form of "economic warfare" and was so damaging that General Washington issued a directive ordering the immediate execution of counterfeiters. It was so dangerous for the British to be caught counterfeiting that much of it was done on ships off the American shore.

Court Martials: British military law required that a court martial be conducted before lashes could be administered. Most sentences were pardoned or commuted. The offender had an appointed lawyer to act in his defense. General Court Martials were reserved for capitol offenses such as repeated desertion, murder of civilians and joining the enemy. Evidence was heard, witnesses testified and the proceedings documented. The jury would consist of officers from several regiments.

"Covenanters": These were militant anti-British Presbyterians who had been pushed out of Britain by the Anglicans to Scotland and then Ireland who fled to America. They were the classic "Scotch/Irish" who in many cases were the backbone of the Continental Army soldiers from the Middle and Southern Colonies.

Convex Order of Battle: The Convex defends the center while other elements advance against the opponents Center.

Crochet: The flank like letter "L" thus offering two faces for defense protecting a flank of a force.

"Crows-Feet": These were mats of iron spikes facing upward to injure and cripple horses. The purpose was to defeat British mounted attacks.

"Custom House Oaths": This was the term given by the Americans and British for Oaths of truthfulness given at Custom House Hearings which were known to be untrue.

"Damn Yankees": There was tension between officers and soldiers from the Southern Colonies and Northern Colonies, not only over the issue of slavery but the manner of "officer ship". It was routine for officers in the Northern Colonies to be elected by their enlisted soldiers, which appalled the officers and enlisted soldiers from the Southern Colonies. Officers from the Southern Colonies were "appointed" not elected. Junior officers from the Northern Colonies would eat with their enlisted soldiers which would not happen in the Southern Colonial units. Leadership from Southern Colonial units was strictly "top down" whereas in Northern Colonial units it was more informal and collaborative which led the Southern Colonials to disparage the military capabilities of Northern Colonial soldiers as "Damn Yankees". The British also on occasion called Americans "Damn Yankees".

Description Books: These were ledgers maintained by British company clerks that recorded the physical attributes of the company's soldiers (height, weight, and eye and hair color) to facilitate their identification if they were recaptured after they deserted.

Desertion: Desertion was not all that difficult for British soldiers serving in America. It is estimated that 5-10 percent of British soldiers deserted. They melded into the American landscape or even joined American units. Because British POWS were not as closely guarded as American POWS it was fairly common for British captives to escape and fail to voluntarily return to their units and thus become deserters. Desertion was a capital offense but execution was done only for deserters who had left their units multiple times.

"Dickinson's Letters": These were essays originally written anonymously which were very popular in pre-Revolutionary America which popularized the notions that the Americans were being victimized by the British. They were first known as "Letters From a Farmer in America" and written by John Dickenson a prominent and highly respected lawyer from Philadelphia. The Letters which were widely read in America gave convincing arguments that the Colonies were being victimized by British Colonial policies. They espoused non-violent opposition to Britain through economic boycotts of British goods.

"Displaying": To "Display" was the act of soldiers moving from column formation to line (file) formations in preparation for battle.

Drafting: The British army was basically an "all-volunteer" organization. The system of leveling the size and experience of the soldiers among regiments was called "drafting" which required that soldiers be reassigned from one regiment to another as necessary. A "draft" might say: Send twelve privates, one corporal and two sergeants from XYZ regiment to ABC regiment. Soldiers took great pride in their regiments so the involuntary transfers (drafting) from one regiment to another was unpopular.

"Dying Speech": Sometimes called a "Last Speech" or "Last Words" these were narrations of British soldiers before their execution. It was their opportunity to tell the story of their lives sometimes as a sort of confessional or testimonial. The few of these documents that exist are of value to historians of the Revolution.

Education of British Soldiers: The British Army knew the value of educating their soldiers. Regimental schools were established to teach soldiers reading, writing, accounting and math. It is estimated that the literacy rate for British soldiers was approximately that of the British population as a whole about (40%).

Enfilade: To enfilade an enemy position was to maneuver so as to fire into the side(s) (flanks) of their position, which created greater casualties and made for the strong possibility of surrounding the enemy. Successfully enfilading an enemy's position frequently caused an enemy to panic and flee the battlefield.

"Entherliche Leute": This is the German term (literally meaning "Expendable People" given to those who had no choice of joining the British Army by order of their German Princes.

Enumeration: Enumerations were the "lists" of American commodities subject to British control. An example of an "Enumeration" would be a British order saying: "The following "enumerated" items are prohibited for export by the Colonies except to Britain: cotton, tobacco, indigo, iron, copper etc."; or an order "enumerating" the non-importation except from Britain of gun powder, flints, muskets, tents etc. The Continental Congress issued its own "enumeration" lists banning the consumption and or purchase of British goods such as glass, silk, ceramics etc. Enumerations by the British were far more common than by the colonies.

"Evacuation Day" March 17, 1776: This is the annual celebration of March 17, 1776 when the last British ship left Boston Harbor for Halifax, Canada when it was determined the city could not be held in the face of American artillery which had been brought from Fort Ticonderoga.

"Evacuation Day" November 25, 1783: On November 25, 1783 the last British solders left America by ships from New York Harbor. This date became known for nearly the next 75 years as Evacuation Day. General Washington rode on horseback into NYC on that day at the head of thousands of celebrating Americans who by Congressional Resolve wore sprigs of green on their hats as symbols of the American Army. In the middle of the 19th Century Evacuation Day was merged with Thanksgiving Day.

"Express": An Express was a time urgent message. The express was sometimes called a "packet". Express riders were messengers who delivered their messages by horseback. They were sometimes called "Outriders". Express ships, sometimes known as "packet ships" were ships carrying mail and communications. During the War the British lost 40 packet ships to the American Navy, privateers and severe weather. Especially sensitive communications were sometimes sent in duplicate on two different ships to ensure their receipt.

"Factors": "Factors" were British and American "Brokers" who negotiated deals between merchants, producers, shippers and sellers of goods. American paper currency was outlawed and the British paid as little as they could in specie. Bartering was common along with writing "Bills of Credit/Exchange". The Factors provided a valuable economic service for both the British and Americans during the Revolution by enabling basic commerce to continue.

Falmouth: Falmouth Maine is the current city of Portland Maine. Falmouth was a significant port for American privateers which caused the British to shell and burn the city.

Farrier: A farrier was a blacksmith and soldier that attended to horses.

Fatigue Party: A fatigue party was a group of soldiers or sailors assigned to do labor such as digging trenches, clearing trees, collecting firewood etc. The term is still used in the military.

Fee Simple: Someone who was "Fee Simple" was an individual who owned property outright with no loan or mortgage. In some instances, individuals could not vote unless they were Fee Simple.

Feed Fighting: This was the term given to fighting the enemy by denying him food by destroying his crops and means of obtaining food. It was commonly used against American Indians who starved and died in great numbers for lack of food resulting from the destruction of their crops. The best example of this was the Gen Sullivan raids in 1779 into the Indian lands of northern Pennsylvania and New York state which all but eliminated Indian raids against American settlers on the western lands.

Feint: A "Feint" is a movement to trap an enemy into thinking a withdrawal, such as was done at the Battle of Cowpens.

Feu De Joie: This was a celebration of gunfire in rapid succession meant as a military salute for exceptional battlefield success. Washington ordered *feu de joie* to be fired after hearing of the American victory at Saratoga.

Fire cake: This was a standard meal of American soldiers consisting to flour mixed with water roasted over a fire either in a pan or on a stick.

Firing Squad: The firing squad was most commonly used method for the execution of military members guilty of serious offenses such as: direct disobedience of orders, mutiny, and cowardice on the battlefield. The firing squad was frequently made up of members of the victim's squad, or hut or friends. The whole unit was formed up to witness the execution.

Flags of Truce: Flags of Truce were accepted in international law as a means whereby non-hostile communications and mutually beneficial commercial exchange could be conducted between enemy lines without combat by displaying white "Flags of Truce". Flags of Truce were not supposed to be used for military missions. For example: they were used in prisoner parole and exchanges and letters between senior British and American commanders. Benedict Arnold illegally used Flags of Truce in his attempt to have the British successfully attack West Point.

Flanking: See Enfilading above.

"Flatter": To "Flatter" was be or make "happy" or pleased. For example: "I am flattered to report the success of …" or" You'll be flattered to know that …"

Flux: Diarrhea. (See Bloody Diarrhea above).

Flying Army: This was the concept of General Nathanael Greene of disbursing his army during the British Southern Campaign in order to confuse British General Cornwallis as to his intensions and to make it easier to obtain provisions for the army from local sources. The Flying Army concept allowed Colonel Morgan to move (be mobile) and take a portion of Greene's forces to Cowpens and defeat Lt Col Banastre Tarleton's British Legion.

Flying Camp: This was a concept by General Washington early during the Revolution for a mobile reserve of militia mostly to be made of very old men. Due to chronic shortages of personnel it was not implemented.

Fodder: Fodder (grain, oats, hay, alfalfa etc.) for army horses, draft animals and oxen was the 18th Century equivalent of oil for modern military forces. Campaigns required massive wagon trains that needed hundreds and sometimes thousands of animals to transport the equipment and artillery. British commanders have been criticized for lack of aggressiveness but their chronic shortages of fodder limited their mobility and ability to launch attacks against the Americans. The British held the major cities but the Americans held the countryside where fodder could only be obtained. This required the British to launch frequent foraging expeditions into the American countryside where they suffered many casualties from attacks by Americans.

Forage Wars: Following Washington's victories at Trenton and Princeton the British settled into cantonment in and around New York City and Washington settled into Morristown New Jersey and Valley Forge. Short of supplies and fodder for animals, the British struck out in the New Jersey countryside for supplies. These British foraging expeditions were met in force by American Militia and Continental forces. Much of what the British plundered was captured by the Americans and ended up in Washington's hands. The vicious combat in these Forage Wars during the winters of 1777 and 1778 is shown by the fact that British suffered an estimated 900 losses in killed, wounded and missing; the equivalent of a major battlefield loss.

Freeholders: These were individuals who held their land outright without debt. They were especially heavily taxed in Britain, but were a powerful influence in British policies and in America.

"Gaol": This was the Revolutionary War spelling and term for "Jail" or prison.

Gaol Fever: This was typhus resulting from the close and unsanitary conditions of American soldiers/sailors held as Prisoners of War in jails and prisons.

Gibbet: This was a type of gallows with a single vertical pole and single horizontal pole whereby the victim could be more easily displayed hanging high in the air. Major John Andre' General Benedict Arnold's cohort in the attempt to surrender West Point to the British was hanged on a gibbet and left for viewing for half an hour. The gibbet was occasionally used to execute deserters from the Colonial army. John Herring a member of Washington's personal guard who was guilty of looting a loyalist's home was hanged on a gibbet as an example of the punishment meted out to those who did not adhere to Washington's high standard of personal conduct.

Gill of Rum: A gill of rum was two ounces of rum frequently given daily to soldiers and sailors and was commonly watered down. Consumed on an empty stomach it had quite an effect.

"Grabs and Lobs": This was the British term for seizing American goods and possessions. To GRAB was to seize by force. To LOB was to seize without opposition. The British practice of plundering, grabbing and or lobbing American property alienated Americans and caused many to join the fight against the British. Despite threats of punishment by British leaders to stop this practice of grabbing and lobbing it was common by English and German troops throughout the Revolution. The Americans were far better disciplined in preventing the practice of plundering and looting during the war.

"Grand Tory Rides": This was the term given for "Riding the Rail" which was the practice of punishing loyalists or British officials by tying the individual to a fence rail between his legs and having two members each at one of the rail yank up and down which caused painful and sometimes deadly injuries.

Gun Powder Barrel: This was a small wooden barrel used for holding gunpowder. A gun powder barrel was a fraction of the size of a hogshead barrel. It was more of a cask than barrel.

"Habitants": Habitants were the French farm laborers in Quebec who were mostly indentured laborers who worked the manors of the wealthy land owners who were called "Seigneurs". The Americans who invaded Quebec solicited the assistance of Habitants against the British officials in the province who tried to align themselves with the Seigneurs.

Half-Johannes: These were Portuguese silver coins that were commonly used by British during the Revolution. They were sometimes called "Half-Joes" and were worth one pound sterling and 16 shillings.

Half-Pay Officers (American): These were American officers who had enlisted for the duration of the Revolution at the promise of ½ pay for life at the end of the War. This was not popular among the American population because it was feared this was unaffordable and created a permanent officer corps. Among officers the difficulty in getting this benefit was a source of considerable discontent.

Half-Pay Officers (British): These were British officers who performed as a sort of Reserve who could be called to full duty when or if there was an open billet and need for their services. Sometimes retired officers would join half pay units.

Hanging: Hanging was usually reserved for spies, traitors and in the "civil" war within the Revolution. Sometimes the victim was left hanging for weeks as a sign to deter others from committing similar offenses.

"Hanging-On": In military literature the term "Hanging-On" meant maintaining contact with an enemy particularly after an engagement so as to determine its further intentions.

"Hillsborough Treat": This was named after Britain's hated Secretary of State in America who supervised many of Britain's tax collectors and administrators in the Colonies. A "Hillsborough Treat" was for American rebels to smear excrement all over a tax collector's or administrator's house.

"His Magistracy's Yankees": This was the name given to the Loyalists who fled America to Nova Scotia after the surrender of the British in 1783. They were sometimes also called "Neutral Yankees".

Hogshead: A hogshead was a wooden cask 4 feet high and 2 ½ feet in diameter commonly used for bulk supplies such as sugar, molasses or tobacco. It should not be confused with a barrel of gun powder which was a fraction of the size of a hogshead.

"Holy Ground": This was the large portion of New York City that became a den of notorious prostitutes, thieves, loan sharks and liquor joints during the British occupation. This was where most British soldiers during the six-year occupation of the city spent their time. Prostitutes with venereal disease in the Holy Ground who had venereal disease were killed or set afire by British soldiers with impunity. These prostitutes were known as "**Fireships**". There were **"Molly Houses"** for gay soldiers in the Holy Ground.

Honors of War: This was the practice of offering surrender terms to an enemy fort. The common practice was for the first offer to be refused so the fighting would resume. This would lead to second and sometimes third offers of surrender terms, each with more harsh conditions. During these negotiations the status of captive soldiers would be a major subject. Sometimes conditions would deteriorate and the soldiers would be slaughtered.

"Houghing": Pronounced "hocking" this was the practice of crippling British soldiers by capturing them and severing their Achilles tendons. This was not a common practice in America, and was more prevalent in Ireland where the hated British occupied their land.

Indent: An "Indent" was a certificate of money owed to an individual, entity, or government office. It was in effect an "IOU". They were exchanged and traded as if they were money. The longer they were held the more they depreciated in value.

"Instant": "Instant" was a common expression used in 18th Century writing which meant in the same month. For example: a writer might say "on 20th instant" the battle commenced. This would mean on the 20th of the current month the battle commenced.

"Insult a Work": To "Insult a Work" was to attack it with a sudden and unexpected force of soldiers and infantry.

Invest: To **"invest"** a fort or town or area was to "surround" it.

Jacobite War: This was a 1745 rebellion of Jacobites in Britain who tried to install the Stuarts on the throne. The British Army put down the rebellion with incredible brutality with hanging, beheading and imprisoning these individuals. This retribution was on the minds of many Loyalists when they decided to leave the United States after the Americans were successful in defeating the British Army in the American Revolution.

"Jockeying": This was the American term of quickly getting rid of American Continental Dollars before they depreciated even further.

Kill Devil: This was the American nickname for a particularly potent type of rum.

King Tree Acts: Main masts for British war ships were highly prized. The Baltic area for many years provided such masts but they became scarce. The colonies of New Hampshire and Massachusetts were found to have superb white pine trees for such masts. By means of the King Tree Acts of 1711/1722 and others the British reserved New England pristine white pine trees of 24 or more inches in diameter for exclusive use by the Crown via marks known as the "King's Broad Arrow". The marking of these trees for exclusive use by the Crown became a major irritant of the New England colonists just as did the 1765 Tea Act.

Kingbirds: This was a nickname Americans used for British officers. When the command went to "Shoot the Kingbirds" the colonials knew that meant to fire at the British officers.

Laboratory: Laboratories were gun powder making facilities. Gun powder was in constant short supply for Americans during the war. Americans could not make enough salt peter which was a key ingredient of gun powder. More than 60% of all gun powder used by Americans during the war was obtained from France and Europe. A single "shot" from large cannon could take as much as forty pounds of gun powder.

Laudanum: Laudanum was a morphine medicine mixed with sweet wine for pain relief, fevers and loose bowels.

Letters From a Farmer in America: See Dickenson's Letters.

Letters of Marque and Reprisal: These were official letters of permission to arm American privateer ships to fight and seize British ships for profit.

"Leveling": Leveling was the disparaging term given by American Southerners that referred to the elimination of the distinctions between the social classes by the peoples of New England. Leveling was particularly prominent and practiced most noticeably in New England American Army units which elected their officers and had casual social interaction between officers and enlisted men. Southern officers, including General Washington were appalled by this situation who considered it a detriment to good order and discipline.

"Levy Money": This was the money Britain paid the German Princes for the services of German mercenaries. It was estimated at the time that the cost to Britain for German soldiers exceeded 1.5 million pounds sterling each year starting in 1776 and ending in 1785. See chapter on German Mercenaries for further details.

Lex Talionis: This is an ancient principle of the Law of War which was intended to keep depredations during war under control. For example, if during a battle soldiers who had surrendered were killed, the retribution had to be in proportion to the offense of the killing of surrendered soldiers. In the case of the Joshua Huddy Affair (see Table of Contents) This principle was violated when an innocent British soldier who had nothing to do with the execution of an American Militiaman was chosen for execution in retribution.

"Liberty Caps": These were distinctive headgear worn by the 3rd South Carolina Ranger Regiment which had the words "Liberty of Death" painted on their upturned visors.

"Liberty's Daughters": This was the term for the young ladies who supported the American Cause by sewing uniforms for American

Soldiers. It was their custom to sew their names into the uniforms to raise the morale of the soldiers.

Liberty Jacket: This was a term used by American rebels for tar and feathering of Loyalists and British officials.

Liberty Poles: In the late pre-War period the New York City patriots emulated the Boston Patriot's "Liberty Trees" with "Liberty Poles" which served the same purpose. It was not uncommon for the crowds around the Liberty Poles to number in the thousands which led to some violence and extra-legal activities.

Liberty Trees: In the late pre-War period starting in Boston, patriots, particularly Sons of Liberty would rally around a "Liberty Tree" to get information and plan activities to start anti-British activities. The trees would be cut down by the British and replaced by the Americans.

Logistics of the Revolution: Even relatively small wars consume mountains of material and resources. For example, the French supply ship *AMPHITRITE* arrived Portsmouth, New Hampshire in June 1777 with, 32,840 cannon balls, 129 barrels of gun powder, 52 cannons, nearly 9,000 grenades, and 219 chests of small arms. A month earlier the French supply ship *MERCURE* arrived at Portsmouth, NH with 12,000 muskets, 1,000 barrels of gun powder, 34 bales of stockings, many more bales of blankets, linen, cloth hats and shoes. Throughout the Revolution the French provided 70 such ship-loads of arms and supplies which were critical to the survival of the Revolution. (See American and British Logistics for further information).

"Long Bobs/Short Bobs": Robert Morris served effectively as the Financier of the Revolution. He obtained critically needed funds at times when the survival of the Revolution was in peril. Much of the money he obtained was in the form of loans. Loans with long repayment times were known as "Long Bobs" and those with short repayment times were known as "Short Bobs".

"Loyal Nine": These were nine Boston merchants and artisans who in 1765 organized the initial opposition to the Stamp Act. The group quickly grew to become the Sons of Liberty.

Loyalist Migration from America: Some 60,000 white Loyalists and 15,000 former slaves left America after the British defeat at Yorktown. They went to Quebec, New Brunswick, Nova Scotia, Britain, West Indies, East Florida, Africa and other locations. Quebec took 6,000 whites, blacks and Mohawk Indians. East Florida took 5,000 whites and 6,500 blacks. Britain took 8,000 whites and 5,000 blacks. The Bahamas took 2,500 whites and 4,000 blacks. Jamaica took 3,000 whites and 8,000 blacks. The migration was in a large part motivated by the fear of retribution by Americans which never materialized in a big way for the Loyalists who remained in America. For the most part the Blacks who left America did so because many had supported or sought protection from the British and feared they would be re-enslaved.

Magazine: Magazines were supply depots where guns, gun powder, weapons, tents, food and all the supplies needed for war were stored. It is commonly misunderstood that the term "magazine" only referred to depots for weapons. Powder magazines were strictly where gun powder was stored.

Maine: Maine during the Revolution was a territory of Massachusetts. Because it had a long coastline it was a haven for American privateers so it became subject to coastal attacks by the British Navy which burned Maine's coastal towns. The town of Falmouth (now Portland) was bombarded by British ships because it was a common port for American privateers. Maine ultimately became a state in 1820.

Manumission: Manumission was the freeing of slaves under specific conditions. Lord Dunmore's 1775 proclamation promising freedom for slaves who joined the British was a form of manumission. Slave holders who "substituted" slaves for their draft notices and promised freedom for the slaves was a form of manumission. overall this process did not work well. Thousands of slaves who were promised freedom if they left their slave masters and fought for the British died of disease and the elements before they could ever be able to taste freedom.

"Market Stoppers": This was the name given to the American soldiers who attacked British forage operations during the winter of January-March 1777. The American capture of the food and fodder the British were plundering from the countryside was a major source of sustenance for George Washington's Army at Valley Forge.

Matross: A Matross was an enlisted artillery gunner. There could be as many as 12 matrosses for a single gun.

Military Medley: These were the drum beat rhythms that all 18th century soldiers had to learn for reveille, assembly, parley, attack, retreat, and wheel and so on. Drum signals were crucial in battle to communicate the commands of officers to soldiers.

Mortification: Mortification was gangrene. To die of mortification was to die of gangrene. It was also used as a term of extreme disappointment and dissatisfaction.

Mosaic Law: This was Biblical Law that limited to 40 the number of lashes to be inflicted on individuals. During the revolution this law limited to 39 the number of lashes to be inflicted by Americans on their soldiers. Washington lobbied Congress to increase the number to 500, but congress raised the number only to 100. British inflicted as many as 1,000 lashes on their soldiers and sailors.

Mushroom Gentlemen: This was the term given to Americans who got rich by war profiteering.

"Necessaries": Necessaries were the latrines, sometimes called "vaults". There were stern instructions to place the Necessaries and vaults a good distance away from where the soldiers ate, camped and drew their water.

Neutral Yankees": This was the name given to Loyalists who fled America to Nova Scotia after the British surrendered in August 1783. They were also known as "His Magistracy's Yankees".

New Hampshire Grants: The New Hampshire Grants was the disputed land from the Western border of New Hampshire on the Connecticut River to Lake Champlain on the Eastern border of New York. New Hampshire Provincial Governor Benning Wentworth began selling "Grants" (titles) to plots of land in the disputed territory in 1741. The grants were six miles square at a price of 20 pounds each. New York claimed the land and began selling grants to the same land. Settlers who had already paid New Hampshire for their "grants" were now being told they had to pay New York for "grants" to the same land. In 1777 the settlers of the area informally created an independent Republic first known as "New Connecticut". When it became known that a Pennsylvania area had already claimed the name "New Connecticut", the name of the Republic was changed to "Vermont" a corruption of French for Green Mountains. Ethan Allen played a major in role keeping New York from seizing the territory through intimidation of New York surveyors and threatening to invite the British to occupy the territory from Canada. New York and New Hampshire almost went to war over the lands, which in 1792 officially became the State of Vermont and subsequently joined the United States.

"New Subjects": This was the name given to the French descendants in Quebec who became new subjects of the British Empire after the

British victory over the French during the Seven Years War. These people were courted by the Americans to support the Revolution with minimal results.

Oaths of Fidelity/Loyalty: These were oaths of the citizens of colonies/states to the American Cause renouncing King George III. They are used as evidence support for the Revolution by the Sons and Daughters of the American Revolution.

Oblique Order: An Oblique Order is the rapidly gathering of an inferior force to support an advance or retreat or advance of a force.

"Old Subjects": These were the Anglo British subjects of Quebec who resided in Quebec after the French and Indian War. They desired to be part of the British Empire during the American Revolution.

Order of Echelon: An Order of Echelon is a movement of an element of a force while holding against an attack by an enemy.

"Out Pensions": These were pensions given to non-hospitalized British veterans who had served a minimum of 20 years' honorable service or had a disabling injury. Upon discharge the soldiers would then apply for a pension of 12 pence per day which for privates would provide a minimum subsistence income for life.

Overshooting: It was learned that when shooting from above (down) there was a pronounced tendency to shoot too high. This was called "overshooting". American soldiers at Bunker Hill were ordered to shoot at the waists and legs of the British charging up the hill so they would not waste their shots by overshooting. At the Battle of King's Mountain, the Loyalists at the top of the hill wasted many of their shots by overshooting at the Americans charging up the mountain.

Parallel Order: Parallel Order is the positioning of opposing sides facing each other prior to battle.

Parricide: A "Parricide" is someone who hates his/her parents. Benedict Arnold was famously called a "Parricide" by Benjamin Franklin after Arnold's treason was exposed.

Peculation: This was the crime of miss-appropriation of public funds or goods in one's care for personal use. This was what Benedict Arnold was accused of and court martialed for doing while he was military governor of Montreal and Philadelphia.

"Petard a Place": This was a method of breaking open the door of a fortified place for soldiers to enter by means of forcing the door open with a sturdy knife-like weapon (petard).

Petit Tories: This was the name given to Americans who tried to stay neutral during the Revolution.

Petite Guerre: Literally this term means "Little War". This was the term used to describe the style of fighting by American militia. It consisted of small unit surprise attacks and ambushes which bedeviled the British and Germans and inflicted a steady stream of casualties and caused them to reinforce their posts and increase their manpower requirements. It was "guerrilla warfare" in every sense of the word.

Phillipsburg Proclamation June 30, 1779: This Proclamation was issued by British General Henry Clinton partly out of moral reasons and also in an effort to bring more manpower to the British cause. It declared that Negroes captured working for American Rebels would be sold as slaves. The Proclamation promised full security for Negroes and prohibited the sale of those who fled their slave holders or those who took refuge with the British. This Proclamation had an electric effect on slaves throughout the 13 States and caused massive migrations of slaves to the British controlled coastal areas and cities of Savannah and New York and Charles Town after it was recaptured by the British in May 1780. The slaves who fled or attempted to flee their slave masters and could not be transported or fed by the British and died by the thousands of disease and privation.

Placeman: A Placeman was a political appointee given a job as a political reward, rather than earned for good service. The appointment of Placemen by the Crown was an irritant to the Colonists because their pay came from levies on local Americans.

Plan of 1776: This was a remarkable plan of the brand new United States to develop a strategy of treaties with neutral countries to protect American trade which was vital to the success of the Revolution. The Plan proposed: "Free goods, free ships, and freedom of neutrals to trade between ports of belligerents." and carefully defined the list of prohibited items. The Plan ultimately formed the basis of trade agreements with most of the neutral European countries during the Revolution.

Platoon Fire: Previous to the Revolution the British procedure for rifle fire was "Line Firing" where a line of infantry soldiers would fire simultaneously on command. This created lulls in firing when the "line" would have to reload. The American innovation of "platoon firing" (elements of a line) would create a constant rate of fire which suppressed bayonet charges by the British. The British were slow to adopt platoon firing because it required more training and was contrary to tradition.

Plundering: To plunder was to confiscate. There were five general rules by the British for plundering during Revolutionary War times:

1. Unoccupied homes could be stripped completely.

2. Resistance by occupiers of a home to plunderers was grounds for complete devastation of the property.
3. The plunder of the home of a military owner was lawful booty.
4. The plunder from the home of a civilian was illegal loot.
5. The families of homes plundered should be left with enough to survive.

Germans were especially noteworthy for their plundering. They had little connection to English speaking Americans and frequently served involuntarily in America. The British were also known for their rapacious plundering. American rebels were far less inclined to plunder the homes of Loyalists because Washington prohibited it to the extent possible.

Poltroon: A poltroon was a lazy coward. It was one of the worst insults one soldier/sailor could inflict on another.

Porter: Porter was dark brown and slightly bitter beer.

Press Act of 1779: This was an act passed by the British Parliament which allowed for the involuntary enlistment of "able bodied souls" who had no gainful employment and in fact might be incarcerated. Initially it applied only to London and its surroundings but by late 1779 was applied to other areas. Individuals were allowed to appeal their impressment. The prospect of impressment motivated a small number of soldiers to voluntarily enlist. In reality, the number of soldiers involuntarily enlisted was quite small. The acts were widely unpopular in the civilian populace and within the military and were repealed in 1780.

Press Warrant: This was the written authorization for British soldiers to plunder the property of American civilian non-combatants.

Privy Council: This was a body of senior advisors to the kings and queens of Britain who were members of the House of Lords and House of Commons, churchmen, judges and military leaders. Many of the decisions to take a hard line with the American Rebels came from this group.

Proclamation of Pacification November 30, 1776: This was a proclamation issued by Admiral Richard Howe British Naval Commander in America and his brother Commander in Chief of British forces in America, LTG William Howe. The proclamation promised protection to American rebels who left the rebel cause and swore allegiance to the Crown. They would be issued "Protection Papers" to certify their protected status. They were also promised amnesty for the previous support they had given to the American rebel cause. Lord George Germain and King George were opposed to this proclamation which failed to produce the expected number of turn coats. Richard Stockton, a lawyer and a signer of the Declaration of Independence, was arrested by the British and imprisoned. In ill health and treated harshly, he swore allegiance to the Crown; and thus became the only signer of the Declaration to switch sides and be given Protection Papers. The Americans responded with their own proclamation promising amnesty for Loyalists who swore for the rebel cause. For either side, the "Promise of Protection" was a false hope because it was impossible to protect anyone from retribution.

Promotions: For a British private to be promoted to NCO grade (corporal or sergeant) it commonly took at least eight years of exceptional service with talents for leadership, management and organization. One of the few avenues for promotion was through advancement to become pay masters, adjutants, commissary and quartermaster sergeants. It was rare but possible for an NCO to be promoted to officer ranks. Approximately one third of officers in the army "Purchased" their commissions. They were very costly. To purchase a commission required a recommendation by the Regimental Commander and approval by the King which kept inept officers in the ranks fairly low.

"Protection Fever": See Tristinania.

"Protection Papers": See Proclamation of Pacification above.

Purchase System: Commissions were sold and bought in the British Army but most promotions were based on merit. General Officer level promotions had to be approved by the Crown. Unqualified officers who had "purchased" their commissions created severe morale problems in the British Army. It was more common for officers to buy commissions in support and non-combat positions. The costs of British commissions were high: 500 pounds sterling for a lieutenant, 1,500 for a captain and 2,600 for a major and 3,500 for a lieutenant colonel. The purchase of a commission required a recommendation by the regimental commander and final approval by the Crown. At the end of a British officer's career he could sell his commission. The purchase system did not exist for the Continental Army. The Continental War Board approved all General Officer appointments and promotions. Promotions based on merit were standard fare in the Continental Army although influence and "connections" were important. Officers from New England colonies were commonly "elected" by their units, much to the dismay of Southern Colonies and General Washington.

Quit-Rent: This was an annual payment to the Crown by landowners in the Colonies. It was defined by the Crown as a "rent" payment, although the landowners may have owned the land outright. It was an obvious "tax" by the Crown which was a burden, irritant and point of contention in the argument about "taxation without representation" which was a flash point that helped ignite the Revolution.

Quittance: A quittance was the repayment or release from a debt.

"Raising for Rank": This was the term used for prominent Loyalists to recruit (raise) at their own expense Americans to fight for the Crown. Their reward was to command the units.

Ravishment: This was the term used for rape of American women by British and German soldiers which was far more common than admitted. Some British soldiers and officers, such as Lt Col Banastre Tarleton bragged about the degree of ravishment of American women they had committed. British and German soldiers guilty of raping American women were only mildly punished, if at all. Washington ordered the execution of Americans guilty of raping Loyalist women, which was very rare.

"Redemptioners": These were Indentured Servants who were brought to America from Britain and then were drafted into the American Army. Masters of indentured servants frequently "substituted" them for their draft notices. Their service in the American Army negated their period of Indenture which was the period of time, usually several years, to work for a master who had paid for their transit to America.

Resolves: "Resolves" were committee, group and Congressional decisions that were frequently issued in the form of directives and then published and publicized. They frequently had many component parts and almost had the force of law.

Returns: "Returns" were lists of officers and soldiers of a unit. In later times, they more commonly known as "Muster Rolls.

Riding the Rail: "Riding the Rail" was a custom adopted from early European times to punish and humiliate violators of laws and regulations. The victim was placed (tied) to a fence rail between his legs where he was bounced up and down by two men yanking up and down on the rail. It was not uncommon for the victim to die or suffer permanent injury from the sanction. This was a common punishment given mostly by Committees of Safety to local loyalists during the Revolution. The term given for Riding the Rail was called a: "Grand Tory Ride".

Rod: A rod was a measure of length equaling 5½ yards or 16 ½ feet.

Royal Wagon Train: During the Revolution the British Army wagon train drivers were mostly civilian contractors. This was expensive and created problems. During combat the contract drivers known as "teamsters" frequently would flee because they were not under strict military control. This was a continuing problem for the British during the Revolution. The British finally established the Royal Wagon Train in 1799 which made wagon drivers military soldiers. From the start, American wagon train drivers during the Revolution were frequently soldiers so they largely avoided the problems that plagued the British.

Running the Gauntlet: Victims of the gauntlet would be sentenced to run between two rows of fellow soldiers or neighbors or friends who would pummel the individual with fists or clubs, frequently until the individual was senseless. This was a favorite treatment by the British of their own soldiers who were guilty of first time desertion or cowardly behavior on the battlefield. An officer would prevent the victim from going too fast by holding the point of his sword to the individual's chest when going through the gauntlet.

Sally: A sally was a quick un-noticed exit of troops from a besieged town or fortress to attack the besiegers and inflict damage on their works and artillery. They would then return under fire to their lines. A Sally was also sometimes called a Sortie.

"Satisfaction": To demand "Satisfaction" was to challenge someone to a duel who had compromised the "honor" of an individual. Restoration of the lost honor was accomplished by a duel either by pistols or foils. "Gentleman's Satisfaction" was a duel with fists. To "refuse" satisfaction was a sign of cowardice and dishonor. The most famous case of "satisfaction" during the American Revolutionary era occurred between Vice President Aaron Burr and former Treasury Secretary Alexander Hamilton. Burr claimed Hamilton had publicly made slanderous remarks about him and demanded satisfaction. A duel by pistols was done on July 11, 1804 in which Hamilton was mortally wounded. The most famous duel during the Revolution occurred on December 23, 1778 between Lt Col Henry Laurens and MG Charles Lee who had disparaged Washington's leadership after the Battle of Monmouth Courthouse. Lee claimed he was slightly injured during the duel which salvaged the honor of both participants.

Sauvegardes: These were American or British officers or sergeants who were left behind to safeguard vulnerable families as their forces moved onward. These individuals were not to be treated as combatants and were free from attack. This was considered a sacred duty so when one of these hand-picked individuals was attacked or killed it caused outrage.

"Scouring": This was the term given to scorched earth policies of both the American Rebels and British Loyalists, particularly in North and South Carolina where the homes of their opponents would be burned, crops ruined, inhabitants uprooted and sometimes murdered.

"Seigneurs": These were the wealthy large land owners of Quebec who were largely French but frequently sided with the British during the American Revolution.

Shirtmen: This was a derisive name the British gave to American soldiers who fought wearing hunting shirts, frequently with fringes. The hunting shirts were sometimes made of leather or cloth for lack of a uniform.

Sinecure: A sinecure was a job for which an individual was paid for doing no work. They were fairly common in civilian life in Britain and even in the British Army and Navy.

"Smart Money": This was a fee of twenty shillings to be paid by a recruit, over and above his bounty, to void his enlistment after the maximum period of four days had transpired since his enlistment. The purpose of this high fee was to deter those who would belatedly change their minds about voluntarily enlisting.

"Smoking": In "Smoking" the victim would be locked in a room with a fire in the fireplace and the chimney blocked so the room would fill with suffocating smoke. Loyalists were "smoked" until they resigned their British appointed positions or recanted their support for the Crown.

Soldatenhandel: This was the practice of "soldier trade" as it was called in the 18th Century, now called mercenary work. The primary source of mercenaries was the German princes. Many of the German mercenaries were forced into service against their will. The practice came into question during and after the American Revolution, partly because of the casualties they endured and the harsh conditions under which they served.

Soldier Servants: British officers, providing they had the personal resources to do so, could select soldiers from the ranks to serve as their "Soldier Servant". The individual selected had to be fully qualified as a combat soldier. He received extra pay and usually experienced a softer side of life than ordinary soldiers. He was responsible for his master's uniform, cut his hair and shaved him, packed and unpacked his baggage and set up his tent and ran personal errands. He also stood guard duty for his master when needed. British officers with ranks as low as captain had Soldier Servants.

Sortie: See "Sally".

Spicketed: This is the term given to the form of punishment given to American soldiers whereby they would be hung by one arm with a bare foot just above a very sharp stick in the ground. The soldier would struggle and soon the sharp stick would cause severe injury to the foot of the soldier.

Spider Catchers: This was the name given to the American whale-boat privateers who operated along the whole American coastline to harass and seize British provisioning and support ships as they approached harbors and ports. Sometimes operating in groups, they used small arms and swivel guns with considerable success.

"Spinners": This was the name given to the hundreds of women who would form in groups to spin cloth for uniforms for American Revolutionary soldiers.

"Spirits and Crimps": This was the nickname given to unscrupulous British tradesmen who sold unsuspecting and unwilling youths for transportation to America for duty as indentured servants.

Sprigs of Green: Because American soldiers almost completely lacked uniforms which were important for morale, cohesion and unit identity, General Washington ordered that soldiers place sprigs of greenery on their hats and blouses. The first American unit to wear sprigs of green was Ethan Allen's Green Mountain Boys just four months after the start of the Revolution. Wearing sprigs had a very positive effect on the morale of the troops. Over and above improving morale there is anecdotal evidence the wearing of sprigs of green helped prevent "friendly fire" incidents. Wearing sprigs of green actually became an iconic symbol of the long suffering, destitute but ultimately victorious soldiers of the American Army. The Continental Congress issued a Resolve in November 1783 directing all Americans to wear sprigs of green to celebrate the November 25, 1783 departure of the last British soldiers from American soil.

St. Eustatius: This was an island possession of the Netherlands in the West Indies that became a major transshipment point of war material, especially gun powder from Europe to the colonies. Individual shipments of gun powder of 4,000 to 49,000 pounds to America were recorded. Eustatius, otherwise known as **Statia** was so profitable to the Dutch that they risked war with Britain by continuing war trade with America. Ultimately, the British declared war on the Dutch on December 20, 1780 after discovering documents that showed their support of the American Revolution. Although the Netherlands did not commit troops to the Revolution they brought fairly significant Naval forces into the conflict after the declaration of war by the British.

"Stonewall": Stonewall was a potent colonial drink consisting of hard cider and rum.

"Stoppages": Stoppages were the deductions made from the pay of British soldiers for uniforms, food, equipment and other things. The stoppages could be so great that there was hardly money left for the soldier. The deductions for American soldiers were called "Allowances".

"Sultana": This was the name given Elizabeth Loring the wife of Joshua Loring who was the British Commissary for American Army Prisoners of War in NYC. It was reliably reported she was paid $30,000 by British Commander in Chief Henry Howe to serve as his open mistress. By siphoning off food and rations for selfish gain Joshua was responsible for the thousands of American POWs who perished in the death ships and prisons in NYC.

Sumter's Law: This was a method by South Carolina American General Thomas Sumter of paying his cavalry by capturing and selling the slaves owned by Loyalist Americans during the Revolution.

"Swamp Fox": This was the nickname given by the British to Brigadier General Francis Marion, a famous South Carolina militia leader. He and his men were known for their hit and run attacks on the British and then disappearing into the swamps and bogs of the Carolinas. Despite the best efforts of the British, including Banastre Tarleton, Marion was never captured. His hit and run and ambush tactics frustrated the British and helped drive Cornwallis out of the Carolinas to Virginia.

Tar and Feathering: The victim, usually a Tory or Loyalist would be stripped, covered with hot tar and covered with feathers. It could take weeks for the tar and feathers to come off. It was a very miserable and wicked experience. This practice was known as giving an individual a "Liberty Jacket".

Tarleton's Quarter: British Cavalry commander Lt Col Banastre Tarleton was known for killing Americans who had surrendered themselves on the battlefield. "Tarleton's Quarter" became a rallying cry of Americans who similarly attacked Provincials and British soldiers who surrendered themselves on the battlefield. Tarleton was nicknamed "The Butcher" and "Bloody Ban".

Test Laws: These were laws primarily in the New England Colonies where individuals were "tested" many times under duress to swear their loyalty to the American Cause.

The Cure: Inoculation for Smallpox was known as "The Cure". During the first year of the War smallpox was the scourge of the American Army. Washington was initially against inoculation of his soldiers but finally completely relented in the face of the huge numbers of men he was losing to the disease and later made it a requirement for newly enlisted soldiers. Puss from an active infection was smeared on a scratch on the soldier which usually created a mild form of the disease which then resulted in lifetime immunity. With "The Cure" smallpox losses were dramatically reduced.

The Great Warpath: The Great Warpath was the name given by early Native American Indians for the Richelieu River, Lake Champlain, and Hudson River corridor from Canada to Albany, New York. Its strategic importance was such that it was a constant source of conflict, between Indian tribes, French and British and ultimately Americans during the Revolution. The British made two serious and failed attempts to split the American Colonies by driving south down the corridor from Canada.

The Lash: This was the most severe punishment given to soldiers short of death. The most serious lashing by the British would be 1,000 strokes which could itself be fatal. The minimum number was usually 25 lashes, commonly called "Strokes". At the start of the Revolution General Washington lobbied Congress to increase the maximum of 39 lashes to 500. Congress agreed to increase it to 100.

Tidesmen: Tidesmen were British customs officials who boarded ships in American ports to inspect the cargo and ensure it complied with the manifest and customs requirements including payment of all duties and fees. Tidesmen were subjected by Americans to threats, tar and feathering and destruction of their homes.

Torture: The use of torture per se was not common by the British, Loyalists or American rebels. However, for American Indians torture was a rite that often preceded death of the victim. Almost every imaginable method of pain was used: burning, skinning alive, disemboweling, castrating, hatcheting and more. These tactics were not just reserved for whites: they used the same for their own Indian enemies.

Tory Rot: See Tristimania.

Tradesmen: British soldiers (like American soldiers) who had a valuable skill such as cobblers, weavers, saddle makers, tailors etc. were called "tradesmen" and sometimes performed these duties in the army full time. They received additional pay for their services.

Traveling Press: Both the Americans and British knew the value of propaganda and used written notices and Broadsides to "spin" stories to their constituents to have them believe their sides of events. The Americans were better at it than the British. George Washington even ordered from Congress what was called his "Traveling Press" to immediately publish newsworthy events to the American advantage.

Trepanning: Trepanning was primitive surgery of the skull to relieve pressure, control bleeding and remove bone fragments from head wounds.

Tristimania: This was a term coined by Dr. Benjamin Rush Surgeon General of the American Army that characterized the despair and depression of "fence sitters" during the Revolution who were for or against the War and were victimized by both those who were for and against the War. It was also sometimes also called "Tory Rot" or "Protection Fever".

"Twin Brothers": This was the name given by the British politicians for the twin actions of repealing the Tea Act and substituting it with the Declaratory Act in 1766. Repeal of the hated Tea Act relieved the colonies of this tax, but substituted it with the Declarative Act which "Declared" Britain right to tax the colonies at their will.

United Colonies: This is the proper name for the 13 colonies for the period 1774-1776 from the First through the Second Continental

Congresses leading up to the July 1776 Declaration of Independence at which time they became the United States of America.

Up and Down Lake George and Lake Champlain: Lake George and Lake Champlain flow **NORTH** towards Canada and the Saint Lawrence River which causes confusion when reading about the battles and campaigns in these areas. For example: the history of Burgoyne's attack from Canada will say he attacked **UP** Lake George and Lake Champlain which appears as if he is attacking towards Canada, when in fact he was attacking **DOWN** these bodies of water towards Albany and New York City.

"Up-Hill/Down-Hill": The term **"Up-Hill"** referred to sailing from Britain/Europe to America. Frequently it took a ship sailing against the westerly winds and the Gulf Current three months or more to reach America from Europe. This amount of time made it nearly impossible for the British to micro-manage their war effort in America. The term **"Down-Hill"** referred to the time it took to sail from America to Europe which at a minimum could take three weeks or more.

Van: The "Van" of a military unit was the leading element, usually containing the leadership of the unit. The Van also applied to ships.

Vaults: This was the term used for latrines during the Revolution. Sanitation management was a priority of General Washington. Every day the vaults of the Army had to be covered with dirt and new vaults dug, always away from the Army's water supply.

Viva Voce Voting: In the years leading up to the Revolution some of the Colonial Assemblies and then State Legislatures permitted "Viva Voce" voting (voting by voice) to prevent possible retaliation from those who opposed their votes.

Volley vs Aimed Fire: British infantrymen were trained to fire on command (volley fire) in the direction of the enemy lines. American infantrymen were trained to fire on command at specific targets (aimed fire). Because American infantry frequently did not form up in battle lines like European soldiers, volley fire was not as effective as aimed fire. Aimed fire was particularly devastating to British and German officers.

War *Ad Terrom:* This was the term for PREDATORY WAR that went on after 1778 in which the Loyalists mostly at the urging of the Refugees (displaced Loyalists) waged wanton destruction of Rebel towns, farms, churches and property. The leader of this effort in the Middle Atlantic States was Royal New York Governor William Tryon. He previously served as a major in the British Army and was Royal Governor of North Carolina. He was nicknamed "The Wolf" for his murderous and merciless actions in New Jersey and Connecticut. His soldiers conducted numerous sweeps through the states to murder and collect prisoners to fill the "death ships" and POW warehouses in New York City. Instead of beating down the rebellion his depredations galvanized the American rebels into further support for rebellion against the British.

White Gold: White gold referred to sugar from the West Indies, the trade of which was extremely profitable to the British, French and Americans. Sugar was the main ingredient of rum which was consumed in great quantities everywhere. The value placed on sugar by the British during the Revolution is reflected in the fact that in 1778 when the French threatened the British islands in the West Indies the British took badly needed troops from America to protect their interests in the Islands.

Whitehall: This was British government headquarters in London.

"Widow Makers": This was the nickname given by the British for American marksmen who were able to shoot and kill at long distances. They were typified by Daniel Morgan's snipers. One of his men, reportedly by the name of Timothy Murphy, using a rifle killed British Major General Simon Fraser on October 7, 1777 with an ultra-long sniper shot. General Fraser was the highest ranking British officer to be killed in combat during the Revolution

Wild Geese: This was the nickname given to the four regiments of Irishmen under command of the French during the Revolution.

Wigwams: These were shelters made of tree branches for British soldiers on campaigns. They helped minimize the burden of carrying tents. It was an obvious sensible copy of the practice of American frontier soldiers and Indians.

Writs of Assistance: Writs of Assistance were search and seizure actions that allowed British sheriffs and customs officials to conduct these activities in the homes and businesses of Americans without an approved specific court approved search warrant. This led to abuse of the system by the British. If they wanted to harass a suspected American Rebel, they would trash his home on the pretext he was breaking the law. This was especially troublesome in the Massachusetts Colony which led the forefront of opposition to the British in the pre-Revolutionary years. The opposition to warrantless search and seizure actions without specific court approved warrants ultimately led to the 4th Amendment of the U.S. Constitution which made such actions illegal.

Yorkers: This was a derisive term given by the people of the New Hampshire Grants for the residents of the colony/state of New York who coveted their lands.

Sources:

Carrington, Henry B. *Battles of the American Revolution 1775-1781.*

Ferling, John. *Almost A Miracle. The American Victory in the War of Independence.*

Hoock, Holger. SCARS of INDEPENDENCE. America's Violent Birth.

Langguth, A. J. *Patriots. The Men Who Started the American Revolution.*

Middlekauff, Robert. *The Glorious Cause. The American Revolution, 1763-1789.*

Scheer, George F. & Hugh F. Rankin. *Rebels and Redcoats. The American Revolution through the Eyes of those who Fought and Lived it.*

TYPES OF SOLDIERS AND UNITS

Alarm Companies: Alarm companies in the Revolution were assemblies of very young boys and very old men who would defend local communities against British forces. The concept was quickly abandoned when these units were faced with hardened and structured British forces.

Black Dragoons: The Black Dragoons were a group of slaves who were given their freedom in November 1781 to fight for the British and Loyalists around Charles Town, S.C. This reflects the desperation of the southern Loyalists after the disastrous battle of Yorktown in October 1781. The Black Dragoons were mounted and were known for their ruthlessness. They continued to fight with the British until November 1782.

Chasseurs: "Chasseurs" were French "Light Foot" infantry. Like British "Light Foot" infantry they were known for skilled combat and mobility on the battlefield.

Civil Affairs Units: In 1777 the U.S. Army established its first Civil Affairs Units, which were designed to have a positive effect on the "Hearts and Minds" of the civilian populace. These units provided funds to compensate for damage done to civilian property by the

Continental Army and provided relief operations and enforcement of laws against local criminals and gangs. Avoiding the alienation of the local populace was a high priority of Washington's Army. While the British Army gave lip service to this concept, it failed miserably in this area.

Cowboys: Cowboys were Loyalist militia around New York City who would rustle the cattle, sheep and farm animals of local Americans and herd the animals to the city to be sold to the British. Their American militia counterparts were called the Skinners after their tendency to burn the skins of Cowboys they captured.

Desperadoes: See "Forlorn Hopes".

Dragoons: Dragoons were infantryman who fought on horseback, i.e. cavalry. There were American, British, Colonial, Loyalist, German and French Dragoon units during the revolution. Most of these fought as regular dismounted infantryman due to the shortage of horses. American mounted soldiers were called cavalry rather than dragoons. They were employed as quick reaction forces and some in reconnaissance roles. The most notable British dragoon unit of the American Revolution was that of Lt Colonel Banastre Tarleton.

File Closers: File closers were soldiers who would step into the line from behind to take the place of wounded and fallen soldiers.

"Foot Soldiers": Foot soldiers were traditional regular English infantry. They were trained to fire on command from "Files" (lines) sometimes two and three lines deep. They were the least skilled of British infantrymen.

Forlorn Hopes: Forlorn Hopes were also known as **DESPORADOES.** They were small American volunteer units which undertook almost suicidal missions to attack enemy fortifications. They were frequently assigned the mission of chopping through the **abatis** in the face of enemy fire to allow the infantry to attack fortified positions. They were sometimes called Pathfinders.

Fusiliers: These were British and French soldiers armed with "Fusils" a shorter barrel musket that was better suited for combat in the colonies where fighting in wooded areas was common. The fusils were frequently the personal possession of the solders.

Grenadiers: These were British, French and German "Shock Troops" who were noted for their size, strength and courage on the battlefield. They were armed with pikes, muskets and short swords for close quarters combat. They got their name from the fact that in earlier wars they were the soldiers that threw explosive "Grenades" which required great strength and courage because these weapons were dangerous to the throwers and unreliable. Grenadiers were distinguishable on the battlefield by their bear skin hats, which were not at all like those seen in current English ceremonial events. The practice of throwing grenades had been almost completely discontinued before the American Revolution. Grenadiers like "Light Foot" soldiers were usually placed at the flanks of battle lines. The common battlefield tactic of Grenadiers was to shoot their weapons and charge with swords.

Hussars: Hussars were British and French light cavalry.

Jaegers: "Jaegers" were traditional German infantry soldiers. They were the equivalent of British "Foot" soldiers.

"Light Foot" Infantry: These were British infantry soldiers lightly equipped for their rapid maneuver and engagement and disengagement. "Heavy Foot" infantry were heavily equipped soldiers for sustained heavy infantry fighting. They were sometimes used in the same role as Grenadiers on the battlefield. Within the standard British regiment, a "Light Foot" infantry company would usually be at one end of the flanks to attempt rapid flanking of the American lines. The typical British "Light Foot" battlefield tactic would be to "shoot and tree". They would fire their weapons, seek cover behind a tree, re-load, fire and seek cover behind another tree. This was known to the British as: "The American Scramble".

Militia: These were armed American Patriot or Loyalist citizens organized by local townships and communities and states. Frequently they operated at the orders of their local officials for extremely limited enlistments of two months. Militia units were under the command of either State or local authorities.

Outliers: These were renegades in the Carolinas who plundered for private gain and blamed their actions on the opposite side of their victims. This helped promote the civil strife and lawlessness that was so prevalent throughout the south during the Revolution. They were neither Rebels nor Loyalists.

Pickets: Pickets were soldiers placed far in front of fortifications or units in the field to alert the main forces of an enemy attack or movement. They would frequently be the first to fire on the advancing enemy.

Skinners: This was the name given to local American patriot militia who operated in contested territory north of New York City. They got their name from the practice of showering their captured enemies (loyalists/cowboys) with hot ashes which would make their skin burn off. It was three Skinners who captured John Andre' as he tried to escape to British controlled territory on September 23, 1780.

State Militia: State Militias were combatants established by individual Colonies/States who owed their allegiance and took their orders from their States. They frequently cooperated with the Continental Army or acted independently. They suffered more casualties in the

Revolution than the Continental Line Army. Their pay came from their individual states.

Teamsters: These were the **civilians** contracted by the British to serve as horse and oxen team handlers that drove their extensive wagons and artillery during the Revolution. This system worked well except when they came under fire at which time they fled, sometimes stranding the artillery and making the wagons subject to capture. The extent of the requirement for civilian teamsters is shown by the fact that the British had a wagon train of 1,500 wagons when they evacuated Philadelphia to relocate to NYC in June 1778. The British Army did not militarize its wagon train driver system until 1799. American wagon masters and teamsters were mostly soldiers which made them subject to military training and discipline and thus were far more reliable on the battlefield.

Vedettes: Vedettes were mounted pickets who guarded fortifications and camps. Their primary purpose was to prevent the enemy from launching surprise attacks.

Whigs: Whigs was the name frequently used by the British and Loyalists to designate supporters of the American Revolution. The term was used both in America and the British Parliament.

Sources:

Ferling, John. *Almost a Miracle. The American Victory in the War of Independence.*
Fischer, David Hackett. *Washington's Crossing.*
Ketchum, Richard M. *The Winter Soldiers. The Battles for Trenton and Princeton.*
Mitchell, Broadus. *The Price of Independence. A Realistic View of the American Revolution.*
Weintraub, Stanley. *Iron Tears. America's Battle for Freedom, Britain's Quagmire 1775-1783.*

ACCOUTREMENTS OF NON-COMMISSIONED AND COMMISSIONED OFFICERS

Epaulettes: These were shoulder devices to indicate an officer's rank. Major Generals wore gold ones on each shoulder with two stars. Brigadier Generals wore gold ones on each shoulder with one star. Colonels, Lieutenant Colonels and Majors wore plain gold ones on each shoulder. Captains wore a silver one the right shoulder. Lieutenants and Ensigns wore a silver one on the left shoulder.

Frog: The "frog" was the loop of leather through which the sword was attached to the scabbard. Only officers and Non-Commissioned officers had swords.

Gaiters: Gaiters were canvas or heavy cloth material from the bottom of the ankle to the top of the knee, usually fixed at the top with a strap.

Gorget: A "Gorget" was a brass or silver crescent plate worn around the neck by officers. It was fairly common among British, French and

German officers, but was never officially adopted by the American Army. The wear of these devices fell out of use early in the Revolution.

Halberd: A "Halberd" was a spear like weapon with a long handle and pointed top with a blade which was used as a badge of authority usually by sergeants. It was also used to ward off bayonet attacks by the British.

Sabretache: This was a leather satchel worn on the left side of a cavalry officer's horse, much like a saddlebag.

Sash: A sash was a long length of red cloth, frequently of silk, which was worn around the waist to indicate officer status.

Spatterdashes: Spatterdashes were protective leather coverings from the tops of the soldier's feet no higher than mid-calf. They were meant to keep mud and debris from getting into the tops of boots.

Spontoon: A "Spontoon" was a spear like weapon on a long pole commonly used by Ensigns and NCOs as a mark of officer status and for close quarters combat where a gun would not be useful.

Swords: Swords were used by officers and Non-Commissioned Officers (NCOs) in infantry combat as well as cavalry combat. Officer swords were curved and had gilded hand cages. NCO swords were straight bladed and had bar hand cages. Many American swords were made from worn out saw mill blades. The sword could be carried by means of a shoulder strap or waist band. The waist band/shoulder strap was attached to the scabbard by a leather loop called a "frog".

Sources:

Wilbur, Keith. *The Revolutionary Soldier.*

SIEGE WARFARE

Siege warfare was the formal process of attacking fortified positions. It was refined into step by step procedures by French engineer Sebastian le Prestre de Vauban. Siege warfare was not common in the classic sense during the American Revolution except for the British siege of the city of Charles Town South Carolina, the American sieges of the British in Boston, the British siege of Savannah, Georgia and American siege of the British army at Yorktown, Virginia. In the case of Boston, the siege consisted of blockading the British ships from entering the port by means of American artillery mounted on the hills surrounding the city. The sieges of Charles Town, Savannah and Yorktown were a combination advancing "parallels, approach and communication trenches" to bring artillery and infantry in range of the forts. These fit the classic mold of European siege warfare. In the case of Charles Town and Savannah, it was the British besieging the Americans and in the case of Yorktown it was the American besieging the British. Rarely in European warfare did defenders successfully repulse formal sieges. The following are the structured steps of a formal siege:

1. Gather supplies, weapons and materials just out of range of enemy artillery.
2. Start by digging an "Approach Trench" perpendicular towards the enemy fort.

3. Dig a trench at right angles from the approach trench. This trench was called the "First Parallel". The First Parallel was dug in crescent shape to avoid enfilading fire from the enemy.
4. Use earth dug from the trenches to make parapets for fighting positions from the First Parallel trench.
5. Use earth dug from the First Parallel to construct redoubts for artillery to fire on the enemy.
6. Construct zig-zag "Communication Trenches" towards the enemy from the First Parallel trench. The purpose of the zig-zag trenches was to minimize casualties from enemy fire from the fort and from enfilading fire.
7. Dig "Second Parallels" from the Communication Trench(s) parallel to the enemy fort.
8. Dig "Demi Parallels" (small shallow trenches) between the First and Second Parallels. The purpose of the Demi Parallels was to get close to the enemy while minimizing casualties.
9. Employ "Sappers" specially trained engineers to dig **"saps"** (narrow and shallow trenches") from the trenches closest to the enemy. The sappers would construct gabions from the earth of the "saps" to build fighting positions. The sappers would construct a "Mantalel" (sap shield) to protect themselves from enemy fire during the process of "sapping". Sappers received enhanced pay due to the very hazardous work they performed much of which was done at night.

The whole purpose of the siege process was to get cannon and soldiers close to attack a fort without sustaining prohibitive casualties.

Sources:

Borick, Carl P. *A GALLANT DEFENSE, The Siege of Charleston, 1780.*
Chartrand, Rene'. *Forts of the American Revolution 1775-1783.*
Greene, Jerome A. *The Guns of Independence.*
Muller, John. *The Attac and Defense of Fortified Places.*
Smith, David. *Camden. The Annihilation of Gates' Grand Army.*

GENERAL FORTIFICATION TERMS

Classic fortifications in the European mode were not common in America. Fort Ticonderoga and Quebec were exceptions. However, forts were built around Charles Town and Savannah in the mode of moats and walls. Battlefield fortifications were built in places such as in combat in Saratoga, NY. It is important to know the terms of fortifications to know how battles involving these structures were won and lost. The terms are also important to know when reading about the how sieges were conducted.

Abatis: These were fallen trees with sharp branches placed in front of fighting positions to delay the advance of enemy attacking forces.

Bailey: A bailey was an external wall enclosing the outer-wall of a castle or fortification.

Banquette: This was a raised step along the inside of a parapet or bottom of a trench upon which soldiers would stand to fire at the enemy.

Barbette: A barbette was a mound or platform from which cannons could be fired over a parapet. Sometimes the cannon could swivel to achieve a large field of fire.

Bastions: These were pointed projections of a fortification thrust out from the face of the main line or at an angle at its corners. Typically, a fort might have six or eight bastions pointing outward. Bastions allowed soldiers to fire at advancing enemy from different angles.

Casemate: A casemate was a bomb proof chamber of a fort or defensive position under siege. At the Battle of Yorktown British General Cornwallis took refuge from the shelling in a "Casemate" dug into the bluff by the York River.

Chandeliers: Chandeliers were wooden frames filled with fascines. The chandelier would hold the fascines in place to form a fortified position.

Chavaux-de-Frise: During the American Revolution these were large logs with sharp spikes which were strung by chains across rivers or sunk in rivers to prevent enemy boats from traveling up or down the river. Their purpose was to impale the boats of the enemy.

Communication Trenches: These were zig-zag trenches between "parallel" trenches in a siege. They were dug in a zig-zag manner to prevent the enemy from attacking soldiers from the flanks.

Counterscarp: A counterscarp was the wall of stone, logs or brick behind the glacis of a fortification where the troops of the fort could assemble for an attack from a fort.

Curtain: The curtain was the part of the wall of a fortification connecting its bastions.

Demilunes: Demilunes were crescent dome shaped structures at the outer-works of fortifications.

Embrasure: An embrasure was the opening in a protective wall through which artillery or soldiers would fire at the enemy.

Epaulment: Epaulements were berms of earth constructed in front of artillery batteries or stalls where cavalry horses were placed and protected from enemy fire.

Fascines: Fascines were bundles of saplings usually six feet long tied together and placed in defensive fighting positions. They could be laid vertically or horizontally and with dug earth used to form strong fighting positions.

Fraise: Fraises were wooden stakes stuck in the earth with the sharpened ends pointing in the direction of the enemy.

Gabions: Gabions were large round woven baskets made of saplings filled with dirt that served as defensive fighting positions. They were commonly used to fortify artillery positions. Very similar devices are still used in rural primitive fighting throughout the world.

Glacis: A glacis was the outward sloped wall of a fortification usually made of earth. Usually the slope of the glacis was so steep that it would prevent attacking soldiers from scaling up it. It also had the effect of deflecting cannon shots as opposed to a vertical wall.

Gorge: A gorge was the entry/exit point from a palisade. A gorge was the equivalent of a Sally Point in a redoubt.

Loopholes: These were cutouts in palisades or stockades where muskets could be fired from the protection of the surrounding wood of the fort.

Maham Towers: Maham towers are named after their inventor Hezekiah Maham an American Militia officer. They are wooden towers constructed high enough for soldiers to fire down into forts. A large one was constructed to fire down into the British Fort Ninety-Six in South Carolina.

Merlons: Merlons were the solid portions of a fortification wall between the openings (embrasures) for artillery or soldiers could fire.

Palings: Palings were wooden fence posts mounted in the earth with vertical sharpened point ends to deter enemy soldiers from breeching the fortification. They were held together by scantlings.

Palisades: Palisades were long sharpened logs driven in the ground to form a fort. They were most common in the fighting on the frontiers during the revolution.

Parallels: Parallels were siege trenches dug parallel to the walls of a fortification. Attacking soldiers could avoid enemy fire from these trenches. During a siege, parallels would be dug closer and closer to the fortification to the point where an attack would be possible. The zig-zag trenches connecting the parallels were known as "communication trenches".

Parapets: Parapets were the defensive works usually of earth or stone in front of a trench or along the top of a rampart.

Redan: A redan was a fortification, usually made of earth shaped in the form of an arrow head with an open end. These were frequently built ahead of redoubts on the battlefield. Because the redans had an open end it was easy for soldiers to retreat from the redans to redoubts ahead of attacking soldiers.

Redoubts: Redoubts were fortifications, usually made of earth, where defenders were protected by the high walls against attackers firing cannons and muskets. Redoubts were frequently hundreds of feet long and were shaped as rectangles, squares, triangles, ovals or circles. The soldiers within the redoubts would fire over the earthen walls against attacking infantry. The most famous redoubt built by the Americans was at the top of Bunker Hill.

Revalins: Revalins were arrow like fortifications built outside the walls of a fortification just ahead of the bastions and behind moats and trenches of the fortification. They were the second line of defense for fortifications.

Sally Point: A sally point was the single point of entry or exit from a redoubt. A sally point made it difficult for attacking soldiers to get into the redoubt. However, once attacking soldiers successfully breeched the walls of the redoubt the defenders were frequently trapped in the redoubt for lack of other ways to retreat than through the sally point. Once the American redoubt at the Battle of Bunker Hill was breeched many Americans were killed in there because the sally point was the only way out and it was blocked by the British.

Saucines: These were long (12-13-foot-long) bundles of branches tied together which could be used for building fortifications and more commonly used by throwing them in stream beds to allow cannons and horse drawn wagons to cross without building bridges. They were essentially oversize Fascines. This was a critical use of these items when moving the large amount of artillery for the Battle of Yorktown in 1781. Benedict Arnold also lashed them to the sides of his ships to deflect enemy fire at the Battle of Valcour Island in 1775.

Scantlings: These were narrow boards nailed laterally to hold palings firm and together for a fort or out-post.

Traverse: A traverse was a device allowing cannons in a fort to sweep from left to right across a battlefield.

Wicket: A wicket was a small door in the large gate of a fortification through which men could enter or exit single file when the door was open.

Sources:

Borick, Carl P. *A GALLANT DEFENSE. The Siege of Charleston, 1780.*
Chartrand, Rene'. *Forts of the American Revolution 1775-1783.*
Greene, Jerome A. *The Guns of Independence. The Siege of Yorktown 1781.*
Muller, John. *The Attac and Defense of Fortified Places.*
Stephenson, Charles. *CASTLES. A History of Fortified Structures, Ancient, Medieval & Modern.*

SURRENDERING TERMS

The surrender of major groups was usually a structured affair. The attacking force would usually offer surrender terms of the force they are attacking by asking for "Quarter". In some instances, those who surrendered were massacred, such as was the case at Fort Griswold outside New London Connecticut in 1781. Knowledge of the terms that follow should help the understanding of this dangerous process.

"Convention Army": This was the group of British and German prisoners of war who surrendered to the Americans after the battles of Saratoga in October 1777. This group of prisoners which consisted of more than 5,600 British and Germans was initially marched to Cambridge, Massachusetts and Rutland where they remained until January 1778 at which time they were marched to Albemarle, Virginia near the present-day Charlottesville. They remained there until the late fall of 1780 at which time they were marched to Winchester, Virginia where they remained for four months. They were then divided into multiple smaller groups and sent to surrounding towns of Berkley, and Martinsville, Shepardstown and Frederick, Maryland and Lancaster and Carlisle, Pennsylvania for the duration of the war. The conditions of the British and German prisoners at Albemarle were starkly different than the way Americans were held. At Albemarle, they had a hospital, entertainment halls, bowling tournaments and horse races. There were no prisoner deaths at the camp associated with their treatment.

Conventions: Conventions were the surrender agreements between major forces; the most famous during the Revolution was the Saratoga Convention where the 5,600+ British and German soldiers surrendered to the Americans after the Battles of Saratoga in October 1777. Other conventions were negotiated at Charles Town, SC and Yorktown, VA.

Grounding Arms: This was a manner of signaling surrender by throwing weapons on the ground. In several instances soldiers (both British and Colonial) ignored this signal of surrender and killed their opponents.

Honors of War: These were the time-honored procedures of surrendering a fort or fortification. It was generally expected that the first surrender demand would be refused and the fight resumed until a second or third set of demands were offered which were increasingly harsh. This system preserved the "Honor" of the commander surrendering. However, it also led to some massacres of occupants of forts.

"Quarter" To Ask For Quarter, Give Quarter, Refuse Quarter:

To Ask for Quarter: This was the act of asking to surrender and for the enemy to cease fighting. This could be done verbally or "grounding" (throwing their weapons on the ground) or by surrender flags.

To Give Quarter: This was acceptance of the enemy's offer (asking for quarter) of surrender and cease fighting.

To Refuse Quarter: This was the refusal to accept an offer of surrender and to continue attacking, frequently to inflict maximum casualties on the enemy often to the death.

Saratoga Convention: The Saratoga Convention terms were the surrender (convention) conditions agreed upon by British LTG John

Burgoyne after his defeat during the September/October 1777 battles in and around Saratoga, New York. The conditions were not approved either by General Washington or the Continental Congress before they were signed by American MG General Horatio Gates. The Continental Congress and Washington considered them far too liberal and full of opportunities for the British to circumvent. They ultimately were voided in January 1778 by the Continental Congress mostly on the basis of technicalities and the fact that captured secret British correspondence also indicated that the British had no intention of complying with the agreement once their captives were returned to their control. The provisions of the Saratoga Convention were as follows:

Article 1. The troops under Gen Burgoyne were to march out of their camp with the honors of war, and the artillery brought to the edge of the river and the arms to be piled by word of the command from their own officers.

Article 2. Free passage to be granted to the army of Gen Burgoyne to Great Britain, on condition of not serving again in North America during the present contest, and the port of Boston is assigned for the entry of transports to receive the troops, whenever British General Howe shall order.

Article 3. Should any cartel take place by which the army under Gen Burgoyne, or any part of it, may be exchanged, the foregoing article to be void as far as possible.

Article 4. The army under Gen Burgoyne to march to Massachusetts Bay by the easiest, most expeditious, and convenient route, and to be quartered in, or near as convenient as possible to Boston, that the march of the troops may not be delayed, when transports arrive to receive them.

Article 5. The troops to be supplied on their march, and during their being in quarters, with provisions, by General Gates' orders, at the same rate of rations as the troops of his own army, and if possible the officer's horses and cattle are to be supplied with forage at the usual rates.

Article 6. All officers to retain their carriages, horses and other cattle, and no baggage is to be molested or searched. Gen Burgoyne giving his honor that there are no public stores secreted therein. Gen Gates will of course take the necessary measures for the due performance of this article. Should any carriages be wanted during the march for the transportation of officer's baggage, they are if possible, to be supplied by the country at the usual rates.

Article 7. Upon the march, and during the time the army shall remain in quarters in Massachusetts Bay, the officers are not, as far as circumstances will admit, to be separated from their men. The officers are to be quartered according to rank, and are not to be hindered from assembling their men for roll call, and other necessary purposes of regularity.

Article 8. All corps whatever, of Gen Burgoyne's army, whether composed of sailors, bateaumen, artificers, drivers, independent companies and followers of the army, of whatever country, shall be included in the fullest sense and utmost extent of the above articles, and comprehended in every respect as British subjects.

Article 9. All Canadians and persons belonging to the Canadian establishment, consisting of sailors, bateaumen, artificers, drivers, independent companies, and many other followers of the army, who come under no particular description are to be permitted to return there, and to be conducted immediately by the shortest route to the nearest British port on Lake George, are to be supplied with provisions in the same manner as other troops, and are bound by the same condition of not serving during the present contest in North America.

Article 10. Passports to be immediately granted for three officers, not exceeding the rank of captain, who shall be appointed by Gen Burgoyne to carry dispatches to Sir William Howe, Sir Guy Carleton and to Great Britain by the way of New York, and Gen Gates engage the public faith, that these dispatches shall not be opened. These officers are to set out immediately after receiving their dispatches, and are to travel the shortest route and in the most expeditious manner.

Article 11. During the stay of the troops in Massachusetts Bay, the officers are to be admitted on parole, and are allowed to wear their side arms.

Article 12. Should the army under Gen Burgoyne find it necessary to send for their clothing and other baggage to Canada, they are permitted to do it in the most convenient manner, and the necessary passports granted for that purpose.

Article 13. These articles are to be mutually signed and exchanged tomorrow morning at 9 o'clock and the troops under Gen Burgoyne are to march out of their entrenchments at 3 o'clock in the afternoon.

(signed) Horatio Gates, Major General and (signed) J. Burgoyne Lieutenant General: October 16, 1777.

Sources:

Ketchum, Richard M. *Saratoga, Turning Point of America's Revolutionary War.*

Mitchell, Broadus. *The Price of Independence. A Realistic View of the American Revolution.*

PRISONER OF WAR (POW) ISSUES, TERMS AND STATISTICS

Statistical Overview (Close Approximates):

225,000 American Militia and Continental soldiers fought in the Revolution.
30,000 became POWs of the British.
18,000 died as POWs of the British.
11,500 died in New York City harbor "Death Ships".
4,500 died in New York City warehouses and prisons.
2,000 died in Charles Town SC Port "Death Ships" and other locations around the world.

Americans Rebels had a 7+% chance of becoming a POW if they fought in the war. Americans had a 60+% mortality rate while being held as POWs of the British. For comparison purposes: Federal Army POWs had a 35% mortality rate during the Civil War; WWI POWs had a 3.6% mortality rate; WWII POWs had a 11.3% mortality rate, Korean War POWs had a 37.8% mortality rate and Vietnam POWs had a 1% mortality rate.

The majority of American POWs were held in New York City with another smaller holding area in Charles Town SC. Most were held in New York City aboard de-commissioned British cargo and troop transport ships in Wallabout Bay on the Hudson River and in former prisons and warehouses. The ships were virtual execution and death chambers. The most famous of the 20+ death ships was the HMS *JERSEY*. The second largest groups of American POWs held in NYC were in warehouses and former jails.

Major Holding Facilities for American POWs:

Because the British held very little territory in America, other than New York City, they were limited in places to hold the large numbers of American POWs that they captured. Therefore, most of American POWs were held in and around NYC. Several thousand captive Americans (mostly Naval Privateers) were held in prisons throughout the world, including the West Indies, Portugal, Ireland, Britain, Africa, Scotland and Canada.

Charles Town SC Harbor POW Ships: Thousands of Americans captured by the British in their Southern Campaign were held in Charles Town Harbor POW ships which were noted for their poor treatment of their captives, many of whom died because of the conditions of their captivity.

Haddrell's Point: This was the main land based facility for American POWs captured in the Southern Campaign, especially from the Battle of Camden and siege and capitulation of Charles Town. It consisted of a barracks type building built on a flat muddy plain next to the city.

***JERSEY* Prison Ship NYC:** This was the most notorious of the "Death Ships" where American and French POWs were held. The ship was a huge broken down former British cargo ship. It was anchored in

Wallabout Bay in New York Harbor. It is estimated that as many as 11,500 American POWs died in that ship alone or other prison ships in Wallabout Bay.

Newgate Prison London: Early in the War American POWs were sent to Newgate prison with the assumption that they might be executed at the Tower of London there. Opposition from local Whigs who protested the harsh treatment of American POWs resulted in most American POWs from this facility being returned to America. Morton and Forton Prisons in Britain were used in Britain were to hold American captives. Their treatment was poor there but in no way on the horrific scale in the prisons of NYC.

"New Jail" Philadelphia PA: Over five hundred Americans captured in the 1777 battles of Germantown and Brandywine were held in a new prison built in 1775 in downtown Philadelphia. The facility was called "New Jail". The prisoners died by the score from starvation, neglect, disease and exposure to the elements. During the change of command celebration for General Howe's return to England and General Henry Clinton's assumption of command, a daring raid on the city was conducted by American Captain Allan McLane. This facilitated the escape of seven officers and 49 enlisted men by tunneling out of the jail. A tunnel collapse buried five of those attempting to flee. When the British evacuated Philadelphia in June 1778 the remaining hundreds of POWs in New Jail were transferred to the death ship JERSEY in New York harbor.

Provost NYC: This was the four-story jail in New York City which was converted to a POW holding facility. It was notorious for its cruelty. The Provost Marshall (Commandant) of the prison was a known sadist even before the Revolution. He would make his rounds throughout the building with a Negro holding a hanging rope for intimidation and would select prisoners at will for whipping. After the War, he returned to Britain without being held accountable for his atrocities.

"Sugar House" NYC: This was a large four story former sugar warehouse in New York City used to hold American POWs. It was noted for being a "Hell Hole" from which almost 50% of the prisoners died of starvation and abuse.

Major Holding Facilities for British and German POWs:

Ultimately, 15,000 British and German soldiers became POWs of the Americans. Very, very few died because of the conditions of their captivity.

Albemarle Camp VA: The main POW camp for captured British and German soldiers was at Albemarle, in south central Virginia. The POWs there developed the camp into a very admirable facility with a hospital, smokehouse, racetrack, and other niceties. It is reported that there were only two deaths during the 18 months the 4,000 POWs were there, one an infant and the other a youngster. Most of the POWs there were captured at the Battles of Saratoga. Over fear they might be liberated during the British Southern Campaign 1979 they were moved to a variety of small camps in Northwest Virginia, Maryland and Pennsylvania.

Simsbury Copper Mines CT: An exception to the humane treatment accorded most British prisoners came from the fact that some were held in old copper mines in Simsbury, Connecticut which they called "Newgate" after the infamous prison in England. No British POWs are recorded as having died there so it was clearly not the nice facility like the one at Albemarle, VA. It was nowhere as horrible as the death ships and hell houses where American were held in NYC. It is said that William Franklin, the son of Benjamin who was known as a cruel Loyalist was held there for some time.

American and British POW Policies

American POW Policies: American POW policy communicated straight from Gen Washington was that British and German POWs were to be treated as humanely as possible in a vain attempt to get the British to improve the treatment of American POWs. When it appeared early in the War that the British might execute high ranking American POWs, such as Colonel Ethan Allen, General Washington made it clear he would in turn execute high ranking British POWs in retaliation which ended any further thoughts of executing POWs. After his exchange, Colonel Ethan Allen took upon himself the trouble and effort to publicize his horrific experience during his 953 days as a POW and the general inhumane treatment of American POWs. This was done at his own expense with a widely read and highly popular pamphlet titled: NARRATIVE OF COLONEL ETHAN ALLEN'S CAPTIVITY WRITTEN BY HIMSELF. This helped educate the world-wide public about the abusive treatment of American POWs by the British. Benjamin Franklin also used his international influence to bring about POW reforms. One of the reforms after the War was the prohibition against separating commissioned officers from enlisted POWs. By keeping officer and enlisted POWs together the general treatment of all the POWs was improved.

British POW Policies: Official British policy straight from King George III was that American captives were "criminals" not POWs. To accord them POW status would acknowledge that the colonies/states were independent; therefore, American POWs were treated as criminals. General Washington did not sanction the mistreatment of British and German POWs. He felt that if British and German POWs were treated humanely he could somehow bargain for similar treatment for American POWs which was folly. There was considerable controversy about the status of American MG Charles Lee who was captured just before the Battle of Trenton. Before the War he was a British officer so some in Britain wanted him tried as a deserter. He was in fact a "Half-Pay" (retired) officer not on active duty in the British Army when he joined the Americans at the start of the Revolution. He was held as a POW of the British while lengthy discussions were held to eventually exchange him for British MG Richard Prescott who had been captured by the Americans in Rhode Island.

The British policy for American POWs captured in their Southern Campaign of 1780-1781 differed from that of the Americans held in NYC. The British were so short of soldiers and sailors in the south that there was a concerted campaign to coerce and entice American POWs to defect to the British forces in return for their freedom. For the most part, the effort failed and many who opted for the deal escaped to American forces to fight the British again. Unlike the POWs in NYC the British in the south offered wholesale exchanges of American POWs for British and Germans mostly held in the main holding area of Albemarle, Virginia. In a painful decision, Gen Washington opposed the exchanges which was also opposed by Congress. The British were starved for soldiers and any exchange would ultimately make it easier for them to crush the American rebellion.

British POW Acts and Legislation:

Sick and Hurt Board: Prior to the 18th Century prisoners of war frequently changed sides or went home. By the middle of the 18th Century warfare had changed with large numbers of POWs being held in foreign countries. This required some internationally accepted "norms" for their treatment. Prisoners could no longer be summarily executed, tortured, starved or mistreated. In 1742 the Sick and Hurt Board was established in Britain to develop policies for the soldiers they held as POWs. The standards of the Board did not apply to American captives because they were officially considered "criminals" by the British, not POWs.

Hulks Act May 1776: This act permitted the long-term imprisonment of British criminals in unusable "Hulks" anchored in the Thames River. Since the British considered American captives as "criminals" the Hulks Act gave legal precedent for holding American POWs in ships.

North Act March 1776: By the spring of 1776 the Americans had captured 2,000 British soldiers which caused Lord North to be concerned about their possible treatment in view of the horrific abuse the British inflicted on American prisoners. There was also pressure from the Whig (anti-war faction) in Britain about the extremely harsh treatment given American prisoners. The North Act gave belligerent rights to American prisoners without giving legitimacy to the American Continental Congress. The Act facilitated the process of cartels, paroles and exchanges of prisoners between the Americans and British, but it did not in any major way lessen the horrific treatment given American POWs were still held

Prisoner Of War Terms:

Cartels: Cartels were the formal agreement under which POWs were exchanged. Cartels were not as common as expected because they were so complex and difficult to negotiate. Cartels consisted of two elements:

Compensation: Compensation was the amount of money that would be included in the exchange between POWs. For example: A major held for two years would require compensation for his care and feeding over that of major held only one year.

Composition: Composition referred to how many of one rank would equate to a number of another rank. For example: Ten sergeants might equate to one captain.

Parole: Officer Prisoners of War were commonly "paroled" after their capture, especially by the Americans who could not afford to maintain them in "prisoner" status. The British commonly sent American parolees to live in areas they controlled, such as New York City. As a condition of **PAROLE** individuals were on their "honor" to remain as non-combatants and not to participate again in the war. They were frequently required to wear their uniforms, pay for their own upkeep and were restricted in their travel, usually to just several miles. Many British and German POWs were paroled and frequently ended up as civilian non-combatants melding into the local populace. Violation of parole status frequently resulted in execution. Parole was almost exclusively limited to officers who could be trusted to abide by their "honor". Because soldiers (Enlisted) men did not have the breeding to have "honor" it was believed they could not be trusted in parole. It was fairly common for officers to first be placed on parole and then be "exchanged' where they could revert to combatant status. Officers from the New England States were more likely to "break" parole than officers from Southern States where "honor" was much more a part of their southern culture.

Prisoner "Commissaries": These were British and American officials responsible for provisioning (food, lodging, medical supplies, clothing, blankets etc.) for prisoners. The British "commissary" for American Army POWs in NYC was Joshua Loring, whose wife was well known as the mistress of General Henry Clinton. Loring used his office to enrich himself by skimming and selling for himself materials intended for American POWs. His corruption was without shame and he completely turned a blind eye to the mistreatment of American POWs. The British "commissary" for American Naval POWs in NYC was David Sproute a notorious criminal and Tory who also made a fortune by confiscating and selling supplies that were supposed to have gone to American POWs. Starting in 1776 with the capture of large numbers of Americans the Continental War Board assigned Elias Boudinot as Commissary and John Pintard as his agent, to provide supplies and sustenance to Americans held by the British. Continental dollars were basically worthless. Each of the individual States had their own POW commissaries which made the jobs of Boudinot and Pintard almost impossible. Both men used their own personal fortunes to the extent possible to provide necessities for the American POWs in their care. In early 1778 the majority of the 5,000+ British and German POWs held by the Americans were consolidated at Albemarle, Virginia. Colonel James Wood Jr. was named the Commissary and then camp Commander where he distinguished himself by the humane treatment he accorded POWs under his care. At the end of the Revolution Joshua Loring and David Sproat fled to England and were never held accountable for their criminal acts.

Prisoner Exchange: This was the opposite of **parole**. These POWs were exchanged for other POWs of the enemy and were free to return to combat. Officer POWs on both sides were frequently "exchanged" for significant numbers of enlisted POWs. A General Officer POW might be exchanged for hundreds of enlisted POWs or for another General Officer. (See Cartels for further information)

Sources:

Allen, Ethan. *The Narrative of Ethan Allen.*

Borick, Carl P. *Relieve Us of This Burthen. American Prisoners in the Revolutionary South, 1780-1781.*

Brown, Wallace. *The Good Americans, The Loyalists in the Revolution.*

Burrows, Edwin G. *Forgotten Patriots. The Untold Story of American Prisoners During the Revolutionary War.*

Cox, Caroline. *A Proper Sense of Honor. Service and Sacrifice in George Washington's Army.*

Ferling, John. *Almost A. Miracle. The American Victory in the War for Independence.*

Fleming, Thomas. *Washington's Secret War, The Hidden History of Valley Forge.*

Hoock, Holger. *SCARS of INDEPENDENCE. America's Violent Birth.*

Kelly, C. Brian. *Best Little Stories from the American Revolution.*
Patton, Robert H. *Patriot Pirates. The Privateer War for Freedom and Fortune in the American Revolution.*
Randall, Willard Sterne. *Ethan Allen, His Life and Times.*
Shomette, Donald Grady. *PRIVATEERS of the REVOLUTION. War on the New Jersey Coast 1775-1783.*

MEDICAL CARE FOR AMERICAN REBELS

Doctors and Hospitals: It shouldn't be a surprise that American Rebel sick and wounded suffered horribly. This situation did not start or end with the Revolution. Approximately 3,500 American doctors and surgeons served in the War. Doctors usually had formal medical training. Surgeons who did operations usually only had on the job training. Of these, approximately 200 had formal medical training. Because of short staffing and lack of trained personnel, many common sense medical procedures were not taken. For example: diseased soldiers were not segregated from wounded ones. Thus, wounded became infected with diseases which further greatly increased their mortality. Family members would frequently come to the hospitals and retrieve their wounded and injured loved ones and take them home to recuperate and recover. Dead soldiers were not quickly removed from hospitals filled with those living. There were severe shortages of medical instruments and medicines. Dr. Benjamin Church the first Continental Army Medical Director was dismissed and convicted of spying for the British. Before he was dismissed he published one of the first medical pamphlets on health for soldiers called: "The Directions for Preserving the Health of Soldiers" which emphasized: proper clothing, cleanliness, diet and encampment. Quakers were not kindly thought of by Rebel Americans because they did not join the cause against the British. It was felt that was tacit support of the

Crown. The fact is that Quakers, specifically the Moravians, volunteered to provide help and comfort to sick and injured soldiers. They did this at considerable risk to themselves because some became infected with smallpox and typhus and died from their service in these hospitals. The service of Moravians in the main American hospital in Bethlehem Pennsylvania is particularly noteworthy. By the end of the War some small improvements were noted in the care of America's sick and wounded soldiers. Sanitation was somewhat improved, the benefits of fresh air in hospitals was realized and inoculation against smallpox was fairly universal. Washington and von Steuben emphasized the need for cleanliness and sanitation. Von Steuben in his Army Instruction Book: "Regulations for the Order and Discipline of the Troops of the United States"._

Scurvy: Another common disease in the Continental Army (and British too) was scurvy. It was the result of insufficient vitamins in their diets, especially vitamin C. The result was severe tooth loss and gum disease, loss of strength and inability to fight off other medical problems. The solution was fruit, especially citrus fruits which were not common in the areas where armies were congregated. Fresh vegetables were emphasized as much as possible in the diets of American and British soldiers. paid great attention to health, sanitation and cleanliness of soldiers and encampments.

Smallpox: Smallpox was the scourge of the American Army. Initially Gen Washington forbade inoculation but completely relented by 1777 when he realized how it was devastating his army. He ordered the American Surgeon General Dr. William Shippen to make sure all new enlistees were inoculated when they were inducted. Washington had undergone a mild case of smallpox in his youth so he did not need to be inoculated.

Treatment of Injuries: Approximately 25% of American wounded died from their injuries. Muskets/rifles caused 60% of battlefield injuries. Projectiles which caused compound fractures usually resulted in amputation. Approximately 45% - 65% of the American soldiers who underwent amputations did not survive. Amputations were done without anesthetic and took about 20 minutes.

Venereal Disease: Venereal disease is shown in the earliest records of world history along with prostitution. It was debilitating and sometimes lethal. During the long term, British garrisons of New York City, NY, Charles Town, SC and Savanna GE, occupation, their soldiers were cooped up for years. British soldiers were paid in specie which made them able to pay for sex which was not the case for most American soldiers who went unpaid or were paid in worthless Continental Dollars. Treatment for venereal disease was frequently done with mercury which in itself was poisonous. There was little shame in having the disease which was sometimes called "Venus Disease", "Lecherous Illness" or "Infectious Malady". Prostitution dens in NYC were known as the "Holy Ground". Houses for British homosexual soldiers in NYC during the Revolution were known as "Molly Houses". Diseased American women in NYC were known as "Fireships" for the British tendency them to set them afire for their diseased condition which spread among British soldiers.

Most armies on the move had so called "Camp Followers" many of whom were women. They followed the army and for the most part provided essential duties: such as nursing, cooking, supply, spying and providing clothing. During the Revolution camp followers were common in both the American and British armies. Prostitution was not uncommon among these individuals of the British and American armies which spread disease.

Sources:

Broadus, Mitchell. *The Price of Independence. A Realistic View of the American Revolution.*

Cox, Caroline. *A Proper Sense of Honor. Service and Sacrifice in George Washington's Army.*

Ferling, John. *Almost A Miracle. The American Victory in the War of Independence.*

Gould, Dudley C. *The Times of Brother Jonathan. What he Ate, Drank, Believed In and used for Medicine during the War for Independence.*

NEW TECHNOLOGIES DURING THE REVOLUTION

Like most wars the American Revolution spurred the development of new technologies and weapons, which are shown in the following:

Breech Loading Rifle: British Major Patrick Ferguson developed the first operational breech loading rifle for use in combat. The Ferguson Rifle could be loaded and fired at twice the rate of the standard British musket. It was expensive to produce and required special training and tactics and thus was only used on an experimental basis during the War.

Germ Warfare: There is evidence that the British sent infected blacks and locals into American lines in order to spread disease, which was a form of "germ warfare". This had reportedly been done with American Indians, but not against Colonists.

Inoculation: British and American recruits were inoculated on a large-scale basis against smallpox which was a revolutionary medical technological development.

Submarine: The Americans developed the first combat submarine named the TURTLE. It was invented by David Bushnell from Connecticut and was designed to carry underwater mines which would be placed against the hulls of British ships. It was nearly successful on September 6, 1776 in its effort to sink Admiral Richard Howe's Flag Ship *HMS EAGLE* which was anchored in NYC Harbor. It failed only due to the inability to attach the mine to the ship's hull. It was never again attempted during the War.

Torpedoes: David Bushnell developed floating mines which were known as "Torpedoes" which were nearly successful against the British Navy. He was better known as the inventor and developer of the *TURTLE*, the first operational submarine.

Sources:

Broadus, Mitchell. *The Price of Independence. A Realistic View of the American Revolution.*

Diamant, Lincoln. *Chaining the Hudson: The Fight for the River of the Revolution.*

Draper, Lyman C. *King's Mountain and its Heroes: A History of the Battle of King's Mountain, October 7, 1780.*

Greene, Jerome A. *Guns of Independence.*

CONSUMPTION OF ALCOHOL

People in Britain and the Colonies during the 18th Century were known for their gargantuan consumption of alcohol. One house in eight in Boston was a pub. There were 48 different drinks in the taverns. Alcoholic drinks were given nicknames such as "Whistle Belly", "Vengeance" "Silabub" and a new concoction called a "Cocktail" which was a mixture of rum, rye and fruit juice. There were 60 distilleries in Massachusetts in 1774 which produced 2,700,000 gallons of rum. It was estimated that each adult American in the Colonies consumed 3 ¾ gallons of rum a year. Pre-breakfast drinks were common. Excessive alcohol consumption by British and German soldiers in America was a major source of their misconduct and desertion. Much of the time in America by these soldiers was spent in garrison duty which was boring and monotonous and was relieved by revelry. German doctors who conducted autopsies on their soldiers who dropped dead concluded they just drank themselves to death. Excessive alcohol consumption in Britain led to a level of moral depravity that did not exist in America. Gambling, whoring, pedophilia, cock fighting, spectacles of group executions and the like were common in Britain. Excessive consumption of alcohol was also a serious problem by American soldiers. Many soldiers were not fit for duty from the effects of alcoholism. Such debilitating effects were called "Barrel Fever". Gills of rum were the commonly given to soldiers on a daily basis. Alcohol was also often sold to the soldiers by sutlers.

Sources:

Archer, Richard. *As If an Enemy's Country. The British Occupation of Boston and the Origins of the American Revolution.*

Covert, Archer. *TAVERNS of the AMERICAN REVOLUTION.*

Hagist, Don N. *British Soldiers, American War. Voices of the American Revolution.*

Martin, James K. & Mark E. Lender. *A Respectable Army. The Military Origins of the Republic, 1763-1789.*

Urban, Mark. *Fusiliers, The Saga of a British Regiment during the American Revolution.*

JEWS DURING THE REVOLUTION

There were approximately 2,500 Jews in America at the time of the Revolution. They mostly resided in the east coast port cities of Newport, RI, New York City, NY, Philadelphia, PA, Charles Town, SC and Savannah, GE, but not so much in Boston, MA. The first synagogue in America was formed in Newport in 1763. They were composed of Sephardic elements, mostly from the Iberian Peninsula and Ashkenazi from Northern Europe. They came to America mostly to escape the oppression and discrimination they face in Europe. Many saw the American Revolution as an opportunity where there was freedom from what they experienced in Europe. Unlike many who came to America they had skills in commercial trading and business. On the whole, many more supported the Revolution than did not, although they did not act in concert together either way. In combat, they were often officers because of their financial well-being and status in the community and some became POWs and were killed fighting the British. Those that were Loyalists supported the British mostly in administrative and supply matters. One of the most senior American Jewish officers was Lt. Col. David Franks who was appointed an aide to General Benedict Arnold at West Point. Franks was suspicious of Arnold's actions before he turned traitor. Like everyone close to Arnold, David Franks was investigated for any complicity in the affair and completely cleared. The biggest and most important contributions by Jews to the American Revolution were in the areas of finance. Many contributed their personal fortunes to the Revolution and never recovered financially after the War. To this day, probably the most well-known Jew who made major contributions to the Revolution was Haym Salomon who was a skilled financier and worked closely with Robert Morris who was critical to the success of the Revolution. He was arrested for allegedly helping free American POWs and was incarcerated in the Prevost. He was released with the influence, reportedly of Hessian General Heister, who interceded with the British on his behalf. Later, working directly with Morris, Salomon performed a key role as a "broker" of French loans to America which were desperately needed. He paid a key role in obtaining money for rebellious American officers in 1782, some of whom had not been paid for years. In the immediate post-war years, he continued to serve in critical financial positions which saved the new Nation from imploding. He died prematurely on January 6th, 1785. Loyalist Jews mostly left America after the War and were compensated for their losses like other British who suffered financially for supporting the Crown. Evidence of Jewish support of the Revolution is documented by many membership applications for the Daughters of the American Revolution. The evidence is also contained in pension applications. In summary, the support by Jews for the Revolution, far exceeds their small numbers.

Source:

Rezneck, Samuel. *Unrecognized Patriots. The Jews in the American Revolution.*

WOMEN IN THE REVOLUTION

In Colonial times women could not vote, own land and had limited rights. During the war, American women organized boycotts of British goods, collected money and made uniforms for soldiers. They also served as spies, signalers, nurses and camp followers who performed essential duties such as preparing food and serving in support roles. A few served in direct combat roles, such as artillery gunners and were wounded and decorated for bravery. Nancy Burgin risked her life by secretly help drug British guards aboard the British POW ship *JERSEY* which facilitated the escape of about 200 American POWs from the ship. The British put a 200-pound price for her head for that act. She was commended by General Washington for her bravery. Sybil Ludington rode 40 miles through British lines to alert American Militia that the British were attacking the military supply depot at Danbury, Connecticut. This courageous act helped rally the Americans to drive the British away. Betty Zane a 16-year-old girl dashed through enemy fire at the Battle of Fort Henry in 1782 to obtain critically needed gunpowder which enabled the fort to survive. The greatest contribution of American women during the war was their essential work in keeping the farms and lands productive during the absence of their husbands and sons. It was not uncommon for senior British and German officers to bring their wives to America where they campaigned with their husbands which not a practice of American senior officers.

Sources:

Berkin, Carol. *Revolutionary Mothers. Women in the Struggle for America's Independence.*

Kelly, Brian & Ingred Smyer-Kelly. *Best Little Stories from the American Revolution.*

Middlekauff, Robert. *The Glorious Cause. The American Revolution 1763-1789.*

Raphael, Ray. *A People's History of the American Revolution, How Common Peoples Shaped the Fight for Independence.*

Smith, Page. *A New Age Now Begins (Volume Two)*

SPYING, SPIES AND TERMS DURING THE REVOLUTION

Spying was relatively easy to do and difficult to expose because Americans and British spoke the same language and had the same cultural background. The British and Americans both had undercover agents in their midst at the highest levels. The Americans had the advantage of knowing who had come to America with the British and who had Loyalist tendencies before the war ever began. Americans displayed better intelligence security than the British. For example; Benedict Arnold when he was assigned the commander of West Point asked to be given the names of local American undercover intelligence agents in his area. His request was denied because he did not have a demonstrated need to know that information. Despite the highly-classified nature of Arnold's willingness to defect that information was known by more than a few individuals in British Headquarters.

NOTABLE AMERICAN AND BRITISH SPIES

Agent 355: This was the code word for the only female agent in the Culper Ring. Although she is still unidentified, there is strong evidence she was a young woman who operated in the highest British military social circles. It is possible she was connected with Major

John Andre' who was an eligible bachelor who was active in the highest military social circles. What is known is that she repeatedly provided at great personal risk intelligence from the highest British levels which was a huge benefit to the American cause. New relevant documents are occasionally found which may result in her positive identification, but for the present time and possibly forever she must remain one of the unidentified heroines of the Revolution.

Anderson, John: This was the code word used by Major John Andre' in his secret communications with Major General Benedict Arnold.

Andre', John: John Andre' was the most famous British spy of the Revolution who was captured and executed by the Americans. As Adjutant to British CINC Henry Clinton, Andre', like Nathan Hale; was captured behind enemy lines, out of uniform, carrying incriminating documents and operating under an assumed name. Andre' was given a trial, found guilty, hanged at Tappan, NY and given a proper burial on October 2, 1780.

Armistead, James: James Armistead was a trusted black servant of General Cornwallis. In his duties, he was trusted enough to be present when Cornwallis would discuss his plans with his staff. As such he became aware of Cornwallis' plan to move his army to Yorktown which was critical information Washington needed. Through his black friends, Armistead had this information passed to General Lafayette whose small force of 1,500 soldiers was nearby. Lafayette passed this information to Washington who began the march of his main army towards southern Virginia. To prevent Cornwallis from escaping the pending trap at Yorktown Lafayette had Armistead pass to Cornwallis false intelligence that Lafayette commanded a far larger army than he actually did. This helped cause Cornwallis to fail to try a break out of Yorktown which ultimately sealed his fate and eventual surrender. Armistead's risky role spying for the Americans was critical to our victory at Yorktown.

Arnold, Benedict: Arnold was a true combat hero of the Revolution who risked his life on numerous occasions when fighting for the American Cause and suffered disabling and painful wounds. However, in May 1779 he offered his services to the British. To prove his traitorous intentions, he had to spy for the British for over a year. However, at that time he was only the Military Governor of Philadelphia which did not give him access to the most sensitive intelligence of the Revolution. This changed in early August 1779 when he became Commander of West Point and the surrounding area. This gave him access to the defensive plans of West Point which was information that was highly sought after by the British. His cohort British Major John Andre' was captured on September 23rd with the plans given to him by Arnold who fled to British controlled territory. So not only was Arnold a traitor his was a spy for the British for an extended period.

Church, Dr. Benjamin: Dr. Church was the first Surgeon General of the American Army and a trusted member of General Washington's inner circle and thus had access to classified information. Benjamin Franklin suspected Church was passing information to the British. He was caught, court martialed on October 4, 1775, found guilty and imprisoned for two years and then released to move to the West Indies. The ship taking him there never arrived or was heard from again. He was one of the most senior members of Washington's inner circle who was found guilty of spying for the British.

Culper Junior: This was the code word for Robert Townsend the leader of the American spy ring (Culper Ring) in New York and Long Island.

Culper Ring: This was the group of six American spies (James Rivington, Abraham Woodhull, Robert Townsend, Austin Roe, Caleb Brewster and Agent 355) who served as Gen Washington's secret service in and around NYC during the Revolutionary War. Reportedly, Washington wanted it called the "Culper" vs "Culpeper Ring" because he thought Culpeper Ring sounded too much like the Rebel town of Culpeper

Virginia. Abraham Woodhull and Robert Townsend were the two main Culper spies in NYC. Their identity as spies was not discovered for nearly 100 years after the Revolution. The Culper Ring was commanded by Major Benjamin Tallmadge who was a Yale College friend of Captain Nathan Hale who was caught and executed by the British on September 22, 1776. The British and American Rebels used spies extensively. Double agents were common. Because English was the common language between Americans and the British spying was difficult to root out. Many long term American Loyalists supported the British by spying but it was a dangerous and risky business with execution the quick penalty for being caught.

Deane, Silas: This Connecticut merchant was sent to France with the unclassified mission of a businessman. In reality, he was a spy for the Americans. He negotiated covert support for the American cause through the French and even travelled to Britain in an attempt to sabotage the British war effort. He was soon discovered as a spy by the British who unsuccessfully tried to capture and possibly assassinate him. Because he had to operate in the murky world of deceit and deception he is often thought of as someone who was out for personal gain rather than for the American cause. In fact, he became destitute in service to America and died as his ship was leaving Europe for America. In reality, he was one of the many unsung heroes of the American Revolution.

Gustavus: This was the code word used by Major General Benedict Arnold in his communications with Major John Andre' during Arnold's betrayal of the American cause.

Hale, Nathan: Nathan Hale was probably the most famous American spy caught and executed by the British during the Revolution. He was a poor choice for spying. He had no spy training and was well known as a superb American infantry company commander. He was betrayed by Rogers Roger to the British. He was captured with the four trademark indicators of a spy: (1) He was out of uniform. (2) He was behind enemy lines. (3) He was carrying incriminating documents. (4) He was operating under an assumed name. He was swiftly given a sentence to be hanged without a trial. He was taken to a secluded orchard on the edge of NYC to be hanged. He asked for a minister which was denied. He asked for a Bible which was denied. He asked to write a note to his family which was granted and then the note was reportedly torn up in his face. The British grabbed a local African American who was passing by and ordered him to hang Hale. It is reported that it was done badly and Hale died from strangulation. His body was stripped and left hanging for days until it reportedly became so offensive it was cut down. Whether the words are exact or not, he is most famous for the oath he gave just before he was hanged: "I regret I have but one life to give for my country".

Honeyman, John: John Honeyman played the role of an American deserter and helped deceive the Germans at Trenton into thinking an attack by Washington was not going to happen. He worked in secret collaboration with Gen Washington for the Battle of Trenton. This incident has largely been discredited by current research.

Tallmadge, Benjamin: Benjamin Tallmadge was Washington's chief of security and was deeply involved in spying operations and was key in helping foil Benedict Arnold's betrayal of the American cause at West Point.

Warren, Dr. Joseph: Dr. Warren was a young celebrated Harvard educated doctor who was a leading patriot in promoting the American Rebel cause. He managed the Boston spy network that discovered the British were going to seize the arms at Concord and Lexington. That information helped the patriots to prepare for the British march on these two towns which resulted in the severe check they received. The resulting casualties suffered by the British pretty much made it impossible to peacefully settle the differences between the Americans and British. Dr. Warren was subsequently killed at the redoubt on Bunker Hill on June 17, 1775.

SPY TERMS

Black Chambers: This was the name given to the were Loyalist and British intelligence operatives who operated in the American postal system to open and read correspondence to obtain intelligence.

Cardano Grille: This was a stiff piece of paper with randomly spaced holes where letters of a message were written. Then a seemingly innocent message was written incorporating the random letters. The receiver of the message had to have an identical grille to place over the whole document to reveal the message.

Cyphers: Cyphers were secret messages were written in letters, numbers or symbols which could be decoded to reveal the information.

Doomed Spy: This was a spy who was given false information to give to the enemy when captured. After divulging the erroneous information which commonly led the enemy astray, the spy was often executed.

Dumbbell Masks: These were hard paper cutouts, frequently in the shape of a dumbbell which when placed over a seemingly innocuous letter would reveal intelligence. These masks were a favorite method by British Gen Clinton of transmitting and receiving intelligence.

Harmonic Alphabet: This was a system of coding intelligence where music notes on music sheets could be translated into secret messages.

Hortalez & Cie: This was a dummy company set up by Silas Dean and Ben Franklin in France through which France would ship arms and supplies to the Colonies without violating French neutrality prior to the time France joined the War with the Americans in the spring of 1778.

Invisible Ink: (See Sympathetic Stain below)

Mono-Alphabetic Coding: This was a rather unsophisticated technique where numbers were substituted for letters or one letter transposition where one letter meant another.

Pigpen Cypher: This technique of sending classified information involved placing numbers which represented letters in pigpen like boxes.

Steganography: This is the term for the physical hiding of classified messages, whether or not they were in code. There were innumerable methods hiding messages such as in hollowed out bullets, the hollow insides of writing quills, hollowed out coat buttons and dead drops.

Sympathetic Stain: Sympathetic stain was an invisible ink used on white paper to conduct secret correspondence by the Americans during the Revolution. The writing would become visible with the application of another chemical to the paper. The stain chemicals were hard to obtain and expensive so the sympathetic chemical was used sparingly.

Visual Transmission: Perhaps the most well-known use of visual transmission of a classified message occurred when American patriots used lanterns in the church tower to indicate "one if by land, two if by sea. In other instances, bond fires were lit to signal the approach of an enemy.

Sources:

Kilmeade, Brian. *George Washington's Secret Six. The Spy Ring that Saved the American Revolution.*

Nagy, John A. *Invisible Ink. Spycraft of the American Revolution.*

Rose, Alexander. *Washington's Spies. The Story of America's First Spy Ring.*

MIRACLE ON THE HUDSON

By the summer of 1780 the American people and Continental Army and Militia were nearing exhaustion and collapse. Soldiers had gone for years without pay and there had been a recent series of battlefield losses by the Americans at Charles Town, Savannah and Camden. The successful betrayal of America's most celebrated combat general and the fall of the key strategic fortress of West Point would have inflicted a mortal blow on the Revolution. The following is the remarkable story of how the plot for the British to capture West Point by the treason of Benedict Arnold was foiled.

In May 1779, General Benedict Arnold indicated his willingness to betray the American cause in a secret communication to British HQ in NYC. Arnold felt unappreciated and neglected and abused. Major John Andre' the Adjutant to the British Commander in Chief, General Henry Clinton was appointed to handle Arnold's defection. In August 1780 Arnold was appointed by Gen Washington as Commander of West Point and the surrounding area. Arnold and Andre' agreed to meet at Dobbs Ferry on September 11th on neutral ground 30 miles south of West Point on the Hudson River. At the meeting Arnold would give Andre' the critical defensive plans of West Point. The plan was accidently foiled by the British when the gunboats of the British sloop *VULTURE* fired on Arnold's personal barge at Dobbs causing him to retreat back up the river to West Point before he could meet with Andre'. A second meeting was planned for September 20th. Due to the inability to get a boat to meet the British ship the meeting was delayed until September 21st. Andre', contrary to orders from Clinton, went up the river to the *VULTURE* to meet with Arnold. In further disobedience of Clinton's orders Andre' went ashore to meet with Arnold in American controlled territory. While Andre' and Arnold were meeting, American artillery fired on the ship forcing it to retreat down river which stranded Andre' behind American lines. Andre' had no choice but to try to return to British lines by horseback down the east side of the river. Escorted by a friend of Arnold by the name of Joshua Smith they successfully passed through a series of check points with safe conduct passes written for them by Arnold. They remained overnight on the eastern shore of the Hudson on the evening of September 22nd. Because they were about to enter British controlled land Smith left Andre' to ride the final short distance. Just as Andre' was about to enter British territory on the morning of September 23rd he was apprehended by three American Militia at the last checkpoint. He was discovered to be a British officer and had the defensive plans for West Point in his possession which showed he was on a spy mission. He was initially sent to Arnold under guard but returned at the last moment on the orders of Benjamin Tallmadge so Andre's mission could be fully investigated. Arnold became aware of Andre's capture just before General Washington was about to arrive at West Point. Arnold fled down the Hudson to the *VULTURE* by his personal barge when he heard Andre' had been captured.

If it were not for the series of highly fortunate circumstances and poor decisions by the British, the plot would have succeeded. The event is known by many as: THE MIRACLE ON THE HUDSON.

Sources:

Brandt, Clare. *The Man in the Mirror; A life of Benedict Arnold.*

Nelson, James L. *Benedict Arnold's Navy. The Ragtag Fleet that Lost the Battle of Lake Champlain but Won the American Revolution.*

Philbrick, Nathaniel. *Valiant Ambition. George Washington, Benedict Arnold and the Fate of the American Revolution.*

Sargent, Winthrop. *The Life of Major John Andre' Adjutant General of the British army in America.*

Sheinkin, Steve. *The Notorious Benedict Arnold, A True Story of Adventure, Heroism and Treachery.*

Van Doren, Carl. *Secret History of the American Revolution.*

THE JOSHUA HUDDY AFFAIR

The Joshua Huddy Affair as it became known showed the fragility of the American Revolution and the degree of animus that existed primarily in South Carolina and New Jersey as late as 1782, a full six months after the disastrous defeat of the British at Yorktown in October 1781.

Captain Joshua Huddy was a passionate American patriot living in central coastal New Jersey. He was an occasional privateer and artillery commander. He was hated and feared by "Refugees" and Loyalists alike. He was momentarily captured by Loyalists in the summer of 1780 but escaped. On February 1, 1782, he was directed with 25 men to take command of the Toms River Fort in NJ. Although there is no evidence Huddy was involved, a local Loyalist named Stephen Edwards was caught masquerading as a woman with incriminating documents. He was tried and hanged as a spy. The local Refugees were out for retribution and Huddy was their target. On March 23, 1782, a capture task force of nearly 120 men left NYC to conquer Toms River Fort and capture Huddy. In the fierce battle that ensued the task force suffered significant casualties. Huddy was captured and the town plundered and an old American patriot named Major John Cook was bayonetted to death.

Huddy was taken and taken to Gen Clinton who had him incarcerated in the infamous British POW Sugar House facility and later the Provost. On April 7, 1782 at the direction William Franklin (son of Benjamin Franklin and head of the New Jersey Board of Associated Loyalists) had Huddy removed from POW status in NYC and put on a sloop to Sandy Hook, NJ. From there he was put in the custody of Loyalist Captain Richard Lippincott with the verbal orders of Franklin to execute Huddy. Lippincott conducted the crude hanging and pinned a note to his body: "UP GOES HUDDY FOR PHILIP WHITE". Philip White was a local Loyalist who had been killed while attempting to escape from his capture by local rebels. Huddy was a POW of the British at the time of White's death and had no complicity in his death. Local Americans petitioned Gen Washington to take retaliatory action who convened a panel of 25 generals to the investigate the situation.

The council unanimously recommended retaliation and an order be sent to Gen Clinton to surrender Lippincott for execution. The Continental Congress concurred with the action which was sent to Clinton on April 21st who ordered Lippincott be court martialed which revealed that Huddy was executed on the direct orders of William Franklin. This freed Lippincott of any responsibility. Franklin fled to Britain and Clinton resigned his command and was temporarily replaced by Lt Gen James Robertson. Under pressure, Washington ordered 13 British officer POWs one of who was to be selected by lottery to executed in retaliation. British Captain Charles Asgill just 19 or 20 years old drew the piece of paper selecting him to be executed. His family was wealthy, well connected and his father was the former mayor of London. The wife of Lord Asgill appealed to George III for assistance who was sympathetic. Soon the Asgill affair became an international an unfavorable cause. French King Louis XVI and Queen Marie Antoinette lent their influence to Asgill's case. Eventually Comte Vergennes who was almost solely instrumental in France's support of the Revolution, wrote Washington asking for relief for Asgill. Tired of the months long affair and afraid of international implications just as peace negotiations were underway, Congress on November 5, 1782 ordered Washington to free Asgill who reluctantly complied. Asgill returned to Britain a free man.

The adroit handling of the affair by Washington and the Congress which could have had damaging effects on the peace agreement with Britain was ultimately negotiated very favorably for America.

Sources:

Chernow, Ron. *Washington, A Life.*

Ferreiro, Larrie D. *BROTHERS AT ARMS. American* Independence and the Men of France Who Saved It.

Hoock, Holger. *SCARS of INDEPENDEWNCE. America's Violent Birth.*

Shomette, Donald Grady. *PRIVATEERS of the REVOLUTION. War on the New Jersey Coast 1775-1783.*

Skemp, Sheila L. *Benjamin and William Franklin. Father and Son, Patriot and Loyalist*

SUCCESSION OF BRITISH COMMANDERS-IN-CHIEFS (CINCs) DURING THE REVOLUTION

LTG Thomas Gage: Gage served in America from 1763 to 1775 and was relieved after the disastrous battle of Bunker Hill. It was also felt he had become Americanized after his long service in America and lacked sufficient enthusiasm for defeating the American Revolution. In fact, his wife was a born American.

LTG William Howe: Howe served in America as British CINC from 1775 to 1778 and was relieved after the disastrous campaign by LTG Burgoyne in his failed campaign to divide the colonies by driving down the Hudson River to Albany, NY where he was to link up with Gen Howe. Burgoyne's drive down the Hudson River might have been successful if Gen Howe had moved up the Hudson River aggressively to link up with him which had long been the plan. Instead Howe took a circuitous route south by ship to Philadelphia thinking the capture of it (at that time it was the American capitol) would end the war. The result was Burgoyne was trapped and defeated at the Battles of Saratoga in mid-October 1777, which gave the France the confidence to openly sign a treaty of cooperation with the American States.

LTG Henry Clinton: Clinton served in America as CINC from 1778 to 1782. He departed America after peace negotiations were initiated with the defeat of the British at the Battle of Yorktown in October 1781. He had an openly adversarial relationship with his major field commander LTG Earl Cornwallis who became trapped at Yorktown after Clinton failed to take aggressive action to support him in time for an effective rescue. After his capture at Yorktown LTG Cornwallis who never served as a CINC was exchanged for Henry Laurens an original signer of the Declaration of Independence who had been captured at sea by the British and held as a POW in the Tower of London. LTG James Robertson, Clinton's second in command briefly served as British CINC after Clinton's resignation and General Carleton's arrival.

LTG Sir Guy Carleton: Carleton served in America as CINC from 1782 to 1783 to complete the British compliance with the Paris Peace Treaty and withdrawal of their troops from America.

Sources:

O'Shaughnessy, Patrick Andrew. *The Men Who Lost America.*

PEACE NEGOTIATIONS

After the defeat of the British at Yorktown the war continued on a small scale, especially in New Jersey and the far southern colonies, but Parliament insisted on peace with America. Negotiations were complicated because they involved not only Britain, but also France, Spain and the Netherlands which had to sign separate treaties. Now that the Americans had the British to the negotiation tables the French worked to make sure that the British did not give too much to the Americans. The French were concerned that the future America would be overly dominant. That is in part why the French opposed Britain giving Canada to the Americans which was an early American demand. The Spanish had significant territorial designs on America: East and West Florida, Louisiana and both banks of the Mississippi River. The American negotiators were Benjamin Franklin, John Jay, Henry Laurens and John Adams. Britain was represented by Member of Parliament David Hartley. France and Spain signed separate treaties with Britain. The American Revolution was ultimately ended with the signing of the September 3, 1783 Treaty of Paris. The provisions of the Treaty were very favorable to America and were as follows:

1. Britain acknowledged America's full independence.
2. The borders between the U.S. and British North America were established.
3. America was granted fishing rights to the Grand Banks, Newfoundland and areas of the St Lawrence River.

4. It was agreed that lawful debts incurred by both parties should be honored.
5. The Continental Congress was to recommend that the States honor rights to all confiscated Loyalist lands.
6. The U.S. would prevent future confiscation of Loyalist lands.
7. Prisoners Of War were to be repatriated.
8. Britain and the U.S. were to be given unrestricted access to the Mississippi River.
9. Territories captured after the treaty were to be returned to their former owners.
10. Ratification of the treaty was to occur within six months of signing.

The U.S. Congress of the Confederation ratified the treaty on January 14, 1784. America largely ignored Articles 5 and 6.

Sources:

Bemis, Samuel Flagg. *The Diplomacy of the American Revolution.*

Ferling, John. *Almost A. Miracle. The American Victory in the War of Independence.*

Ferreiro, Larrie D. *Brothers At Arms. American Independence and the Men of France and Spain Who Saved It.*

Martin James K. & Mark E. Lender. *A Respectable Army. The Military Origins of the Republic, 1763-1789.*

Mitchell, Broadus. *The Price of Independence. A Realistic View of the American Revolution.*

POST-REVOLUTION WAR DEBTS

American National Debt: Not including worthless paper Continental Dollars, the Colonies and the Continental authorities spent approximately 150 million dollars during the American Revolution, most of it borrowed from Europe. The U.S. debt was only settled during 1790s by the U.S. National Bank which was established by Alexander Hamilton, the first American Secretary of the Treasury and notable Revolutionary War hero.

British National Debt: At the end of the French and Indian War (1763) the British National debt was 122,603,336 pounds sterling with annual interest payments of 4,409,797 pounds, equaling more than ½ of the British national budget. By 1766 the debt had increased another 14 million pounds. The dire circumstances of the British debt was a major force behind the multiple Colonial revenue producing acts (Sugar Act, Stamp Act etc.) instigated by the British which were major contributors to the eruption of the American Revolution. At the end of the American Revolution (1783) the British National debt was 250 million pounds with annual interest payments of 9.5 million pounds; twice the debt they experienced before the Revolution.

Dutch National Debt: The Dutch initially gave America a loan of 5 million Guilders in 1782 and by 1793 the amount of loans had ballooned to 30 million Guilders. These loans were crucial in keeping America solvent. However, the loans were largely unrepaid by America and played a significant part in weakening the Dutch government which contributed to their own subsequent revolution.

French National Debt: The French spent about 56 million Livre supporting the American Revolution, which was almost 1/3 of their total national debt. The French debt crisis was generated in a significant way from expenses to support the American Revolution and was one of the causes of the subsequent French Revolution.

German Princes: The British paid dearly for the German mercenaries who served in America. The salaries for even the lowest ranking mercenaries were very generous. The German mercenaries were paid by the British and the British matched their salaries in direct payments to the Princes. Extra pay was provided to the Princes for Germans who were killed and wounded. Financially, the German Princes were handsomely rewarded but the seeds for discontent were sown for future change much to the detriment of the Princes.

Spanish National Debt: Spain spent 246 million Reales in support of the American Revolution from 1776-1779. Spain incurred additional significant expenses and losses after its declaration of war with the British and from the disruption of trade with America.

Sources:

Butler, Judge Ed. *Galvez. Our Forgotten Ally In The American Revolutionary War.*

Butler, Nick. *An EMPIRE on EDGE.*

Ferreiro, Larrie D. *Brothers At Arms. American Independence and the Men of France and Spain Who Saved It.*

Middlekauff, Robert. *The Glorious Cause. The American Revolution 1763-1789.*

Tuchman, Barbara W. *The First Salute, A View of the American Revolution.*

REVOLUTIONARY WAR PENSIONS

The promise of pensions and land grants were used partly for recruiting and reenlistment inducements and reward for faithful war-time service. American officers were promised half pay for life after faithful service of three or more years in the war. This issue became a point of contention during and after the war between civilians and military officers. Ultimately 80,000 individuals applied for pensions and approximately 60,000 were approved. The following reflects the major pension acts and legislation for Revolutionary War veterans. The two most important and comprehensive pension acts were the 1818 and 1832 acts.

1. **August 26, 1776:** Continental Congress provided ½ pay for enlisted and officers disabled in service and unable to earn a living for the duration of the disability.
2. **May 15, 1778:** Provided ½ pay for officers for seven years who remained on duty for the duration of the war. Enlisted were to receive $80 at the end of the war.
3. **August 24, 1780:** Provided ½ pay for seven years to orphans and widows of soldiers who died in the service.
4. **October 21, 1780:** Provided ½ pay for life for officers, later amended to full pay for five years.

5. **September 29, 1789:** Expanded previous eligibility for pensions.
6. **April 10, 1806:** Extended some pensions for militia and state troops.
7. **Service Pension Act of 1818:** This act required two things: (1) Proof of at least a total of six months War service in the Continental Army and (2) financial need. If an applicant was not destitute, he did not qualify for a pension. If the soldier was a militia or state veteran, he did not qualify.
8. **Service Pension Act of June 1832:** This was the last pension legislation for Revolutionary War Veterans. It deleted the financial need requirement, retained the minimum of six months' total service and opened pensions for state troops and militia. A Revolutionary War veteran who served at least two years got his pay according to his rank for life. If the service was for less than 2 years, the applicant got a pro-rated annuity according to his rank and service.

Applicants for pensions needed to submit their cases to local county courts which ruled on the documentation provided. Because of the age, infirmity and lack of education of many of the individuals, the applications were mostly orally given to local courts and clerks and transcribed on paper. Once the county court was satisfied with the documentation the case was forwarded to the Commissioner of Pensions in Washington D.C. which ruled on the case. Approximately 80% of cases approved by county courts were accepted by the Commissioner. Approximately 10% of American Revolutionary War Veterans were African Americans. There were some obvious cases of discrimination in the awarding of pensions for these veterans, but for the most part they received pensions according to the documentation that was available. Unfortunately, there are few records to document the service for Revolutionary War participants, especially those of the militia. Revolutionary War pension and bounty applications serve a major resource to fill this void.

Revolutionary War pension application records now constitute the largest oral history archive in our Nation's history. The applications are part of the Veterans Administration Record Group 15. They can be purchased from the National Archives Publication M804 and consist of 2,670 reels of microfilm.

Sources:

Dann, John C. (Editor) *THE REVOLUTION REMBERED. Eyewitness Accounts of the War for Independence.*

Fleming, Thomas. *Washington's Secret War. The Hidden History of Valley Forge.*

Martin, James K. & Mark E. Lender. *A Respectable Army. The Military Origins of the Republic, 1763-1789.*

Mullen, Jolene Roberts. *Connecticut Town Meeting Records during the Revolution.*

Resch, John and Sargent Walter Editors. *War and Society in the American Revolution Mobilization and Home Fronts.*

MAJOR BATTLES AND CAMPAIGNS OF THE REVOLUTION

The following are what many historians consider the most important and major battles and campaigns of the Revolution. To constitute a MAJOR event, it had to have a significant good or bad impact on the outcome of the War. Many individuals will undoubtedly disagree with these personal assessments. Formal US Army records show there were 69 battles in the Revolution. The following major battles and campaigns are listed in chronological order:

LEXINGTON/CONCORD

Date: April 19, 1775.

Location: Northwest of Boston, Massachusetts.

The Fighting Forces: 700 British Infantry later reinforced with 1,000 during their retreat. 270 Americans at Lexington/Concord were reinforced by nearly 6,000 militia after the battle started.

The Situation: Tensions between the British occupiers of Boston and the local American insurgents were escalating daily. British General

Gage ordered his soldiers to reduce the military capability of the Americans by launching a secret expedition to the nearby towns of Lexington and Concord to seize munitions the American had stored there. The news of the pending expedition became well known so the Americans mobilized and hid the munitions.

The Battle: Two hundred British soldiers under the command of Marine Major John Pitcairn and Lt Col Francis Smith marched on Lexington en-route to Concord to seize the American munitions. At Lexington Green, they were met by 70 American Minutemen commanded by Captain John Parker. A confusing confrontation occurred with no record of who shot first, but eight Americas were killed and 10 wounded. The British resumed their march to Concord. News of the shooting spread like wildfire and 200-400 Americans assembled at Concord. Fighting broke out and British Lt Col Smith realizing he was about to be outnumbered, started a retreat back to Lexington and Boston. By now several thousand Americans had converged on the road from Concord to Lexington and a running battle ensued. The Americans fired from behind trees and stone walls forcing the British to retreat for their lives. The British lost 73 killed, 174 wounded and 26 missing. The Americans lost 49 killed, 41 wounded and 5 missing.

Assessment: Significant American victory that demonstrated the British were not invincible. It also served to alarm the British that they could expect similar casualty rates in future battles.

Sources:

Kelly, C. Brian. *Best Little Stories from the American Revolution.*

Borneman, Walter R. *American Spring. Lexington, Concord and the Road to Revolution.*

Rae, Noel. *The People's War, Original Voices of the Revolution.*

Savas, Theodore P. & J. David Dameron. *A Guide to the Battles of the American Revolution.*

Ward, Christopher. *The War of the Revolution.*

BUNKER/BREEDS HILL

Date: June 17, 1775.

Location: Charleston, (Boston) Massachusetts.

The Fighting Forces: 2,500 British: 3,000 American.

The Situation: The British were seeking to avenge their losses at Lexington and Concord of April 19, 1775. The British disrespected the American ability to fight professional British soldiers. To win the battle, the British needed to successfully take the commanding heights of Breeds/Bunker Hill. The Americans occupied the heights before the battle and had time to construct a massive redoubt of earth and defensive fortifications.

The Battle: The British debarked from boats in the harbor at the base of the heights of Charleston and made three up-hill frontal assaults. Twice they were beaten back with serious losses. By the third assault the Americans were seriously low on ammunition and the British succeeded in breaking the American lines and captured the redoubt. The British suffered 226 killed and 1,154 wounded for an astounding casualty rate of 46%. Especially serious was the loss of officers. The Americans suffered 140 killed and 301 wounded. The stunning British casualties emboldened the rebel Americans and caused General William Howe who had been in the midst of the slaughter on the battlefield to be disastrously cautious during his subsequent service as Commander-In-Chief of all British forces in America. This cautiousness caused him to miss several golden opportunities to trap and defeat General Washington. After the battle, the Americans surrounded the city of Boston and brought in cannon captured from Fort Ticonderoga which caused the British to evacuate their forces to Halifax on March 17, 1776 and never again return to the city during the war.

Assessment: Huge American victory.

Sources:

Cutter, William. *The Life of Israel Putnam.*
Ketchum, Richard M. *Decisive Day, The Battle for Bunker Hill.*
Nelson, James. *The Battle of Bunker Hill.*
Rose, Ben Z. *John Stark, Maverick General.*
Savas, Theodore P. & J. David Dameron. *A Guide to the Battles of the American Revolution.*
Ward, Christopher. *The War of the Revolution.*

BATTLE OF FORT MOULTRIE (ALSO KNOWN AS THE BATTLE OF FORT SULLIVAN)

Date: June 28, 1776.

Location: Charles Town Harbor, South Carolina.

Engaged Forces: 2,900 British soldiers and sailors: 1,175 American soldiers.

The Situation: The British aimed to open a southern campaign to seize the colonies of South and North Carolina, Georgia and Virginia. They needed to capture a major port from which to conduct operations and Charles Town provided the best choice. In February 1776, the British assembled a fleet with 1,500 soldiers under the command of General Henry Clinton and set out from Boston for a base of operations in the area of Cape Fear/Wilmington, NC. A fleet of troop transports and battleships under the command of Gen Cornwallis arrived in the area from England on May 3, 1776. The Cape Fear/Wilmington area of North Carolina proved totally unsuitable as their base of operations, due in a significant part to the lack of expected local Loyalist support.

This caused the objective to be changed to Charles Town, SC. The major fort (Fort Moultrie) guarding the harbor had been under construction by the Americans for nearly a year.

The Battle: The British attacked the fort with tremendous volumes of cannon fire from their ships. Three of their ships ran aground trying to get close to the fort which resulted in the destruction of one by the fort's cannon. The volume of cannon fire from the ships is reflected in the fact that after the battle the Americans collected 7,000 British cannon balls from the battlefield. The fort absorbed without major damage most of the British cannon fire because the walls of the fort were made of sand and Palmetto logs which did not shatter like hard wood. British infantry attacks failed in the marshes and sand dunes around the fort. The British lost one major ship and suffered 195 killed and wounded and withdrew eventually to NYC. The Americans lost just 37 men.

Assessment: This was a significant victory for the Americans because the British did not attempt to conquer the southern states again for another two years.

Sources:

Savas, Theodore P. & J. David Dameron. *A Guide to the Battles of the American Revolution.*

Ward, Christopher. *The War of the Revolution.*

BATTLES FOR NEW YORK CITY

Dates: Long Island, August 27-29, 1776; New York City, September-November 1776; White Plains, October 28, 1776; Forts Washington and Lee, November 1776.

Locations: In and around NYC.

Engaged Forces: Battle of Long Island British 26,600 soldiers and 5,000 German mercenaries, British Navy 10,000; American soldiers 10,000: Battle of NYC same as above: Battle of White Plains 13,000 British and German mercenaries; Americans 5,000 soldiers.

The Situation: The British sought to seize New York and its fine harbor as soon as possible. The Americans hoped they could somehow hold the city like they held Boston, but it was a false hope.

The Battles: On August 22, 1776 the British landed 15,000 soldiers from 400 boats at Long Island (Brooklyn) and an additional 4,300 Germans on August 25th. They consolidated their positions and moved forward mostly without opposition from the Americans. In the fighting on August 27th the British and Germans suffered approximately 360 killed and wounded and the Americans about 800, mostly captives. On the evening of August 29th while facing the likelihood of annihilation by being pinned against the Hudson, Washington secretly, against odds, moved his Army across the East River to Manhattan. On September 16th, the British landed thousands of soldiers on Manhattan Island and in the subsequent fight the Americans lost two key combat leaders, LTC Thomas Knowlton and Major Andrew Leitch and 40 killed and wounded as they withdrew. Fort Washington was captured by the British on November 16, 1776. Gen Washington had wanted to evacuate the fort but Gen Greene, the on-scene commander, felt it could be held. Washington regretfully deferred to Greene. The British (mostly Germans) lost 300 killed and wounded. The Americans lost 160 killed and wounded and a staggering 2,830 prisoners. On November 20, 1776, the Germans captured Fort Lee across the Hudson which the Americans evacuated just before its capture. The material losses, mostly from Fort Lee, were staggering; amounting to 146 cannons, 12,000 shot and shell, 2,800 muskets and 400,000 cartridges and mountains of other war material.

Assessment: The capture of approximately American 4,000 soldiers and loss of extremely critical war supplies made the New York campaign by the British a catastrophic defeat for the Americans.

Sources:

Rae, Noel. *The People's War, Original Voices of the American Revolution.*
Savas, Theodore P. & J. David Dameron. *A Guide to the Battles of the American Revolution.*
Schecter, Barnet. *The Battle for New York.*
Ward, Christopher. *The War of the Revolution.*

BATTLE OF VALCOUR ISLAND

Dates: October 11-13, 1776.

Location: Middle section of Lake Champlain, New York State.

Engaged Forces: 697 British soldiers and sailors; 873 Americans.

The Situation: The British under the command of Lord LTG Sir Guy Carleton, commander of British forces in Canada sought to drive south from Canada via Lake Champlain to the Hudson River and link up with British forces from Albany NY. This would divide the New England American States from those of the Mid Atlantic and Southern States and would allow the states to be defeated in detail and prohibit them from reinforcing each other. He needed inland ships to sail the length of the lake. However, they could not be transported intact from the Saint Lawrence River over the falls on the Canadian end of the lake. Due to the thick ice, disassembly and construction of new ships he could not start until June 1776. They had to build combat ships, in addition to transports because the Americans were building their own fighting ships to counter the British. The Americans had the challenge of building from scratch its fleet and forming crews to battle the British on the lake. This was done under the command of the extremely able Brigadier General Benedict Arnold, who was not just a battlefield general but an accomplished blue water sailor.

The Battle: The British raced to build their ships at the northern end of the lake and the Americans at the southern end. Both finished their ship building at about the same time (early October 1776) and readied themselves for battle. Arnold hid his ships behind Valcour Island as the British sailed south. The British fleet consisted of one three masted ship, two sloops, one massive gun platform, one gondola and 48 gunboats which engaged Arnold's fleet consisting of one sloop, two schooners, four galleys and eight smaller gondolas. The American navy was outgunned but inflicted considerable damage on the British. After the battle, Arnold sailed what was left of his fleet in the middle of the night to the southern end of the lake saving the last of his sailors. The Americans lost 673 sailors and the British 50. By the time the British had built their ships and defeated the Americans winter was upon them and they withdrew back to Canada. The controversial decision by Carleton to abandon the campaign gave the Americans another whole year to prepare for Britain's second attempt to attack south towards Albany and divide the northern colonies from the others.

Assessment: The battle itself was a clear victory for the British. However, the time consumed in building their navy to do battle with Arnold would later have disastrous consequences for the British. After the battle, it was too late in the fall to campaign further south so they had to retreat back to Canada in the face of the upcoming winter. Their second attempt a year later to strike south via Lake Champlain resulted in the British catastrophe at Saratoga in October 1777.

Sources:

Bratton, John R. *The Gondola Philadelphia and the Battle of Lake Champlain.*

Nelson, James L. *Benedict Arnold's Navy. The Ragtag Fleet that Lost the Battle of Lake*
Champlain but Won the American Revolution.
Savas, Theodore P. & J. David Dameron. *A Guide to the Battles of the Revolution.*
Ward, Christopher. *The War of the Revolution.*

BATTLE OF TRENTON NEW JERSEY

Date: December 26, 1776.

Location: Trenton, New Jersey.

Engaged Forces: 1,500 Hessian Mercenaries; 2,400 Americans.

The Situation: The American Army was near collapse from its losses during the British campaign in and around New York City. Enlistments were about to expire at the end of December. Many of the American soldiers were shoeless and dressed in nothing but worn out blankets. Desperate action was needed by General Washington to turn the tide of the war. Instead of pursuing the Americans after his victories around New York British General Howe emplaced his army in winter cantonments in and around NYC and a string of outposts along the New Jersey side of the Delaware River. In a desperate gamble, General Washington saw an opportunity to strike the vulnerable outpost at Trenton, NJ which was manned exclusively by Hessians under the command of Colonel Johann Rall.

The Battle: In a complete surprise maneuver Washington moved his army across the Delaware River at night in the middle of a fortuitous storm. Contrary to stories that the Hessians were hung over from Christmas drinking, they had been on exhausting full alert for days on end because they knew they were vulnerable. They were completely surprised and overwhelmed as the Americans struck at dawn on December 26th. The Hessians lost 106 killed and wounded and 918 captured while the Americans lost four who froze to death and twelve wounded. American morale soared and soldiers were convinced to extend their enlistments in turn for cash which was scraped up by Robert Morris the American financier of the revolution. Not wanting the world to think this battle was a fluke, Washington eight days later out maneuvered the British at the Battle of Princeton (January 3, 1777) which further stunned them and gave international notice of the American's capability to successfully fight the British and their German mercenaries.

Assessment: The Battles of Princeton and Trenton were stunning American victories which gave international credit to the generalship of Washington and the American Army.

Sources:

Dyer, William M. *The Day is Ours. November 1776-1777. An Inside View of the Battles of Trenton and Princeton.*

Ferling, John. *Almost A. Miracle. The American Victory in the War of Independence.*

Fischer, David Hackett. *Washington's Crossings.*

Ketchum, Richard M. *The Winter Soldiers. The Battles of Trenton and Princeton.*

Savas, Theodore P. & J. David Dameron. *A Guide to the Battles of the American Revolution.*

Tucker, Phillip Thomas. *George Washington's Surprise Attack. A New Look at the Battle That Decided the Fate of America.*

Ward, Christopher. *The War of the Revolution.*

BATTLES OF SARATOGA NEW YORK

Dates: Hubbarton, July 7, 1777; Oriskany, August 6, 1777; Bennington, August 6-16, 1777; Freeman's Farm, September 18, 1777; Bemis Heights, October 7-17, 1777.

Locations: Hubbarton in the southwest part of modern Vermont; Oriskany in the forests west of what is now known as Rome, New York; the town of Bennington then part of New Hampshire Grants, and in the forests of what is now known as Saratoga, New York, forty miles south of the end of Lake Champlain and 45 miles north of Albany.

Engaged Forces: Hubbarton, 1,030 British; 1,100 Americans: Oriskany, 900 British, Germans and Indians; 800 Americans: Bennington, 900 Germans, 2,000 American militia: Freeman's Farm, 6,000 British, Germans and Indians; 7,000 Americans: Bemis Heights, 5,500 British and Germans; 11,000 Americans.

The Situation: This was the second British attempt to drive a wedge between the New England States and the rest of the newly declared independent states. LTG John Burgoyne had personally briefed the three-prong battle plan to King George III, Lord George Germain the Minister of Colonies and Lord North the Prime Minister with their full approval. General Burgoyne was to lead the major element and strike south via Lake Champlain. The plan was for General Howe Commander In Chief to command the second element with the objective of moving up the Hudson River from NYC to link up with General Burgoyne at Albany. This part of the plan was not firmly put in place. The third element consisted of a diversionary force commanded by Lt Col Barry St. Ledger who was to strike east from Lake Oswego via the Mohawk River and link up with Howe and Burgoyne around Albany. Command of the American Northern Army was in disarray. First it was commanded by MG Schuyler and then MG Horatio Gates who gained the position by political maneuvering. The British force moved south via Lake Champlain without significant opposition and seized Fort Ticonderoga without much difficulty on July 6, 1777. The British had unexpectedly moved their artillery to Independence Hill above the fort which caused the quick evacuation of the fort by the Americans. The British were now faced with moving their army south of the lake through densely forested land which was largely without roads or even trails. Burgoyne decided to send half his forces south via Lake George and the other half through the forests. The Americans did everything possible to slow the British advance by felling gigantic trees in their way, diverting streams to create swamps and rolling huge boulders in the way of possible paths. The timetable of the British soon became completely disrupted. The Lake George route required that he move his boats and material up steep falls to get to the lake which further upset his timetable. Soon getting supplies south from Canada became a critical problem.

The Battles: (**Hubbarton, July 7, 1777**) A trailing element of the withdrawing Americans unexpectedly clashed with the advancing British at the small town of Hubbarton on July 7th. In the battle the British lost 185 killed and wounded and Americans lost 80. Although the battle did not stop the advance of the British, it slowed them significantly enough to cause disruption to their critical timetable to advance south towards Albany. **(Oriskany, August 6, 1777)** The diversionary force led by Lt Col Barry St. Ledger had been moving east via the Mohawk River with the objective of diverting Americans away from Burgoyne and eventually linking up with British forces in Albany, NY. On August 6, 1777, his force of 900 Loyalists, British, Germans and Indians collided with a force of 800 Americans led by BG Nicholas Herkimer at Oriskany six miles from Fort Stanwix. The Americans were defeated and Herkimer killed, but St. Ledger was shaken. He demanded the surrender of Fort Stanwix which the commander bravely refused. Hearing of the threat to the fort, General Gates asked for volunteers to relieve the fort and drive St. Ledger back to Lake Oswego. Gen

Benedict Arnold volunteered for the task with an initial group of 950 men. Arnold approached the fort with just a few soldiers, but convinced a local German American by the name of Hon Yost Schuler to go to St. Ledger to tell him Arnold had an overwhelming force of 3,000. The Indians in St. Ledger's force panicked and fled causing St. Ledger to retreat back to Lake Oswego which ended that element of Burgoyne's master plan. **(Bennington, August 6-16, 1777)** Seeking desperately needed supplies, especially horses, Burgoyne at the urging of German MG Baron von Riedesel sent a force east to an area around the town of Bennington in the New Hampshire Grants where there was reported to be a huge store of supplies and horses. The 900-man German force was led by Lt Col Friedrich Baum. His force was successfully attacked by New Hampshire American militia led by the indomitable BG John Stark. German reinforcements under the command of Lt Colonel Heinrich von Bergmann were sent to relieve Baum and were attacked by Stark's men. In the ensuing battle the Germans lost 207 killed and wounded and 700 captured while the Americans lost 30 killed and 40 wounded. Baum was killed. These losses reduced Burgoyne's force by a full 15%. **(Freeman's Farm, September 19, 1777)** Unwilling and unable to return to Canada (the Americans had cut his supply lines and ability to go back north) and hoping General Howe was driving north from Albany to link up with him, Burgoyne decided to engage the Americans in a decisive battle at a location called Freeman's Farm where both the American and British armies collided. Colonel Daniel Morgan's expert riflemen exacted a terrible toll on British and German officers. The fighting was hand to hand in places and artillery pieces on both sides were captured and recaptured. The British and Germans suffered 600 killed, wounded and missing and the Americans 65 killed and 254 wounded. It became clear Burgoyne's army was now trapped. **(Bemis Heights October 7-17, 1777)** Knowing Burgoyne was trapped and sensing victory the American forces were flooded with militia reinforcements. Burgoyne's forces were on severely reduced rations and there was no indication of serious help from General Howe, who contrary to the operational plan, had moved his army south to seize the American capital of Philadelphia rather than move north up to the Hudson to link up with Burgoyne. Hoping against hope that he could win a climactic battle, Burgoyne engaged the Americans again at a site one mile from Freeman's Farm called Bemis Heights. Seeing that Gen Gates was overly cautious Gen Arnold seized the initiative without authority or approval from Gates and personally led troops on repeated and successful attacks on the British lines and fortifications. In the process, he was seriously wounded by a gunshot which shattered his thigh bone. The British and Germans suffered another 600 killed, wounded and captured and the Americans 150 killed, wounded and captured. Burgoyne sought counsel from his senior generals, most of which advised surrender, which he did on October 17, 1777. The surrender agreement became known as the Saratoga Convention. The 5,600+ British and Germans became Prisoners of War and thereafter were known as the Convention Army.

Assessment: Between the battles of Hubbarton, Oriskany, Bennington, Freeman's Farm and Bemis Heights the Americans lost 800 killed and wounded; the British and Germans 1,700 killed and wounded and 6,463 British and Germans became POWs. Fully one fourth of all British forces in America were captured. The series of battles in Burgoyne's campaign were catastrophic defeats for the British. The victorious battles by the Americans had a direct impact on the French decision to enter the war on the side of the Americans. This was formalized by the Treaty of Alliance of February 6, 1778. This internationalized the war and added greatly to the strain of Britain's war effort.

Sources:

Ketchum, Richard M. *Saratoga, Turning Point of the American Revolutionary War.*

Kidder, Frederic. *History of The First New Hampshire Regiment.*

Loqusz, Michael. *With Musket and Tomahawk. The Saratoga Campaign and the Wilderness War.*
Nielson, Charles. *Original and Corrected Accounted of Burgoyne's Campaign.*
O'Shaughnessy, Andrew Jackson. *The Men Who Lost America. British Leadership, the American Revolution and the Fate of the Empire.*
Savas, Theodore P. & J. David Dameron. *A Guide to the Battles of the American Revolution.*
Ward, Christopher. *The War of the Revolution.*

BATTLE OF MONMOUTH COURTHOUSE

Date: June 28, 1778.

Location: Monmouth Courthouse area north central New Jersey.

Engaged Forces: 10,000 British and Germans; 12,000 Americans.

The Situation: The capture of Philadelphia by Gen Howe had not produced the intended effect of crippling the Revolution. With the capture of the city the American capitol was simply moved to Baltimore. The occupation of Philadelphia was a drain on British resources now that France had entered the war which required Britain to send forces throughout the globe, especially to the West Indies. In May 1778 Lord North ordered Gen Clinton (who had replaced Howe) to move his army back to NYC. This presented Washington a golden opportunity to strike against Clinton's 1,500 wagons and long lines of soldiers.

The Battle: MG Charles Lee, Washington's second in command became confused as the battle began and ordered a retreat instead of an advance as he was ordered to do. Washington personally took charge and restored order. Both armies lost hundreds of soldiers due to heatstroke. The overall battle degraded into a series of localized vicious engagements between elements of their whole armies. Due to the poor performance of Lee the opportunity to deal Clinton's army a decisive defeat was lost. The British lost 370 killed and wounded and the Americans 350. More than 400 Germans deserted to the Americans shortly thereafter. As a result of his incompetence Gen Lee was court martialed and found guilty on all counts and cashiered from the army.

Assessment: Draw. The Americans were able to demonstrate they could fight toe to toe with the best of the British Army. However, despite significant losses, the British were able to successfully withdraw to NYC.

Sources:

Bilby, Joseph G. & Katherine Bilby Jenkins. *Monmouth Court House.*
Fleming, Thomas. *Washington's Secret War – The Hidden History of Valley Forge.*
Savas, Theodore P. & J. David Dameron. *A Guide to the Battles of the American Revolution.*
Ward, Christopher. *The War of the Revolution.*

SIEGE OF SAVANNAH GEORGIA

Dates: September 16 - October 9, 1779.

Location: Savannah Harbor, Georgia.

Engaged Forces: 3,000 British: 3,000 American and 4,000 French.

The Situation: From the start of the Revolution to December 1778 Savannah had been occupied by American soldiers. American occupation ended on December 29, 1778 when the British retook the city. A combined French/American effort was undertaken to retake the city starting in September 1779. The French contributed 4,000 soldiers and sailors who were commanded by Admiral Comte d'Estaing. The British forces were commanded by MG Augustine Prevost a well-known and capable combat leader. American forces were led by MG Benjamin Lincoln. After they seized Savannah in 1778 the British had built impressive fortifications, redoubts and trenches so retaking the city from the British was a serious challenge.

The Battle: Although this is called a siege it was not one in the classic sense with communication trenches and parallels. The first effort to take the city by bombardment failed. d'Estaing then opted against the advice of others to take the city by infantry assaults on October 9, 1779 which failed. The famous Polish Count Kazimierz Pulaski who had volunteered his services for America was killed in the assaults and d'Estaing himself was wounded. The Americans lost 250 killed, wounded and captured; the French lost 828 killed and wounded and captured. The British lost 140 killed and wounded. It was one of the most lopsided British victories of the Revolution.

Assessment: A serious defeat for the Americans, which was also a sour note in French-American relations.

Sources:

Mattern, David B. *Benjamin Lincoln and the American Revolution.*

Savas, Theodore P. & J. David Dameron. *A Guide to the Battles of the American Revolution.*

Ward, Christopher. *The War of the Revolution.*

Wilson, David K. *The Southern Strategy. Britain's Conquest of South Carolina and Georgia, 1775-1780.*

SIEGE OF CHARLES TOWN SC

Date: April 18, 1780 – May 12, 1780.

Location: Charles Town South Carolina Harbor and City.

Engaged Forces: 13,500 British soldiers and Sailors; 7,000 Americans.

The Situation: The British were fought to a standstill in the northern states by Washington. General Clinton and the British leadership in London thought the key to winning the war might be in capturing the southern states. This would have to start with the capture of Charles Town, SC. In December 1779 and January 1780, the British landed 13,500 soldiers and sailors from over 90 troop ships below Charles Town with the support of 14 war ships. MG Benjamin Lincoln the commander of American forces in the city had far too few soldiers to defend it.

The Battle: British war ships successfully entered Charles Town harbor and cannonaded the city, setting it on fire. Despite the desperate situation, the city's leaders refused to let Lincoln evacuate his soldiers from the city which was soon surrounded. On May 12th Lincoln surrendered to the British. In November 1780 Lincoln was exchanged for British MG William Phillips and German MG Friedrich Adolph von Riedesel both of whom had been captured at the Battles of Saratoga in October 1777. The British lost 78 killed and 140 wounded with the Americans losing 89 killed, 138 wounded and 6,684 soldiers and sailors captured.

Assessment: The battle was a catastrophe for the Americans. The total Americans killed and captured far exceeded any previous battle of the Revolution. The battle gave the British new hope that defeating the Revolution would come from their new "Southern Campaign".

Sources:

Borick, Carl P. *A GALLANT DEFENSE. The Siege of Charlestown, 1780.*

Ferling, John. *Almost A. Miracle. The American Victory in the War of Independence.*
Mattern, David B. *Benjamin Lincoln and the American Revolution.*
Savas, Theodore P. & J. David Dameron. *A Guide to the Battles of the American Revolution.*
Smith, David. *Camden. The Annihilation of Gates' Grand Army.*
Stephenson, Michael. *Patriot Battles. How the War of Independence was Fought.*
Ward, Christopher. *The War of the Revolution.*
Wilson, David K. *The Southern Strategy. Britain's Conquest of South Carolina and Georgia*

BATTLE OF CAMDEN SC

Date: August 16, 1780.

Location: Camden, South Carolina (South Eastern, SC)

Engaged Forces: 2,238 British soldiers; 3,700 Americans.

The Situation: After the capture of Charles Town in May 1780 General Clinton gave LTG Earl Cornwallis command of all British forces in the southern theatre of operations. Due to the capture of American General Benjamin Lincoln at the Battle of Charles Town, General Horatio Gates was made commander of American southern forces.

The Battle: Advance elements of both armies clashed and the armies withdrew for a major battle at Camden. Gates deployed his forces badly and his army was overwhelmed. He was out flanked by cavalry and his militia fled in the face of British bayonet charges. Gates fled north by horseback and did not stop for 60 miles. The British lost 68 killed and 256 wounded and the Americans lost 250 killed and wounded and 800 captured. MG Nathanael Greene Washington's second in command was named as the replacement for the disgraced Gates.

Assessment: Disastrous defeat for the Americans.

Sources:

Savas, Theodore P. & J. David Dameron. *A Guide to the Battles of the American Revolution.*
Siry, Steven E. *Liberty's Fallen Generals. Leadership and Sacrifice in the American War of Independence.*
Smith, David. *Camden. The Annihilation of Gates' Grand Army.*
Ward, Christopher. *The War of the Revolution.*

BATTLE OF KING'S MOUNTAIN

Date: October 7, 1780.

Location: King's Mountain, South Carolina (Rural NW South Carolina/ North Carolina border).

Engaged Forces: 1,075 British Loyalists: 910 American Militia.

The Situation: British Loyalists from South and North Carolina were emboldened by the British victory at the Battle of Camden. They flocked to the command of British Major Patrick Ferguson who was the leader of Loyalist forces in the region. Ferguson's threats to rampage through the border area brought many America militiamen, especially those called the "Over the Mountain Men" to come together under the command of militia Colonel William Campbell. Ferguson thought he was safe by withdrawing to the top of King's Mountain while waiting for reinforcements from General Cornwallis. In fact, he was vulnerable and became surrounded.

The Battle: Campbell's forces launched simultaneous attacks on all sides of the mountain. It was not long before the mountain top was overrun. Because the Loyalists were shooting from above, they "over shot" (shot too high). This limited the casualties of the American Militia who were advancing up the mountain. Ferguson was killed. The Loyalists lost 244 killed, 163 wounded and 688 captured. The Americans lost 29 killed and 58 wounded.

Assessment: This was a decisive American victory which helped put a huge dent in Loyalist support for the British in the south. The British had badly miscalculated in thinking they would get overwhelming support from Loyalists during their southern campaign.

Sources:

Draper, Lyman C. *King's Mountain and its Heroes.*

Savas, Theodore P. & J. David Dameron. *A Guide to the Battles of the American Revolution.*

Ward, Christopher. *The War of the Revolution.*

BATTLE OF COWPENS

Date: January 17, 1781.

Location: Northwest South Carolina (Near the present city of Spartanburg).

Engaged Forces: 1,100 British: 910 American.

The Situation: The British were determined to make their southern campaign a success despite the Loyalist defeats at King's Mountain and Blackstock's Plantation (November 20, 1780). General Cornwallis sought to destroy General Nathanael Greene's newly appointed southern army command. Contrary to accepted combat doctrine,

Greene divided his inferior force in the face of Cornwallis's greater numbers. Col Daniel Morgan was assigned to command the "Flying Wing" (mobile element) of Greene's army. Cornwallis assigned the job of destroying Morgan to Lt Col Banastre Tarleton.

The Battle: The overly aggressive Tarleton was pursuing Morgan to the near ruin of his own soldiers. Being the pursued, Morgan could pick the battlefield of his choosing. He staged his men in three battle lines; the first consisting of militia whose orders were to fire two shots and retire to the back of the second line of militia marksmen who were given the same order to fire two shots and retire. The third line consisted of battle hardened Continentals who would stand and fight no matter how hard the British charged. Tarleton was over anxious to start the battle and did not give his soldiers a chance to rest or eat before charging at 7AM in the morning. This charge resulted in especially grievous casualties among officers who were targeted by the marksmen. Thinking the first line retreat was a sign of panic the British continued to charge and ran headlong into the second line which inflicted further serious losses on them. Finally, the British reached the Continentals where the battle in many places was hand to hand, bayonet to bayonet and charge and counter-charge. Completely devastated, the British fled to Cornwallis who was 20 miles away. The British lost 100 killed, 200 wounded and 529 captured. The Americans lost 12 killed and 60 wounded. Morgan and his men quickly withdrew from the battlefield with their captives. Cornwallis was very angry and bent on revenge which led to his hell bent for leather pursuit of Morgan and Greene.

Assessment: This was a clear battlefield victory for the Americans. The subsequent ruinous pursuit by Cornwallis of Morgan's men who had joined General Greene after Cowpens set the stage for the victorious Crossing of the Dan River by the Americans.

Sources:

Aaron, Larry. *Crossing the Dan. The Retreat that Saved the American Revolution.*

Babits, Lawrence. *A Devil of a Whipping. The Battle of Cowpens.*

Buchanan, John. *The Road to Guilford Courthouse.*

Higginbotham, Don. *Daniel Morgan, Revolutionary Rifleman.*

Savas, Theodore P. & J. David Dameron. *A Guide to the Battles of the American Revolution.*

Tonsetic, Robert L. *1781. The Decisive Year of the Revolution.*

RACE TO THE DAN RIVER

Dates: January 18 – February 13, 1781.

Locations: Northwest South Carolina (From the Cowpens Battlefield to the north central border of Virginia).

Engaged Forces: 2,036 American: 2,100 British.

The Situation: Cornwallis was determined to avenge the battlefield loss at Cowpens and set out in hot pursuit of Morgan's men who had rejoined General Greene's forces. Any pitched battle would likely have been a disastrous loss by the Americans so Greene fled with utmost speed north to safety in Virginia. At times, the armies were within sight of each other across many swollen rivers. Cornwallis had to destroy his baggage train to help speed his pursuit. Greene destroyed all boats he used at river crossings and deceived Cornwallis into guessing the direction he was going. Both armies suffered terribly from sickness and fatigue. With their last bit of energy, the Americans crossed he Dan River just ahead of Cornwallis who could not ford the flooded river.

Assessment: While this was not a battle per se, the losses suffered by the British were the equivalent of a battlefield loss. Supplies had been burned, horses crippled and destroyed, and his army sick, dispirited and exhausted. Cornwallis had to retreat to Hillsboro, NC for rest and refitting. The Americans were resupplied, re-nourished and reinforced from Virginia and states from the north.

Sources:

Aaron, Larry. *Race to the Dan. The Retreat that Saved the American Revolution.*

Buchanan, John. *The Road to Guilford Courthouse: The American Revolution in the Carolinas.*

BATTLE OF GUILFORD COURTHOUSE

Date: March 15, 1781.

Location: North Central NC (Now known as Greensboro NC).

Engaged Forces: 2,100 British: 4,500 American.

The Situation: General Greene had safely taken his army across the Dan River to be rested, resupplied and reinforced in southern Virginia. General Cornwallis had taken his exhausted army to Hillsboro, NC to be resupplied and rested. With rest and reinforcements Greene moved into North Carolina to do battle with Cornwallis.

The Battle: General Greene developed a battlefield plan similar to what Morgan had at Cowpens and staged his men in three lines. Greene's soldiers fired devastating volleys into the advancing British. Desperate close quarters fighting erupted. At one point Cornwallis ordered his artillery to fire into the struggling melee knowing he would be killing some of his own men in the process. In another incident,

Cornwallis had to be evacuated from the battlefield to avoid being captured. Eventually Greene knew he had done all he could and withdrew. The British lost 93 killed, 413 wounded and 26 missing; the Americans lost 70 killed, 185 wounded and 46 missing.

Assessment: Despite the fact that Cornwallis retained the battlefield, he suffered ruinous losses, especially among key officers. It was another example of how the Americans could stand and fight, inflict grievous losses and depart to fight again. With the string of losses at King's Mountain, Cowpens, Race to the Dan and now Guilford Courthouse, Cornwallis then began to believe success would come from moving north. This led him to invade Virginia and the catastrophe at Yorktown which ultimately ended the war against the Americans.

Sources:

Buchanan, John. *The Road to Guilford Courthouse.*

Nelson, James A. *George Washington's Great Gamble and the Sea Battle that Won the American Revolution.*

Savas, Theodore P. & J. David Dameron. *A Guide to the Battles of the American Revolution.*

Tonsetic, Robert L. *1781. The Decisive Year of the Revolution.*

Ward, Christopher. *The War of the Revolution.*

NAVAL BATTLE OF THE CAPES

Dates: September 5-8, 1781.

Location: Off Chesapeake Bay, Virginia.

Engaged Forces: The British - 27 ships, 13,000 sailors and 1,400 guns: The French - 23 ships, 18,000 sailors and 1,600 guns.

The Situation: The American Revolution was on the brink of collapse and disintegration. Officers and men had gone for years without pay. There were recent mutinies of major units in Pennsylvania, Connecticut and New Jersey. Northerners were refusing to deploy south because they thought they would be protecting slavery which they abhorred. They also were reluctant to be exposed to the tropical diseases more common to the south. People from the southern states disliked and distrusted the people from the northern states who for them practiced too "democratic" forms of life. Soldiers from the northern states elected their officers which appalled those from the south. Washington needed a winner take all victory to salvage the Revolution or it would implode. Ultimately, he realized that such a victory would have to come with a battle with Cornwallis who was in southern Virginia, but not yet trapped at Yorktown. Washington could surround him on land but could not prevent him from being either reinforced or evacuated by sea. He needed the assistance of the French Army to encircle him on land and the French Navy to defeat the British Navy to prevent Cornwallis' reinforcement or evacuation by sea. There was dissention in the senior leadership of the British Navy in America. There was little cooperation between British Admirals Rodney, Arbuthnot and Hood. By seniority Rodney was in overall command much to the displeasure of Hood and Arbuthnot. On July 4, 1781 Admiral Thomas Graves was given command of the British fleet in America. There was no such "friction" in the French and American leadership. The French Navy in American waters was under the command of French Admiral Compte de Grasse. Early on, French General Rochambeau ordered Admiral de Grasse to move his fleet from the West Indies to the Chesapeake Bay. Washington deceived Clinton into thinking he was going to attack NYC but instead moved his forces to southern Virginia to trap Cornwallis.

The Naval Battle: On September 1, 1781 British Admiral Sir Thomas Graves sailed his fleet south from NYC in search of the French fleet. On August 30, 1781 Admiral, de Grasse arrived from the West Indies at Lynnhaven on the Chesapeake and began debarking 3,200 French soldiers and Marines to aid in the entrapment of Cornwallis. Admiral Graves arrived unexpectedly with his fleet at Lynnhaven on September 5th just as de Grasse was disembarking his troops and resupplying his ships. Leaving as many as 1,200 soldiers and sailors ashore de Grasse immediately got underway. As is usual in naval battles both fleets maneuvered for advantage, especially trying to get the "Weather Gauge" (the up-wind position) which could steal the wind from the downwind enemy's ability to maneuver. Neither fleet was able to come to engage completely so the contest degraded into multiple battles of portions of their fleets. Admiral Graves gave confusing commands to his ship captains via his signal flags, which to this day are the subject of analysis and controversy. Both fleets inflicted serious damage on each other. The British 74-gun ship *TERRIBLE* was so severely damaged it was burned and scuttled. On September 11th Admiral Graves sailed his damaged fleet back to NYC. Graves was accused of dragging his feet in repairing his fleet in New York to avoid confronting de Grasse again. After more than a month of repairs Admiral Graves set out with 5,000 soldiers on October 19th from NYC to rescue Cornwallis. He arrived at the entrance to the Chesapeake on October 24th only to be told that Cornwallis had surrendered his army a week earlier. Graves immediately dispatched one of his ships, the *RATTLESNAKE,* to take the bad news to London.

Assessment: A near draw on the water, but a catastrophe for the British once their fleet left for repairs in NYC. The battle could not have been managed worse by the British. It was a clear case of confusion brought on by ego centric Admirals and Generals who were more interested in their legacies than in committing themselves to attain victory. The departure of Graves from the Capes to NYC and his subsequent foot dragging in making repairs to his fleet doomed Cornwallis.

Sources:

Nelson James L. *George Washington's Greatest Gamble and the Sea Battle that Won the American Revolution.*

Savas, Theodore P. & J. David Dameron. *A Guide to the Battles of the American Revolution.*

Tuchman, Barbara W. *The First Salute. A View of the American Revolution.*

BATTLE (SIEGE) OF YORKTOWN

Dates: September 28 – October 17, 1781.

Location: Yorktown, Virginia (Southeast coast of Virginia).

Engaged Forces: 8,000 British soldiers, sailors and Germans: 8,845 American soldiers and 7,800 French soldiers.

The Situation: After failing to secure the states of South and North Carolina and suffering a series of costly defeats in the process, LTG Cornwallis in the absence of clear orders from Clinton moved north into southern Virginia. Cornwallis needed a good coastal port to be either evacuated or reinforced by sea. He initially chose Portsmouth, but on the advice of his engineers he moved down to Yorktown which had deeper waters for ships, although it had the disadvantage of presenting the possibility of him becoming trapped there. General Clinton then proceeded to issue a series of contradictory orders: First: For Cornwallis to send reinforcements to NYC and Second: To stay in place and await reinforcements from NYC. General Washington appeared to want to attack Clinton in NYC, but was dissuaded from doing so by French General Rochambeau whose army had been stationed in Rhode Island. The prospect, however remote, of being attacked by Washington, made the paranoid Clinton hunker down in NYC. In the meantime, Washington and Rochambeau stole a march on Clinton and headed south for an as yet and hoped for climatic battle with Cornwallis. The longer Cornwallis stayed in Yorktown the better it appeared he could be trapped there which caused American forces to converge on southeast Virginia. By the time Clinton learned Washington was headed south with Rochambeau it was too late for him to intercede. He was forced to decide whether to reinforce Cornwallis or evacuate him. The French success at the naval Battle of the Capes (September 5-8, 1781) precluded any realistic possibility of Clinton reinforcing or evacuating Cornwallis by sea.

The Battle (Siege): With great good fortune French Admiral de Barras was able to sail from Rhode Island past the British fleets on the open seas without being intercepted to bring critically needed siege cannon to the area of Yorktown. Using classic siege warfare tactics with communication trenches and advancing parallels the French and Americans were able to bring artillery in range of the British positions at Yorktown. The siege was made easier by the soft soil which made digging of trenches easier than normal. The artillery bombardment began when Washington touched off the first round on October 6th. The bombardment got worse as artillery was moved closer and closer and new trenches and revetments were built. Knowing that reinforcements were not possible Cornwallis on October 16th tried a breakout by attempting to send his forces across the Bay of Gloucester at night by barges and large boats. The effort was ruined by a late-night storm. A series of successful French and American infantry attacks on the British redoubts around the town sealed Cornwallis' fate. His army was facing around the clock bombardment, sickness, and starvation with no prospect for relief in sight. He offered to surrender on October 17, 1781 which was accepted by Washington and Rochambeau. The British lost 156 killed, 326 wounded and 7,157 captured. French losses were 52 killed and 134 wounded. Americans lost 23 killed and 65 wounded.

Assessment: This was a catastrophic defeat for the British. It made winning the war to defeat the American Revolution politically impossible in Britain and militarily impossible in America.

Sources:

Greene, Jerome A. *The Guns of Independence.*
Hallahan, William H. *The Day the Revolution Ended.*
Leepson, Marc. *Lafayette, Lessons in Leadership from the Idealist General.*
Lockhart, Paul. *The Drillmaster of Valley Forge, The Baron de Steuben.*
Savas, Theodore P. & J. David Dameron. *A Guide to the Battles of the American* Revolution.
Tuchman, Barbara W. *The First Salute. A View of the American Revolution.*
Tucker, Glenn. *"Mad" Anthony Wayne and the New Nation.*
Ward, Christopher. *The War of the Revolution.*

BIBLIOGRAPHY

The following books from my personal library on the American Revolution are the source material for this document. As I read and learn more, additional material and sources will be added. The "**Summaries**" are entirely mine and are in no way endorsed by the Sons of the American Revolution or any other individual or organization.

Aaron, Larry. *The Race to the Dan; The Retreat That Rescued the American Revolution.* Halifax County Historical Society, South Boston, VA. Published 2007, 222 pages.

Summary: This excellent book uniquely presents the critical retreat to the Dan River by General Greene after the Battle of Cowpens through narrative, biographies and memoires of participants. It describes in considerable detail the chess game between Cornwallis and Greene in the 200 + mile journey from the battle to Virginia which tested the endurance of the soldiers of both armies to their absolute limits. Not only did Greene outlast Cornwallis but he out witted him several times over. This book helps elevate the Dan River Crossing to the group of the most critical events of the American Revolution.

Alden, John R. *A History of the American Revolution.* De Capo Press, New York, NY. Published 1969, 557 pages.

Summary: This is not a "survey" book of the Revolution. It covers the period from 1763 through 1789. It is well written and very readable. It has details without being confusing. Unlike some books, it does not dwell on arcane thoughts and policies. Its strengths are in recording the social and economic conditions of both America and Britain. A book like this which covers the pre-war, conflict period and post war era must have some "light" spots. It is "light" on POWs and the Major John Andre'/General Benedict Arnold treason affair but it is hardly possible for any single book to cover every aspect of such a world changing event that lasted over a period of 30 years without having soft spots. This book is highly recommended for anyone who wants a serious but very readable single volume on the Revolution. It shows the: who's, where's, when's and how's of the event. The book's Bibliography is different in that it is organized by time and subject and is lightly annotated. Overall the book is excellent.

____________. *The American Revolution.* Harper and Row Publishers, New York, NY. Published 1954, 293 pages

Summary: The book has annotated book notes which are useful. It has an excellent account of the flawed decision making by British leaders in London and British Generals and Howe regarding the attack south from Canada via Lake Champlain to Albany NY. There was no clear plan agreed by all and no coordination between the major players before or after the start of the operation. The author makes the interesting assertion that that capture of the waterway from Canada to Albany was not worth the effort or risk by the British. They did not have enough soldiers to prevent cross communication from the Northern Colonies which was the stated objective. In reality, most of the land cross communication of supplies and soldiers between the northern and lower colonies by the Americans was done below Albany, NY.

Allen, Ethan. *The Narrative of Colonel Ethan Allen by Himself.* Bennington. Published March 25, 1779, 124 pages.

Summary: This book was written by Ethan Allen himself to chronicle his mistreatment as a British Prisoner Of War for 953 days. It was intended to, and did, expose for America and the world to see how Britain was effectively murdering American prisoners through deprivation, starvation, abuse and in some cases torture. This book shows Allen was genuinely brilliant, despite not having a formal education. He was a prolific pamphleteer second only to Thomas Paine during the Revolution.

Allen, Thomas B. *Tories, Fighting for the King in America's First Civil War.* HarperCollins Publishers, 10 East 53rd St., New York, NY. Published 2010, 468 pages.

Summary: In many ways this book could be a substitute for a detailed general history of the American Revolution. It shows that the Tories were almost completely involved in all aspects of the Revolution so the book is the story of the Revolution from start to its ending. The author attempts to debunk the generally accepted assertion that 1/3 of the American populace were Rebels, 1/3 uncommitted and 1/3 Tories. Allen's research shows that the Rebels and Tories each had no more than 20% of the population and the uncommitted 60% who would tilt either way as the War ebbed and flowed.

Anderson, Mark R. *The Battle for the Fourteenth Colony. America's War of Liberation in Canada: 1774-1776.* University Press of England. Published 2011, 356 pages.

Summary: This book has considerable value from the fact that it adds new perspective of the campaigns to capture Canada. It shows that the Canadians were in a similar dilemma as American Indians. If they sided with the British, the Americans would attack them and if they sided with the Americans the British would attack them. Frankly, most wanted no part of the conflict. The book shows how important the St. Lawrence River was to all parties concerned.

Archer, Richard. *As If an Enemy's Country: The British Occupation of Boston and the Origins of the Revolution.* Oxford University Press, New York, NY. Published 2010, 284 pages.

Summary: The focus of this book is not on the military aspects of the Revolution. This book works to understand the depth of the emotions that would lead tens of thousands of American soldiers to fight without pay, no uniforms and little sustenance against the British. This book helps to bring that into focus. It concentrates on the beginning of the struggle in Boston and how the independence effort took root there. It shows how the British made the huge mistake of sending four regiments of soldiers to Boston in 1768 which was more than twice the number needed for basic security. The "friction" between local residents and British soldiers of this unnecessary force which lacked quarters and proper logistics, helped bring about the high-level developments that led to the outbreak of violence between the soldiers and residents of Boston. This is a good book that should be acquired and read by any serious reader of the Revolution.

Aron, Paul. *FOUNDING FEUDS. The Rivalries, Clashes, and Conflicts That Forged a Nation.* Source Books, Williamsburg, VA. Published 2016.

Summary: The vast majority of the conflicts detailed in this book occurred in the Post-Revolutionary period. However, it does contain a nice piece on General Washington and his slave Harry Washington who escaped in 1771 from Washington's work in the Dismal Swamp. In the summer of 1776 Harry Washington joined the British and served with them in the far south. Initially, General Washington in 1776 prohibited the enlistment of slaves in the American Army who had escaped their owners. However, later that year, desperate for recruits, he allowed the enlistment of black freemen who helped swell the American ranks. Harry Washington escaped from Charles Town SC to New York City when the British evacuated the city in 1782. The conflict in this case was between British LTG Guy Carleton and General Washington over the evacuation of Blacks with British troops. The Peace of Paris of 1783 prohibited the British from withdrawing the Blacks that had served with them. General Washington regretfully agreed to let many Blacks depart America with the British mostly because he did not have the means to stop it. Harry escaped from New York City in the Fall of 1783 to Nova Scotia with many British where he remained until 1792 and then left for Sierra Leone in Africa where he remained until sometime in 1780.

Babbitts, Lawrence E. *A Devil of a Whipping: The Battle of Cowpens.* University of North Carolina Press, NC. Published 1988, 231 pages.

Summary: Of the many books on the Revolution this is one of just a handful that deserves the notation MUST READ by all serious readers of the struggle between America and Britain. It teaches tactics, leadership at the unit and strategic levels, and battlefield management. It shows how Colonel Morgan out-thought and out-generaled Banastre Tarleton. It gets down into the "weeds" of how units were structured to fight and how their weapons were used. It is a classic example of the integration of militia and continental soldiers to maximum effect. The British should have learned from the lessons that Morgan taught them at this battle. The book also has an excellent "Order of Battle". The book also points out Tarleton's mistakes of failing to let his exhausted men nourish and rest themselves before rushing into the battle. This is the kind of book that should be required reading by all aspiring military officers.

Bennett, David. *A Few Lawless Vagabonds. Ethan Allen, The Republic of Vermont and the American Revolution.* CASEMATE Publishers, Havertown, PA. Published 2014, 276 pages.

Summary: This book paints Allen as nothing more than a self-promoter who was mostly out of control. The book says he was hardly a true patriot. The book jumps from one date to another which makes it hard to determine what happened when. It has next to nothing to say about Allen's 953 days as a POW in Britain, Canada and New York City. It brands Allen as someone who tried to negotiate with the British for selfish gains. The truth is that Allen was playing a very difficult game of playing off against each other, the "Yorkers", British, New Hampshireites and Continental Congress to preserve Vermont. Allen negotiated with the British to secure the release of American POWs the British had captured in raids along the shores of Lake Champlain. Allen also made it appear he was making a deal with the British in Canada to pressure officials in New York and New Hampshire to begin to accept the fact that the area between the two states needed to become a separate state. The book seems to be well researched, but draws conclusions that are not supported by the author's own facts.

Berkin, Carol. *Revolutionary Mothers. Women in the Struggle for America's Independence.* Vintage Books, New York, NY. Published 2005, 194 pages.

Summary: More American women supported the Revolutionary cause than supported the Crown. Female supporters of the Revolution collected clothing, made uniforms, ran fund drives, donated their own personal jewelry and collected food for the troops. The American women suffered mightily during the War. Rape by German and British soldiers was prevalent, but greatly under reported due to the humiliation of making it public. Female supporters of the war frequently had no other option than to become "camp followers" which was a miserable existence. They heroically performed dangerous duties such as nurses in hospitals where infectious diseases were common, serving as spies and couriers and collectors of intelligence. There are also documented cases where women performed heroically in direct combat. This book should be added to any Revolutionary War library.

Bilby, Joseph G. & Katherine Bilby Jenkins. *Monmouth Court House; The Battle that Made the American Army.* Westholme Publishing, LLC., Yardley, PA. Published 2010, 310 pages.

Summary: From the start this book MUST BE READ by any and every serious reader of the Revolution. The first three chapters give an excellent very readable account of the War in New Jersey from the beginning to the start of the Battle of Monmouth Court House in June 1778. Chapter 4 is a superb tutorial on tactics, training, muskets, rifles, bayonets, artillery, uniforms, firing procedures and more. This information is supplemented with actual test information to confirm its accuracy, including rates of fire and speed of loading. Even if someone is not interested in the Battle of Monmouth Court House they should acquire the book to get information in Chapter Four. The actual battle starts with Chapter Five. The book goes on to show that Philadelphia was no longer affordable by the British from the standpoint of resources and manpower. The movement of tens of thousands of soldiers and 1,500 wagons from Philadelphia to New York presented a golden opportunity for a great victory by Washington. However, MG Charles Lee who was in operational command repeatedly gave confusing orders which resulted in a lost opportunity for the Americans to inflict a severe defeat on British General Clinton.

Blackmon, Richard D. *Dark and Bloody Ground; The American Revolution on the Southern Frontier.* Westholme Publishing, LLC, Yardley, PA. Published 2013, 215 pages.

Summary: This book concentrates on the American Indian situation in the south. Despite the serious efforts by the author to clarify locations, rivers, and American Indian tribes it becomes very difficult to determine who was doing what or where. Partly to address this problem the book contains a good number of maps showing rivers whose names have likely changed over time and are not currently so identified. The American Indians were in an impossible position. They were being used by the British and American Rebels to their detriment. The American Indians were equally at war with each other so there was no unity which diluted their efforts on either side of the conflict. Due to the never-ending number of tribes who fought over land that is not easily identified, the book is a difficult read, although it is extremely well done in face of these difficulties. This book is probably one of the premier books on Indians and the American Revolution.

Bobrick, Benson. *Angel in the Whirlwind.* Penguin Books, New York, NY. Published 1997, 553 pages.

Summary: Although John Alden's *A History of the American* Revolution mentioned above has some similarities to this book they have enough differences to make it worthwhile to read them both. Bobrick's book essentially ends with the Treaty of Paris 1783 while Alden's goes through 1789. Bobrick's book has more detail. For example: it has a paragraph on Jews in the American Revolution who numbered about 3,000 and mostly supported the rebel American cause. It also contains information about spying not covered elsewhere. Its account of the Arnold/Andre' affair, while not faultless, is far better than Alden's. It's a long book but worthwhile for a serious reader of the Revolution.

Bonnel, Ulane. *The French Navy and the American War of Independence.* Commemorative Brochure by The Ambassador of France, Bicentennial of the American Revolution. November 8, 1975, Paris, France, 18 pages.

Summary: This is an excellent article on the contributions of the French Navy to the American Revolution. It covers the strengths and weaknesses of the French and British Navies and the strategic situation that existed during the Revolution. The article also discusses the methods the Spanish Navy used with the French Navy to achieve ultimate success.

Borick, Carl P. *A Gallant Defense. The Siege of Charleston, 1780.* University of South Carolina Press, SC. Published 2003, 332 pages.

Summary: This good book goes a long way in vindicating the reputation of Gen Benjamin Lincoln who has far too often been maligned as a poor general in charge of the defense of Charles Town. He faced an almost impossible situation with too few soldiers defending overwhelming British and German forces. Unlike the 1776 successful American defense of Charles Town where the British were unable to penetrate the seaward defenses of the city; in this case the British brought their ships into the inner harbor which enabled them to bombard the city. The enemy forces from the land effectively surrounded the city. Lincoln was an activist general who used every trick to defeat the enemy. He could see that defeat was at hand and wanted to withdraw his soldiers before they became trapped. However, the South Carolina Governor John Rutledge and city leaders all but demanded he fight off the enemy which resulted in the capture of the largest number of American during the whole war. He became a POW and was ultimately exchanged for British Major General William Phillips who had been captured at the Battle of Saratoga in October 1777. Officers aspiring to senior levels should read this book to learn how Lincoln creatively used every possible technique to successively defend the city. The book has excellent annotated Chapter End Notes and an extensive bibliography.

___________. *Relieve Us of This Burthen. American Prisoners of War in the Revolutionary South, 1780-1782.* University of South Carolina, South Carolina University Press, SC. Published 2012, 170 pages.

Summary: This is a companion book by Borick mentioned above. Six thousand American Continental soldiers, militia and seamen were captured during the siege of Charles Town SC. Throughout the South, Charles Town became the hub for captive Americans. While the book does not give more definitive numbers, it goes on to say THOUSANDS of American POWs in Charles Town died because of the abuse they endured during their captivity. The general accepted number is approximately 2,000. Obsolete troop transport ships in Charles Town Harbor were used as holding pens just as they were in New York City. By the summer of 1780 the British were severely short of soldiers which caused them, unlike those held in NYC, to offer to exchange American POWs for British POWs. This "hot potato" was handed to Gen Washington who opposed exchange but passed the buck to the Continental Congress who decided against the exchange offers. Unlike the situation in NYC there were sizeable numbers of American POWs who escaped from their captivity from the barracks at Haddrell's Point. The British also offered freedom to those held in and around Charleston in exchange for their service in the British Navy, which was mostly declined. All serious readers of the Revolution should read both of Borick's books.

Borneman, Walter R. *American Spring. Lexington, Concord and the Road to Revolution.* Little, Brown and Company, New York, NY. Published 2014, 469 pages.

Summary: This book is more story telling than history. It is well written and easily readable. It gives the American perspective to the reasons why the New Englanders were so opposed to the British presence in the Colonies.

____________. *The French and Indian War, Deciding the Fate of America.* HarperCollins Publishing, 10 East 53 St., New York, NY. Published 2006, 359 pages.

Summary: This book provides a good understanding of the French and Indian War and how it was a prelude to the American Revolution. It is a good book and an easy read. Many of the generals who fought with the British during the French and Indian War subsequently fought for the American cause during the Revolution.

Bowler, R. Arthur. *Logistics and the Failure of the British Army in America 1775-1783*. Princeton University Press, NJ. Printed 1975, 291 pages.

Summary: This superb book, expensive as it is ($79.00 used) goes a long way to explain the failure of the British to exploit great opportunities to take the initiative to crush the American Revolution. The personal caution of both Howe and Clinton was heightened by the tenuous logistics situation of the British Army in America. They were afraid to take the initiative for fear they might run out of supplies, especially food if they did not have at least six months' reserves which was rarely the case. They could not sustain their Army from local American sources because they did not occupy enough land to do so. If they obtained food by plundering local citizens, they turned these otherwise neutral Americans into active supporters and enemies of the British. The crisis of British logistics during the American Revolution was in a large part caused by fundamental erroneous assumptions made by senior British leaders at the start of the war. They assumed they could overwhelm the Americans with a quick victory and thus did not think from the start there was a need to develop a robust logistics system. They erroneously assumed the logistics system used for the French and Indian War in America would suffice for the Revolution. These were two highly different situations. They falsely assumed large supplies could be obtained from the American land and economy. They way over estimated the support they would get from American Loyalists. They underestimated the difficulties of a large-scale logistics operation across a three-thousand-mile ocean in the face of severe weather, the American privateers and Navy. The significance of British logistics problems merits a separate and detailed section in this document. The book addressed the corruption of the British commissaries it did not mention David Sproate and Joshua Loring who were the notoriously corrupt commissaries for the thousands of American Naval and Army POWs held in NYC "Sugar Houses" and Death Ships.

Braisted, Todd W. *Grand Forage 1788. The Battleground Around New York City.* Westholme Publishing, Yardley, PA. Published 2016, 223 pages.

Summary: This book shows how the confused fighting around New York City contributed to the British foraging operations to obtain critically needed supplies. It is hard to believe that a book that has Foraging in its title would not site Arthur Bowler's *Logistics and the Failure of the British Army in America* as a source!

Brandt, Clare. *The Man in the Mirror; A life of Benedict Arnold.* Random House, New York, NY. Published 1994, 364 pages.

Summary: This book is one of the better biographies of Benedict Arnold. Unfortunately, it does not provide a crystal-clear account of the Andre'/Arnold affair, which is admittedly complicated and subject to interpretation because it was a highly secretive event at that time. The book does not delve in sufficient depth into Andre's disobedience of Clinton's orders. Andre' was instructed by Clinton to **have the order delivered** to the Captain of the HMS *VULTURE* to move the ship south down to Dobb's Ferry. Instead, Andre' personally delivered the order to the ship. If Andre' had stayed at Dobbs Ferry and the Captain of the ship had moved the *VULTURE* south to Dobbs as he was ordered to do, Andre' could never have been stranded behind American lines and captured. Read this book and then read Carl Van Doren's *Secret History* and you'll get the true story of the betrayal of Arnold and his actions with Andre'.

Bratten, John R. *The Gondola PHILADELPHIA, and the Battle of Lake Champlain.* Texas A&M University, Austin, TX. Published 2002, 235 pages.

Summary: This is a good book about Benedict Arnold's critical role in the important Battle of Valcour Island. As is indicated in its title, the book focuses on the USN ship *PHILDELPHIA* which was built under the direction of General Benedict Arnold on Lake Champlain in response to British General Sir Lord Carleton's movement down the lake during the fall of 1776. The value of the book really comes from the realization of how complex it was to build a ship in those times. The parts list is incredibly long and detailed. In 1935 the ship was raised from the bottom of Lake Champlain where it sank after the battle. The ship can be viewed at the Smithsonian Museum in Washington, D.C. This book also educates the reader how difficult it is to do modern battlefield archeology.

Breen, T. H. *American Insurgents, American Patriots, The Revolution of The People.* Hill and Wang, 18 West St., New York, NY. Published 2010, 337 pages.

Summary: This book explains the feelings, especially among those in New England, of "rage militiare". This was the feeling that the situation had to be settled by force of arms. It was recognized that successful resistance required communication and cooperation between the colonies which gave birth to the "Committees of Communication and Cooperation". Demographics played a part in events. America was doubling its population every 25 years. During the Revolution 50% of the colonists were less than 16 years of age. America was very different from Europe. Ownership of land was much higher in America than Europe. New England had a literacy level of 80%. The book has good coverage how religion played into the outbreak of the Revolution. All this shows how during the two years before the Revolution (1774-1776) America morphed from an insurgency to a full-fledged revolution. This book is not for the casual reader of the Revolution. It is full of philosophical material that makes it a hard read.

Brown, Wallace. *The Good Americans, The Loyalists in the Revolution.* William Morrow and Company, New York, NY. Published 1969, 302 pages.

Summary: The book explores the specific motivations of Loyalists to stay the course with George III rather than supporting the Revolution. For many it was money. They could see that they would be financially better off under the Crown than not. For others, it was resistance to change. Many thought the Crown as their heritage. They saw American rebels as radicals rather than revolutionary reformers. The book shows the conditions the British POWs and captive loyalists experienced in the copper mines of Simsbury Connecticut. The book chronicles the financial losses the loyalists experienced after they left America. Free transportation was provided Loyalists who left America and compensation for the material and financial losses they experienced. The resettlement of loyalists to Canada cost Britain an estimated 30 million pounds. Many former Loyalists were given lifetime annuities for their support of the Crown. The book shows that Loyalists many times over paid a dear price for their choice to stay with the Crown. The book also shows how religion was a factor in Loyalist tendencies to stay with the Crown.

Buchanan, John. *The Road to Guilford Courthouse, The American Revolution in the Carolinas.* John Wiley and Sons, 605 3rd Ave., New York, NY. Published 1997, 452 pages.

Summary: This book covers in great detail how the American Revolution was won in the south. It shows the threads between the battles of Sullivan's Island, Charles Town, Camden, King's Mountain, Cowpens, Race to the Dan and Guilford Courthouse. The American commander Nathaniel Greene tried at Guilford to emulate the successful tactics used by Daniel Morgan at Cowpens. However, the circumstances were different. General Cornwallis was almost captured on the battlefield. He had to use exploding shells over the heads of his own soldiers to stop the Americans. In the end, Greene left the battlefield but the British suffered irreplaceable casualties. The needed replacements could never come from General Clinton. This is probably the best currently researched and written book of Britain's southern campaign.

Buker, George E. *The Penobscot Expedition, Commodore Saltonstall and the Massachusetts Conspiracy of 1779.* Down East Books, Camden, Maine. Published 2002, 204 pages.

Summary: In July 1779 the Americans launched their largest amphibious assault against the British during the Revolution. The mission was to capture the British forts in and around Penobscot in the territory of Maine. The expedition was commanded by Commodore Dudley Saltonstall from start to finish. The American fleet consisted of 21 transports, 6 armed brigs, 9 armed privateers, and two armed sloops and nearly 2,000 soldiers and marines. This was the largest U.S. Marine Corps land based action of the Revolution. The expedition resulted in catastrophe with nearly all ships lost. The thesis of this book is that Saltonstall was unfairly blamed for the disaster. It is true he was railroaded by his subordinate Army commanders after the disaster but he was in command and by no possible measure can he be absolved of his full responsibility for the event.

Buker, Nick. *An EMPIRE on EDGE.* Alfred A. Knoff, New York, NY. Published in 2014, 429 pages.

Summary: This book chronicles in multiple ways the way Britain miss-managed its finances from the 17th Century onward through the end of the American Revolution. It did this at home, in America and throughout its whole empire. Corruption was rife and funds were squandered. Wars were funded on loans that could never be repaid. Britain made fundamentally flawed assumptions about how much revenue could be obtained from taxes in America. They made equally flawed assumptions about their ability to force Americans to bend to Britain's will. The costs of Britain's Army and Navy escalated just as its world-wide commitment grew larger and larger. The book has a lengthy and excellent account of how tea came to be an important rupture between Britain and America. The book concludes with the start of the Revolution. It is a somewhat difficult read for anyone whose focus is not solely on the finances of the pre-Revolutionary years.

Burrows, Edwin G. *Forgotten Patriots; The Untold Story of American Prisoners During the Revolutionary War.* Perseus Books Group, 387 Park Ave., New York, NY. Published 2008, 364 pages.

Summary: There will never be a better book than this one on American Revolutionary POWs. It is meticulously researched and documented. It has over 60 pages of "End Notes" for documentation. Read this book to get a full appreciation of how so many Americans suffered and died at the hands of their British captors. An American who was captured had a 60+% chance of dying from the abuse meted out by the British. Americans under Washington's leadership took the high moral road and treated British and German captives with great humanity. It was hoped that this would result in the British treating Americans similarly, which was a false hope. It is a bothersome fact that our leaders did not attempt to hold accountable those who were responsible for the atrocities committed against our POWs. The Treaty of Paris talks did not even rate the final resolution of the POW situation as a high priority. This book should be another MUST READ by all students of the Revolution.

Butler, Judge Ed. *Galvez. Spain – Our Forgotten Ally In The American Revolutionary War: A Concise Summary of Spain's Assistance.* Southwest Historic Press, San Antonio, TX. Published 2014, 301 pages.

Summary: Judge Butler served as President General of the Sons of the American Revolution from 2009 to 2010 and is credited with raising the consciousness of historians and Americans alike to the major contributions that Spain made to the success of the American Revolution. It is now recognized that without Spain's assistance the Revolution would likely have failed. This book details the financial, logistical and direct military assistance provided by Spain which enabled American Rebels to survive and win against the British Army and Navy which were recognized as the most powerful in the world at that time. In fact, the assistance provided by Spain rivals that provided by France. Spain's involvement was motivated largely to regain what she lost to the British during the French and Indian War. In the end, like France despite being on the winning team, Spain paid a severe financial price for supporting the American cause and never realized the territorial gains she had hoped for. Its Index is difficult to use because individuals are listed first by rank, then first name and last name. For example: If you want to find references to John Paul Jones he will not be listed under Jones or John but under the letter "C" for Captain John Paul Jones. If you don't know an individual's rank or title rank, you'll not be able to find him or her in the Index. Despite these problems, the book is otherwise a significant contribution to the body of knowledge of the history of the American Revolution.

Carbone, Gerald M. *Nathanael Greene, The Remarkable Life of an Unsung Hero of the American Revolution.* Palgrave MacMillan, 175 5th St., New York, NY. Published 2008, 268 pages.

Summary: Nathanael Greene does not get the credit he deserves for his contributions to the American Revolution. He was a self-educated

Quaker from Rhode Island who had a knack for leadership and organization from his earliest days. As head of the Quartermaster Corps, a job he hated, he was responsible for saving the Revolution from ruin for lack of supplies and material. He went on to become Washington's second in command and led the American southern army to repeated victories over the British which ultimately set the stage for America's triumphal battle at Yorktown.

Carlisle, Rodney P. (General Editor) *One Day In History, The Days That Changed History, July 4, 1776.* Harper-Collins Publishers, New York, NY. Published 2006, 272 pages.

Summary: This book is a collection of 255 essays on events and prominent people of the Revolution. It concentrates on the events surrounding July 4th. It has brief histories of each of the 13 colonies which are useful.

Carrington, Henry B. *Battles of the American Revolution 1775-1781.* Promotion Press, New York, NY. Published 1887 (originally two volumes), 712 pages.

Summary: This is a "must read" book of the battles of the Revolution written in the traditional old style of 19th Century historians. The most informative chapters are one through fourteen. They describe the laws of war during the Revolution, logistics, tactics and strategy. The book describes the "run-up" to each battle in detail. The accounts of the battles are "personalized" by quotes attributed to the participants. It contains excellent maps of the battle fields along with many "Orders of Battle". There are no Footnotes or End Notes and the Bibliography is sparse. However, the Index is massive and is especially useful.

Cecere, Michael. *Wedded to My Sword, The Revolutionary War Service of Light Horse Harry Lee.* Heritage Books, 100 Railroad Ave., Westminster, MD. Published 2012, 303 pages.

Summary: Right from the start this is a refreshing work by a contemporary historian who uses "Footnotes" vs "Endnotes". Having come from a distinguished family of Virginians Harry Lee used his connections to get appointed a captain of Virginia dragoons in June 1776. He first served in combat under Washington in the "Forage Wars" (January – March 1777) in northern New Jersey. He continually distinguished himself and came to the attention of Gen Washington who offered Lee the prestigious position of aide-de-camp. Lee graciously declined preferring to personally lead his men in battle. He later proved invaluable in the service of Gen Greene in defeating the British in several battles. He resigned from the Army in a dispute over perceived disrespect for his services. His service to Virginia and our new Republic continued during his three terms as Governor of Virginia after the war. Due to bad land investments, he spent two years in debtor prison (1809-1811). He then fled to the West Indies where he spent five years. He returned to Georgia in 1818 and soon thereafter died. He was no relation to MG Charles Lee of the American army but he was in fact the father of Robert E. Lee of Civil War fame. Cecere has written numerous books on the American Revolution and it is hoped they are all as good as this one.

Chadwick, Bruce. *The First American Army. The Untold Story of George Washington and the Men behind America's First Fight for Freedom*. Sourcebooks, Inc., Naperville, IL. Published 2005, 399 pages.

This book chronicles in their own words the Revolutionary War experiences of four enlisted soldiers, two officers, one doctor and one chaplain. The real value of the book is in the detail of the doctor and chaplain during the War. The horrific situation of thousands of wounded and sick soldiers during the failed 1775 attack towards Canada almost defies description. Neither the chaplain nor doctor had the resources to provide the basic means of solace or care for these soldiers who died miserable deaths by the hundreds at a time.

How or why the American Army held together during this time is nothing short of a miracle.

Chartrand, Rene'. *Forts of the American Revolution.* Osprey Publishing, Oxford Britain. Published 2016, 64 pages.

Summary: This excellent short book gives brief histories with illustrations of all the forts and sieges of the American Revolution. It has a very helpful Glossary of the terms regarding forts and sieges.

Chernow, Ron. *Alexander Hamilton.* Penguin Press, 375 Hudson St., New York, NY. Published 2004, 848 pages.

Summary: This is probably the best single volume biography that will ever be written about this truly remarkable individual, who was raised fatherless in poverty in the West Indies and who overcame incredible adversity to rise to great heights through grit and god given talents. He became Washington's personal secretary, then a combat hero, and ultimately America's first Secretary of the Treasury. His financial fingerprints are still present on America's fiscal system very much to our Nation's benefit. There is speculation that he might have spun out of control in some way had he not been killed in a duel with Aaron Burr. His story should be told to those who don't think they can overcome the disadvantages that life has thrown in their paths.

____________. *Washington, A Life.* Penguin Books, 80 Strand, London England. Published 2010, 904 pages.

Summary: This has got to be one of the best if not the best and most comprehensive single volume biography of Washington. This book is not for the casual reader. It shows that Washington was far and away more intelligent than he was given for being then or even now. He was multi-tasked with political, military and international challenges that were nothing short of awesome. Only someone of his special character could have surmounted the stresses he endured. He survived and thrived through determination, intelligence, strength of character and remarkable steadiness.

Cohen, Eliot A. *Conquered Into Liberty. Two Centuries of Battles Along the Great Warpath that Made the American Way Possible.* Free Press, a Division of Simon and Schuster, New York, NY. Published in 2012, 405 pages.

Summary: This book covers the Canada to southern New York corridor which covers the area of Lake Champlain, Lake George and Richelieu River. It explains why this area was the source of almost constant combat from the 17th Century through the 19th Century. Its coverage is very broad that so that Revolutionary War historians can appreciate why the British made two serious attempts down the Great Warpath to exploit its obvious potential to divide and destroy the American Revolution.

Commager, Henry Steele, & Robert B. Morris. *The Spirit of '76, The Story of the American Revolution as Told by Participants.* Castle Books, Edison, NJ. Published 1958, 348 pages.

Summary: This book is written by two distinguished historians in a rather unique format. Each subject, and there are 196 of them, is usually preceded by the authors' comments and historical accounts which are then followed by letters, memoires and accounts of the participants. The reader then gets the analysis of the authors followed by the word for word accounts by multiple participants. Some of the participant material is tedious and others fascinating. The book is massive in heft and length which makes it a little difficult to hold comfortably while reading, otherwise it is excellent. The great number of topics makes it a valuable resource for a serious reader of the Revolution.

Corbett, James David. *Dunmore's New World. The Extraordinary Life of a Royal Governor in America.* University of Virginia Press, Charlottesville, VA. Published 2013, 270 pages.

Summary: Lord Dunmore had more influence on Revolutionary War events than most colonial governors. His times as Royal Governor of New York (1770-1771) and Virginia (1771-1776) were characterized by drunkenness, debauchery, influence peddling and money grubbing through illegal land speculation. He was a disaster for the British cause because his 1775 proclamation to free slaves and indentured servants to fight for the British turned the land (slave) owners of the south into the arms of American rebels.

Covert, Adrian. *TAVERNS of the AMERICAN REVOLUTION.* Insight Editions, San Raphael, CA. Published 2016, 191 pages.

Summary: This book has some interesting facts about consumption of alcohol by Americans during the Revolution. The value of the book is that it contains a State by State listing and many histories of the great taverns of the Revolution. Many of these watering holes are still in use, with more in use as museums. It could be used as a tour guide for Revolutionary War enthusiasts.

Cox, Caroline. *A Proper Sense of Honor, Service and Sacrifice, in George Washington's Army.* University of North Carolina, NC. Published 2001, 338 pages.

Summary: This is a well written book, but its contents go well before and after the American Revolution. Soldiers (non-officers) were mostly considered worthless and they themselves did not consider each other much better. This explains the relative lack of upward mobility in the ranks – if you did not have education and breeding you did not have the "Honor" to be an officer. This situation also explains the tolerance of "soldiers" for their abysmal treatment - corporal punishment, lack of burial ceremonies, deaths frequently unrecorded and bodies thrown in ditches and pits without remorse. The book shows the rather ugly side of being a grunt soldier in the Revolution.

Cunningham, Noble E. *The Life of Thomas Jefferson.* Ballantine Books, New York, NY. Published 1987, 414 pages.

Summary: Thomas Jefferson is another of the "Giants" of the Revolution. He was cautious from the start and then warmed up to the Revolution. He was the first choice to draft the Declaration of Independence which has defined his life ever since. As President, he faced serious issues which he successfully navigated. This is a very good work on Jefferson among many other good works on him.

Cutter, William. *The Life of Israel Putnam Major General of the Army of the American Revolution.* John Philbrick, 62 Hanover St., Boston, MA. Published 1854, 383 pages.

Summary: This is a reprint of the original 1854 publication. It shows Putnam as a tough as nails battlefield general whose main contribution to the Revolution came at the Battle of Bunker Hill where he steadied the soldiers and deployed them to achieve maximum effect. He was affectionately known as "Old Put" and could out ride, outmarch and outsmart his opponents, either British or American Indian. In the best of times he was a lot savvier that he was given credit for being. There is an account, if true, that shows the true grit of Putnam. During the French and Indian War, he was challenged to a duel by a British officer. Putnam chose the method which was for both participants to sit on kegs of gunpowder with lighted fuses. The Brit soon ran away after his fuse was lit and Put stayed until the fuse sputtered out.

Dann, John C. (Editor). *THE REVOLUTION REMEMBERED. Eyewitness accounts of the War for Independence.* University of Chicago Press, IL. Published 1980, 446 pages.

This book has significant value for all serious students of the Revolution. It contains the word for word transcriptions of 79 pension applications from Revolutionary War veterans. In total, over 80,000 pension and land bounty applications were filed by these veterans. They are all in National Archives Publication M804, comprising 2,670 microfilm reels. The Introduction gives an excellent description of how the applications were mostly orally given to town clerks and court recorders. The applicants described their experiences and the names of their commanders and events to substantiate their participation in the War. Thus, the pension applications on file constitute the largest oral history project in our Nation's history. The 79 pension applications in this book are mostly from local militia and show that there was an almost constant low level of deadly and bloody local combat far apart from the major battles of the War. This type of combat is not covered in detail by major histories of the War which makes this book of significant value to the Militia's contribution to the war effort.

Daughan, George C. *REVOLUTION on the HUDSON. New York City and the Hudson River Valley in the American War of Independence.* W. W. Norton & Company, Independent Publishers, New York, NY. Published 2016, 416 pages.

Summary: The focus of this book is how NYC and the Hudson River Valley were central to the American Revolution, even as it went south. The book covers in detail the battles in and around NYC. As expected it also covers the first attempt by Lord General Carleton to drive down Lake Champlain to NYC in 1776 and the second attempt by Gen Burgoyne in 1777, both of which were foiled in a large part by American Gen Benedict Arnold. The book gives details not shown in most histories about the specifics of the 1776 North Peace plan and Carlisle Peace plans. Like many other histories, it shows the dysfunction between Generals Howe, Clinton and Lord Germaine regarding the plans to drive down Lake Champlain in 1777. The book also shows how the fear by the British leaders of the Americans attacking

NYC, time and again, adversely effected their efforts to successfully their conduct combat operations. That fear played a significant part in "freezing" the British in place in NYC while Americans moved south to trap Cornwallis in Yorktown.

Diamant, Lincoln. *Chaining the Hudson: The Fight for the River of the Revolution.* Fordham University Press, New York, NY. Published 2004, 233 pages.

Summary: This is a very valuable book that shows in great detail the five major efforts to block the British from sailing up the Hudson River. First it was forts with artillery along the shores of the river; next it was *Chevaux-de-Frise;* then it was a submarine (The Turtle), then Fire Ships and last huge chains across the river. All failed except the last one, chains across the river, which the British never really attempted to breach. It also gives interesting information into the iron mining and smelting operations in and around northwest Connecticut and New York which were critical to the Revolutionary War effort. The book also shows how some of the chains used to block the river are still available for viewing at West Point. This is a very entertaining and well documented book. It is excellent!

Dorwart, Jeffery M. *Fort Mifflin of Philadelphia, an Illustrated History.* University of Pennsylvania Press, PA. Published 1998, 211 pages.

Summary: This book gives an excellent history of Fort Mifflin an important fort which was one of the many forts along the Delaware River that guarded the approaches to Philadelphia. It was actually on an island known as Hog Island which gave it advantages against land attack but left it vulnerable to 360-degree attack once the land on the Pennsylvania and New Jersey sides of the Delaware River had been captured by the British. British General Howe has been universally criticized for not attacking up the Delaware River when campaigning to capture Philadelphia in the fall of 1777. It was the forts of

Red Bank on the New Jersey side of the Delaware and Fort Mifflin hugging the Pennsylvania side of the river that spooked Howe into a costly and time-consuming end run to Philadelphia via Head of Elk in Maryland. The book gives an excellent description of the daunting challenges Benedict Arnold faced when he was named military governor of Philadelphia in 1778. The book finally gives an excellent tutorial of the extraordinary challenges in restoring and maintaining an old fort at the edge of a modern city. This book is a worthy addition to anyone's library of Revolutionary books.

Draper, Lyman C. *King's Mountain and its Heroes; History of the Battle of King's Mountain, October 7th, 1780 and the Events Which Led to It.* South Carolina University Library. Published 1881, 612 pages.

Summary: There will probably never be another more detailed account of King's Mountain Battle than this one. It has an excellent account of Major Patrick Ferguson during his service in America. The actual battle starts on page 236 of the book. The book goes on to detail the events after the battle, especially the retribution exacted on some of the senior officers who surrendered after the battle. These individuals were hanged, not because they fought the American militia, but for the crimes they committed against civilians and innocents before the battle. The book may be very long but it cannot be faulted for lack of detail or documentation.

Dwyer, William M. *The Day is Ours! November 1776-January 1777: An Inside View of the Battles of Trenton and Princeton.* The Viking Press, New York, NY. Published 1983, 426 pages.

Summary: This book and David Hackett's book *Washington's Crossing (2004)* both cover the Battles of Trenton and Princeton. The difference between them comes from the fact that Hackett's book has extensive information about training, tactics, uniforms, objectives and terminology not contained in this book. There are no discrepancies between them. They are both excellent. Hackett's book is more informational and Dwyer's book is more pure history of the Battles of Trenton, Assunpink and Princeton.

Ellis, Joseph J. *American Creation, Triumphs and Tragedies at the Founding of the Republic.* Random House Inc., New York, NY. Published 2006, 284 pages.

Summary: This book is more about the political miracle of the Revolution, without which the military miracle would have been a waste. The actual material about the military component of the Revolution is somewhat of an overview. The subsequent material about the transition from the Articles of Confederation to the Constitution is far more worthwhile. The book goes on to the Louisiana Purchase. The book's primary value is its accounting of the transition from the Articles of Confederation to the Constitution.

____________, Founding *Brothers.* Alfred A. Knopf, New York, NY. Published 2001, 287 pages.

Summary: This book is about the relationships between George Washington, Thomas Jefferson, Aaron Burr, James Madison, Alexander Hamilton and Benjamin Franklin. The book has one of the best descriptions of the duel between Hamilton and Burr available. The book goes on to chronicle the events after the duel with Hamilton. Burr was rightfully accused of disregarding the rules of duels, by shooting the defenseless Hamilton. The book is more about post-Revolution events than the actual Revolution. The book clearly shows that America was blessed with extraordinary great fortune to have such world class talents at such a critical time in its history. This is a Pulitzer Prize winning book.

__________. *Revolutionary Summer: The Birth of American Independence.* Vintage Books, Random House, New York, NY. Published 2013, 265 pages.

Summary: The three books by Ellis shown in this bibliography cover much common ground. Ellis postulates that Washington's early military failures were in significant part because he felt to retreat was dishonorable so he engaged in loosing battles that he never should have fought. This was particularly true of the 1776 New York Campaign. When Washington finally realized, it was not dishonorable to avoid major battles, and retreat to inflict more punishment on the British, is when he really began winning the war. From this he developed his strategy of "War of Posts" where he attacked British posts that could not be supported by large elements of British troops. Although this strategy required much time and suffering to implement by the American Army, it made it impossible for Americans to lose and impossible for the British to win their effort to conquer the Revolution.

Ferling, John. *Almost a Miracle, The American Victory in the War of Independence.* Oxford University Press, New York, NY. Published 2007, 679 pages.

Summary: The title is incorrect! It should say: "The Miracle ..." because it was in fact a miracle many times over. The Prefix explains it well. It was a miracle the Americans did not win quickly. It was a miracle the British did not win quickly. It was a miracle the Americans finally won. It was a miracle the war did not come to a negotiated settlement after hostilities started. This book explains how all this played out. The book is necessarily long but contains detail not revealed in other books. This book is often cited by historians in their works. The bibliography is unique because it is separated by areas of interest. It is a little less detailed than Ward's work but still superb. It is another book that serious Revolutionary readers must have in their libraries.

____________. *INDEPENDENCE: The Struggle to Set America Free.* Bloomberg Press, New York, NY. Published 2011, 434 pages.

Summary: John Ferling is a highly-respected author of many books on the Revolution. This book focuses on the events that led up to the struggle. It details the conflicts between the anti and pro American Independence personages and groups on both sides of the Atlantic. It shows the incredible complexity involved in the decisions and actions undertaken during this critical period. This is a good book which should be part of the library any serious reader of the Revolution, but be careful of factual errors.

____________. *WHIRLWIND. The American Revolution and the War That Won It.* Bloomsbury Press, New York, NY. Published 2015, 409 pages.

Summary: Like most other of Ferling's books this is more great story telling than factual history. It is easy and enjoyable to read but lacks factual details that historians crave. For example: It mentions the Coercive/Intolerable Acts without specifics, the same for the Revenue Acts and Suffolk Resolves and other areas. However, the book gives good coverage of how the French and Indian War soured the Americans on the British. For example: The British promised. American privates who fought for the British 50 acres of land and American field officers 5,000 acres. This promise was broken in 1772 much to the discontent of these men. The book also shows how the American Colonies were burdened by debt from the from the War. For example: Virginia owed 600,000 pounds sterling and Massachusetts even more. Retiring these debts caused the colonies to enact burdensome taxes on themselves. The book has generous annotated chapter "End Notes". It also has a unique and very helpful 150 book bibliography which is segregated by subjects, such as; Key Leaders, Armies and Navies, Battles and Campaigns, Diplomacy, African Americans, Women in the Revolution and more. Serious readers of the Revolution should concentrate on the Bibliography to direct their study on more serious reading.

Fleming, Thomas. *The Perils of Peace: America's Struggle for Survival After Yorktown.* HarperCollins Publishing Inc., 10 East 53rd St., New York, NY. Published 2007, 352 pages.

Summary: This details how Washington kept the American Army intact throughout the period after Yorktown in October 1781 and the Treaty of Paris. The book goes into the logistical and financial support provided to the Americans after Yorktown. The book shows the political mayhem that existed in America and in Europe after that great battle. There were internal forces (soldiers wanted to be paid and to return to their homes and families) and external forces (budgetary and fear of a standing army) that drove the Army into possible disintegration. Even after Yorktown there were forces in Britain which wanted to continue the war. It was Washington's force of character and personal connection with his officers and men that saved the day by keeping the American Army intact during this critical period.

Ferreiro, Larrie D. *Brothers At Arms. American Independence and the Men of France and Spain Who Saved It.* Random House LLC., New York, NY. Published 2016, 429 Pages.

Summary: This superbly researched and extraordinarily detailed history for the France and Spanish military and diplomatic contributions to America's war of Independence is recommended only for the very knowledgeable historians of the Revolution. The book describes Spain and France's desire for revenge after their losses in the French and Indian War. It accurately describes the fact that Spain and France considered their financial support as "loans" while the American considered them as "gifts". The book has excellent coverage of the French and Spanish navies. It also goes into great length about the contributions that these countries, especially France made to the Revolution in the critical areas of engineering and artillery. The book has a superb bibliography and index which can be used for further research of specific subjects.

Fischer, David Hackett. *Washington's Crossing.* Oxford University Press. Published 2004, 564 pages.

Summary: The title of this book is a little deceiving. It sounds as if it is just another book about the Battle of Trenton. It is far more than that. The first one third of the book is extensive instruction on tactics, strategy, terms, training and a whole host of other interesting and important things that serious readers of the Revolution should know. Once the battle is engaged the book goes into great detail on how good luck on the part of the Americans and missed opportunities on the part of the British and Hessians contributed to the disaster that befell the Germans at Trenton. The book also discusses the "Second Battle of Trenton" a little-known event and it also details how the decision was made to proceed to attack the British at Princeton. This is another of book that is a MUST READ by those seriously interested in the Revolution!

Fleming, Thomas. *Washington's Secret War – The Hidden History of Valley Forge.* HarperCollins, New York, NY. Published in 2005, 384 pages.

Summary: Washington has been accused by some as being at best a mediocre general, but he achieved victory with vastly inferior human and material resources. He grew into being an excellent strategist and battlefield manager. This book shows that he was also politically very sophisticated and a savvy negotiator of the mind-field that was the Continental Congress. This was shown best while he was at Valley Forge during the winter of December 19, 1777- June 19, 1778. Washington's appointment of General Nathanael Greene as the Quartermaster General replacing the inept and corrupt Thomas

Mifflin eliminated a point of contention between him and the Congress. Washington's political mastery was best demonstrated by his crushing of the "Conway Cabal". Brigadier General Thomas Conway was behind the covert effort to discredit Washington and possibly get General Horatio Gates the so called "Victor of Saratoga" appointed commander in chief. By artfully disclosing the correspondence to discredit Conway, Washington displayed the leadership and political acumen needed to carry on through the war as the commanding general of the Continental Army. The book also contains excellent accounts of General von Steuben's transformation of the Continental Army at Valley Forge and General Nathanael Greene's rescue of the Quartermaster department.

Fowler, William M. Jr. *Rebels Under Sail, The American Navy During the Revolution.* Scribner's Sons, New York, NY. Published 1976, 320 pages.

Summary: This excellent book details the struggle to create an American Navy that could contest with British ships of the line which was a false hope. Getting funding, recruiting sailors and obtaining the expertise to build big combat ships proved almost impossible. Politics, much like today was a problem. Each State wanted the ships to be built in their turf for the jobs they would create (sound familiar)? The book also gives a good accounting of the Battle of Valcour Island. The book assumes a degree of nautical knowledge that the average reader does not have.

Goolrick, John T. *The Life of General Hugh Mercer.* The Neale Publishing Company, New York and Washington, DC. Published 1906, 140 pages.

Summary: This proves that a book does not have to be long to be very good. Mercer was a highly-regarded physician and hero of the French and Indian War where he was seriously wounded three times.

After that war he moved from Pennsylvania to Fredericksburg, VA where he became friends with George Washington who promoted him to Brigadier General of Virginia troops in June 1776. He needlessly died at the Battle of Princeton on January 3, 1777 where he refused "quarter" by the British who then repeatedly clubbed him with their muskets and bayonetted him multiple times. If he had accepted "quarter" it is highly likely he would have either been "paroled" or "exchanged" like almost every other American or British General captured during the War. If he had lived it is likely he would have been one of Washington's most trusted and celebrated generals on the level of Nathanael Greene.

Gould, Dudley C. *Times of Brother Jonathan. What he Ate Drank, Wore, and used for Medicine during the War of Independence.* Southham Press, Middletown, CT. Published 2001, 336 pages.

Summary: Brother Jonathan was the name Gen. Washington used when he referred to common American soldiers. It derived from Governor Jonathan Trumbull of Connecticut who was an extremely strong supporter of the Revolution. Connecticut became the commissary and armory of the War for the northern and middle colonies. The book does not completely cover the areas mentioned in the title. It covers far more territory than just the period of the Revolution. The book has interesting things to say about American Indians and the consumption of alcohol during the Revolution. The book also debunks Washington's relative lack of religiosity. The book is recommended only for very well read Revolutionary War souls who can glean the few nuggets of useful information contained therein.

Greene, Jack P. & J. R. Pole (Editors). *The Blackwell Encyclopedia of the American Revolution.* Blackwell Publishers, Malden, MA. Published in 1991, 850 pages.

Summary: This book is not an encyclopedia of terms as might be thought. It is a collection of 75 essays regarding the American Revolution. The vast majority of the essays concern very early pre-war or later post-war matters. The focus of this document is on the War itself so this book does not contribute much to this effort. The only exception is the essay by Robert A. Becker *Currency, Taxation and Finance 1775-1787*. This article goes into great detail how the 13 Colonies and then States financed the War. The War was significantly financed by loans from France, the Netherlands and Spain which were largely never repaid. Other than foreign loans, the Revolutionary War was mostly financed by taxes the individual States imposed on their own people. This ultimately set the stage for centralized finance and taxation imposed by the Federal Government after the passage of the Constitution in 1789.

Greene, Jerome A. *The Guns of Independence: The Siege of Yorktown 1781*. Savas Beatie, 521 5th Ave., New York, NY. Published 2005, 507 pages.

Summary: This book is a MASTER TUTORIAL about everything you would ever want or need to know about period artillery and siege warfare. You'll be far and away smarter about these two subjects after you read this book. Read this superb book before you visit the battlefield of Yorktown. The book contains excellent descriptions of the technical process of conducting a siege. The book also describes the archaeological research done on the battlefield to reconstruct trenches, redoubts and gun positions. It also has contemporary pictures of the battlefield. This is another book that every serious reader of the Revolution must have in their library.

Griffith, Samuel B. *The War for America's Independence*. University of Illinois Press, Urbana, IL. Published 1976, 725 pages.

Summary: Any single book that attempts to cover the whole eight years of the Revolution and run-up to it is bound to have strong and weak points. Rightfully or wrongly, before taking the time to read a very long book on the Revolution it is recommended to do some fact checking so as not to waste too much time on the book. The book is not error prone like some

Gross, Robert A. *Minutemen and Their World.* Hill and Wang, New York, NY. Published 1976, 242 pages.

Summary: This book chronicles the life of the town of Concord, Massachusetts from the pre-war period through the end of the 18th Century. It serves as a good example of how the American Revolution impacted a typical New England town. It shows how the town went from religious strife to unity against the Crown. For at least the first two years the town was an enthusiastic supporter of the revolt but as very hard times appeared it lost its appeal. The wealthy could avoid the draft by paying for "substitutes". Farms went into decay for lack of young men to work them. Currency inflation destroyed businesses. At the end of the War the town was irrevocably devastated and changed. The town only rebounded with industry and small farms in the last decade of the century. Concord claims to be the birthplace of America's Revolutionary "Minutemen" but that is in dispute by other New England towns. This is a good book that shows how the War impacted the civilian population that initially was a strong supporter of the break with Britain.

Hagist, Don N. *British Soldiers, American War. Voices of the American Revolution.* Westholme Publishing, Yardly, PA. Published 2012, 356 pages.

Summary: With fairly extensive individual introductions written by the author, this book contains the narrative experiences of nine British soldiers during the American Revolution. The book is fascinating and convincingly demolishes the common thoughts that British soldiers were "pressed" into service and brutally treated in training. It goes into significant detail as to how British soldiers were recruited and trained and their motivations for enlisting. Although this is only nine soldiers it gives a good glimpse that they and their comrades were motivated to enlist to better their miserable existence on farms, mills, factories and mines where they were in fact badly mistreated. It also goes to show that alcohol abuse was a very significant problem in the British service and in America. The excessive consumption of alcohol was a major factor in much of the misconduct and desertion by British soldiers. This is another book that is highly recommended for serious readers of the Revolution.

Hallahan, William H. *The Day The Revolution Ended: October 17, 1781.* Castle Books, 114 Northfield Ave., Edison, NJ. Published 2004, 292 pages.

Summary: For ease of reading this book deserves an A+. Take this description of LTG Henry Clinton Commander-In Chief of British forces in America: "His neurotic, indecisive, often paranoid manner cost him friendships of most important colleagues in America. Few people liked him, fewer trusted him. He was isolated." This is probably the best book in existence of the 12 months leading up to the battle of Yorktown in October 1781. The book is genuinely good.

Harris, Michael C. *Brandywine. A Military History of the Battle that Lost Philadelphia and Saved America.* Savas Beatie, El Dorado Hills, CA. Published 2014, 483 pages.

Summary: This book is another that must be read by serious readers of the Revolutionary War. It does a superb job of detailing Commander-In-Chief General William Howe's irrational and inexplicable decision making in moving his army south to capture Philadelphia, contrary to the plan to assist Burgoyne who was attacking south from Lake

Champlain. Howe also compounded his error by unnecessary delays, and procrastination followed by his decision to withdraw down the Delaware River and waste another three weeks to sail up the Chesapeake to disembark at Elk Head, MD. This gave Washington critical time to recruit more soldiers and reorganize for the forthcoming battle. The days leading up to the battle were consumed by the American and British armies marching and countermarching in attempts to flank each other. Once the battle was joined Washington received faulty intelligence which resulted in him being outflanked. Washington was saved by the last-minute movements of the divisions of General Greene and Sullivan. Although Howe captured Philadelphia his losses at Brandywine were ruinous and convinced many that the British were never going to be able to bring the Americans to heel. This is an EXCELLENT, EXCELLENT book.

Hart, Gary. *James Monroe*. Time Books, Henry Holt & Co., New York, NY. Published 2005, 170 pages.

Summary: This book gives a good appreciation of Monroe's Revolutionary War service which began when he was commissioned a Second Lieutenant in the Third Virginia Regiment stationed around Williamsburg. He participated in the Battles of Harlem Heights and other early battles. He was one of the first of Washington's infantrymen to enter Trenton on December 26, 1776. He was wounded in the shoulder at the Battle of Trenton and was saved from bleeding to death by a surgeon who had joined the unit just hours before. The best description of Monroe's service at the Battle of Trenton is described in Phillip Tucker's book *George Washington's Surprise Attack* shown in this bibliography. Monroe then served at Valley Forge and ultimately ended his service as a Colonel of Virginia Troops. He went on to become President and is famously known for his Monroe Doctrine. The book is another of many that show how America was blessed with world class talents during the struggle for independence.

Hibbert, Christopher. *Redcoats and Rebels; The American Revolution Through British Eyes*. W. W. Horton Co., New York, NY. Published 1990, 375 pages.

Summary: The purpose of this is book is to show both the British and American perspectives of the Revolution. The book has good detail of the major battles of the Revolution but so do many other books. The book reveals that morale among British soldiers, especially the non-careerists was a problem. It also reveals the devastating impact on the soldiers of the inability of senior British leaders to cooperate on common goals and strategies. The value of this book is in its reporting of the struggles between the senior leaders in Britain and the inability of British generals to work effectively together. These are problems common to most wars and like many wars the results were devastating. To get the full flavor of these problems read and re-read chapter: Fifteen "The English Debate" and Chapter Twenty "Quarrels in New York". At the end of the book there are brief biographies of 70 important figures of the time which are interesting and helpful.

Higginbotham, Don. *Daniel Morgan, Revolutionary Rifleman.* University of North Carolina Press, Chapel Hill, NC. Published 1961, 239 pages.

Summary: This good book was obviously written by a traditional historian with annotated footnotes, except for the fact that it does not have a traditional bibliography. It chronicles the entire life of Daniel Morgan who fought with Benedict Arnold at Quebec and Saratoga. At Quebec, he was injured while scaling a wall causing a painful back problem that plagued him for the rest of his life. He was also held as a POW for nine months. He is most known for his defeat of LTC Banastre Tarleton at the Battle of Cowpens in January 1781 which set the stage for the collapse of the British southern campaign. He retired in Winchester, Virginia where his remains are buried in the beautiful

Mount Hebron Cemetery along with dozens of other Revolutionary War and War of 1812 Veterans.

Higgins, David R. *THE SWAMP FOX. Francis Marion's Campaign in the Carolinas 1780.* Osprey Printing, New York, NY. Published 201, 80 pages.

Summary: This is not a biography of Francis Marion. It is a narrative of Marion's engagements with Loyalists and the British in the Carolinas in 1780.

Hoock, Holger. *SCARS of INDEPENDCNE. America's Violent Birth.* Penguin Press LLC., Random House Group, New York, NY. Published 2017, 559 pages.

Summary: This great book could easily be titled: THE CIVIL WAR within the AMERICAN REVOLUTION. As advertised, it graphically describes the threats, beatings, intimidation, torture, rape, wounding, war crimes and murder of Loyalists by Americans and vice versa by British and Germans. It starts with the run-up to the war with threats, intimidation and occasional murder of Loyalist by American Rebels. Interestingly, it suggests that many of the "Loyalty/Fidelity Oaths" to the American Cause found in contemporary records might have been coerced rather than genuine. It has a long-detailed chapter on plundering which was done far and away more by British and German soldiers. Americans did it more by absolute necessity than retribution. British and German plundering caused many fence sitting Americans top join the American cause. Included in the book is a good description of the miserable conditions experienced by the British in the Simsbury Copper mine POW camp. The book has multiple pages describing the ravishment (rape) of American women and girls by British and German soldiers. Lord (Lt Col) Francis Rawdon and Lt Col Banastre Tarleton, both high profile British commanders, bragged about their ravishment of American women and girls. The book also has extensive chapters on Prisoners Of War, the Sullivan Indian expedition, war crimes, the Joshua Huddy Affair and evacuation of thousands of Loyalists and Afro-Americans from America after the War's end. This book is highly recommended for all serious readers of the Revolution.

Isaacson, Walter. *Benjamin Franklin, An American Life.* Simon and Schuster, Rockefeller Center, New York, NY. Published 2003, 586 Pages.

Summary: This excellent book shows Franklin's extraordinary talents, intellect and abilities as a thinker, philosopher, inventor, scientist, researcher, diplomat and patriot. As American Ambassador to France he played a central role in France's entry into the American Revolution. He was an extraordinary individual regardless of his role in the Revolution for which he paid a significant personal price: the permanent estrangement of his son who was for two years a prisoner of the Americans and then an un-repentant Loyalist far beyond the end of the Revolution. This is another book that should be read regardless of whether or not you are a serious reader of the American Revolution.

Jasonoff, Maya. *Liberty's Exiles, American Loyalists in the Revolutionary World.* Random House, Inc., New York, NY. Published 2011, 468 pages.

Summary: If you want to see exceptional historical research read this book! Documented to the absolute degree it seems errorless. It reveals in remarkable detail the exodus of American Loyalists from America after Britain's defeat after in October 1781 at Yorktown. While there was some retribution by American Rebels against Loyalists it was, in fact isolated and not severe. Loyalists fled in a significant part because they felt insecure without the Crown. The book describes in considerable depth the diaspora of the Loyalists and African Americans and American Indians. Unlike many books this one contains many maps which are helpful in understanding the whole issue. The book describes in multiple pages the locations and travails of Loyalists and others to Nova Scotia, New Brunswick, Quebec, East Florida, Britain, Jamaica, The Bahamas, and Africa. The book is an "enjoyable read" primarily because it goes into such infinite detail, and should be read by serious student of the Revolution!

Kaminski, John P. *The Founders on the Founders; Word Portraits from the American Revolutionary Era.* University of Virginia Press, Charlottesville, VA. Published 2008, 589 pages.

Summary: This book does not provide much information on the "Founders". It is a detailed collection of correspondence from and with the major civilian officials of the Revolution. The format of letter/response is unique.

Kelly, C. Brian, & Ingred Smyer-Kelly. *Best Little Stories from the American Revolution.* Cumberland House, Nashville, TN. Published 1999, 464 pages.

Summary: This book contains (in brief) 125 stories of the Revolution. It is noticeably lacking on specific dates. It does not have end or foot notes. The bibliography is very sparse. The book's redeeming feature is the good material regarding the many specific women who made significant contributions to the success of the Revolution at great personal risk. The material containing the information about women is the thing that makes the book worthwhile.

Kelly, Jack. *Band of Giants.* Palgrave MacMillan, 175 Fifth Ave., New York, NY. Published 2014, 276 pages.

Summary: This book is much like Ward's acclaimed War of the Revolution except that it lacks the depth of Ward's two volume book that has nearly 900 pages. This book does not seem to have the factual errors that are contained in many of the recently written books on the Revolution. It is recommended for a reader who would like a good and accurate account of the military aspects of the Revolution without going into the events that led up to the start of the conflict.

Ketchum, Richard M. *Decisive Day, The Battle for Bunker Hill.* Doubleday & Co. Inc., Garden City, New York, NY. Published 1962, 282 pages.

Summary: This is among the best written accounts of the Battle of Bunker Hill. The print is small but the book is supported by generous "notes". The Battles of Lexington/Concord followed by Bunker Hill caused shocking casualties and came as real eye openers to British military and civilian leaders. Their reaction, as might be expected, was to send more troops and further dig in their heels. If it were not for the fact that the Americans had run out of black powder and ammunition the slaughter of the British at Bunker Hill would have been much worse.

____________. *Saratoga, Turning Point of America's Revolutionary War.* Henry Holt & Co., New York, NY. Published 2008, 456 pages.

Summary: This may be the best and ultimate book on the battles in and around Saratoga. It is infinitely detailed, but in a very readable and enjoyable style. It covers the whole push south from Canada by Burgoyne during 1777. Read it and enjoy it several times over, especially if you want to go visit the battlefields there. It should have covered the travails of the "Convention Army" more thoroughly at the end of the book. Curiously, the book does not mention the fact that a courier was found with a secret message that indicated the British had no intention of sending its captive soldiers back to Britain. It also does not mention that the fleet of ships Britain was assembling to send the soldiers back to Europe were coastal ships not capable of Atlantic crossings which is another indication the British were secretly planning to sail their captives from Boston to New York City in violation of the surrender agreement. The book is superb!

Kidder, Frederic. *History of the First New Hampshire Regiment in the War of the Revolution.* Albany, NY. First published 1868, 184 pages.

Summary: This book shows actual copies of militia Paymaster Records, Returns (muster Rolls) and Battle Casualty Lists not seen elsewhere. The book was written with the benefit of first and second-hand accounts of participants in the battles of the regiment. Some of the battle scenes are gruesomely described in the book.

Kiernan, Denise & D'Agnese. *Signing Their Lives Away, The Men Who Signed their Lives Away. The Fame and Misfortune of the Men who signed the Declaration of Independence.* Quick Books, 125 Church Street, Philadelphia, PA. Published 2009, 255 pages.

Summary: This book gives short bios of the 56 men who signed the Declaration of Independence.

Kilmeade, Brian. *George Washington's SECRET SIX: The Spy Ring that Saved America.* Penguin Group, 375 Hudson Street, New York, NY. Published 2013, 235 pages.

Summary: For a while this book was on the Washington Post's top ten non-fiction books for 2014. Readers should compare this book with *Washington's First Spies* by Alexander Rose shown in this bibliography.

King, Dean. *A Sea of Words.* Henry Holt and Company, New York, NY. Published 1995, 411 pages.

Summary: This book contains the hundreds of naval terms of the Eighteenth and Nineteenth centuries, many of which are applicable to Revolutionary War ships. It helps to know naval terminology especially when reading the many sea engagements that occurred during the Revolution.

Kranish, Michael. *Flight from Monticello. Jefferson at War.* Oxford University Press, New York, NY. Published 2010, 388 Pages.

Summary: The heart of this book starts with chapter: *This Dangerous Fire is Only Smothered.* Up until October 1780 Virginia had largely escaped the ravages of the Revolution. This stopped with the British invasion from NYC to the Elizabeth River area around Norfolk by General Leslie on October 16, 1780. This caught Jefferson and all Virginians by surprise and completely unprepared. Leslie was in a position to crush the Revolution in Virginia but after pleading for instructions to attack Virginia he was told to leave the state on November 15 and go south to support Cornwallis in the Carolinas which wasted a golden opportunity to strike a severe blow. At this time Jefferson had been Governor of Virginia for 15 months. The governor of Virginia had limited power to draft militia, build fortifications and prepare for war. When Jefferson tried to pass draft legislation there were draft riots. He was roundly criticized then and even now by historians for his lack of preparations to confront the British who attacked in force in January 1781 with British General Phillips and Benedict Arnold in charge. Initially Arnold very favorably impressed the British for his field generalship and aggressiveness which led to many successes against the weak Virginia militia. Arnold in his perpetual quest for wealth made a deal with British Commodore Thomas Symonds to split the spoils captured in Virginia. Instead of destroying valuable goods he set aside hogsheads of tobacco and other valuables for himself and soon fell into conflict with Symonds and other British officials who saw Arnold's personality faults which got him in so much trouble with his American superiors before he defected. Arnold was recalled back to NYC under mysterious circumstances to later lead an invasion of New London, CT which ended in controversy involving the slaughter of surrendered Americans at Fort Griswold. The value of this book rests in the fine detail of Arnold's devastation of Virginia and the nearly impossible situation Jefferson faced with defending Virginia against the invading British in the spring of 1781.

Lancaster, Bruce. *The American Revolution.* Houghton Mifflin Co., Boston, MA. Published 1987, 368 pages.

Summary: The introductory chapter by J. H. Plumb is the most valuable part of the book. Unlike most relatively recent written books on the Revolution this one does not seem to have many glaring factual errors. When starting to learn about the Revolution one should first learn the basics of what happened, where, when, how and why.

Langguth, A.J. *Union of 1812, The Americans who Fought the Second War of Independence.* Simon and Schuster, 1230 Independence Ave., New York, NY. Published 2006, 486 pages.

Summary: This book covers in considerable detail the successive miracles of the Revolution concerning: Issues of succession, geographical divisions (North vs South), Federalism vs Republicanism, proactive vs isolationist foreign policy, military weakness vs strength and the financial crises that followed the Revolution. The successful resolution of these serious issues reflects well on the strengths of our new constitution and form of government.

Lanning, Lee Michael. *The American Revolution 100. The People, Battles and Events of the American War for Independence Ranked by their Significance.* Source Books, Naperville, IL. Published 2008, 373 pages.

Summary: This book "attempts to rank the War's leaders, battles and events in terms of their influence on the Revolutionary War". Anyone who attempts to rank order the top 100 events of such a world changing event as the American Revolution is up for a difficult challenge. The top ten events listed by the author are as follows:

1. George Washington as the leader of the Revolution. He successfully led a half starved, poorly armed, ill fed, unpaid army for six years, a feat that others could not possibly do. He ultimately understood that as long as the Americans did not quit, the British would lose. It was a war of wits and attrition and he was the master of it.
2. The Battle of Yorktown. The American Army was ready to shred itself. It needed a titanic war ending victory. With an extremely high stakes strategy, collaboration with the French, skill by his subordinate generals (Steuben, Lafayette, Wayne, Lincoln and others) Washington was able to con Clinton into thinking New York was going to be his next target. This eliminated any chances of timely evacuation or relief of Cornwallis in Yorktown.
3. The Battle of Saratoga. This was a case of "over reach" by the British at Whitehall and Burgoyne. The Americans under the leadership of General St Clair retreated to the point where Burgoyne was beyond logistical support and any means of retreat. Americans smelled victory and converged by the thousands to defeat him in battle. The capture of five German and British generals and surrender of over 5,600 soldiers convinced France the Americans could win the Revolution and joined in a war winning alliance with the United States.
4. General Nathanael Greene. Greene was a natural born leader who quickly won acclaim as a battlefield commander and administrator. He took over the job of Quartermaster General when American logistics were in crisis condition. After succeeding in that endeavor he commanded American forces in the south and through cunning and grit soundly defeated Cornwallis which led to his retreat to Yorktown and catastrophe.

5. American Allies. Through a combination of savvy diplomacy and clandestine intrigue the Americans were able to bring the sworn enemies of Britain into the conflict which made the American Revolution a world war that the over stretched British could not win.
6. American Financier Robert Morris. He was a genius at finance and shipping and commerce. Where there was no money he found money. Through con games and Ponzi schemes he managed to keep the Revolution solvent enough to prevent it from imploding.
7. The Continental Army. Total enlistments came to 231,771, with a high total at one moment of 35,000. It endured unbelievable hardship and failed to quit.
8. The Battle of Trenton. After a string of battlefield losses in and around New York and enlistments expiring at the end of December a clear victory over the enemy was needed to prevent the total defeat of the Americans. That victory came at the Battle of Trenton which sparked enlistments and raised morale to the point where the army held itself together.
9. British Secretary of State George Sackville Germain. Through his incompetent management of the war effort there was no cohesion between British generals which directly led to the British defeats at Saratoga and Yorktown.
10. Continental Congress. The two notable achievements of the Continental Congress were the Declaration of Independence and Articles of Confederation which laid the groundwork for our Constitution.

Leake, Isaac Q. *Memoir of the Life and Times of General John Lamb. An Officer of the Revolution*. Applewood Books, Bedford, MA. Published 1857, 431 pages.

Summary: This is an extensive old biography of a true American patriot who was raised in New York City and was one of the original

"Liberty Boys" who organized and led the anti-British activities in the city. He was very intelligent and was fluent in Dutch and very proficient in math which led him to service in the artillery during the Revolution. He participated in the assault on St. John's with artillery and the subsequent failed attack to seize Quebec with Benedict Arnold on December 31, 1775. At the battle he was gravely wounded by grapeshot to his face which was very disfiguring. After spending six months as a Prisoner of War he was exchanged and returned for service with the Second Continental Artillery Regiment at West Point New York. He and his deputy LTC James Livingston were the artillerymen who fired on the HMS *VULTURE* on the Hudson River on September 22, 1780. This caused Major John Andre' to become stranded ashore and ultimately led to his capture. Lamb was eventually promoted to BG before his ultimate death in retirement on May 31, 1800.

Leepson, Marc. *Lafayette, Lessons in Leadership from the Idealist General.* Palgrove MacMillan, 175 Fifth St., New York, NY. Published 2011, 202 pages.

Summary: Lafayette was one of the most prominent European idealist volunteers who came to America to provide their services free of charge for the success of the Revolution. Again and again he demonstrated his high ethical principles and courage on the battlefields of America. He was considered the equivalent of a son by Washington and sacrificed everything short of his life for the Revolution. The scores of cities and highways in the US that are named after him reflects the degree of high esteem he is held in America. After the War he barely escaped the gallows in the French Revolution and suffered imprisonment and poverty.

Lefkowitz, Arnold S. *Benedict Arnold in the Company of Heroes.* Savas Beatie, El Dorado Hills, CA. Published 2012, 294 pages.

Summary: This book follows Arnold's service in America and those who served with him, primarily in his attempt to conquer Quebec. The book attempts a more "balanced" approach to Arnold. However, the author does not excuse Arnold's hot headedness, abrasiveness, arrogance, egomania and lack of ability to cooperate with others for his problems that were ultimately his undoing. The book has little good to say about Ethan Allen who with Arnold captured Fort Ticonderoga in 1775. It is refreshing to see the author uses "footnotes" vs "endnotes".

Lenk, Torsten. *The Flintlock, Its Origin, Development, and Use.* Skyhorse Publishing, 555, 8th Ave., New York, NY. Published 1939, 188 pages.

Summary: The book has everything you want, or there is to know about muskets. It has multiple pictures which should help the readers visualize the guns, most of which pre-date the Revolution by many years.

Linklater, Andro. *An Artist in Treason, The Extraordinary Double Life of General James Wilkinson.* Walker Publishing Co., New York, NY. Published 2009, 392 pages.

Summary: This is a biography of a seriously flawed American Revolutionary general who networked himself to ultimately be promoted to the rank of MG and Commander of the U.S. Army on May 19, 1813. During the Revolution, he sought advancement by scheming against Generals Gates, Arnold, George Washington, Alexander Hamilton, Thomas Jefferson and Aaron Burr. His motives were greed, self-aggrandizement and ego gratification. He secretly arranged to have Spain go to war with the U.S. and for Spain to lay claim to Kentucky, Tennessee, Mississippi, West Florida and Louisiana for a huge personal fee and secret deal. When overwhelming evidence of his betrayal started to become evident he asked for trial by court martial which ended up in a sham, finding him not guilty. Through his political connections he was ultimately promoted to command the U.S. Army. The upshot is that this was another post-Revolutionary crisis that was avoided and could have had disastrous consequences for the country.

Lockhart, Paul. *The Drillmaster of Valley Forge, The Baron de Steuben and the Making of an American Army.* HarperCollins Books, 10 East 53 St., New York, NY. Published 2008, 337 pages.

Summary: This book places Baron de Steuben in the pantheon of heroes of the American Revolution who volunteered their services from abroad free of charge. Without his discipline, standardization, and combat training the American Revolution would not likely have succeeded. Some of the routines he instilled in the Army are still used, such as the traveling inspection teams and formal in-unit training teams which rotated among units. The book does an especially good job of describing Steuben's service in Virginia. The book also gives him the credit he deserves for not only training American soldiers but leading them in battle in and around Yorktown.

Loqusz, Michael. *With Musket and Tomahawk, The Saratoga Campaign and the Wilderness War.* Casemate Publishers, 908 Darby Road, Havertown, PA. Published 2010, 418 pages.

Summary: This book is a masterpiece of military reporting. It starts with the British planning for the campaign by Gen Burgoyne to capture Fort Ticonderoga via Lake Champlain and drive down to Albany New York to link up with General Howe. It shows the flaws in the planning and execution and problems with logistics. The book has a unique and very helpful day by day format so there is never a doubt what is happening when. The book has a wealth of detail including the classic structure of British regiments: Eight "Center Companies" combined with two "Flank Companies" one a "Grenadier Company" and the other a "Light Foot Company". The book covers the preliminary battles of Hubbarton, Bennington and Fort Stanwix in considerable detail. The details of the Battles of Freeman's Farm and Bemis Heights are superb. This book has more detail than Ketchum's *SARATOGA* but both should be read and made part of the libraries of Rev War enthusiasts.

Lowell, Edward J. *The Hessians and the other German Auxiliaries of Great Britain in the Revolutionary War.* Edward J. Corner House Publishers, MA. First published 1887, 301 pages.

Summary: This book from the "rare book" section of the George Mason University Library describes in significant detail the trauma experienced by the average German villagers when they were subject to the "requirement" to provide soldiers for Britain's war with America. Mutinies were not uncommon along with desertions and suicides. The book clearly indicates how many German soldiers served and returned from what they considered a losing war in America.

Mackesy, Piers. *The War for America, 1775-1783.* Harvard University Press, MA. Published 1964, 565 pages.

Summary: This book is about the British conduct of the American Revolution from their strategic perspective. Once the war went international in 1778 the book covers the world-wide aspects of the conflict. It covers in detail the stresses endured by Lord North and Germain in trying to protect Britain's global possessions from attacks by the French, Spanish and Dutch. It covers in great detail every petty squabble and insult experienced by any Admiral ever promoted to that grade. The value of the book is in its coverage of the problems of supplying (victualizing) its forces. It covers the waste that came from having separate transport administrations for the Navy and Army. Fully 11% of all supplies shipped to America were lost to privateers, storms, spoilage and corrupt suppliers. The book overall gives high marks to the British for overcoming the difficulties of supplying their forces in time of war.

Martin, James K & Mark E. Lender. *A Respectable Army. The Military Origins of the Republic 1773 – 1789.* Harlan Davidson Inc., Wheeling, IL. Published 1982, 240 pages.

Summary: This book covers the relationship between the American military and civilians at the start of the Revolution and how it evolved to a wary co-existence. At the start of the Revolution there was enthusiasm for the military which quickly disappeared when the war became long and drawn out. The book then covers very well the issues of recruiting, training and fighting. The book indicates the Conway Cabal never was a conspiracy which is a view not shared by other historians. The book also covers in interesting detail other issues such as abuse of alcohol and pensions for the war's veterans.

Mattern, David B. *Benjamin Lincoln and the American Revolution.* University of South Carolina Press, Columbia, SC. Published 1995, 307 pages.

Summary: This is a great biography about a very interesting hero of the Revolution. Lincoln was deeply religious which put him apart from most leaders of the Revolution. He was seriously wounded at Saratoga and nearly had to have his foot amputated, and then walked with a limp the rest of his life. He was unfairly blamed for the loss of Charles Town SC to the British where he was in command. He knew the condition inside the city was untenable and wanted to withdraw but the citizens of the city opposed his retreat. The result was he and thousands of Americans were captured and the British held the city to the end of the war. More Americans were captured at the siege of Charles Town than in any other single battle of the Revolution.

Mayers, Robert A. *The War Man. The True Story of a Citizen-Soldier Who Fought from Quebec to Yorktown.* Westholme Publishing, LLC., Yardley, PA. Published 2009, 284 pages.

Summary: This book is not one of the many memoires of Revolutionary Soldiers. It is record of a soldier who served from the beginning to the end of the Revolution, based not on solely on his recollections, but mostly on official records. It gives a good perspective of combat at the individual soldier level on the battlefield. It gives good information about the recruiting of American soldiers. It shows how the heroism of small units of Americans, several times, over saved Washington's whole army by sacrificing themselves to overwhelming numbers of British and Germans.

McBurney, Christian M. *Kidnapping the ENEMY. The Special Operations to Capture Generals Charles Lee and Richard Prescott.* Westholme Publishing, New York, NY. Published 2014, 334 pages.

Summary: This book fills in many holes left by many other works on the Revolution. In effect, it contains biographies of: American MG Charles Lee, British MG Richard Prescott and Colonel William Barton. The book explains Lee's capture and dispels rumors he was cavorting with a woman at the time of his capture. It also goes into the complex legal issues regarding whether he was a deserter from the British Army at the time of his capture. He was in fact a "Half-Pay" (retired) officer from the British Army at the start of the Revolution. The book chronicles his capture, life as a POW, exchange and disastrous service at Monmouth Courthouse after he was returned to service in the Continental Army. The book does much the same for MG Richard Prescott who after his exchange with Lee was eventually returned to Britain and promoted to Lieutenant General. The real tragic hero of the book is Colonel William Barton who conceived of and led the high-risk operation to capture Prescott from Rhode Island in 1777. Barton was in many ways a victim of his own doing. He fell onto hard times and actually spent time in prison. The book is documented to the highest possible degree with annotated end-notes and a very extensive bibliography. The book does not have much information concerning Prescott's first capture at the Battle of Montreal in November 1775. The book is rated very high on my recommended books concerning the Revolution.

McCullough, David. *John Adams.* Simon & Schuster Paperbacks, New York, NY. Published 2001, 751 pages.

Summary: If you have ever attended any of McCullough's lectures you are likely to have been overwhelmed with his story telling of the American Revolution. He made three perilous crossings of the Atlantic in the face of British capture and severe weather, two of which were with his sons. His descriptions of these events along with his first-person description of the failed Long Island Peace conference are very worthwhile.

____________. *1776.* Simon and Schuster, Rockefeller Center, New York, NY. Published 2006, 386 Pages.

Summary: This well written book is more for the casual reader than a serious reader of the Revolution. Like the title says, it covers the war up to and through 1776 and then ends. McCullough through his lectures and public appearances has done a great service in raising the consciousness of the American public about the Revolution.

McDowell, Bart. *The Revolutionary War.* Published by the National Geographic Society, Washington, DC. Published 1996, 200 pages.

Summary: This is a professionally prepared work of pictures and illustrations of the Revolution. It is a helpful read for those who need a review before they might visit a Revolutionary War battlefield or location. The pictures (actual photos) are impressive and worth seeing! Before going to a Revolutionary War event take this book and get a fresh look at the events and their descriptions. You can bet the National Geographic did this FIRST CLASS!

McGrath, Tim. *Give Me a Fast Ship. The Continental Navy and the American Revolution.* The Penguin Group, New York, NY. Published 2014, 543 pages.

Summary: This is a superbly researched and written book. It contains 500+ pages of an infinite number of big and small naval battles. It shows how John Adams was almost singularly responsible for the creation of the American Navy through persistence and tireless work. The book contains more about "privateer" battles and engagements than most other books. It also shows that if you were a ship's captain you had to be a very good leader, very brave and a skilled seaman or at the very least you would lose your reputation if not your life. The book does an excellent job of telling the adventures of America's Revolutionary Naval heroes: Nicholas Biddle, John Paul Jones, Gustavus Conyngham and John Barry. The book also shows how the incompetence of Dudley Saltonstall, who gained command of the Penobscot Expedition to the District of Maine in July-August 1779, led its catastrophe.

McGuire, Thomas J. *Battle of PAOLI. The Revolutionary War Massacre Near Philadelphia, 1777. STACKPOLE BOOKS, Mechanicsburg, PA.* Published 2000, 270 pages.

Summary: This is a book sponsored by the Pennsylvania Sons of the American Revolution, which is rare. It uses the original documents of the court martial of General "Mad" Anthony Wayne among others for source material. General Wayne was cleared of responsibility for the British assault on his men. This book is valuable from the standpoint it part of the campaign by the British to capture Philadelphia which ultimately proved useless. Nine months after Philadelphia was captured by the British it was abandoned resulting in one of the biggest battles of the Revolution: Monmouth Courthouse.

Middlekauff, Robert. *The Glorious Cause, The American Revolution 1763-1789.* Oxford University Press Inc., 198 Madison Ave., New York, NY. Published 1982, 696 pages.

Summary: This book is rated as a masterpiece by historians. It covers the history of America from 1763 through 1789. Because of the length of this period it does not cover the period of actual armed conflict in great depth. Its strengths are in the lead up to the armed conflict and the post war period through the Constitutional Convention.

___________. *Washington's Revolution. The Making of America's First Leader.* Alfred A Knopf Random House Publishers, New York, NY. Published 2015, 358 pages.

Summary: This book presents Washington from his time in the French and Indian War through the end of the Revolution. You don't need to read the nearly 1,000 pages from other books to read about and understand Washington's growth to become the commander of a nearly starving and non-paid force to mature as the leader of an international force that won the revolution at the Battle of Yorktown. This is a good book that many should read.

Miller, John C. *Origins of the American Revolution.* Brown & Little Co, Standford, CA. First published in 1943, 530 pages.

Summary: This excellent book covers in depth the pre-War origins both in Britain and America. It has "classic" footnotes which are helpful and contains a voluminous bibliography. It shows the stresses that were pulling apart the 13 Colonies and the stresses that existed on the British home front. Conversely, it shows the elements which caused the Colonies to unify which were mostly the desires by the

Americans to be treated as ordinary British citizens in accordance with the British Constitution and not as "subjects". They wanted relief from "mercantilism" which was the equivalent of a huge tax. They would have accepted taxes but with representation. Its coverage of the religious stresses in America is particularly excellent along with the material on the background of the East India Company crisis.

Mitchell, Broadus. *The Price of Independence. A Realistic View of the American Revolution.* Oxford University Press, New York, NY. Published 1974, 374 pages.

Summary: Rather than a beginning to end history of the Revolution the book focuses hard on 19 issues such as POWs, medical care for wounded soldiers, the Hessians and end of War peace negotiations etc. Some of the areas are covered well in other books and others hardly at all until this book. The sections on the care of the sick and wounded and final peace negotiations are exceptional along with others. No factual errors were found. The bibliography is a treasure. It points to many books particularly 18th Century and early 20th Century sources that need further exploration and should be read. The book does not have either footnotes or endnotes. However, the bibliography will well tell where the factual material in the book came from. Serious readers of the Revolution should include this book in their libraries.

Mullen, Jolene Roberts. *Connecticut Town Meeting Records during the American Revolution.* Volume I, Towns Ashford – Milford. Heritage Books, Westminster, MD. Published 2011, 742 pages.

Summary: This is a two-volume series. The books are a treasure for documenting the patriotic service of thousands of Connecticut citizens. The volumes are word by word transcripts of the town meeting records of the 80 Revolutionary War towns in CT. The town meeting records for three towns (Barkhamsted, Lyme and Waterbury) could not be located. The research was done by Ms. Jolene Mullen, the Senior Director of Research for the Daughters of the American Revolution who is a nationally recognized expert on American Colonial records. The records for Volume I, alone document at least: 1) The names of 5,400 patriots who took Oaths of Fidelity to the State rejecting King George III; 2) The names of individuals who provided uniforms and food for Continental Soldiers; 3) The names of those who participated in recruiting soldiers; 4) The names of citizens who were members of the Committees of Safety and Correspondence; 5) The names of soldiers who enlisted for the American Cause. The names of the 75,000 individuals who are mentioned are all listed in the massive index of the volume. The volumes also show how the recruitment of soldiers in CT was managed. The CT Assembly would generate a gross number of recruits for each town that had to be provided for the Continental Army. The number was based on the population of the town. The towns would then raise taxes to the extent necessary to obtain the required number of recruits. If the required number of recruits was not provided, the town had to pay the CT Assembly a certain amount of money. The volumes also surprisingly show the significant opposition to compensating officers at "Half Pay" for their service at the end of the Revolution.

Muller, John. *The Attac and Defense of Fortified Places in Three Parts (1757)*. London, England. Published 1757, 248 pages.

Summary: This is truly an outstanding instructional book consisting of three major parts: (1) The Attac of Fortified Places (2) The Defense of Fortified Places and (3) Mines. The book is superbly organized starting with definitions of the terms that will be used in each part. There were only four major sieges during the Revolution: The Siege of Boston, Siege of Charles Town, Siege of Savannah and the Siege of Yorktown. In the case of Boston, it was a siege by "Blockade" (cannons capable of shooting down into the harbor) eventually denying the British supplies needed to hold the city. In the case of Yorktown, it was a classic case of siege by artillery supported by infantry reducing the fortifications to the point of surrender by the British. The book shows the professionalism of the engineers in conducting attack and defense of fortified places. Serious math (algebra, geometry, hydraulics, trigonometry, laws of motion etc.) were applied along with serious planning for supplies, strategy and methods of counteracting enemy actions. The challenge for the reader is to determine what from the book applies to the study of the American Revolution. The book is highly recommended for any serious reader of the Revolution and 18th Century Warfare. **Note the publication date 1757!**

Murphy, Daniel P. *The Everything Revolution Book*. Adamsmedia, 57 Littlefield St., Avon, MA. Published 2008, 305 pages.

Summary: Written in mostly a Q&A format it might be useful for a teacher at the grade school level, otherwise it is of little use to a serious reader of the Revolution.

Nagy, John A. *Invisible Ink. Spycraft of the American Revolution*. Westholm Publishing LLC., Yardley PA. Published 2011, 381 pages.

Summary: This book is especially strong in showing the multiple methods used in spying and transmitting classified intelligence by the Americans and British. It also gives a complete accounting of the spying of Dr. Benjamin Church the first Surgeon General of the American Army. The book is detailed in describing the technical aspects of coding and decoding messages. Probably the best portion of the book is the description and methods Gen Washington used to deceive Gen Clinton into thinking he was going to attack NYC when in fact he was moving his army and the French south to trap Gen Cornwallis at Yorktown.

Nash, Gary B. & Graham R. Gao Hodges. *Friends of Liberty*. Perseus Books Group, New York, NY. Published 2008, 328 pages.

Summary: This book covers in significant detail the more than six-year Revolutionary War experiences of Agrippa Hull a black freeman from Connecticut. It does the same for Tadeusz Kosciuszko a Polish volunteer who also fought for the American Rebel cause throughout the Revolution. Tadeusz and Hull often served together. Hull was eventually assigned to BG John Paterson also from CT. The book is an excellent read on Hull, Kosciuszko and Paterson. Thomas Jefferson is also cited in the book mostly from his complicated views on the issue of slavery. The book's account of blacks and slaves in New England is very interesting and worthwhile reading.

Nelson, James L. *Benedict Arnold's Navy. The Ragtag Fleet that Lost the Battle of Lake Champlain but Won the American Revolution.* McGraw-Hill, Camden, ME. Published 2006, 386 pages.

Summary: This book covers the incredible military contributions of Benedict Arnold from the capture of Fort Ticonderoga, to his assault on the fortress of Quebec, his time as Military Governor of Montreal and finally his heroic actions at the Battle of Valcour Island on Lake Champlain. If anything, this book shows the best sides of Arnold. He was faced with building an American Navy on Lake Champlain under impossible time constraints, shortages of shipwrights, materials and resources of every kind. Despite this, he managed to construct a fleet with enough fire power to force the British to take the time to build their own combat fleet on the lake. The result was the Battle of Valcour Island. Arnold was an accomplished blue water sailor and put up such a fight during the battle that the British, despite winning the battle, retreated back to Canada in the face of the oncoming winter. This controversial decision was probably warranted because he would have faced the same problems that caused the defeat of Burgoyne a year later. The year long wait to try another assault down the lake led to the disaster for the British at Saratoga in October 1777.

Nelson, James L. *George Washington's Greatest Gamble and the Sea Battle that Won the American Revolution.* McGraw Hill, New York, NY. Published 2010, 376 pages.

Summary: Two thirds of the book is material that leads up to the sea battle. There is not enough to say about the actual battle to fill a chapter of the book. The battle among the British Admirals is quite interesting and shows that their posturing, egos and concern for their careers were as much to blame for the defeat as anything else. The book shows that the poor leadership of the British Admirals and Generals combined with the excellent leadership of General Washington and General Rochambeau and a large dose of good fortune were the factors that resulted in the American victory at Yorktown.

___________. *The Battle of Bunker Hill and the Beginning of the American Revolution.* St. Martin's Press, 175 Fifth St., New York, NY. Published 2011, 364 pages.

Summary: This is a good account of the battle. The author and many other historians believe that British General Howe who was in the middle of the battle and splashed with the blood of his beloved grenadiers was forever adversely affected by the slaughter of his soldiers to the point that he was chronically over cautious in committing his troops in the future to the great advantage of the American cause.

Nielson, Charles. *Original and Corrected Account of Burgoyne's Campaign and the Memorable Battles of Bemis Heights September 19 and October 7, 1777.* J. Munsell, 58 State St., Albany, NY. Published 1844, 291 pages.

Summary: This book was written from still surviving members of the battle and second-hand accounts. It accurately describes Benedict Arnold's heroic actions which helped turn the tide of the battles of the British Saratoga campaign.

O'Donnell, Patrick K. *WASHINGTON'S IMMORTALS. The Untold Story of an Elite Regiment Who Changed the Course of the Revolution.* Atlantic Monthly Press, New York, N.Y. Published 2016, 463 pages.

Summary: This is a book that should be owned and read by every member of the SAR chapters in Maryland and Delaware too. The book covers pretty much the whole Revolutionary War with emphasis on the contributions of the Marylanders, sometimes known as the Immortals or Maryland 400. The unit was formed in 1774 under the leadership of Mordecai Gist who was an upper-class businessman in Baltimore. Their fancy uniforms, the fact that most came from the upper class and their special training set them apart as an elite unit. Their leaders (Major Gist, Lt Colonel John Edgar Howard, Captain William Smallwood and Lieutenant William Washington) were some of the most legendary combat leaders of the Revolution. The book is especially good at recounting how the Marylanders through near suicidal attacks on advancing British and Hessian soldiers during the battles around New York City in 1776 gave Washington time to withdraw and thus saved the American Army from destruction which could have ended the war at that early point. The book does not have a bibliography but has generous "Chapter Notes" which can be used as a substitute.

O'Shaughnessy, Andrew Jackson. *The Men Who Lost America - British Leadership, The American Revolution and the Fate of the Empire.* Yale University Press, New Haven and London. Published 2013, 466 pages.

Summary: This is an excellent book that shows that British politics was a "blood sport" far and away more vicious than anything experienced in America then or now. It actually shows that George III was more of a "hands on" ruler than most people think. Prime Minister Lord North and Minister of the Colonies George Germain were highly capable leaders and administrators who were faced with almost insurmountable problems. The Whig opposition led by Edmund Burke and William Pitt the Elder which opposed the American War were very vocal and powerful. Senior British generals were not enthusiastic about serving in America and were more concerned with their careers and legacies then winning the War. They were frequently at odds with each other to the point of non-cooperation which severely hindered their efforts to crush the American Rebellion. This book should be high on the reading list of anyone seriously interested in the Revolution.

Paine, Thomas. *Common Sense, The Crisis & Other Writings from the American Revolution.* Eric Foner Editor. Penguin Random House Inc., New York, NY, Published 2015, 450 pages.

Summary: This good book contains the most significant writings of Thomas Paine from his 1774 arrival in America through his last writings in Europe in 1808. The book contains the verbatim writings, letters and pamphlets starting with his famous *Common Sense* written in February 14, 1776 which stirred Americans in opposition to occupation by the British. Paine's even more famous pamphlet *The American Crisis* (more commonly known as *The Crisis*) written on December 19, 1776 on the eve of the potential disintegration of the American Army is included. The book also contains Paine's writings which have surprising relevance to modern times such as the need for taxation, the necessity of post war commerce with Britain and paying off war debts.

Palmer, David R. *George Washington and Benedict Arnold, A Tale of Two Patriots.* Regency Publishing Inc., One Massachusetts Ave., Washington DC. Published 2006, 424 pages.

Summary: The book focuses more on character, leadership and ethics than on substantive history. It does however, describe General Washington's cautious trip across the Hudson returning from

Wethersfield, CT from his meeting with French General Rochambeau. The fact that Washington was delayed in crossing the Hudson to West Point allowed Arnold to escape capture after his plot had been discovered. This important fact is commonly unreported by most historians of the Arnold/Andre' affair.

__________. *George Washington's Military Genius.* Regency Publishing, One Mass Ave., NW Washington, DC. Published 2001, 254 pages.

Summary: This book is not for the casual reader of the Revolution. It starts with an interesting exposition of strategy and tactics in the 17th and 18th Centuries. The book proceeds to defend Washington from critics who disparaged his lack of "strategic vision" and then shows how Washington effectively took four steps to achieve victory. It is another book which vindicates Washington from criticism for his seeming lack of clear strategic vision during the War.

Patton, Robert H. *Patriot Pirates, The Privateer War for Freedom and Fortune in the American Revolution.* Pantheon Books, New York, NY. Published 2008, 291 pages.

Summary: Privateers working on behalf of the American Revolution significantly increased Britain's cost to support their war in America. Convoys had to be escorted with armed ships and considerable losses had to be replaced. The privateer situation was so severe for Britain that Lord North had Parliament pass the **Pirate Act of March 1777.** Under this act pirates who were captured could not be exchanged or paroled and had life terms in prison unless they joined the British Navy, an offer very few accepted. A great many of the naval POWs in the prisons and the death ships held in New York Harbor were captured privateers. Privateers stood to make far greater money than standard sailors which aggravated the job of recruiting sailors for the American Navy. Some pirates were still held in the British prisons of

Mill and Forton even after the War ended. This is probably the best and most authoritative book on the subject of privateering during the Revolution.

Paul, Joel Richard. *Unlikely Allies, How a Merchant, A Playwright and a Spy Saved the Revolution.* Penguin Group Inc., 375 Hudson St., New York, NY. Published 2009, 405 pages.

Summary: This book tells the true story of Silas Deane who has been unfairly scarred with false claims about his character. He was an under-cover spy posing as a merchant, mostly in France. As a spy, he had to be untruthful and deceitful to be successful. He was largely responsible with Benjamin Franklin for the covert funding and arms transfers to America from France. Dean frequently lived under death threats by British agents and endured sacrifice and danger no less than American infantrymen who faced enemy fire.

Phelps, M. William. *Nathan Hale, The Life and Death of America's First Spy.* St. Martin's Press, 175 Fifth Ave., New York, NY. Published 2008, 306 pages.

Summary: Nathan Hale was a highly Yale University but naïve patriot who never should have volunteered or been accepted for duty as a spy. He was an expert and seasoned Ranger infantryman, with powder burns on his cheek from the firing of his musket which was a dead giveaway he was not a teacher which he professed to be. Like Major John Andre' he was caught out of uniform, operating under an assumed name, carrying incriminating documents behind enemy lines all of which under international norms made him a spy. It is shocking to read the disgusting manner Hale was treated during his execution, compared with how Andre' was treated. He was marched to a remote site of New York, and was denied a pastor and Bible. A letter he wrote to his family was reportedly torn up in his face. A passing black man was ordered by the British to do the deed. He was strangled and suffered. His body was stripped naked and left to hang for days until it became so offensive passersby cut him down and buried his remains. It is not positive he uttered the words: "I regret I have but one life to give for my country" but that would have been entirely within his character.

Philbrick, Nathaniel. *VALIANT AMBITION. George Washington, Benedict Arnold and the Fate of the American Revolution.* Penguin Random House LLC, New York, NY. Published 2016, 427 pages

Summary: The book is a pleasure to read. John Andre' should be have been added to the title along with Arnold and Washington. The author has excellent Chapter End Notes. The following is the timeline for the Arnold/Andre/Smith travails:

Robinson and Andre' await Smith in vain on board VULTURE on Hudson River all day 20 September
Cahoons and Smith depart for Vulture from Hudson shore 9 PM 21 September
Cahoons and Smith Arrive at Vulture: 12:30 AM 22 September
Andre'/Arnold meet ashore and at Smith's house 2:30 AM
Andre'/Arnold depart after meeting 10:00 AM
Andre'/Smith depart Smith's House for Safe Haven (British Lines) 7:00 PM
Andre'/Smith remain overnight on the east side of Hudson River 11:00 PM Smith/Andre' resume trip to British Lines 6:00 AM 23 September
Smith leaves Andre' to go lone to British Lines 7:00 AM
Andre' apprehended by American Militia 9:00 AM 23 September

Philipps, Kevin. *1775. A Good Year for Revolution.* Viking, Penguin Group, New York, NY. Published 2012, 628 pages.

Summary: No factual errors could be found in this long and comprehensive book that leads up to and through the early months of 1776. The book revealed many new aspects of the Revolution not found in other books on the conflict. The thesis of the book is that the American Revolution was well underway two years before 1776 and that the seeds for America's success were sown by British mismanagement of the colonies. The book covers the economic, cultural, religious, demographic, geographic and military aspects of the pre-1776 period in both the Colonies and Britain. All serious readers and students of the American Revolution should read and add this book to their Revolutionary libraries.

Piecuch, Jim (editor). *CAVALRY of the American Revolution.* Westholme Publishing, Yardley, PA. Published 2012, 284 pages.

Summary: This book consists of nine essays concerning the use and development of cavalry during the Revolution by both the Americans and British. Because of the different geography of America which included stone walls, dense forests, and numerous rivers and near jungle environment the British had to modify their European style of cavalry operations. Americans had to start from scratch. The two essays that best tell the story of British and American cavalry operations are: "Anthony Walton White a Revolutionary Dragoon" and "Cavalry Action at Pound Ridge, New York". Cavalry was rarely a decisive factor in major Revolutionary battles, except for Cowpens, Guilford Courthouse and Camden. Nevertheless, cavalry was essential for recon, quick strike, intelligence gathering, security, foraging, confiscation and destruction of enemy supplies and the infliction of constant painful and debilitating casualties for both the American Loyalists and British. This book is recommended for the addition to the library of any serious reader of the Revolution.

Puls, Mark. *Henry Knox, Visionary General of the American Revolution.* MacMillan, 175 Fifth Ave., New York, NY. Published 2008, 282 pages.

Summary: This is a superb book about a remarkable self-taught artillerist, who learned his very technical trade from reading about the subject. He played a crucial role in orchestrating the movement of artillery from Fort Ticonderoga to Boston Heights in the middle of winter in 1776, which ultimately led the British to evacuate Boston for the duration of the War. He quickly became the trusted commander of American's artillery corps. He expertly handled the complex job of obtaining ammunition, forging cannons and training gun crews. The book does not describe how artillery was integrated into the infantry and used on battlefields and how gun crews were composed with firing procedures and the like. Knox went on to serve in distinguished roles after the Revolution. He retired to a mansion called Montpelier, in Thomaston, Maine which is currently a tourist attraction.

Rae, Noel. *The People's War, Original Voices of the American Revolution.* Lyons Press, Guilford, CT. Published 2012, 614 Pages.

Summary: The author has a unique format for telling about the Revolution from the actual letters and diaries of participants. It shows the fear and trauma of the civil war (Loyalists vs Rebels) within the overall Revolution. The letters are from Americans and British and show the humanity and inhumanity of the war. Battles are described in the letters in graphic terms. Overall the book is an enjoyable read and worthwhile. It provides insights that are not found in ordinary histories. For example: The book describes the campaign to eradicate the Indians of Pennsylvania and upstate New York. Per direction of General Washington, it was to be a cruel campaign that was to destroy any further Indian attacks. The result was thousands of Indians were displaced in the dead of winter and starved. Soldiers who were unfortunate enough to be captured by Indians were tortured to death. All this is described in the letters of those who were part of the campaign.

Rakove, Jack. *Revolutionaries, A History of the Invention of America.* Houghton Mifflin Harcourt, 215 Park Ave., New York, NY. Published 2010, 487 pages.

Summary: This book concentrates on the how the war evolved from the actions taken by the leaders in Britain and America. It was a case where the moderates on both sides of the Atlantic who could have prevented the revolution lost out to the hardliners. Samuel Adams and Dr. Joseph Warren among others were the hardliners in America. Prime Minister Lord North and Minister of Colonies Lord George Germain were the hardliners in Britain with, of course, King George III. Thomas Jefferson and James Madison were the moderates in America. Moderates in Britain were led by Member of Parliament Edmund Burke who correctly predicted war with America would lead to disaster for Britain. Throughout the war American and British moderates were sucked into the conflict and either came to support the Revolution or became marginalized. The book concentrates on politics vs the war so it should be read from that perspective.

Randall, Willard Sterne. *Benedict Arnold, Patriot and Traitor.* William Morrow & Co., 105 Madison Ave., New York, NY. Published 1990, 667 pages.

Summary: This is a long and detailed account of Benedict Arnold with considerable documentation. It helps to clear the air on some of the confusion surrounding his betrayal. There are multiple books on Benedict Arnold and this is one that should be read on the subject of his betrayal of the American Cause.

____________. *Ethan Allen, His Life and Times,* W. W. Horton & Co., 500 Fifth Ave., New York, NY. Published 2010, 617 pages.

Summary: Right up front, this is a MUST-READ book by anyone interested in the American Revolution. Ethan Allen was born in poverty in rural Connecticut. He grew to become a multi-talented, highly intelligent, courageous battlefield leader, philosopher, writer, successful businessman and preacher. He spent 953 days as a Prisoner of War of the British and endured horrific treatment. Allen and Benjamin Franklin raised the consciousness of the international community about the brutal treatment of American POWs. This caused some reforms which resulted in improving the treatment of POWs in subsequent conflicts. Ultimately, and almost singlehandedly, Allen was responsible for the creation of the State of Vermont from the lands of the New Hampshire Grants which both New Hampshire and New York coveted.

Rankin, Hugh F. *Greene and Cornwallis, The Campaign in the Carolinas.* Raleigh Archives, Raleigh, NC. Published 1976, 91 pages.

Summary: In a new twist not spoken of by many other historians Rankin postulates that the British turned south after failing to subdue the north because the American generals in the south were less competent than those in the north. He also indicates the British went south because resources there (hemp, indigo, tobacco and rice) were far more prevalent and valuable to the British than the resources that came from the north. The book also indicates that the British turned to the south erroneously thinking they would be welcomed by legions of supportive Loyalists which never happened. The book along with others gives a good account of the battles of the British southern campaign.

Raphael, Ray. *A People's History of the American Revolution. How Common People Shaped the Fight for Independence*. The New Press, New York, NY. Published in 2001, 506 pages.

Summary: This book superbly covers the following seven issues: Rank and File Rebels, Fighting Men and Boys, Women, Loyalists and Pacifists, Native Americans, African Americans and the Body of the

People. It shows more clearly than other works that the American Revolution was the uprising of common men and women. After the initial enthusiasm for service in the Rebel Army and Navy recruiting soon became difficult with the resort to the draft in 1777 by the Continental Congress. It became more of situation where the low class common men were required to serve or did serve after being paid to serve as substitutes for the well-connected and well to do. The book shows the very significant contributions of women through "spinning bees" to make uniforms for soldiers, supporting boycotts of British goods, keeping farms intact during the absence of their husbands and sons, fighting, spying, nursing and "shaming" the members of their families not to quit the fight. It also details the ugly Civil War fought in America. Every section is extremely well done. There are also extensive annotated end-notes to further explain the material.

Rappleye, Charles. *Robert Morris, Financier of the American Revolution.* Simon and Schuster, 1320 Avenue of the Americas, New York, NY. Published 2010, 625 pages.

Summary: Although Robert Morris never wore a uniform he deserves as much credit for the success of the American Revolution as Washington's most successful generals. He was a man of enormous energy and talents who was a virtual working machine. Washington constantly depended on him to pull financial rabbits from hats to obtain pay, food and materials for the troops. He succeeded through con schemes, tricks, deception, lies and Ponzi schemes. Ultimately, after the War he made bad land speculation deals and the promissory notes he made during the war came due which caused him to go broke and land in debtor prison.

Resch, John & Sargent Walter (Editors). *War and Society in the American Revolution Mobilization and Home Fronts.* Northern Illinois Press, Dekalb University Press, IL. Published 2007, 318 pages.

Summary: Any book that brings new information and insights of the Revolution is worthy of reading. However, in this case this book is recommended only for the most serious readers of the revolution. The book consists of eleven essays by very highly respected Revolutionary authors who address a variety of academic subjects on the Revolution. It discloses the significant motivations of the northern colonies to join the revolution vs the southern. In the northern colonies enlistees were motivated more by "Republican" principles such as taxation without representation and heavy handed British policies that violated local government policies. Southern land holders were more hierarchical and were concerned the British would do away with slavery. Most land owning or slave owning southerners felt it was the duty of the poor whites to fight the British. The Southern poor whites would only enlist in the American army for high bonuses. The book also revealed interesting information about the 1818 and 1832 pension legislation for Revolutionary War veterans.

Rezneck, Samuel. *Unrecognized Patriots. The Jews in the American Revolution.* Greenwood Press, Westport, CT. Published 1975, 299 pages,

Summary: Jews numbered at approximately 2,500 in America during the Revolution comprised and less than 1% of the 2.5 million Americans who lived in the colonies. They did not act cohesively, but most supported the American Cause than those who supported the Crown. This excellent book documents the many contributions by individual Jews to the Revolution. While some served in combat as officers and suffered death and imprisonment as POWs, their main contributions came in the areas of finance and brokers of foreign loans. Their contributions to the Revolution far out-weigh their small numbers.

Rose, Alexander. *Washington's First Spies: The Story of America's First Spy Ring.* Bantam Books, New York, NY. Published 2006, 369 pages.

Summary: This is an excellent book that details the spy network Washington used to infiltrate British Headquarters. Spying for either the British or American rebels was high risk business where the result of being caught was death as evidenced by the high-profile executions of Major John Andre' and Captain Nathan Hale. The book gives no mention of Dr. Benjamin Church, America's first Surgeon General and member of Washington's inner circle who was caught as a British spy. Church was tried, convicted, imprisoned, released due to ill health and allowed to sail to the West Indies. His ship never reached its destination. The book details the code used for the secret communications and other interesting information.

Rose, Ben Z. *John Stark, Maverick General.* Treeline Press, Waverly, MA. Published 2007, 199 pages.

Summary: General John Stark's contributions to the Revolution were significant but brief. He threw himself into the battles of Bunker Hill and Bennington which helped to make them victories for the Americans. He then mostly retired from the scene. Combative and fiercely independent up to his death at age 92 in 1822; his words "Live Free or Die" have become the official New Hampshire State Motto. The book is one if not the only available work on this cantankerous individual.

Ross, John F. *War on the Run, The Epic Story of Robert Rogers and the Conquest of America's First Frontier.* Bantam Books, Random House, New York, NY. Published 2009, 549 pages.

Summary: This book is the true story of how Rogers betrayed Nathan Hale which is described quite well. Rogers was the epitome of the American Special Forces soldier, which is understandable except for the fact that he betrayed Hale who was a true American hero. Other than the description of how Hale was discovered to be an American spy, the book does not have much information on the Revolution.

Royster, Charles. *A Revolutionary People at War. The Continental Army & American Character, 1775-1783.* University of North Carolina Press, Chapel Hill, NC. Published 1979, 452 pages.

Summary: This book covers the motivations of soldiers to serve in the American Army. It was at first patriotism and later more desperation to improve one's lot and finally the draft. It then covers methods to instill discipline and training in the ranks. It shows the ill effects of excessive alcohol consumption. It also shows methods of recruiting new soldiers. It does not cover combat to any significant degree whatsoever. The book is a generalist's look at issues that occurred during the Revolution.

Sargent, Winthrop. *The Life of Major John Andre' Adjutant General of the British army in America.* D. Appleton and Company, 549 Broadway, New York, NY. Published 1871, 478 pages.

Summary: This is likely to be the most comprehensive biography that will ever be written on Andre'. He was a multi-talented individual who was completely fluent in German, Italian and French and was an artist, playwright and musician. His ambition was his undoing. Written in the style of the 1800's it is somewhat hard to understand. However, it contributes much that needs to be known about Andre' and his relationship with Arnold.

Savas, Theodore P. & J. David Dameron. *The New American Revolution Handbook, Facts and Artwork for Readers of All Ages.* Savas Beatie, New York, NY. Published 2011, 360 pages.

Summary: If you are interested in the military aspects of the Revolution READ THIS BOOK! If you are going to visit a Rev War battlefield TAKE THIS BOOK! If you want more information on the battles (all 69 of them) covered in this book ORDER THE FURTHER READINGS for each battle covered in this book. If you want to know who the battlefield commanders were THIS BOOK WILL TELL YOU! If you want to know the near and long-term impacts of the battles THIS BOOK WILL GIVE THEM TO YOU. If you want to research the Rev War military units of a particular state or colony THEY ARE IN THIS BOOK! If you want to know how the American allies contributed to the battles (French, Spanish and Dutch) you'll find them in this book! If you want to see well drawn battlefield maps YOU'LL FIND THEM IN THIS BOOK! This book is a masterpiece, front to back.

Schama, Simon. *ROUGH CROSSINGS, Britain, The Slaves and the American Revolution.* BBC Books, London, England. Published 2005, 478 pages.

Summary: This book requires concentrated reading to get good to its good information. Ultimately it proves to be worthwhile. It documents the dilemma of African Americans, slaves and free men during the Revolution. Their situation was not unlike the situation of American Indians. They were going to be victimized no matter whether they sided with American Rebels or the British. The British promised "British Freedom" if they supported the Crown. Southern whites were terribly afraid their slaves would flee their bondage so the slave holders sided with American Rebels. The British did not have the resources to feed and care for the thousands of slaves that fled their masters and showed up in the cities they held; primarily Savannah, Charles Town and NYC. These slaves died by the thousands of starvation, small pox and privation. In a few instances Rebel American blacks fought directly against British freed slaves. At the end of the War the tens of thousands of blacks who had fled to the protection of the British had to flee America fearing they would be enslaved again.

Schecter, Barnet. *The Battle for New York, The City at the Heart of the American Revolution.* Walker and Company, 435 Hudson St., New York, NY. Published 2002, 454 pages.

Summary: Just as the title of the book suggests, it focuses on the political/military role of New York City in the American Revolution which makes it useful for that purpose. It does not have new or interesting material unrelated to NYC. The book is useful by unravelling what happened in the many battles in and around NYC when the British invaded the city in 1776.

Severe, Richard & Milford Lewis. *The Wages of War. When America's Soldiers came Home – From Valley Forge to Vietnam.* Simon & Schuster, New York, NY. Printed 1989, 495 pages.

Summary: The thesis of this book is that veterans of all of America's wars have been short changed, ignored, neglected and deliberately victimized by the U.S. Government and its citizens. The book starts with a chronicle of the post-Revolutionary soldiers of America. Less than half of America's citizens were active supporters of the war. After the war, many individuals became rich and felt that they had no obligation to help those who bore the dirty burden of doing the fighting. Upon demobilization in 1783 America's soldiers were owed back pay, land and bonuses that were never given. Pay was given in worthless "Bills of Credit". The veterans, many of whom were former farmers, could not pay the taxes owed on their land. Confiscation of land to pay back taxes was not uncommon as was placing those in arrears in debtor prisons. These outrages led to "Shay's Rebellion" in the early months of 1787 which failed to resolve their grievances. The State treasuries were empty so paying pensions was nearly impossible. It was not until 1818 that the United States had a National Bank with sufficient funds to begin paying pensions. The Revolutionary War portion of the book is brief and adds very little to what is already written about this period.

Sheinkin, Steve. *The Notorious Benedict Arnold, A True Story of Adventure, Heroism and Treachery.* Roaring Book Press, 175 Fifth Ave., New York, NY. Published 2010, 341 pages.

Summary: This is another of many books on Arnold. Its broad-brush approach to the actual interactions of Andre' and Arnold might be helpful for the first-time reader of this event. Works like this help clarify this event which is quite confusing especially considering the correspondence between Andre' and Arnold which was written in code and meant to be deceiving. Read this book and then read some of the more substantive books on the Andre'/Arnold affair to get the best possible picture of this complicated event.

Shelton, Hal T. *General Richard Montgomery and the American Revolution from Redcoat to Rebel.* New York University Press, NY. Published 1994, 245 pages.

Summary: This is an excellent book which describes how Richard Montgomery converted from a former loyal and valorous British officer in the French and Indian War to a leading general of the Revolution. It describes in great detail the assault and capture of Fort St. Johns in Canada which Montgomery successfully managed to lead despite great obstacles. Contrary to other histories it indicates that British Brigadier General Richard Prescott Military Governor of Montreal was tricked into surrendering by Montgomery. If General Montgomery had not been killed in the assault on Quebec, he certainly would have had an even more distinguished leadership role in the Revolution such as Daniel Morgan eventually had.

Shomette, Donald Grady: *PRIVATEERS of the Revolution. War on the New Jersey Coast, 1775-1783.* Schiffer Publishing Ltd., Atglen, PA. Published 2015, 447 pages.

Summary: This long book with small very print goes into infinite detail on privateering by the New Jersey and Pennsylvania Colonies. It gives graphic details of privateer battles both won and lost by the Americans. Because American privateer and naval Prisoners of War were primarily held in the British ships in New York harbor, the book has excellent coverage of the atrocities committed against these individuals. The book confirms the fact that nearly 11,500 Americans perished on the HMS JERSEY alone and as many as 9,000 more on the other prison ships in NYC. The book gives excellent coverage of the importance of salt in the War. It was needed by both the British and Americans for diet, curing and preservation of meat. The British imported salt for their forces and battles were fought for the American salt works along the New Jersey coastline. The book also gives rare coverage of the conditions the British endured as POWs in the Simsbury copper mines. The book also gives excellent coverage of the illegal execution of American Militia Captain Joshua Huddy by the British. Ultimately this affair rose to international attention resulting from the fact that the Americans selected by lottery a captive British officer (Captain Charles Asgill the son of a prominent and influential baronet who was the former Mayor of London) to be executed in retaliation. Under pressure from the French, the execution was never carried out. The book seems very factually accurate. The detailed account given in the book of six British troop ships one made a successful voyage. Two were sunk with all hands during a vicious storm at sea. Two ships, one carrying 214 Hessians, were so damaged by the storm that they were captured by American privateers and returned to Philadelphia again as POWs. The remaining ship was also severely damaged by the storm and captured by American privateers, only to be recaptured and rescued by the British before it reached American waters. The book should be an excellent addition to all serious readers of the Revolution.

Sirey, Steven E. *Liberty's Fallen Generals. Leadership and Sacrifice in the American War of Independence*. Potomac Books, Dulles, VA. Published 2012, 146 pages.

Summary: This great little book contains the biographies and facts and circumstances of the 10 American generals (BG Joseph Warren, BG Richard Montgomery, BG Nathaniel Woodhull, MG Hugh Mercer,

BG David Wooster, BG Nicholas Herkimer, BG Francis Nash, BG Casimir Pulaski, MG Johann de Kalb, and BG William L. Davidson) who died in combat during the during the American Revolution. Two of these generals (Pulaski and de Kalb) came from Europe to serve in the Revolution. Other American generals were wounded in battle which shows the high degree of dedication and commitment to the American cause by the senior military leaders of the Revolution. The high rate at which American generals were wounded and killed versus that of British generals is a credit to the dedication of our Revolutionary combat leaders. In addition, those senior officers who survived the war were frequently poverty stricken because of their selfless service to our new nation. Twelve other American generals died during the Revolution of non-combat causes.

Skemp, Sheila L. *Benjamin and William Franklin. Father and Son, Patriot and Loyalist.* Bedford Books of St. Martin's Press, Boston and London. Published 1994, 205 pages.

Summary: This book details the tortured relationship between Benjamin, a founding member of the Revolution, and his Loyalist son William.

Smith, David. *Camden. The Annihilation of Gates' Grand Army.* Osprey Publishing, Oxford, England. Published 2016, 96 pages.

Summary: This book proves great amounts of good history can be packed in a limited number of pages. Not only does this book cover Camden but it also covers in considerable detail the Siege of Charles Town and the Battle of Waxhaws. It has Orders of Battle, short biographies of the important combat leaders, excellent battlefield maps and contemporary photos. It also delves into the complex relationships of the most senior British Generals and Admirals. It ends with an excellent list of Suggested Further Reading. It is hard to say too much good about this book.

Smith, Page. *A New Age Begins.* Volumes One and Two, McGraw-Hill Book Company, New York, NY. Published 1976, Volume One pages 1 to 875, Volume Two pages 875-1,899.

Summary: This massive work is recommended only for the most serious readers of the Revolution if only because of its very long length. It is suggested the reader scan the Table of Contents and pick and choose topics of interest and then decide whether to tackle the whole work. Volume One covers the Revolution from its start through the Declaration of Independence. It starts with the many things that made the thirteen colonies different from the people of Britain. The colonies were made of immigrants, many of whom fled Britain for economic opportunity and oppression. This volume has excellent material on American Indians and the settlers of western North and South Carolina. Unlike Volume Two the early battles of the conflict are covered in-depth. Volume Two starts after the Battle of Princeton. The book's account of the John Andre'/Benedict Arnold affair is worth reading in depth. Considering the depth of material in these two volumes, it is remarkably error free. The book does not have foot or end notes; however, it is excellent!

Smith, Richard B. *The Revolutionary War in Bennington County; A History and Guide.* The History Press, Charleston, SC. Published 2008, 160 pages.

Summary: This is a surprisingly good book that gives the run-up to the Battle of Bennington and the battle itself. Not only that, it provides superb information for anyone who would want to visit the battlefield because some of the buildings of the period are still extant. It is disconcerting to note that the 200 or so Germans killed in the battle and 30 American killed there were buried in a common grave, for which there is now a large memorial stone placed at the site.

Stein, Mark. *How the States got their Shapes*. Smithsonian Books, Harper Collins, New York, NY. Published 2008, 334 pages.

Summary: This New York Times best seller gives a state by state history of how each of our states were formed which should be of particular interest to all serious readers of the Revolution. From the times of their Colonial Charters up to and through the Revolution the 13 Colonies/ States were in serious conflict over territory they claimed, which at times led to open warfare which could have destroyed the unity that was critical to the successful Revolutionary struggle with Britain. The fact that the colonies were at such adds with each other was part the thought process of the British leadership that the colonies could be defeated easily because of their inability to bind together in a cohesive group.

Stephens, Karl F. *Major General John Sullivan, Neither the Charm Nor the Luck*. Outskirts Press Inc., Denver, CO. Published 2009, 145 pages.

Summary: This small book did not reveal much about this Revolutionary War general. There must be a more comprehensive book on this officer who served throughout the War and followed in official government capacity.

Stephenson, Charles. *CASTLES, A History of Fortified Structures, Ancient, Medieval and Modern*. St. Martin's Press, New York, NY. Published 2011, 288 pages.

Summary: The only serious classic fort that existed during the Revolution was Fort Ticonderoga. However, in the literature of the Revolution there are terms regarding the assault of fortified places that need explanation. This book provides the needed definitions to fulfill this void.

Stephenson, Michael. *Patriot Battles. How the War for Independence was Fought.* Harper Perennial, New York, NY. Published 2007, 421 pages.

Summary: Chapters one through eleven – Part One (The Nuts and Bolts of War) are fabulous! The subjects in these chapters (the first 200 pages) are the stuff of things rarely talked about in histories such as: medical care, feeding the soldiers, weapons, officers, artillery, women, blacks, Indians, organization and motivation of Americans soldiers to fight and much more. This is absolute must-read material. Part Two: (The Battles): Chapters twelve through twenty-two are descriptions of the major battles of the War. This is good but this material is covered in multiple other histories, so for the serious reader of the Revolution it is recommended Part One be read very seriously and just scan Part Two.

Steuben, William Baron. *Baron von Steuben. Revolutionary War Drill Manual.* Dover Publications LLC., New York, NY. (A Facsimile Reprint of the 1794 Edition). Reprint published 1985, 158 pages.

Summary: This book is an actual copy of the comprehensive instructions for the American Continental Army compiled by Baron von Steuben. It contains everything from camp sanitation, camp set up (castrametation) weapons care, formations, customs and courtesies, fighting tactics, battle field maneuvers and much, much more. This book shows it is a misconception that American forces almost always fought from behind stone walls and trees. This book will show you that was not the case. Boy Scouts of America might have a similar book for camp set up etc. etc. and no doubt that much of it must come from von Steuben's Drill Manual because so much of it is common sense. This Drill Manual was the US. Army's official procedures manual up until 1812. It was known with affection as "The Blue Book". It is very worth reading and acquiring.

Stewart, David O. *American Emperor, Aaron Burr's Challenge to Jefferson's America*. Simon & Schuster, New York, NY. Published 2011, 410 pages.

Summary: The American Revolution and the birth of our new nation were successful due to the great good fortune of world class leaders like Washington, Jefferson, Franklin, Madison, John Adams and many others. However, the fragility of our new Nation was shown by the ego centric Aaron Burr who with the conniving of the Army Commander MG Wilkinson almost brought it to its knees. The book covers Burr well beyond the Revolution. America is fortunate he fell victim to his own devices.

Stoll, Ira. *Samuel Adams, A Life*. Free Press, New York, NY. Published 2008, 338 pages.

Summary: This is a very good "quick read" of Samuel Adams. A comprehensive biography of him like Ron Chernow's bio of George Washington's with thousands of pages is certainly in print. This is far from the definitive work on him, but a very good work without having to delve into a 1,000-page work.

Thatcher, James. *A Military Journal During the American Revolutionary War from 1775-1783*. Plymouth, MA. Published 1827, 487 pages.

Summary: This book was written in 1827 by a former Surgeon General of the Continental Army. It is long with small type. Although it was written by a former surgeon general during the Revolution it has very little to say about medical issues. It does not describe military hospitals, but it indicates that the British medical staff was well trained and competent, and the Germans hardly trained at all. American doctors under-went a half day interview process to determine their suitability. Only half survived the interview. The value of the book is contained in the "Revolutionary Annals" at the end which contains biographies of revolutionary personages. It is not an easy read and is recommended only for serious readers of the Revolution.

Tonsetic, Robert L. *1781, The Decisive Year of the Revolutionary War.* Casemate Publishers, Darby Road, Havertown, PA. Published 2013, 258 pages.

Summary: This book convincingly shows that in 1781 Washington was focused on attacking the British in NYC despite the impossible odds against success in the effort. What changed his mind was the firm stand taken by French General Compe de Rochambeau who convinced Washington that the culmination of the war would occur in the south not the north. Washington began moving his army south completely deceiving Gen Clinton that the attack was going to come on British HQ in NYC. It also gives one of the best accounts of Benedict Arnold's devastation of southern Virginia when serving as a British Brigadier. There are many good books about the events of 1781 and this is one of the best that can be found.

___________. *Special Operations During the American Revolution.* CaseMate Publishers, Darby Rd, Haverford, PA. Published 2013, 272 pages.

Summary: The author has personal experience as a decorated Special Operations Officer in Vietnam which is unique. The book chronicles eight combat events which he believes qualify as Special Operations.

Trevelyan, George Otto. *The American Revolution: A Condensation of the Original Six-Volume Work.* David McKay Company, Inc., New York, NY. Published 1899, 580 pages.

Summary: This book's concentration is on the war from the perspective of British politicians. It shows the dis-function that existed in

Britain that contributed to paralysis in many areas that led to in-effective action.

<ins>**Tuchman, Barbara W.**</ins> *The First Salute, A View of the American Revolution*. Ballantine Books, New York, NY. Published 1988, 347 Pages.

Summary: Barbara Tuchman is one of America's most highly regarded and awarded historians. It is a gift to those of us who treasure the Revolution that she brought her talents to write this book. As well as any book, this book shows the utter dysfunction that existed in the British military leadership during the Revolution, especially in 1780-81. Tuchman makes extremely telling statements that would make Clausewitz proud, such as when referring to the inability of British Admirals to understand Cornwallis' predicament she wrote: "Preconceived notions can be more damaging than cannon". She goes on further to say: "Pessimism is a primary source of passivity", and "A negative mission lacks the propelling impulse of a positive one". Tuchman most aptly describes the British inaction because they: "Were in do nothing trances because they were caught in a war they did not know how to win". The book does an excellent job of describing the paralysis that permeated the British leadership in times of stress. It also does an excellent job of describing in detail the extremely long odds of successfully trapping Cornwallis. Any and every serious reader of the Revolution must add this book to their collection.

<ins>**Tucker, Glenn.**</ins> *"Mad" Anthony Wayne and the New Nation. The Story of Washington's Front Line General*. Stackpole Books, Harrisonburg, PA. Published 1973, 287 pages.

Summary: This book should be required reading for all military officer candidates. It shows Wayne as a savvy tough disciplinarian and superb battlefield general who learned from multiple books he acquired how to fight, deploy soldiers and retreat and assault under fire. Once when his "Van" (lead element) was captured the British were amazed to find that his personal wagon was filled with books on battlefield strategy and tactics rather than fine wine and expensive linen. He believed in leading from the front and practiced what he preached which is shown in the fact that he was wounded five times in battle. He earned the sobriquet (MAD) not because he was crazy, or angry; but because he practiced things that others thought mad (crazy), like his penchant for night fighting, fighting without artillery, fighting only with the bayonet and fighting in the dead of winter. This is an excellent book about a giant of the Revolution. His contributions to our country continued even after the Revolution. He actually died in uniform in 1792 as Commander of the Army after returning from final negotiations with the British regarding the Battle of Fallen Timbers.

Tucker, Philip Thomas. *George Washington's Surprise Attack. A New Look at the Battle that decided the Fate of America.* Skyhorse Publishing, New York, NY. Published 2014, 627 pages.

Summary: This long book covers in infinite detail the Battle of Trenton. The first 220 pages cover the run-up to the battle describing over and over again how the Continental Army was suffering from lack of food, clothing and supplies. The book seems to credit Washington with the precise placement of each and every one of his 18 artillery guns during the battle which is improbable. The book correctly indicates the Germans were very alarmed over a possible attack by Washington and were exhausted from standing ready around the clock for several days fearing an attack. They were not in any way hung over celebrating from Christmas cheer. Each time a new individual, German, British or American is mentioned (Rall, Stephen, Hamilton, Monroe, Weedon, Mercer, Glover, Dechow, Bisenrodt, St Clair and on and on) is followed by a chronology of their life which is unnecessary and adds to the length of the book. The book correctly absolves Colonel Rall of major responsibility for the disaster. He repeatedly asked for reinforcements which were denied by both his German and British superiors. His soldiers were on constant high alert and their placement during the battle was without fault. Curiously, and much to the book's detriment it does not contain an Index which would have been very helpful.

Unger, Charles Giles. *Improbable Patriot. The Secret History of Monsieur de Beaumarchais the French Playwright Who Saved the American Revolution.* University Press of England, London. Published 2011, 236 pages.

Summary: This book shows again how America was blessed with highly favorable international circumstances and exceptional talent which made it possible for the American Revolution to succeed. The geopolitical scene consisted of Spain and France being anxious to avenge their losses to Britain during the Seven Years War and the Netherlands willing to risk war with Britain to trade war provisions with America. The talent came from Augustin Caron de Beaumarchais who was a commoner who became wealthy through his inventions, and world-famous plays and financial skills. Beaumarchais convinced the French Foreign Minister Comte de Vergennes, King Louis XVI and the Spanish King to start secretly bankrolling the American Revolution in 1776 through a dummy trading company called "Roderigue Hortalez and Cie". Spain and France both agreed to provide one million Livre "loans" to start arming America. The book details the enormous amounts of weapons and supplies provided by France. America eventually considered the money from France and Spain gifts while they considered the money loans. Read this book to see the depravity of French King Louis VI. You'll get it in spades from this book. This book is a worthy addition to the library of any serious reader of the Revolution.

Unger, Harlow Giles. *Lion of Liberty, Patrick Henry and the Call to Liberty.* De Capo Press, 11 Cambridge Center, MA. Published 2010, 384 pages.

Summary: Virginia born, Patrick Henry was home schooled by his highly-educated parents. Although he looked, dressed and acted like a crude back woodsman, he was able to pass the bar without any formal legal training. He was a passionate defender of the poor and underdogs and an inspiring and intimidating firebrand as an orator. His March 20, 1775 "Give Me Liberty or Give Me Death" speech at the Second Virginia Convention caused a sensation and helped bring the southern colonies into the Revolutionary fold. This is a very good book about a very complicated hero of the Revolution.

Urban, Mark. *Fusiliers, The Saga of a British Regiment during the American Revolution.* Walker and Company, 104 Fifth Ave., New York, NY. Published 2007, 384 pages.

Summary: This book was written by a British historian, using British documents and sources. The author pulls no punches as it documents the six years of service in America of the much loved and honored 23rd Fusilier Regiment, otherwise known the Royal Welch Fusiliers. It dispels the notion that British officers were inept and that their soldiers were motivated only by the lash. It documents atrocities perpetuated by the British and how common the "ravishment" (rape) of American women was during the war. This is a very good book!

Van Doren Carl. *Mutiny in January.* The Viking Press, New York, NY. Published 1943, 288 pages.

Summary: Van Doren is the author of many biographies, histories and novels. His histories are superb. This is the story of the January 1781 Mutiny of the Pennsylvania Line, which at that time was commanded by the famous American General "Mad" Anthony Wayne.

Soldiers throughout the Continental Army had suffered through privation and lack of pay; however, they usually enlisted for just one year. Those from Pennsylvania were an exception: they enlisted for three years or duration of the war. With the decline in the value of the Continental Dollar this put them both at a disadvantage. In frustration, while Wayne was absent, large elements of the Pennsylvania Line decided against orders to march on the Continental Congress. Wayne and Washington negotiated with the leaders and with promises to give them back pay and straighten out enlistment papers the soldiers eventually relented. In June 1781, there were some refusals of orders and threats of another mutiny, which Wayne crushed with brutal executions (see pages 254-255 for gruesome details). The book graphically demonstrates how the Continental Army was unraveling after six years of war. A superb book!

____________, Secret *History of the American Revolution*. Viking Press, New York, NY. Published 1941, 534 pages.

Summary: Although the title does not indicate it, this book is about the Major John Andre' and General Benedict Arnold affair. It was written with the benefit of previously classified material from the British archives. It is likely to be the best and most accurate accounting of Arnold's betrayal that will ever be written. It shows how Andre' with a few simple actions that were in direct disobedience of General Henry Clinton's orders caused the unraveling of the plot and resulted in his hanging and Arnold fleeing to the British in disgrace. This requires a careful read. The style of writing in 1941 was not as clear as it is now. This is a MUST-READ book if you really want to know the details and truth about the Andre'/Arnold affair.

Ward, Christopher. *The War of the Revolution*. Skyhorse Publishing, 307 West 36th St., New York, NY. Published 2004, 989 pages.

Summary: This is unquestionably the best and most comprehensive book that concentrates on the military aspects of the Revolution. Other books of this length (this copy is actually two volumes bound together) include the politics of the Revolution. This one almost exclusively concentrates on the war itself. It is reported that this is the most quoted book of all Revolutionary War histories. Despite its length, it is an easy and enjoyable read. I would have preferred for the author to have indicated the dates of events more frequently; however, it clearly is another of my MUST-READ books.

Wilbur, C. Keith. *Revolutionary Soldier, 1775-1783*. Philadelphia, PA. Published 2008, 96 pages.

Summary: This book not only gives information about weapons, uniforms and instruments of the Revolution, but it also gives very helpful illustrations. It is highly recommended.

Wilson, David K. *The Southern Strategy. Britain's Conquest of South Carolina and Georgia 1775-1780*. University of South Carolina Press, Columbia, SC. Published 2005, 341 pages.

Summary: This absolutely superb book reports in great detail the battles of Britain's southern campaign up until 1780. It also contains the thoughts of British leaders concerning their strategy of the campaign, with analysis of the erroneous assumptions, primarily the belief that they would get strong support of local loyalists. Orders of Battle are contained for each of the battles which is somewhat unique and very helpful. The style of writing is exceptionally clear and engaging. The book has extremely detailed annotated "end notes" which every reader should review in depth. The bibliography is also a treasure. This book is very highly recommended.

Winkler, John F. *Point Pleasant: Prelude to the American Revolution*. Osprey Publishing, Oxford, England. Published 2014, 96 pages.

Summary: This is a surprisingly detailed account of the October 10, 1774 Battle of Point Pleasant in the Ohio/Virginia territory. The battle is considered by many historians as the first battle of the Revolution. It is commonly also known as Lord Dunmore's War as he was the Royal Governor of Virginia and took action to initiate the battle. American Indians were killing and terrorizing American settlers and someone had to put a stop to it. Dunmore organized an army of 2,400 Virginia and Pennsylvania militia to battle the Indians and put a stop to their attacks. He divided his army into two elements, north and south with the object of consolidating them to do battle with the Indians. The battle was initiated before the two elements were joined and the southern element conducted the battle. The battle lasted from dawn to dusk with the militia suffering 80 killed and 140 wounded and Indians suffering 40 killed and 70 wounded. The Indians could not endure such losses and agreed for peace which did much to bring reduce Indian attacks on the western border of Virginia. The book has many current pictures of the battlefield which would be of great help to anyone touring the area. A good and very informative book!

INDEX WITH "QUICK LOOK INFORMATION"

Abatis (Tangle of sharp tree branches in front of fortifications) ----- 204

Accoutrements of Officers and NCOs (Distinctive uniform items) ----- 200

Adams, John (Bio. by D. McCullough)

Adams, John (Boston Revolutionary leader and later US President) ----- 19, 372

Adams, Samuel (Bio. by I. Stoll)

Additional Companies (Recruiting companies in Britain from regiments sent to the US) ----- 149

Administration of Justice Act May 20, 1774 (One of the Intolerable Acts) ----- 17

Adjutant's Daughter (Nickname for a flogging post) ---- 149

African Americans and Slavery ----- 50

Agent 355 (Unknown female American spy from Culper Ring) ----- 149, 237

Ague (Flu like disease which could be fatal) ----- 149

Aimed Fire (See Volley Fire)

Alamance Battle May 16, 1771 (Battle of "Regulators" in South) ----- 140

Alarm Companies (Early concept by Washington of old men and very young boys) ----- 195

Albany Plan of Union 1754 (Plan to unite colonies by B. Franklin) ----- 23

Albemarle Virginia POW Camp (Main camp where British and Germans POWs were kept) ----- 218

Albion (Early name given to Britain) ----- 149

Alcohol Consumption (Over consumption a big problem for British and Americans) ----- 231

Allen, Col Ethan (Bio. by W. Randall) ------ 41

Allen, Col Ethan (Rev War hero largely responsible for creation of State of Vermont) ---- 41, 219

Allowances (Name for deductions from pay of American soldiers for food, uniforms etc.) ----- 150

Ambuscade (Word for Ambush) ----- 150

American Army (See Continental Army) ------ 43

American Army Infantry Center Ft Benning GE (Rev War Army records are located) ---- 43

American Army Organization (Very similar to British Army organization) ------ 85-87

American Army, Recruiting, Enlistments (Methods and challenges) ----- 110, 111

American Army Strategic Options ----- 116

American Colonies Act March 18, 1766 (AKA as Declaratory Act) ----- 11

American Command Philosophy (Washington's approach to battlefield decision making) ----- 88, 89

American Crisis (By T. Paine late 1776 – stirred Americans to support the Revolution) ----- 156

American Duties Act 1764 (Known as Sugar Act - decreased tax but increased enforcement) ------ 9

American Generals Killed In Action (See book by S. Sirey)

American Indians ----- 52

American Indians, History of during Revolution (See book by R. Blackmon)

American Infantry Tactics (Less structured and more fluid than standard European tactics) ------ 90

American Marines (Founded Nov 10, 1775 primarily for ship security) ------ 49

American Militia ------ 43, 54, 91

American National Post-War Debt (See Debts American Post War)

American Naval Privateers (Private American ships authorized to attack British ships) ------ 47

American Prohibitory Act Dec 22, 1775 (Act blockading American ports, an act of war) ----- 18

American Scramble (American style of fighting from behind trees and walls) ----- 92

American Volunteers (Group of Americans who fought for the British) --- 143

Amputations (Common surgery after battles) ----- 227

Amuse the Enemy (Get the attention of, or confuse an enemy) ------ 150

Anderson, John (Spy code name for John Andre') ------ 238

Andre', Maj John (Bio. by S. Winthrop)

Andre', Maj John (British spy caught behind American lines and executed) ----- 141, 166, 237, 244-246

Anglicans (Followers of the Church of England) ------ 25

Appalachian Mountains (Western boundary of Colonies created by Proclamation Act of 1763) ------ 3

Approach Trenches (Siege trenches approaching an enemy fortification) ------ 202

Aranjuez Treaty Jun 21, 1779 (Treaty between France and Spain declaring war against Britain) ----- 64

Armistead, James (American Spy) ------ 237

Army Infantry Center Ft Benning GE (See American Army Infantry Center)

Arnold, MG Benedict (Bio. by A. Lefkowitz)

Arnold, MG Benedict (Bio. by C. Brandt)

Arnold, MG Benedict (Bio. by S. Sheinkin)

Arnold, MG Benedict (Bio. by W. Randall)

Arnold, MG Benedict (American general betrayed the American Cause) ----- 41, 239, 244-246

Articles of Agreement (Contracts with Privateer crews and ship captain) ----- 150

Articles of Confederation (US Government from 1777 to 1781 replaced by Contl Congress) ----- 36

Articles of War (Codes which described punishments for violations military rules) ----- 150

Artificers (Skilled American soldiers who made weapons, medical instruments, etc.) ---- 150

Artillery Carcase (See Carcase)

Artillery Parks (Formal term of placement of artillery being readied for combat) ----- 133

Artillery Terms (Descriptions of unique artillery terms) ------ 133

Artillery Types (Descriptions of three types of artillery, accuracy, rates of fire) ------ 130

Asgill, Charles (British officer held in Huddy Affair) ----- 249

Assunpink Battle Jan 2, 1777 (After Trenton before Battle of Princeton Jan 3, 1777) ----- 320

Attempt to Make Quebec the Fourteenth Colony ----- 40

Attempt to Make Quebec the Fourteenth Colony (History of by M. Anderson)

Attesting (Confirmed British soldiers had been read their rights on enlistment) ----- 114, 150

Attrition from Atlantic Crossings (Losses of ships, soldiers, matl, horses etc.) ------ 151

Bailey (External wall of a fortification) ------- 151, 204

Banquette (Raised step in bottom of trench for soldiers to stand on and shoot) ----- 204

Bar Shot (Two artillery shots connected by a bar usually for ship fighting) ------- 133

Barbette (Platform on which artillery was mounted) ----- 204

Barge (Personal boat of senior general or admiral) ----- 151

Barras, de Jacques-Melchior (French Admiral brought siege arty to Yorktown) ----- 60

Barrel Fever (Term for sickness from over consumption of alcohol) ----- 151

Barry, John (American Naval War Hero) ----- 344

Basic Military Training (Initial training given to soldiers) ----- 30

Bastions (Pointed projections from fortifications) ----- 205

Bateaux (Large inland flat bottomed boats used in American lakes and rivers) ------ 68

Batman (Personal assistant to a senior British officer) ----- 151

Battalion Boxes (Ammo holders on shoulder straps of soldiers) ------ 96

Battalions (Combat units usually consisting of 260 soldiers from four companies) ----- 86

Batteries (Groups of usually three artillery guns together) ----- 133

Baum, Lt Col Friedrich (German officer KIA at the Battle of Bennington Aug 14-16, 1777) ----- 270

Bayonets (Main British infantry weapon along with muskets) ----- 94

Beaumarchais, Pierre Monsieur (Bio. by C. Unger)

Beaumarchais, Pierre Monsieur (Advisor to French King Louis XVI) ---- 354-376

Belly Boxes (Ammo boxes strapped to waists of soldiers) ----- 96

Bemis Heights Battle Oct 7, 1777 (Battle in Saratoga resulted in defeat of Gen Burgoyne) ----- 273

Bennington Battle Aug 14-16, 1777 (Early battle in the Saratoga Campaign of Gen Burgoyne) ----- 270

Biddle, Nicholas (American Naval War Hero) ----- 344

Big Battle Strategy (Strategy of British to trap Americans into a war ending single defeat) ----- 122

Bill Hook (Short stout curved bladed weapon to cut abatis and trees in front of fortifications) ----- 94

Bills of Credit or Exchange (IOUs used instead of currency during the Revolution) ----- 2, 4, 151

Black Chambers (British spies in US postal system) ----- 242

Black Dragoons (African American mounted soldiers who fought the British) ----- 109, 195

Black Loyalists (African Americans who sided with the British during the Revolution) ---- 143

Black Pioneers (Unit of former slaves created by Gen Clinton to fight American Rebels) ----- 143

Black Powder (See Gun Powder)

Blackstock's Plantation Battle Nov 20, 1780 (British defeat in their Southern Campaign) ----- 123

Blockade (Economic warfare - usually restricted commerce or trade) ---- 120, 152

Bloody Ban (Derisive American name for Banastre Tarleton) ----- 188

Bloody Flux (Bloody diarrhea) ----- 152

Blue Book (Army regulations and instructions written by Gen von Steuben) ---- 152, 371

Board of Associated Loyalists (Rabid Anti-American Loyalists in New Jersey) ----- 138, 144

Board of War (See War Board)

Bomb Ketch (Inland boat strongly built to fire artillery) ----- 68

Bonus for Enlisting ----- 157

Bonus Signing (See Rifle Dress)

Boston Resolves (Resolutions sent to 1st Continental Congress against Britain) ----- 35

Boston Tea Party (December 16, 1773) ----- 16, 20

Boudinot, Elias (American Commissary official charged with feeding American POWs in NYC) ----- 222

Bounties (Bonuses given American soldiers for enlisting and re- enlisting in the army) ---- 110

Bounty Jumping (Act of enlisting in multiple units to collect several bounties) ----- 152

Boycotts (Rules against use, sale, importation/exportation of goods) ------ 35

Branding (Branding a soldier's thumb or foot to indicate he had been punished) ----- 153

Brandt, Joseph (Indian leader of Six Nations Confederacy) ----- 145

Brandywine Battle Sep 9, 1777 (Battle before British occupation of Philadelphia) ----- 325

Brandywine Battle (History of by M. Harris)

Breaming (Process of removing vegetation from the hulls of ships) ----- 68

Breech (The non-firing end of a gun or artillery piece) ------ 95

Breech Loading (New method of loading ammo into rifles from the breech) ----- 95, 229

Brevet (Temporary promotion of an officer for an event or victory) ----- 153

Brewster, Caleb (Famous American Spy - part of Culper Ring) ----- 239

Brigades (Combat group usually consisting 1,620 soldiers from two regiments) ----- 86

Brigantines (Two masted ships with square sails) ----- 69

British Admirals (Richard Howe, Gage, Rodney etc. – See book by A. O'Shaughnessy)

British Army ----- 55

British Army Enlistments and Recruiting Methods ----- 113, 114

British Army Organization (Served as the model for American Army) ----- 89

British Army Strategic Options----- 120

British Command Philosophy (British "Top Down" approach to making decisions) ----- 89

British Currency (Values of British specie) ----- 153

British East India Company (Large British company mostly involved in trade of tea) ----- 13

British Infantry Tactics (Standard European style of "Stand and Fight") ----- 92

British Leaders ----- 251, 327

British Leaders (See book by A. O'Shaughnessy)

British Moral Depravity (A cause for British emigration to America) ------ 153

British Navy (In terms of size and modernization the best in the world) ----- 56

British Need for Revenue ----- 9

British Royal Marines (Naval infantry) ----- 58

British Sergeant's System (Method of training new recruits) ---- 153

Broadsheets (Large two-sided paper notices pasted to walls announcing events etc.) ---- 154

Broadsides (Notices posted on walls and public places announcing events, battles etc.) ---- 154

Brown Bess (British infantry musket) ----- 97, 98

Buck and Ball (American musket "Load" consisting of one "Ball" and multiple smaller "Bucks") ----- 95

Bumper (A drink consisting of rum and sider to make toasts) ----- 154

Bunker Hill (Battle History of by B. Ketchum)

Bunker Hill (Battle History of by J. Nelson)

Bunker Hill Battle Jun 17, 1775 (Severe defeat of British at Boston) ---- 262-263

Burgin, Nancy (Heroine who helped American POWs escape from JERSEY) ----- 235

Burgoyne, LTG John (British Cmdr. of failed assault on Lake Champlain towards Albany) ------ 272-273

Burr, BG Aaron (American who killed Hamilton in a Post-War duel) ----- 184, 316

Bushnell, David (Inventor of American Submarine) ----- 229

Caissons (Two-wheel ammo carriages attached to the limbers of artillery pieces) ----- 134

Caliber of Guns (Diameter of the hole in the muzzle) ----- 95

Camden Battle Aug 16, 1780 (Severe defeat of Americans in SC) ------ 278-279

Camels (Inflatable devices attached to sides of ships to float them over sandbars) ----- 69

Camp Difficulty (Diarrhea) ----- 154

Camp Followers (Sutlers and women who followed armies on the move) ------ 227

Campbell, Col William (Commander of American militia at the Battle of King's Mountain) ----- 279

Canadians (Very early white residents of Canada) ----- 154

Cannon Fever (Fear of cannons) ----- 134

Cannons, accuracy, rates of fire etc. (See Artillery Types) ----- 131, 134

Cantonments (Stand-down periods for an army for rest and refitting usually in winter) ----- 154

Capes Naval Battle Sep 5-8, 1781 (French and British Naval Battle off Chesapeake VA) ----- 284-285

Carbines (Short barreled muskets/rifles used by cavalry) ----- 95, 102

Carcase (Artillery round filled with flammable material to spread fire on impact) ----- 133

Cardano Grill (De-cypher system for coded messages) ----- 242

Careening (Cleaning the vegetation from the hull of a ship by laying it on its side) ----- 69

Carleton, LTG Sir Guy (British Canadian Governor Genl and CINC in US from 1782-1783) ----- 50, 252

Carlisle Commission (Spring 1778 failed Commission instigated by British to end hostilities) ----- 38

Carolina Gamecock (Name for Gen Thomas Sumter famous SC militia leader) ----- 154

Carriage Gun (See Gun Carriage) ------ 134

Cartels (Formal POW exchange agreements) ----- 221

Cartouche Box (Ammo box carried by soldiers) ----- 96

Case Shot (Artillery shot enclosed in a case similar to grape/canister shot) ----- 134

Casemates (Bomb proof shelters from artillery) ----- 205

Caisson (Two-wheel cart towed behind Artillery Limber to store Ammo and Equipment) ----- 134

Castrametation (Structured method of setting up a military camp) ----- 154

Catherine the Great of Russia (Solicited by British to provide soldiers) ----- 61

Catholics, Roman (Mostly located in Quebec and Maryland) ---- 17, 113

Caught In Irons (A ship stalled by heading directly into the wind) ----- 69

Cavalry (Horse mounted soldiers) ----- 104

Cavalry Terms (Terms unique to cavalry) ----- 102

Cavalry Units (British and American) ----- 106

Chain Shot (Two artillery shots attached by chains frequently used in naval combat) ---- 134

Chamade (Beating by a drummer to signal surrender parley) ----- 155

Champlain Lake (Key lake on west border of NY from Canada) ----- 46, 73-74, 122, 189

Champlain Lake Battles (1775 – 1777) ----- 73-74

Chandeliers (Wooden frames to hold fascines in forts) ----- 205

Charles Town (Major Colony Port – Name changed to Charleston after the War) ----- 155

Charles Town POW Ships ----- 216

Charles Town Siege April 18, 1780 - May 12, 1780 (British captured Charles Town SC) ----- 276-277

Charleville (French made musket used by Americans) ----- 96

Chasseurs (French "Light Foot" infantry) ----- 195

Chavaux-de-Frise (Obstacles made of wood and iron placed in rivers to snare ships) ---- 69, 205

Church, Dr. Benjamin (First Surgeon Gen of American Army – later guilty of spying for British) ----- 239

Civil Affairs Units (American Army created to lessen the trauma of combat on local civilians) ---- 195

Civil War in Revolution (Rebel and Loyalist militia fighting each other) ----- 93, 138, 328

Clinton, LTG Henry (British CINC in America from 1778 - 1782) ---- 252

Clippers (Fast multiple masted light ships used for recon and communications) ----- 69

Close Hauling (Sailing a ship nearly head on into the wind) ----- 69

Club (Bundle of hair at the back of a soldier's head, frequently worn by officers and NCOs) ----- 155

Coercive and Intolerable Acts 1774-1775 (Punishment for Boston Tea Party) ----- 16

Cohorn (Small American mortar) ----- 132, 134

Colors of British and German Uniforms ----- 155

Column Marching (Soldiers marching in a line one behind another) ----- 92

Commissaries for POWs (See Prisoner Commissaries)

Commissioner of Customs Act 1767 (Townshend Act meant to enforce anti-smuggling) ----- 13

Committees (System of coordinating actions by American Rebels) ----- 138

Committee of 51 (Proposal to create Continental Congress) ---- 17

Committees of Correspondence (Committees for information sharing and dissemination) ----- 138

Committees of Inspection and Compliance (Ensured compliance with their orders) ----- 138

Committees of Safety (Conducted drafts and organized defense against the British) ----- 138

Committees of Supply (Gathered supplies for the American Army) ----- 139

Common Sense (Famous early 1776 pamphlet by T. Paine stirred Americans to action) ----- 155

Communication Trenches (Zig zag trenches between "Parallel" trenches in sieges) ------ 202, 205

Commutation (One-time payment for services of a soldier) ---- 157

Companies (Small infantry fighting elements, usually consisting of 65 soldiers) ----- 86

Compensation (Term of negotiating transfer of money with exchange of POWs) ----- 221

Composition (Term of negotiating exchanging POWs of different ranks) ---- 221

Conciliatory Proposal (See North Peace Plan) ----- 37

Concord/Lexington Battle Apr 19, 1775 (First major battle of Revolution) ---- 260-261

Congregationalism (Strict New England religious teaching against Anglicanism) ----- 26

Congress of the Confederation (US governing body from March 1, 1781 – March 4, 1789) ----- 36

Connecticut (One of the 13 Colonies known for its support of the Revolution) ----- 144

Connecticut River (River that formed the western border of New Hampshire) ----- 144

Continental Army (Established Jun 16, 1775 main combat army of Americans) ----- 43

Continental Army Casualties ----- 43

Continental Army Signing Bonus (See Rifle Dress)

Continental Association 1774 (Group of Committees established to oppose British) ----- 35, 36

Continental Congress First, Sep 5, 1774 – Oct 22, 1774 (First American Rebel government) ----- 34

Continental Congress Second, Established May 5, 1775 (Second American government to 1781) ----- 36

Continental Dollars (Depreciation of) ----- 157, 158

Continental Line (Name given to "Regular" soldiers of the American Army) ----- 90

Continental Navy (Founded Oct, 13, 1775) ----- 45

Convention Army (Name given to British Army captured at Saratoga) ----- 210

Conventions (Process of coming to agreement for the surrender of an army) ----- 211

Convex Order (Order to protect center of a combat line) ----- 159

Conway, BG Thomas (Irish - later French officer who tried to have Washington replaced) ---- 158

Conway Cabal (Group instigated by American BG Thomas Conway to discredit Washington) ----- 80

Conyngham, Gustavus (Famous American naval hero) ----- 344

Copper Mines of Simsbury CT (See Newgate)

Coppering (Lining the hulls of wooden ships with copper plating to prevent vegetation growth) ----- 70

Cornwallis, LTG Charles (British Army leader of Southern Campaign, captured at Yorktown) ----- 251

Counterfeiting (Printing counterfeit American money to destroy its value) ----- 158

Counterscarp (Wall behind outer fortification for soldiers to assemble) ---- 205

Court Martials (Formal trials of soldiers for major offenses of military discipline) ----- 158

Covenanters (Presbyterians persecuted out of Britain – served mostly for American Cause) ----- 159

Cowboys (Loyalists north of NYC who "Rustled" livestock for sale to British in NYC) ----- 141, 143, 196

Cowpens Battle (History of by L. Babbits)

Cowpens Battle Jan 17, 1781 (Major defeat of Tarleton by Gen Greene) ----- 280-282

Crisis (See American Crisis)

Crochet (Flank defense) ----- 159

Crossing the Dan River Jan 18-Feb 13, 1781 (Escape to Virginia by Americans after Cowpens) ----- 290

Crows-Feet (Iron spikes linked together on the ground to deter soldiers on horseback) ----- 159

Culper Junior (Code name for Robert Townshend leader of American Culper spy ring) ----- 239

Culper Ring (Name of group of six American spies in NYC) ------ 239

Cures (Names for influential Canadian Catholic Priests) ----- 40

Currency (American) ----- 153

Currency Acts 1764 (Several acts meant to further restrict use of American currency) ----- 2, 10

Curtain (Part of a fort connecting the "Bastions") ----- 205

Custom House Oaths (Name for false oaths) -----159

Cutlass (Short sword used by cavalrymen) ----- 96

Cutters (Smallest of commissioned ships - had single mast with multiple sails fore and aft) ----- 70

Cyphers (Coding systems for classified messages) ----- 242

Damn Yankees (Derisive name given to American Rebels from Northern Colonies) ----- 159, 159

Dan River (See Race to the Dan)

Dean, Silas (American agent who arranged for French support of the Revolution) ----- 240

Dean, Silas (Bio. by J. Paul)

Debtor's Prison (Post-War place where many individuals ended after the Revolution) ---- 308

Debts (American Post-Revolutionary War debts - most never were repaid) ----- 255

Debts (British Post-French and Indian War debts British to tax the colonies) ----- 255

Debts (British Post-Revolutionary War debts) ----- 255

Debts (Dutch Post-Revolutionary War debts) ----- 255

Debts (French Post-Revolutionary War debts - a significant contributor to French Revolution) ----- 256

Debts (German Post-Revolutionary War debts) ----- 256

Debts (Spanish Post-Revolutionary War debts) ----- 256

Declaration of Independence (July 4, 1776) ----- 33

Declaratory Act March 18, 1766 (AKA American Colonies Act) ----- 11

Deism (American religious philosophy that preached self-reliance) ----- 26

Delaware Colony (Provided highly regarded combat soldiers for the American Cause) ---- 268

Delaware River (Important river separating NJ from PA) ----- 268

Demi Parallels (Small parallel approach trenches just before enemy forts during sieges) ----- 203

Demilunes (Crescent shaped domes at the walls of fortifications) ----- 205

Demographics of America (Exploding American population helped Revolution) ----- 29, 356

Denmark (Provided covert assistance to American Cause) ----- 79

Depravity of British Society (Part of the reason for America's break with Britain) ----- 153

Description Books (Books maintained by British clerks describing each soldier of the unit) ----- 160

Desertion (Willful absence of a soldier from his unit) ----- 160

Desperadoes (See "Forlorn Hopes")

D'Estaing, Admiral de Compte (French Admiral who fought for America) ----- 59

Dickinson Letters (Essays giving reasons for split with Britain) -----160

Discipline of Soldiers (Methods and reasons for disciplining – See Obedience of Orders)

Displaying (Unit reforming from column formation to line formation for battle) ----- 160

Divide and Conquer (British Strategy against Northern Colonies, then Southern Colonies) ----- 120, 122

Divisions (Military unit composed of two or more brigades - approximately 3,240 soldiers) ----- 85

Dobbs Ferry (Hudson River crossing 30 miles below West Point) ----- 245

Doctors/Surgeons (Always in chronic short supply) ----- 225

Doctrine of Free Ships-Free Goods (Allowed neutral countries to ship non-military material) ----- 70

Doomed Spy (Spy who gives false info on interrogation) ----- 242

Donop, Col Carl (German commander killed at battle of Ft Mercer/ Red Bank Oct 22, 1777) ----- 321-327

Double Shot Range (See Naval fighting tactics) ----- 73

Down Hill (See "Up Hill – Down Hill")

Draft Boards (Local American boards to identify individuals for mandatory military service) ---- 114

Draftees (Individuals involuntarily selected for military duty) ----- 111, 114

Drafting (British practice of moving soldiers from one unit to another) ----- 160

Dragoons (Horse mounted cavalrymen) ----- 102, 196

Dueling (Disparaged but done between Hamilton and Burr and Charles Lee and H. Laurens) ---- 184

Dumbbell Masks (System for de-coding classified messages) ----- 242

Dunmore, Lord John Murray (Bio. by J. Corbett)

Dunmore, Lord John Murray (British appointed Colonial Governor of NY and then VA) ----- 21

Dunmore's Wars (Point Pleasant and Great Bridge) ----- 21, 29

Durham Boats (Flat boats of Delaware River used by Washington to cross to Trenton) ----- 70

Dutch (Netherlanders – provided much gun powder for the American Cause) ----- 27

Dying Speech (Speech given by soldiers just prior to their execution) ----- 161

East India Company (See British East Company)

Economic Conditions (Britain and America) ----- 4

Economic Differences between Colonies ------ 24

Economic Warfare (Blockades, boycotts etc.) ----- 35

Education of British Soldiers (Improving their literacy and skills) ----- 161

Efforts to Negotiate an End to Hostilities ----- 37

Embrasures (Openings in the protective walls of forts) ----- 206

Enfilade (To successfully attack a unit from its sides - usually causing panic of soldiers) ------161

Enlistments American (See American Army Recruiting)

Enlistments British (See British Recruiting)

Entherliche Leute (German for expendable people) ----- 161

Enumeration (Goods prohibited from consumption, sale, purchase, exportation/import) ---- 4, 161

Epaulettes (Devices worn on shoulders of officers indicating their rank) ----- 200

Epaulements (Berms of earth constructed in front of artillery or horses) ----- 206

Ethiopian Regiment (Dunmore's regiment of freed slaves at Battle of Great Bridge) ----- 50, 143

Evacuation Day Mar 17, 1776 (Day British evacuated Boston to Halifax, never to return) ----- 162

Evacuation Day Nov 25, 1783 (Day last British soldiers left from NYC at War's end) ----- 162

Evacuation of Loyalists (Departure of Loyalists from America at the end of the War) ---- 162

Evacuation of Loyalists (History of by M. Jasonoff)

Exchange of Prisoners (Formal process of trading prisoners) ----- 223

Executions (Methods and reasons) ----- 147

Express Riders (See Packet Riders)

Expresses (Time urgent messages) ----- 162

Factors (British and American commerce "Brokers") ----- 162

Falmouth (Sea coastal city in Territory of Maine attacked by British) ----- 163

Farrier (One who cares for horses) ----- 163

Fascines (Long bundles of tree branches tied together for defense of fortifications) ----- 206

Fathom (A measure of distance of six feet) ----- 71

Fatigue Party (Work detail of soldiers) ----- 163

Federalism vs Republicanism (Strong central government vs strong state government) ----- 334

Fee Simple (Property owned without a mortgage or debt) ----- 163

Feed Fight (Fighting to deny an enemy food from local sources0 -----163

Feint (Movement to trap an enemy) ----- 163

Ferguson, Maj Patrick (British inventor- rifle - KIA at Battle of King's Mountain Oct 7, 1780) ----- 96, 97

Ferguson Rifle (Revolutionary breech loading rifle invented by Ferguson) ----- 96

Feu-de-Joie (Celebratory firing of muskets) ----- 163

Fibiger, Hans Christian (Notable Danish volunteer soldier in America) ----- 79, 80

Field Artillery (Artillery capable of being towed around a battlefield) ----- 134

File Closers (Soldiers designated to fill in files for those who fell from enemy fire) ----- 196

Files (Line formations of soldiers standing shoulder to shoulder, usually before battle) ------ 92

Finances (American) ----- 5, 323

Finances (British) ----- 9

Fire Cake (Fried flour, common food for American soldiers) -----163

Fireships (Boats set afire and floated towards enemy ships) ----- 71

Fireships (Name given by British soldiers to prostitutes in NYC with venereal disease) ---- 227

Firing Squads (Execution squads – usually conducted by members of victim's unit) ---- 164

First Congress (See Continental Congress First) ----- 34

First Parallels (First trenches dug towards an enemy fort in siege operations) ----- 203

First Rhode Island Infantry Regiment (Famous African American Rebel unit) ----- 50, 139

Fishing Rights (Negotiated at Treaty of Paris 1783 – See Treaty Negotiations)

Flags of Truce (White flags used to temporarily cease combat action) ----- 164

Flanking (See Enfilading)

Flanking Companies (British Light Foot and Grenadier companies at flanks of files) ----- 339

Flatter (Expression in correspondence indicating to be pleased or make happy) ----- 164

Fleury, de Francois (French volunteer engineer in America) ----- 80, 81

Flint (The "Pebble" that strikes the frizzen to cause sparks to ignite the powder of a musket) ----- 97

Flintlock Muskets (The standard firearm used by almost all armies in the Revolution) --- 97, 98

Flintlock Muskets (Major Infantry weapon of American Revolution history of by T. Lenk)

Florida (The land south of Georgia contested mostly by the British and Spanish) ----- 1, 64

Flying Army (Successful concept of Gen Greene of a mobile force in the Southern Campaign) ----- 164

Fodder (Food for animals, always in short supply) ----- 165

Foot Soldiers (Ordinary infantry soldiers) -----196

Forage Wars (Jan-Apr 1777 where there was heavy fighting for forage around NJ & NY) --- 165

Forlorn Hopes (American soldiers who of attacked enemy head-on, AKA Desperadoes) ----- 196

Fort Griswold Battle - AKA Groton Heights Battle (History of by B. Harris)

Fort Griswold Battle Sep 6, 1781 (New London CT battle where Rebels were slaughtered) ----- 333

Fort Lee Battle Nov 20, 1776 (American defeat with huge loss of critical war material) ------- 265

Fort Mercer Battle Oct 22 - Nov 15, 1777 (Where German Col Donop was killed) ----- 321-322

Fort Mifflin Battle Sep-26 Nov 16, 1777 (Battle for fort on Delaware River) ----- 314

Fort Moultrie Battle Jun 28,1776 (British defeated trying to capture Charles Town SC) ---- 264-264

Fort Stanwix Battle Aug 2-22, 1777 (Where British advance from Oswego was stopped) ----- 270-271

Fort Sullivan Battle (See Fort Moultrie)

Fort Ticonderoga Siege Jul 2-6, 1777 (Was abandoned by Gen St. Clair to British) ----- 271

Fort Washington Battle Nov 16, 1776 (American defeat with many captured) ----- 265

Fortification Terms ---- 204

Fourteenth Colony (American attempt to conquer Quebec) ----- 40

Fourteenth Colony (American attempt to conquer Quebec, History of by M. Anderson)

Fourth Amendment (See Writs of Assistance) ---- 7

Fowling Pieces (Name given for shot guns for bird hunting) ----- 98

Fraise (Wooden stakes stuck in the ground facing outward from a fort) ----- 206

Franklin, Benjamin (Bio. by W. Isaacson)

Franklin, Benjamin (Famous American diplomat, inventor and revolutionary) ----- 23, 329

Franklin, William (Loyalist son of Benjamin - permanently estranged from father) ----- 218

Fraser, MG Simon (British general killed at Battle of Saratoga) ----- 193

Free Ships - Free Goods (See Doctrine of Free Ships – Free Goods)

Freeholders (Landowners who owned their property outright) ----- 165

Freeman's Farm Battle Sep 18, 1777 (Battle where British were defeated) ----- 273

French and Indian War 1754-1763 (Known in Europe as the Seven Years War) ----- 127

French Army (Key contributor in success of American Revolution) ----- 59, 60

French Foreign Minister (See Vergennes Peace Plan)

French Navy (Key contributor to success of American Revolution) ----- 59, 60

Friendly Fire (Accidently shooting of fellow soldiers) ----- 186

Frigate (Three masted war ship with a single gun deck) ----- 71

Frizzen (Piece of steel struck by the flint to create sparks to fire a musket) ----- 99

Frog (Leather cup like device attached to the shoulder straps to hold a sword) ----- 200

Fusiliers (French and British soldiers armed with short barrel muskets) ----- 197

Gabions (Basket like structures filled with earth for fortifications) ------ 206

Gage, LTG Sir Thomas (First British CINC In America – relieved after Battle of Bunker Hill) ----- 251

Gaiters (Canvas or heavy cloth material worn by soldiers from ankle to knee) ----- 200

Galloway, Joseph (Famous Pennsylvania Loyalist) ----- 34

Galloway Plan (Plan for Peace, AKA Grand Council) ----- 34, 35

Galvez, BG Bernardo (Bio. By E. Butler)

Galvez, BG Bernardo (Spanish Gen who led Spain's support of American Rev – Book by E. Butler)

Gaol (Revolutionary War term for "Jail") ----- 166

Gaol Fever (Flu or pneumonia from dank conditions in gaols) ----- 166

GASPEE Affair Jun 9, 1772 (British ship captured and burned by Americans) ----- 20

Gates, MG Horatio (American general victor at Saratoga, later disgraced at Battle of Camden) ----- 278

Gauntlet Running (Punishment by being beaten between lines of comrades) ----- 146

Gentleman's Satisfaction (Duel with fists vs weapons) ----- 183

Geography ----- 1, 2

Geology ----- 1

George III (King of Britain) ----- 28, 37

Germ Warfare (The British reportedly sent sick slaves to American lines to infect Rebels) ----- 229

Germain, Lord Sackville (British Minister of Colonies – see book by A. O'Shaughnessy)

German Army Mercenaries (Soldiers from German Princes to fight for British) ----- 61, 62

Gibbet (Type of gallows with one pole) ----- 166

Gill of Rum (Daily ration of rum for soldiers/sailors - usually 4 ounces) ----- 166

Glacis (Sloped embankment in front of a fort) ----- 206

Gloucester (Area across from Yorktown River where British tried to escape) ----- 288

Gold Ores (Absence of in Colonies) ----- 1

Gondolas (Large flat bottomed boats constructed for combat on Lake Champlain) ----- 71

Gorge (Exit point from a palisade fort, similar to a Sally Point in a redoubt) ----- 206

Gorgets (Crescent like metal devices worn on breasts of some British officers) ----- 200

Governance Conditions (How American government operated under British) ----- 4, 5

Grabs and Lobs (British plundering – informal rules) ----- 166

Grand Council (Compromise called Galloway Plan rejected by First Continental Congress) ----- 34

Grand Tory Rides (Term given for Loyalists punished by "Riding the Rail") ----- 166

Grape Shot (Iron balls in a canvas bag shot from cannons) ----- 135

Grasse, de Francois Joseph (French Admiral in command at Battle of Capes) ----- 60, 288

Grasshoppers (Three pound cannons) ----- 131, 135

Graves, Sir Thomas (British Admiral in command at Battle of Capes) ----- 60, 285

Great Awakening (Religious turn away from Anglican Church by Americans) ----- 6

Great Bridge Battle Dec 9, 1775 (Defeat of British by Americans south of Norfolk VA) ----- 22

Great Masts (Ship masts 27+ inch in diameter - reserved for use by British war ships) ----- 71

Great Warpath (Route from Canada via Lake Champlain to New York/ Albany) ----- 3, 293, 310

Green Mountain Boys (American militia soldiers from CT, NH, MA) ----- 139

Greene, MG Nathanael (Bio. by G. Carbone)

Greene, MG Nathanael (Washington's second in command) ----- 278, 280

Grenadiers (British, French and Spanish soldiers known for their strength and courage) -----197

Grounding Arms (Method of surrendering by throwing guns on the ground) ----- 211

Guerrilla Warfare (Hit and run warfare used by American militia) ----- 90-91

Guilford Courthouse Battle Mar 15, 1781 (British suffered heavy losses) ----- 283-284

Gun Carriages (The wooden frames on which cannons/artillery were mounted) ----- 134

Gun Powder (Mixture of potassium nitrate, sulfur and charcoal at 75/15/10 ratio) ---- 99

Gun Powder Barrel (Small wooden cask - not to be confused with a hogshead) ---- 99, 152

Gustavus (Spy code name used by Benedict Arnold) ----- 240

Habitants (French farmers in Quebec) ----- 40

Haddrell's Point (Infamous POW prison in SC) ------ 216

Halberd (Spear like weapon with blade) ----- 200

Hale, Capt. Nathan (American spy executed by British) ----- 240

Hale, Capt. Nathan (Bio. by M. Phelps)

Hale, Capt. Nathan (Description of his execution) ----- 240-241

Half-Joes (Portuguese coin used by Americans during the Revolution) ----- 167

Half-Pay Officers (Retired American and British Officers) ----- 167

Halifax Canada (Major port for British operations during the Revolution) ----- 303, 329

Halyards (Lines - ropes - used to raise/lower sails on ships) ----- 72

Hamilton, Alexander (Bio. by R. Chernow)

Hamilton, Alexander (Revolutionary War hero and first Secretary of Treasury of the US) ----- 184

Hammer of Musket (The part of firing mechanism that held the flint) ----- 99

Handspikes (Iron bars used to align cannons) ----- 135

Hanger (Another word for sword) ----- 99

Hanging (Common method to execute criminals) ----- 167

Hanging-On (Maintaining contact with the enemy after an engagement) ----- 168

Hat Act 1732 (Act that limited trade of American made hats) ----- 7

Head of Elk (Point in Maryland were Gen Howe began his attack on Philadelphia) ----- 128-129

Hearts and Minds (Efforts to maintain good will of civilians) ----- 195-196

Heaving Down (Laying a ship on its side to remove marine growth from its hull) ----- 72

Heavy Cavalry (Cavalry used to assault enemy front lines) ----- 102

Heavy Foot Soldiers (British infantry soldiers the same as Grenadiers) ----- 104

Heeling (A ship leaning over while sailing underway) ----- 72

Henry, Patrick (Bio. by H. Unger)

Henry, Patrick (Famous orator who roused Virginians to the American Cause) ----- 27

Herkimer, BG Nicholas (Commander killed at Battle of Oriskany – Oct 1777) ----- 368

Hessians (Name given to all German soldiers in America – See German Mercenaries) – 48

Heurtoirs (Platforms where artillery was placed in fortifications) ----- 135

Hillsborough Treat (Smearing excrement on the homes of Loyalist and British officials) ----- 168

His Majesty's Yankees (Name given to Loyalists who fled to Halifax and Canada from America) ----- 168

HMS GASPEE (See GASPEE Affair) ----- 20

HMS JERSEY (See JERSEY)

Hogshead (Large barrel to hold tobacco or commercial goods) ----- 168

Holy Ground (Area of NYC occupied by prostitutes visited by British soldiers) ----- 168

Honeyman, John (American spy) ----- 241

Honor (Code of conduct) ----- 222, 311

Honors of War (Procedures of surrendering to an enemy) ----- 168, 211

Horses (Few survived the trip from Britain and were always in short supply in America) ----- 128

Hortelez and Cie (Dummy business company in France to spy, operated by Silas Deane) ------ 242

Houghing (Method of crippling British soldiers by cutting their Achilles tendons) ----- 169

Howe, Admiral Richard (British naval commander in America) ----- 38

Howe, LTG William (Second British CINC in America – older brother of Richard) ----- 38, 250

Howitzers (Type of artillery that fired explosive shells) ----- 131, 135

Hubbarton Battle Jul 7, 1777 (Early battle in Burgoyne's drive south of Lake Champlain) ----- 270

Huddy Joshua (American patriot killed by NJ militia) ----- 248

Hudson River (Major river running north to south from upper New York) ----- 270

Hulks Act May 1776 (British Act that made it legal to imprison criminals in ships) ----- 221

Hussars (British and French cavalry) ----- 197

Impressment (See Press Acts)

Incident on King Street (British name for Boston Massacre) ----- 19

Incidents that Precipitated the Revolution ----- 19

Indemnity Act 1767 (Townshend Act - raised price of tea) ----- 13

Indents (Name for IOUs in business actions and loans in absence of currency in America) ---- 169

Indentured Servants (Servants who paid for their transit to America with their labor) ----- 22, 29, 111

Independence Hill (Hill above Ft Ti where British placed artillery that caused Americans to flee) ----- 271

Indian Tribes (Frequently described as "Nations") ----- 52-53

Indians (Original inhabitants of America) ----- 52-53

Indigo (Valuable dye grown in American southern plantations) ----- 5

Infantry, American Tactics (See American Infantry tactics)

Infantry, Weapons (British and American) ----- 94

Infectious Malady (Name for venereal disease) ----- 227

Inoculation ----- 229

Inspector of the Army (Title of von Steuben to establish and Army procedures) ----- 82, 83, 226

Instant (Expression in writing meant to convey same month) ----- 169

Insult a Work (To suddenly attack a fort without notice) ----- 169

Intolerable Acts 1774-1775 (British acts to punish the Colonies for Boston Tea Party) ----- 16

Invest (To surround a fortification or place) ----- 169

Invisible Ink (See sympathetic stain)

Iron Act 1750 (Another British restrictive trade act that aggravated Americans) ----- 7

Iron-Sick Ship (A ship with a weak hull due to corroded iron bolts) ----- 72

Iroquois Confederacy (Group of five Indian tribes that later became Six Nations Confederacy) ----- 52

Jaegers (German infantrymen) ----- 167

Jay, John (American Ambassador to Spain) ----- 118

Jefferson, Thomas (Author of Declaration of Independence and later President of US) ----- 312

Jefferson, Thomas (Bio. by M. Kranish)

Jefferson, Thomas (Bio. by N. Cunningham)

JERSEY HMS SHIP (Notorious British prison ship for American POWs in New York Harbor) ----- 216

Jews in the Revolution (Approximately 2,500 in US most supported American Rebel Cause) ----- 233

Jews in the Revolution (History of by S. Rezneck)

Jockeying (Getting rid of paper money quickly) ----- 170

Jones, John Paul (American naval hero) ----- 344

Judges (British appointed judges who had obvious biases against Americans) ----- 17

Kalb, de Johann (French General fighting for America killed at Battle of Camden) ----- 81

Keel Haul (British method of punishing sailors by dragging them under the hull of their ship) ----- 72

Kennebec River (Place where Arnold expedition started for Quebec) ----- 41

Ketch (Small boat with two masts used mostly on Lake Champlain and inland waterways) ----- 72

Kill Devil (Name for potent rum drink) ----- 170

King Carlos III (King of Spain, supporter of American Cause) ----- 64

King George III (See George III)

King Tree Acts 1711-1722 (British acts reserved large American trees for British Navy) ----- 170

King's Broad Arrows (Marks on American trees reserved for British ships) ----- 170

King's Mountain Battle (History of by C. Draper)

King's Mountain Battle Oct 7, 1780 (Southern Loyalists were decisively defeated) ----- 140, 279

Kingbirds (Name given by Americans for British officers) ----- 170

Knox, MG Henry (Bio. by M. Puls)

Knox, MG Henry (Chief of Artillery of American Army) ----- 357-357

Kosciuszko, Tadeusz (Pole who volunteered for duty with Americans – was Chief of Engineers) ----- 83

Laboratory (Gun powder making facility) ----- 170

Lafayette, de Marquis (Bio. by M. Leepson)

Lafayette, de Marquis (French volunteer who served with distinction in America) ----- 81, 82, 337

Lake Champlain (Major lake from Canada to NY) ----- 31

Lake George (Lake south of Lake Champlain in Burgoyne's campaign) ----- 271

Lamb, Col. John (Bio. by I. Leake)

Lamb, Col. John (Prominent American combat leader and artillery officer) ----- 336

Land Pattern Musket (Standard infantry musket used by British, also called Brown Bess) ----- 97

Land Taxes (British were as high as 20% annually) ----- 14-15

Langrage (Scrap metal and objects fired from cannons in the absence of metal balls) ---- 135

Lanteen Sail Boat (Boat with a single mast and triangular sail for use on inland waterways) ----- 72

Lash (Whip used for punishment) ----- 147

Laudanum (Morphine and wine mixed medicine) ----- 170

Laurens, Henry (Fifth President of Continental Congress) ----- 184

Lead (Critical use in bullets, little found in American ores) ----- 1

League of Armed Neutrality (Group of European nations neutral in American War) ----- 139

Lecherous Disease (Name for venereal disease) ----- 227

Lee Gauge (Sailing position below other ships in combat which usually was a disadvantage) ----- 72

Lee, Maj Harry ("Light Horse" celebrated American cavalry combat leader) ---- 106

Lee, Maj Harry (Bio. by M. Cecere)

Lee, MG Charles (American Gen dismissed for miss-mismanagement of Monmouth Battle) ----- 184

Leeward (Nautical term meaning the direction the wind is blowing TO) ----- 73

Legions (Cavalry units of dismounted and mounted soldiers, usually 1,000 men) ----- 102

Letters of Marque and Reprisal (Letters authorizing sea captains to capture enemy ships) ----- 47

Leveling (Elimination of social classes in New England society) ----- 26, 171

Levy Money (Money paid by Brits to German Princes for service of their soldiers) ----- 62

Lexington/Concord Battle Apr 19, 1775 (American Militia inflicted heavy losses on British) ----- 260-261

Liberty Boys (Group of New York City rebel rousers like Boston Sons of Liberty) ---- 139, 140

Liberty Caps (Distinctive caps worn by South Carolina militia) ----- 171

Liberty Jacket (Term for giving a victim a coat of tar and feathers) ----- 172

Liberty Poles (Rallying points in New York City like Liberty Trees in Boston) ----- 172

Liberty Trees (Rallying points in Boston for Sons of Liberty) ----- 172

Liberty's Daughters (Young girls supporting the American soldiers by sewing uniforms) ----171

Light Cavalry (Cavalry used for intelligence gathering and reconnaissance) ----- 103

Light Foot Soldiers (Infantry trained and equipped for mobility on battlefield) ----- 197

Light Horse Legion Harry Lee (See Lee, Maj Harry)

Light-Ball (Artillery shell on fire shot at night to illuminate an area) ----- 73

Limber (The two-wheeled cart attached to the tongue of artillery to enable it to be towed) ----- 135

Lincoln, MG Benjamin (Bio. by D. Mattern)

Lincoln, MG Benjamin (American general who was captured at Charles Town SC) ----- 277, 341

Line Firing (British method of an infantry "Line" firing on command) ----- 92

Linstock (Wick used to ignite gun powder in cannons) ----- 130

Lippincott, Richard (Militia captain who executed J. Huddy) ----- 229

Logistics American (No experience with a nationwide army) ----- 124, 125

Logistics British (Severe problems supporting British forces across the Atlantic) ---- 126, 127, 128, 129

Long Arm of the Army (Name given for artillery) ----- 136

Long Bobs/Short Bobs (Long and Short loans negotiated by Robert Morris) ------ 172

Long Land Pattern Musket (Standard British infantry musket from 1722-1768) ----- 97

Loopholes (Cutouts in walls of stockades for firing muskets) ----- 206

Loose File and American Scramble (American infantry combat behind trees, walls etc.) ----- 92

Lord Dunmore (See Dunmore's Wars)

Loring, Elizabeth (Mistress of British Gen Howe) ----- 222

Loring, Joshua (British Commissary for American POWs - husband of Elizabeth Loring) ----- 222

Louisiana (Area sought by Spain during and after the Revolution) ----- 64

Loyal Nine (Nine early prominent Massachusetts opponents of British) ----- 173

Loyalist Integration into British Army ----- 93

Loyalist Migration (Post-War History of by M. Jasonoff)

Loyalist Migration from Post-War America (Statistics) ----- 173

Loyalist Militia (Loyalists who took active combat against American Rebels) ----- 328

Loyalists (Those who sided with the British in America) ----- 144

Ludington, Sybil (Heroine who alerted Americans that British were attacking Danbury CT) ---- 235

Lutherans (Germans, Dutch and Scandinavians mostly settled in PA, DE and MD) ----- 26

Made Masts (Ship masts made from slabs of wood due to shortage of traditional masts) ----- 73

Madison, James (Signer of Declaration of Independence and later President of US) ----- 330

Magazines (Supply depots) ----- 173

Maine (At the time of Revolution a Territory of Massachusetts) ----- 173

Man of War (The very largest of war ships) ----- 73

Mantalel (Shield pushed ahead of sappers as they dug final trenches in a siege) ----- 203

Manumission (Process of freeing slaves to fight American Rebels or British) ----- 174

Marham Towers (Towers built to assault British forts in the Southern Campaign) ----- 206

Marines United States (See American Marines)

Marion, Francis (See Swamp Fox)

Market Stoppers (American soldiers who intercepted British plundering for supplies) ----- 174

Mason Dixon Line (Pennsylvania/Maryland/Delaware borders established by British in 1767) ----- 32

Massachusetts Government Act May 20, 1774 (Act limited government of Massachusetts) ----- 17

Matchlock Muskets (Muskets that predated the Flintlock Musket) ----- 99

Matross (Artillery soldier) ----- 174

Medical Care (Description and conditions of care) ----- 225

Mercantilism (Economic policy practiced by European colonial powers towards their colonies) ---- 1, 6

Mercenaries (Statistical summary) ----- 61

Mercer, BG Hugh (American Gen killed at the Battle of Princeton) ----- 321, 367

Mercer, BG Hugh (Bio. by J. Goolrick)

Merlons (Part of fort wall between embrasures) ----- 136, 207

Middle Colonies (NJ, PA, MD, DE) ----- 25

Military Medley (Drum rolls (beats) to signal commands - retreat, reveille, advance, taps etc.) ----- 174

Militia (See American Militia) – 43, 54

Minutemen (New England citizens ready for quick duty against the British) ----- 324

Miracle on the Hudson (Improbable disclosure of B. Arnold's betrayal of the American Cause) ----- 245

Mississippi River (Major commerce river on western frontier of US) ----- 45

Molly Houses (Houses for British gay soldiers in NYC) ----- 227

Monmouth Association for Retaliation (Group of NJ Loyalists who fought against Americans) ------ 140

Monmouth Courthouse Battle Jun 28, 1778 (British left Philadelphia to return to NYC) ---- 274-275

Monmouth Courthouse Battle (History of by J. Bilby)

Mono-Alphabetic Coding (Coding system for secret messages) ----- 243

Monroe Doctrine (American doctrine limiting European powers from American territories) ----- 326

Monroe, James (American Revolutionary combat officer, later President of US) ----- 326

Monroe, James (Bio. by G. Hart)

Montgomery, BG Richard (American general killed during attack on Quebec) ----- 41, 366

Montgomery, BG Richard (Bio. by H. Shelton)

Montreal Battles Sep-Nov 13, 1775 (Battles for St Johns and Montreal Canada) ----- 41

Montreal City (Key Canadian city south west of Quebec) ---- 41-

Moors of Morocco (Solicited by the British for duty in America) ---- 61

Moravians (Quakers who served in non-combat duty during the Revolution) ---- 226

Morgan, Col Daniel (American combat leader defeated Tarleton at Cowpens) ----- 79, 327

Morgan, Col Daniel (Bio. by D. Higgenbothem)

Morris, Robert (Wealthy American major finance manager for American Cause) ----- 234, 310

Morris, Robert (Bio. by C. Rappleye)

Mortars (Short stubby artillery pieces) ----- 132

Mortification (Expression of severe disappointment/unhappiness/displeasure) ----- 174

Mortification (Gangrene, to die of mortification was to die of gangrene) ----- 174

Mosaic Law (Biblical law regarding flogging) ----- 170

Murphy, Timothy (American sniper who shot British MG Fraser at Saratoga) ----- 193

Mushroom Gentlemen (War profiteers) ------ 175

Musket Loading Process (Fifteen step sequence to load the weapon) ----- 98

Musket Range (Naval term where ships in combat are with musket firing range) ----- 73

Muskets (Standard infantry weapons of soldiers of the Revolution) ----- 338

Muster Rolls (Rosters of soldiers assigned to a unit) ---- 128

Mutiny by American Soldiers Jan 1781 (History of by C. Van Doren)

Narrative by Colonel Ethan Allen (Allen telling his horrific experience as a POW) ----- 219, 292

NANCY (British ship captured Nov 27, 1775 with major arms haul for Americans) ----- 47

Naval Fighting Tactics (French vs British) ----- 73

Naval Terminology (Terms helpful in understanding naval warfare of the period) ----- 67

Navigation Acts (Series of multiple acts starting o/a 1700 restricting American trade) ----- 24

Necessaries (Latrines, sometimes also called "Vaults") ----- 175

Need for Revenue (British Debts from French and Indian War) ----- 9

Netherlands (Dutch were powerful merchantmen who benefitted from the Revolution) ---- 66

Neutral Yankees (Name given to Loyalist New Englanders who fled to Nova Scotia) ----- 175

New Connecticut (The original proposed name for the Republic of Vermont) ----- 175

New Hampshire Colony (Provided critical soldiers for New England Battles) ----- 175

New Hampshire Grants (This contested land between New Hampshire and New York) ----- 175

New Jail (Name of a notorious prison for American POWs In Philadelphia) ----- 217

New Jersey Board of Associated Loyalists (Rabid loyalist in NJ) ----- 144

New Lights (Followers of new religious thinking who rejected strict British Anglican thought) ----- 6

New Subjects (French who were in Canada after the F&I War) ----- 40, 175

New York City Battles Aug-Nov 1776 (Disastrous battles that left NYC in British hands) ---- 264-265

New York Colony (Less enthusiastic for Revolution than most colonies) ----- 14, 17

New York Restraining Act 1767 (Act - forced NY to quarter British soldiers) ----- 14

Newgate (Notorious American prison for British POWs in Simsbury CT copper mine) ---- 217

Newport Rhode Island Battle August 29, 1778 (Americans ousted by British from area) ----- 23

Norfolk Port (See Port of Norfolk) ------ 22

North Act March 1776 (Gave belligerent status to American POWs) ----- 221

North, Lord Frederick (British Prime Minister throughout the American Revolution) ----- 14

North, Lord Frederick (See book by A. O'Shaughnessy) ------ 14

North Peace Plan Feb 20, 1775 (AKA "Conciliatory Proposal" British effort to avoid war) ---- 37

Northern Colonies (MA, RI, NH, NY, CT) ----- 24

Northern Department (The collection of all American fighting forces in New England) ----- 40

Northern vs Southern Colonies (Differences) ----- 232-24

Oakum (Calking between planks of ships) ----- 73

Oaths of Fidelity (Oaths swearing allegiance to America) ----- 176

Obedience of Orders (Methods and reasons for discipline of soldiers) ----- 146

Oblique Order (Rapid gathering of soldiers) ------ 176

Old Lights (Supporters of British Anglican Church in America) ----- 6

Old Subjects (Original British subjects of Canada after the F&I War) ----- 40, 176

Olive Branch Petition July 5, 1775 (Proposal by Americans to prevent war with Britain) ----- 37, 38

Order of Battle (Composition of forces of an army) ---- 176

Order of Echelon (Movement of soldiers in battle) ----- 176

Organization of American Army ----- 85, 86

Organization of British Army ----- 85, 86

Oriskany Battle Aug 6, 1777 (Battle where British defeated Americans but then retreated) ----- 271

Out Pensions (Pensions that were awarded to disabled and retired British officers) ----- 176

Outliers (Renegades of North and South Carolina) ----- 198

Outriders (Message carriers on horseback) ----- 162

Over Mountain Men (American militia from the mountains of NC, SC and GE) ----- 140

Packet Ships (Ships designated to carry messages) ----- 73

Paine, Thomas (Author of "The Crisis" and "Common Sense") ----- 156-157

Palings (Fence made of sharp sticks driven into the ground) ----- 207

Palisades (Heavy logs driven vertically into the ground to create a fort) ----- 207

Pan (Place where the powder was placed for guns prior to "Firing") ----- 97

Paper Money (Continental Dollars) ----- 2

Paoli Battle (History of by Thomas McGuire)

Parallel Order (Order to move soldiers facing each other in battle) ----- 177

Parallels (Siege trenches dug parallel to the walls of an enemy fort) ----- 202, 207

Parapets (Defensive works in front of forts and trenches) ----- 207

Paris Peace Treaty Sep 3, 1783 (Terms and conditions for ending the Revolution) ----- 253

Parker, Capt. John (Commanded the American militia company at the Battle of Lexington) ----- 261

Parole (Status of a POW released on terms of good behavior and no further combat) ----- 222

Parricide (Parent hater - a nickname given to B. Arnold by B. Franklin) ----- 177

Peace Negotiations (Treaty of Paris 1783) ----- 177

Pebble (Nickname for flint in guns) ----- 97

Peculation (Misappropriation of public funds - charge against B. Arnold) ----- 177

Pennamite War (Conflict between CT and PA over land in Pennsylvania they both claimed) ----- 32

Penobscot Bay Expedition Aug 1779 (Failed American expedition into Territory of Maine) ----- 49, 58

Penobscot Bay Expedition Aug 1779 (History of by G. Buker)

Pensions and Pension Acts (American Pension Acts for Revolutionary War veterans) ---- 258-259

Petard a Place (Force open the door of a fort with a petard - large sturdy blade) ---- 177

Petite Guerre (Expression that meant "Little War" or guerrilla warfare waged by Americans) ----- 177

PHILADELPHIA (American War Ship on Lake Champlain) ----- 73, 74

PHILADELPHIA American Warship on Lake Champlain (History of by J. Bratten)

Philadelphia (First capitol of America – occupied by British from Oct 1777 – Jun 1778) ----- 36

Phillipsburg Proclamation Jun 30, 1779 (British Act giving freedom and protection to slaves) ----- 50

Pickets (Sometimes called Piquet's - soldiers ahead of camps on alert to enemy) ----- 198

Picquets (Sharp sticks soldiers must stand on for punishment) ----- 147

Pig Pen Cypher (Classification technique for secret messages) -----243

Pintard, John (American commissary agent for Rebel POWs) ----- 222

Pirate Act March 1777 (British act that mandated life in prison for captured American pirates) ------ 47

Pistol Range (Naval term meaning the ships in combat were within 50 yards fighting distance) ------ 73

Pistols (Rarely used usually only by officers) ----- 99

Pitcairn, Maj John (Commander of British Marines killed at Bunker Hill) ----- 261

Pivot Guns (Small caliber cannons mounted on a pivot, frequently used on small boats) ----- 131, 136

Placeman (An individual given an official position based on connections - not merit) ---- 178

Plan of 1776 (Plan to protect American trade with European nations) ----- 178

Plantation Culture (Built around slave labor on large farm estates in southern colonies) ------ 25

Platoon Firing (Aimed fire on command by American platoons) ----- 90, 178

Platoons (The smallest of infantry combat elements - usually just 10 to 15 soldiers) ----- 86

Plundering (Confiscation of civilian property - caused Americans to turn against enemy) ----- 178

Point Pleasant Battle (History of by J. Winkler)

Point Pleasant Battle Oct 10, 1774 (Thought of as the first battle of the Revolution) ----- 21-22

Political Conditions in America and Britain ----
Poltroon (Name for a cowardly inept soldier) ----- 179
Poneau, du Peter Stephen (French volunteer who acted as interpreter for Gen von Steuben) ------ 82
Poop-Deck (Elevated deck at the stern of a ship) ----- 74
Port of Norfolk Virginia (Major port on south east coast of Virginia abandoned by British) ----- 22
Port Side of a Ship (The left side of a ship when facing the bow from the stern) ----- 74
Porter (Dark brown and slightly bitter beer) ----- 179
Post-War Improvements in the treatment of POWs ----- 219
Powder Horns (Devices usually made of cattle horns to hold and pour powder for muskets) ----- 100
Powder Monkeys (Very young boys who would work in the powder magazines of British ships) ----- 74
Presbyterians (Protestants who moved from Ireland to America) ----- 22, 141
Pre-War Issues (Which led to the Revolution) ----- 16-18
Predatory War (See War Ad Terror)
Predestination (Anglican preaching that individuals predestined for privilege and life of ease) ----- 141
Prescott, MG Richard (British general twice captured by Americans) ----- 38
Press Acts May 28, 1778 & Feb 9, 1779 (Allowed impressment of civilians into British Navy) ----- 179
Press Gangs (Gangs of British seamen or soldiers who would force civilians into military service) ----- 74
Press Warrants (Written authorization for British to plunder American property) ----- 179

Prevost (Famous former NYC jail converted to horrific POW prison for American captives) ---- 287

Prevost, MG Augustine (British general at Siege of Savannah, Sep 16 - Oct 1779) ----- 276

Pre-War Legislative Acts and Issues ----- 16-18

Pricker (Sharp device used to puncture bag of gunpowder in a cannon) ----- 130

Princeton Battle Jan 3, 1777 (Battle after Trenton again defeating the British) ------ 315

Princeton Battle (History of by C. Dwyer)

Prisoner Commissaries (Individuals responsible for feeding and caring for POWs) ----- 222

Prisoners Of War (British and German) ----- 63, 219

Prisoners Of War Exchanges (Difficulty in exchanging differing ranks etc.) ----- 223

Prisoners Of War Issues (Treatment of and legal status) ----- 220

Prisoners Of War (Statistics and Information) ----- 215

Privateering (Act of attacking ships for profit) ----- 45-46

Privy Council (Senior British leaders - clergy, generals, politicians etc. to advise on War) ---- 180

Prize Gangs (Gangs of sailors to abduct individuals for privateer duty) ----- 74

Prize Money (Money from the sale of prize ships and cargo to be split by crew and officers) ----- 75

Prize Ships (Ships captured by privateers) ----- 47, 75

Proclamation Act Oct 7, 1763 (Land west of Appalachians off limits to Americans) ----- 6, 52

Proclamation of Pacification Nov 30, 1776 (Protection given to those went American cause) -----180

Proclamation of Rebellion Aug 23, 1775 (George III rejection of Olive Branch Petition) ---- 38

Proclamation for Suppressing Rebellion and Sedition (Same as Proclamation of Rebellion) ----- 38

Promise of Protection (See Proclamation of Pacification)

Promotions (How conducted by British) ----- 180

Protection Fever (See Tristinania)

Protection Papers (See "Proclamation of Pacification")

Provincials (Another name for Loyalists) ----- 144

Provisional American Loyalists (Americans who fought with British against American Rebels) ----- 144

Provost (Former NYC jail used as POW camp by British) ----- 287

Pulaski, Casimir (Polish volunteer in America killed at the Battle of Savannah October 1779) ----- 84

Pulaski's Continental Light Dragoons (Unit of dragoons led by Casimir Pulaski) ----- 106

Punishment (Methods and rules for the punishment of American and British soldiers) ----- 146

Purchase System (System in Britain where officer commissions could be bought and sold) ----- 181

Puritanism (Strict New England body of religious practice) ----- 26

Putnam, MG Israel (Bio. by W. Cutter)

Putnam, MG Israel (Famous elderly combat leader of Americans in New England) ----- 312

Quaker Guns (Logs painted black to look like cannons to scare the enemy) ----- 136

Quakers (Religious sect believed war was immoral and refused combat in Revolution) ----- 26

Quarter (Asking to Surrender) ----- 211

Quarter-Bill (List of officers and men on a ship similar to a Muster Roll for the army) ---- 75

Quartering Act 1765 (Act requiring Colonies to provide lodging/provisions for British soldiers) --- 11

Quartering Act Second Jun 2, 1774 (Intolerable Act requiring the colonies to provide lodging) --- 11

Quartermaster General (American official responsible for supplying the American Army) ----- 125

Quebec (See Fourteenth Colony)

Quebec Attempt to Conquer ----- 40

Quebec Act Oct 7, 1774 (Intolerable Act expanded British control of western colonial lands) ----- 17

Quebec City (Place where B. Arnold was wounded in attempt to capture the city) ----- 41

Quebec Province (West of PA, VA and NY ceded to Quebec by Quebec Act of Oct 7, 1774) ----- 40

Quit-Rent ("Rent" paid to Crown by American and British landholders - a tax) ----- 181

Quittance (Repayment or release from a debt) ----- 181

Quoins (Screw like devices under the breech of cannons to lower or raise elevation of the gun) ----- 136

Race To The Dan River (American retreat to Dan River after Battle of Cowpens) ----- 282-283

Rage Militaire (Name for desire by Colonists to break with Britain by military force) ----- 302

Raising for Rank (Loyalists raising at their own expense units to fight Americans) ----- 182

Rall, Col Johann (German Commander killed at Trenton Battle Dec 26, 1776) ----- 268

Randolph, Payton (President of First Continental Congress) ----- 28

Ranger Units (American and British) ----- 103

Rape (See Ravishment)

Ratline (Ladder like system of ropes to climb a ship's rigging) ----- 75

RATTLESNAKE (British warship that carried the news of Yorktown defeat to Britain) ---- 286

Ravishment (Rape – a scourge of British and German soldiers in America) ----- 182

Reconnaissance (Major role of cavalry) ----- 103

Recruiting American (See Enlistments American)

Recruiting British (See British Recruiting)

Red Bank Battle (Otherwise known as Battle of Ft Mercer Oct 1777 – See Ft Mercer)

Redans (Arrow like defensive structures usually made of earth and logs) ----- 207

Redemptioners (Indentured servants drafted into US Army for their freedom) ----- 111

Redoubt Number 10 (Key British defensive position captured at Battle of Yorktown) ----- 82

Redoubts (Large earthen fortifications) ----- 207

Refugee Club (This was a group of New Jersey radical loyalists displaced by the war) ---- 144

Refugees (Individuals displaced by the revolution) ----- 248

Regiments (Large infantry combat units of 810 soldiers usually composed of 10 companies) ----- 86

Regional Differences between the Colonies ----- 23

Regulations for Order and Discipline of Troops (von Steuben's "Blue Book") ----- 226

Regulators (NC and SC Americans who opposed British lawlessness) ----- 140

Reinforcement of British soldiers in Boston (4,000 soldiers added to Boston) – 19

Religious Conditions in America ----- 25, 26

Republic of Vermont (Earliest independent government of Vermont) ----- 32

Resolves (Group decisions that nearly had the force of law) ----- 182

Returns (Another term for Muster Rolls) ----- 182, 332

Revalins (Arrow like structures built in front of bastions of forts) ----- 208

Revenue (British need for after French and Indian War) ----- 9

Revenue Act 1767 (Townshend Act that levied taxes on goods from Britain) ----- 14

Revere, Paul (Influential Boston patriot) ----- 35

Revolutionary Fervor (Differences in the colonies for enthusiasm for the Revolution) ----- 26, 27

Ricochet Firing (Intentional ricochet firing by cannon to cause great damage and casualties) ----- 136

Riding the Rail (Common punishment given to loyalists with rail between legs) ----- 182

Riedesel, MG von Friedrich (Senior German officer captured at Battle of Saratoga) ----- 272

Rifle Dress (Equipment issued to new American recruits) ----- 157

Rifles (Guns with grooved "rifling" inside barrels) ----- 100

Rights of Man (Liberal document written by Thomas Paine after the Revolution) ----- 156

River Gods (Wealthy Royalist large land owners around the Connecticut River) ----- 144

Rivington, James (American spy part of Culper Ring) ----- 239

Rochambeau, de Compte (French Gen who fought along-side Washington at Yorktown) ----- 267

Rod (Measure of length equal 5 1/2 yards or 16 1/2 feet) ----- 183

Roe, Austin (American spy part of Culper Ring) ----- 239

Rogers, Maj Robert (Bio. by J. Ross)

Roman Catholics (See Catholics)

Royal Army (See British Army)

Royal Mortar (A very large mortar with a 5 ½ inch diameter bore) ----- 136

Royal Wagon Train (The British wagon system which was largely run by civilians) ----- 183

Rum (Rum was a major factor in trade and revenue for Britain and the Colonies) ----- 231

Running the Gauntlet (See Gauntlet Running)

Rutledge, John (President of First Continental Congress) ----- 298

Sabots (Wooden disks placed in cannons to hold the shots in place) ----- 136

Sabres (Cavalry swords – shorter than infantry swords) ----- 103

Sabretache (Leather or canvas satchel worn by cavalrymen) ----- 201

Saint-Simon compte de (French General at Yorktown) ----- 59

Sally (To "Sally" was to rush unexpectedly from a fort and attack) ----- 183

Sally Point (A single entry/exit point from a redoubt) ----- 208

Saltonstall, Dudley (Leader of America Penobscot expedition into Maine in 1779) ----- 304

Saltpeter (Key component of gun powder) ----- 152

Salutary Neglect (Neglect by British of customs and tax laws in Pre-Revolutionary America) ----- 7

Sandwich Earl (Corrupt British Minister of the Navy – see book by A. O'Shaughnessy)

Sappers (Soldiers who dug trenches in siege operations) ----- 203

Saps (Final trenches before an enemy fort) ----- 203

Saratoga Battles (History of by C. Nielson)

Saratoga Battles (History of by M. Loquat)

Saratoga Battles (History of by R. Ketchum)

Saratoga Battles Jul 1777-Oct 1777 (British defeats in Northern Campaign – Book by M, Loquez)

Saratoga Convention (The surrender agreement of Burgoyne) ----- 211

Sash (Red waist band to signify an officer) ---- 201

Satisfaction (Challenge to a duel) ----- 208

Saucines (Long bundles of sticks tied together for protection in forts) ----- 208

Sauvegardes (American or British officers left to protect vulnerable civilians after battles) ----- 184

Savannah SC Siege Sep-Oct 9, 1779 (Site of serious defeat of Americans) ----- 275-276

Scantlings (Narrow boards nailed to hold picket boards of a fort together) ----- 208

Scouring (Name given to scorched earth campaigning) ----- 184

Schooners (Sailing vessel with two masts mostly used for inland and coastal work) ----- 75

Schuler, Hon Yost (The individual B. Arnold used to spook the enemy at Oriskany) ----- 272

Schuyler, MG Philip (General who commanded Americans before battle of Saratoga) ----- 40

Scotch/Irish (An immigrant group in America that strongly opposed the British) ----- 140, 141

Scurvy (Dietary disease common on ships and in American and British armies) ----- 226

Second Parallels (The second trenches constructed in a siege) ----- 203

Second Quartering Act Oct 7, 1774 (Intolerable Act required the quartering of British soldiers) ----- 17

Seigneurs (Wealthy land owners along the St. Lawrence River in Canada) ----- 40, 184

Seven Years War – 9, 176

Shay's Rebellion (Rebellion in MA & NH of Post-Rev War veterans over taxes) ----- 365

Ships of the Line (Large combat ships) ----- 75

Shipwrights (Ship builders and carpenters) ----- 76

Shirtmen (Derisive name given by British to American soldiers who had no uniforms) ----- 184

Shock Troops (Grenadiers - sometimes called "Forlorn Hopes") ----- 196

Shrechlichkeit (German term for "Total War") ----- 120

Shrouds (Lines in the rigging of ships) ----- 76

Sick and Hurt Board (British board in 1742 to develop treatment policies for POWs) ----- 220

Siege Artillery (Heavy caliber artillery made to destroy a fort) ----- 136

Siege Warfare (Warfare that focused on sieges of enemy forts) ----- 202

Signing Bonus (Money paid to "Recruits" for enlisting frequently called a "Bounty") ----- 110

Silver Ores (Absence of in Colonies) ------ 1

Simcoe, John LTC (British commander of Queen's Rangers) ----- 108

Simcoe's Queen's Rangers (Ruthless British Ranger unit) ----- 108

Simsbury Copper Mine (Site of mine in CT where British POWs were held) ----- 218

Sinecure (Position appointed where individual was paid but did no work) ----- 185

Six Indian Nations Confederacy (Loose group of Indian Nations - tried to protect themselves) ----- 145

Skinners (Militia north of NYC who fought local loyalists called the "Cowboys") ----- 141, 198

Slaves/Slavery (How it differed between Northern, Middle and Southern Colonies) ----- 28, 29, 30

Sleeping in Arms (Soldiers on very high alert who would sleep with their weapons) ----- 100

Sloops (Ships larger than cutters, used mostly for coastal work) ----- 76

Smallpox (The highly contagious disease contained by inoculation) ----- 226

Smallpox Inoculation (Smearing infected material on small abrasion to induce immunity) ----- 226

Smart Money (Money paid by a British enlistee to void his enlistment) ----- 114, 185

Smith, Joshua (Involved with B. Arnold in his betrayal of the American Cause) ----- 246

Smithsonian Museum (Place where American ship PHILADELPHI is currently housed) --- 74

Smoking (Punishment of Loyalists blocking the chimney filling house with smoke) ----- 185

Social Conditions ----- 4

Social Stratification in Colonies ----- 23

Solano, Don Jose (Spanish Admiral who supported French Navy to Yorktown) ----- 60

Soldatenhandel (German term for mercenaries) ----- 185

Solemn League and Covenant (Boston response to Port Act) ----- 16, 141

Soldier Servants (Soldiers who were paid as attendants to senior officers) ----- 185

Sons of Liberty (Early Boston group of rebel rousers) ----- 141

Sons of Neptune (American sailors who supported the Revolution) ----- 141

Sons of Violence (Name given by the British for Sons of Neptune) ----- 142

Sortie (See "Sally")

Southern Campaign (See History of by D. Wilson)

Southern Colonies (VA, NC, SC, GE) ----- 25

Southern British Strategy (Strategy to defeat Revolution by winning in South) ---- 123

Spain (Spain lost land to Britain in F&I War) ----- 64, 319

Spanish Army Mostly fought the British in Florida, Louisiana and Mississippi River) ----- 64, 65

Spanish Navy (While not modernized was still a potent threat to the British) ----- 64, 65

Spatterdashes (Protective covers at the ankles and tops of soldier's feet) ----- 201

Special Operations during the Revolution (See history of by R. Tonsetic)

Specie (Absence of in Colonies) ----- 2

Spider Catchers (New Jersey Privateers who attacked British shipping from whale boats) ------ 76

Spider Shot (Cannon shots linked together by chains mostly used in naval battles) ----- 137

Spiking of Cannons (Disabling cannons by driving a spike of metal or into the vent hole) ----- 137

Spinners (American volunteer women who made cloth and uniforms for soldiers) ----- 186

Spirits and Crimps (Unscrupulous British agents who tricked youngers into indenture) ----- 186

Spontoon (A spear like weapon on a pole to help deter bayonet charges) ----- 100, 201

Spreading Ink Stain (Strategic concept considered by British – rejected) ----- 121

Sprigs of Green (Greenery worn by American soldiers to identify them as Rebels) ----- 186

Sproat, David (The corrupt British appointed official for feeding American Naval POWs in NYC) ----- 222

Spying during American Revolution, History of by B. Kilmeade

Spying during American Revolution, History of by A. Rose

Spying and Terms ----- 237

St. Augustine Florida (Place of significant combat occurred between British & Spanish soldiers) ----- 306

St. Clair, MG Arthur (Commanded Ft Ticonderoga at Saratoga Battle – Book by Loquez)

St. Eustatius (Dutch Island where much of America's black powder was shipped to US) ----- 66, 187

St. Johns Fort (Canadian fort 30 miles south of Montreal which saw heavy combat) ---- 41

St. Lawrence River (Key river between Canada and Northern Colonies) ----- 41

St. Ledger LtCol Barry (British Commander of force that tried to assist Burgoyne) ----- 270

Stacking Arms (Method of storing guns in the field for quick action) ----- 100

Stamp Tax Act of 1765 (Repealed 1766 - source of great ire by Americans) ----- 10

Staple Act 1763 (Prohibited exports direct to Europe) ----- 5

Starboard Side (Right side of a ship when facing the bow from the stern) ---- 76

Stark, BG John (NH General - Leader of Americans at Bennington & Bunker Hill) ----- 332, 362

Stark, BG John (Bio. by B. Rose)

State Militia (Militia organized and paid by the States vs Local Militia) ----- 198

Staten Island Peace Conference Sep 11, 1776 (Effort by the British to stop the Revolution) ----- 38

Statia another name for St. Eustatius (See St. Eustatius)

Steganography (Techniques of hiding secret information) ----- 243

Steuben, MG Drill Manual ("Blue Book" gave rules and regulations for American Army) ----- 152, 339

Steuben, MG William von Frederich (German volunteer who trained and led Americans) ----- 82, 83

Steuben, MG William (Bio. by P. Lockhart)

Stockton, Richard (Only Signer of Declaration Independence to re-cant – See book D. Kiernan)

Stony Point Battle Jul 16, 1779 (American morale boosting victory by Gen Wayne) -----

Stoppages (Deductions of pay of British soldiers for uniforms, food, medical care etc.) ----- 187

Strategies (American Army Options – See American Army Strategic Options)

Strategies (British Army Options –See British Army Strategic Options)

Strength Accounting (Method of totaling numbers of soldiers) ----- 86

Strokes (Whips with a lash) ----- 189

Subordination (Willingness to submit to superiors) ----- 30, 31

Submarine (American submarine named the TURTLE invented by American D. Bushnell) ----- 229

Substitutes (Individuals who "substituted" for those who received "Draft" notices) ----- 111

Succession of British Commanders in Chief in America ----- 251

Suffolk County Resolves (See Boston Resolves) ----- 35

Sugar (Called "White Gold" because of its value, it was the major component of rum) ----- 192

Sugar Acts 1773 & 1774 (British tax acts on sugar which infuriated Americans) ----- 7, 9

Sugar House (Former sugar warehouse in NYC and notorious prison for American POWs) ----- 218

Sullivan, MG John (American Gen lead campaign in PA and NY to punish American Indians) ----- 52

Sullivan, MG John (Bio. by K. Stephens)

Sulphur (Crucial component in gunpowder, absence of in American Colonies) ------ 2

Sultana (Name given to Elizabeth Loring, mistress of British Gen Howe) ----- 187

Sumter, BG Thomas (Famous South Carolina militia commander) ------ 188

Sumter's Law (Policy of Sumter's men selling captured Loyalist slaves) ----- 188

Surgeons (Performed operations and frequently had less medical training than "doctors") ----- 225

Surrendering (Methods, Protocols and Terms) ----- 210

Susquehanna Valley (Area pf central Pennsylvania sometimes called Wyoming) ----- 32

Swamp Fox (Name given to Francis Marion a famous South Carolina militia leader) ----- 188

Sweeps (Oars for rowing boats) ----- 76

Swivel Guns (Cannons on a swivel so they could be fired around the battlefield) ----- 131, 137

Swords (American swords were frequently made from saw mill blades) ----- 101, 201

Sympathetic Stain (Invisible ink used by Americans for spying) ----- 243

Tallmadge, Maj Benjamin (Spy Leader - Washington's Chief of Intelligence) ----- 240, 241

Tar and Feathering (Common punishment given loyalists) ----- 188

Tarleton, Lt Col Banastre (Notorious British Legion Commander) ----- 108, 109

Tarleton's Quarter (No quarter or forgiveness or surrender) ----- 188

Taxation (The way to fund British soldiers in America) ----- 14-15

Taxes Without Representation (Considered a major violation of British law by Americans) -----

Teamsters (Civilian wagon masters) ----- 199

TERRIBLE (Major British Ship sunk at Battle of Capes) ----- 286

Territorial Disputes (Description of territorial disputes between the Colonies) ---- 31, 32, 33

Test Laws (new England laws to test loyalty to American Cause) ----- 188

The Cure (Inoculation for smallpox) ----- 188

The Great Warpath (Water route from St Lawrence River via Lake Champlain to NY) ---- 189

The Lash (The whip for punishment) ----- 189

The Wolf (Nickname given for Lord Tryon as British Colonial appointed Governor of NY) ----- 192

Ticonderoga Fort (Major fort at the southern end of Lake Champlain) -----

Tidesmen (British appointed customs officials) ----- 189

Tobacco (Highly valued export product to Britain and Europe) ----- 25, 29

Tomahawk (Somewhat unique hand held American fighting weapon) ----- 101

Tories (Another name for Loyalists) ----- 145

Torpedoes (Explosive "mines" floated in the water to sink ships) ----- 230

Torture (More common with American Indians than with British or Colonists) ----- 189

Tory Rot (See Tristimania)

Tow (Wadding used in musket shots) ----- 101

Town Meetings (Unique New England meeting for locals to discuss issues) ----- 17

Townshend Acts 1766-1767 (Five acts passed to make Americans pay for F&I War) ----- 11, 13, 14

Townshend, Lord Charles (Britain's Chancellor of the Exchequer from 1766 - 1767) ----- 13

Townsend, Robert (American spy and member of Culper Ring) ----- 240

Tradesmen (British soldiers who had special skills which exempted them from line combat) ----- 190

Traveling Press (Washington mobile press to get propaganda out) ----- 190

Traverse (The part of a cannon's platform that allowed it to aim across a battlefield) --- 208

Treaty of Alliance Feb 6, 1778 (French treaty with America following defeat of British defeat) ----- 273

Treaty of Paris 1783 (Treaty that ended the American Revolution) ----- 253

Treaty of Aranjuez Jun 21, 1779 (Treaty where Spain joined France in war against Britain) ----- 64

Trench Pikes (Spear like weapons to deter bayonet charges and trench attacks) ----- 101

Trenton Battle (History of by W. Dwyer)

Trenton Battle (History of by P. Tucker)

Trenton Battle Dec 26, 1776 (Crucial battle that saved the American army) ----- 48, 268-269

Tristimania (Depression and despair over the long fight for independence) ----- 190

Trepanning (Operations on the skulls of injured soldiers) ----- 190

Troop (Proper Name for a Cavalry Unit) ----- 103

Troopers (Proper name for cavalrymen) ----- 103

Trunnion (Frame of an artillery piece) ----- 137

Tryon, William (British Governor of Colony of NY) ----- 192

TURTLE (World's first submarine developed by American inventor D. Bushnell) ----- 76, 77

Twin Brothers (Name for British repeal of Stamp Act and passage of Declaratory Act) ----- 11

Types of Units and Soldiers ----- 195

United Colonies (Early term for colonies) ----- 190

Up and Down Lake Champlain (Lake Champlain flows north towards Canada) ----- 191

Up Hill and Down Hill (Atlantic Crossings - sailing east or west to and from Europe) ----- 29

Valcour Island Battle Oct 11-13, 1775 (Delayed British advance south from Canada one year) ----- 46

Valley Forge (Place of Washington's cantonment during Winter 1777-Spring 1778) ----- 84, 320

Van (Lead element of a force) ----- 191

Vauban, Sebastian (French engineer who developed siege procedures) ----- 202

Vaults (Latrines) ----- 191

Vedettes (Pickets on horseback) ----- 199

Venereal Disease ----- 227

Vent Holes (Small holes in barrels of cannons where powder charge was ignited) ----- 137

Vergennes, Charles (French Foreign Minister who supported the American Revolution) ------ 39

Vergennes, Charles Peace Initiative (Early 1779 initiative to possibly end the Revolution) ----- 39

Vermont (Formerly the territory called the New Hampshire Grants) ----- 32

Vice Admiralty Act 1767 (Townshend Act - appointed British officers to courts) ----- 14

Volley vs Aimed Fire (Volley was fire on command, aimed fire was at specific targets) --- 192

VULTURE (British Ship on Hudson River involved with Andre'/Arnold) ----- 245

Wallabout Bay (Cove in New York harbor where POW ships were anchored) ----- 217

Wagon Department (Created May 14, 1778 to solve wagon train problems) ----- 125

War Ad Terror (Wage unrelenting war) ----- 192

War Board (Group of American Committees to manage the War) ----- 36, 124

War of Posts (Washington's defensive strategy of attacking/defending posts) ---- 317

War of 1812 (History of by W. Borneman)

Warner, Colonel Seth (Commanded Green Mountain Boys after Colonel Ethan Allen) ----- 139

Warren, Dr. Joseph (Revolutionary Boston doctor who was killed at Bunker Hill) ----- 241

Washington, LTG George (Bio. by R. Chernow)

Washington, LTG George (Commander of American forces 1775-1783) ----- 157

Washington, Harry (escaped slave of General Washington) ---- 51

Wayne, MG Anthony (American general who commanded the Pennsylvania Line) ----- 80-81

Wayne, MG Anthony (Bio. by G. Tucker)

Weather Gauge (The upwind position in naval combat) ----- 76

West Point (Key fort on Hudson River) ----- 245

Whigs (Those who supported the American Cause) ----- 142, 199

White Ash Sail (Nickname given to oars) ----- 77

White Gold (Nickname given to sugar) ----- 192

Whitehall (British Government Headquarters in London) ----- 192

Wicket (Small door in the entrance of a fort) ----- 209

Widow Makers (Name given by British for American snipers) ----- 193

Wigwams (Shelters made of local field material on campaigns) ----- 193

Wild Geese (Name for four Irish regiments under French) ----- 193

Wilkinson, BG James (Bio. by A. Linklater)

Wilkinson, BG James (American Gen who tried to discredit Gen Washington) ----- 338

Williamsburg Virginia (Virginia capitol until moved to Richmond by Gov. T. Jefferson) ----- 27

Windage (The space between the bullet and barrel of a gun) ----- 101

Windward (Direction the wind is blowing FROM) ----- 77

Wings (Major combat unit composed of two or more divisions) ----- 85

Women in the Revolution (Rolls and their participation) ----- 235

Wood, Col James II (American Commander at Albemarle VA POW camp) ---223

Woodhull, Abraham (American Spy – member of Culper Ring) ----- 240

Woolens Act 1699 (One of early Navigation Acts limiting American trade in wool) ----- 7

Xebecs (Inland sailboats with two masts and overhanging bow and stern) ----- 77

Yorkers (Derisive name given New York Staters by New Hampshireites) ----- 193

Yorktown (Place in south east coast of Virginia where Cornwallis was trapped) ----- 287

Yorktown Siege (History of by J. Greene)

Yorktown Siege Sept 28-Oct 17, 1781 (Battle where British Southern Army surrendered) ----- 287

Yorktown Casemate (Shelter taken by Cornwallis during Yorktown Siege) ----- 205

Zane, Betty (American heroine at Battle of Ft Henry 1782) ----- 235

ACKNOWLEDGEMENTS

When I retired "for good" in 2010 I decided to dedicate myself to community service through the Veterans of Foreign Wars (VFW) and the Sons of the American Revolution (SAR). These two outstanding organizations have very similar values, goals and objectives. I joined the VFW as a Life Member in 1986 when I was still on active duty. I joined the SAR in 2010 with my four sons, five grandsons, two brothers and four nephews. My maternal grandfather joined the SAR in 1953 and maternal grandmother joined the Daughters of the American Revolution also in 1953.

After joining the SAR, I started an intense reading program on the Revolution. I was surprised at how much I did not know and began taking informal notes, especially on the multitude of terms that abound about the Revolution. After two years, I showed my notes to the Virginia Society SAR Historian the Reverend Larry Aaron, who is a published historian on the Revolution. He encouraged me to proceed to possibly publish my work. He deserves full credit for any success from this effort. Despite his extremely busy schedule he read my drafts and provided critical advice, especially as pertains to organization and content.

I also want to thank my personal friend Colonel William Schwetke, USAF (Ret) President of the Culpeper Minutemen who encouraged me to power through this journey. He is a leader of awesome capability and dedication.

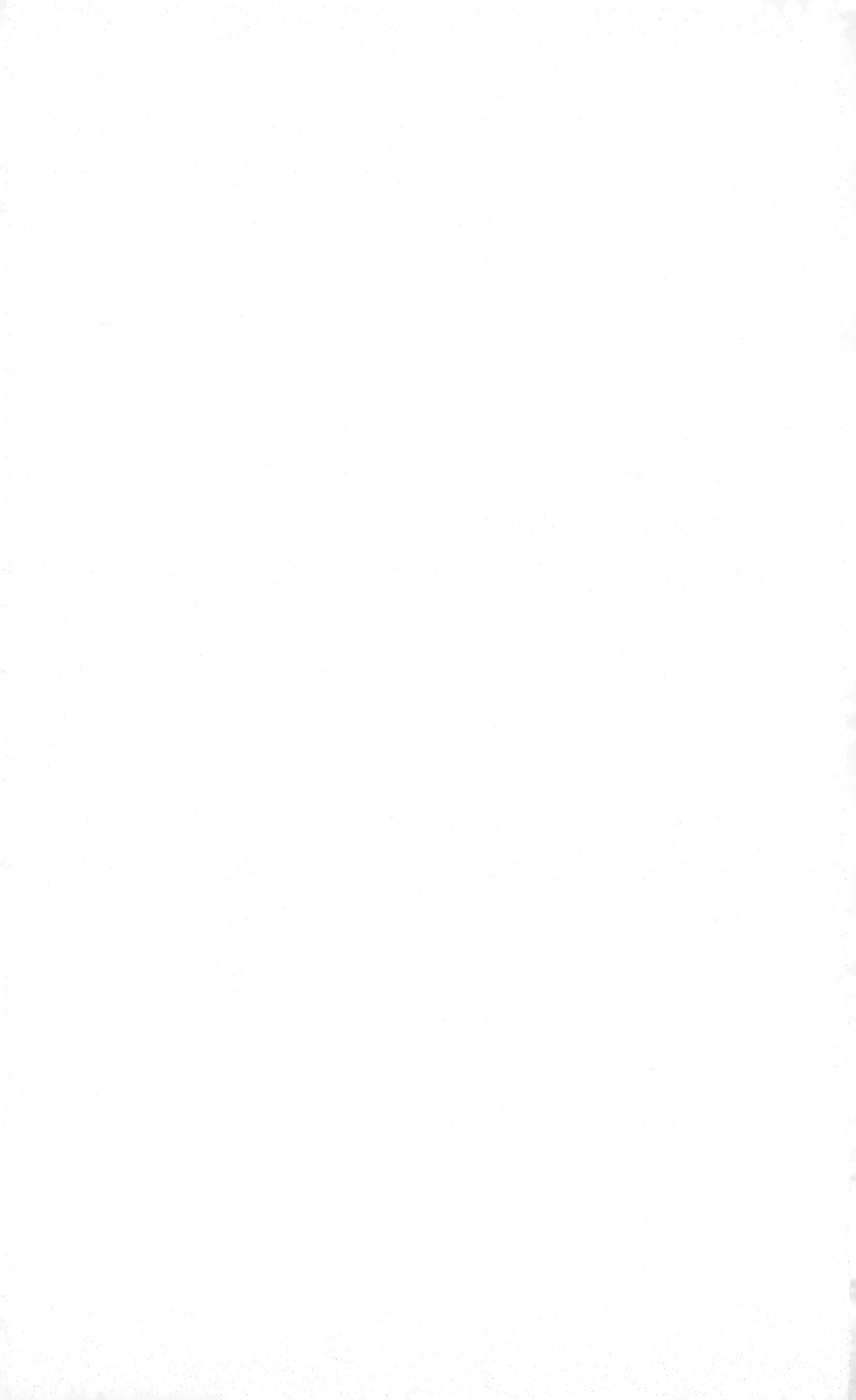

CPSIA information can be obtained
at www.ICGtesting.com
Printed in the USA
BVOW06s1657230917
495487BV00004B/7/P

9 781478 791836